Religious Truth

A Volume in the Comparative Religious Ideas Project

Edited by
ROBERT CUMMINGS NEVILLE

Foreword by
JONATHAN Z. SMITH

STATE UNIVERSITY OF NEW YORK PRESS

Published by
State University of New York Press, Albany

Printed in the United States of America

For information, address State University of New York Press,
90 State Street, Suite 700, Albany, NY 12207

Production by Marilyn P. Semerad
Marketing by Dana E. Yanulavich

Library of Congress Cataloging-in-Publication Data

Religious truth / edited by Robert Cummings Neville; foreword by Jonathan Z. Smith.
p. cm.—(The comparative religious ideas project)
Includes bibliographical references and index.
ISBN 0-7914-4777-4 (alk. paper)—ISBN 0-7914-4778-2 (pbk. : alk. paper)
1. Truth—Religious aspects. 2. Religions. I. Neville, Robert C. II. Series.
BL492 .R45 2000
291.2—dc21 00-020268

10 9 8 7 6 5 4 3 2 1

To

William Eastman, Publisher

*Who, as Director of the State University of New York Press,
fostered the extraordinary variety and depth of studies of
world religions, and the careers of young scholars working
with novel approaches, that have made possible such
ambitious comparative inquiries as this one.*

Contents

Foreword

Jonathan Z. Smith

Unlike so many theological and philosophical terms, our English word, "truth," is set wholly within a Germanic and Anglo-Saxon provenance. In its roots, it is a botanical noun denoting trees and products made from wood. This xyloid meaning is extended to connote solidity, durability, and, therefore, steadfastness and trustworthiness. It is a semantic movement from "tree" to "troth" and "trust," and, then, to "truth." In this ambitious work, *Religious Truth*, Robert Cummings Neville and his colleagues ask, above all, for the reader's trust. They have taken extraordinary care to be worthy of it.

This is an undertaking carried out, quite self-consciously, in the face of a widespread contemporary academic ethos and ethic of extreme localism along with a concomitant distrust of comparison. While comparison was once seen as a cosmopolitan undertaking, it is now often abjured in the name of responsibility toward the concrete specificity of the objects of study within the human sciences. The older nomothetic ideal has yielded to one that is uncompromisingly idiographic.

However, one cannot simply impose a cordon sanitaire around the impulse to compare. Comparison is fundamental to intellection. The compulsion to compare persists, whether we will it or not. The task is to do it right. This requires a conceptualizing confidence that is grounded in an articulate theory of comparison. The latter is a hallmark of this volume along with its two companions.

The Boston University Cross-Cultural Comparative Religious Ideas Project is the most ambitious, collaborative, comparative enterprise since the Cross-Cultural Survey, founded in 1937, of the Institute for Human Relations at Yale University, whose emblem remains those ranks of gray cabinets containing the Human Relations Area Files. (The Survey, by the way, yielded more than twenty thousand statistically significant correlations from a sample of some sixty societies.) While its methods and goals are utterly distinct, the Boston University Project shares an ethos of corporate work along with a high profile theory that is subjected to public testing against a set of carefully selected data. The members of the Project are now submitting the results of their experiments to the criticism of their peers. In so doing, they have reiterated, quite properly, that their results remain "vulnerable" and corrigible.

As an enterprise of thought and method, this volume skillfully steers a path between two notions that have proven, for good reasons, difficult to defend: that of the singular or unique, and that of the universal. Rather, the team members, while comparing religious ideas across recognized and indissoluble difference, have wisely chosen to situate themselves at the level of generalization. In older handbooks of logic, the 'general' is usefully placed as greater than the individual but as less than, even in opposition to, the universal. A generalization admits to significant exceptions. Generalizing is a comparative and taxonomic activity that intentionally focuses attention, across differences, on co-occurrences of selected, stipulated characteristics while ignoring others. Both of these qualifications—not universal, and highly selective—are central. Exaggerated, they lead to the pejorative sense of 'generality' as exhibiting vagueness or indeterminacy. Employed properly, as they are here, these same qualifications ensure that generalizations are always useful and corrigible.

While the scarcely concealed antagonist of *Religious Truth* is a sort of popular relativism, I wish the Project had taken aim at a more carefully formulated position that affects every aspect of its work: that of incommensurability. This would have required a major, additional theoretical undertaking, the development, for purposes of the Project, of an adequate theory of translation. This latter remains one of the most urgent areas for thought within the human sciences in general, and in the study of religion in particular.

This said, *Religious Truth* contains a sentence that ought to be inscribed on the lintel of every academic program devoted to the study of religion: "comparison is unavoidable and . . . religion is complicated." The Project, in its way, has been trustworthy with respect to both of these principles. How students of religion respond intellectually to these two axioms will determine the future of the field.

Preface

Robert Cummings Neville

The Comparative Religious Ideas Project, based at Boston University, ran from the fall of 1995 through the spring of 1999, meeting as a seminar for twenty-five days in total. Its results are published in three volumes: *The Human Condition*, *Ultimate Realities*, and *Religious Truth*. The conclusion of the project was a conference in May, 1999, at which the participants in the project were joined by a number of distinguished scholars of world religions, including Anne Birdwhistell, Jose Cabezon, Julia Ching, Jordan Pearlson, Arvind Sharma, Jonathan Z. Smith, Max Stackhouse, Tu Weiming, and Lee Yearley, who had not been involved in the project save for Stackhouse and Tu as mentioned below. The conference reflected on drafts of the volumes and produced helpful insights into what we had done and not done with the special virtue of external but experienced perspectives. Although the three volumes were drafted sequentially, they are published together and thus benefit from a retrospective overview in the form of this preface, which appears in each volume.

Two purposes motivate the project: to develop and test a theory concerning the comparison of religious ideas, and to make some important comparisons about religious ideas of the human condition, ultimate realities, and religious truth. These two aims are intimately connected: the theory cannot be tested without putting it to work making comparisons, and comparisons are not to be trusted without a justified second-order reflection on the nature of comparison.

In the study of religion in Western cultures today, the making of comparisons among religions on topics such as ours is not novel or surprising. Despite the fact that scholars are worried about the imperialism of interpretive categories, comparisons are standard fare in undergraduate religion courses—how else can people learn about religions new to them? Moreover, ignorance of the world's major religions is simply unacceptable today in any discipline within religious studies, even in confessional theologies, if only for the sake of keeping imperialist prejudices in check. The larger worlds of politics, economics, and cultural communications are deeply shaped by conceptions of how religions relate comparatively to one another, often conceptions that are unnecessarily ignorant and parochial. So what we propose here is to offer some better comparisons on very important religious topics, better for having been refined through the comparative methods of the theory.

The careful presentation of an elaborate theory of comparison for religious ideas, by contrast, is extremely surprising in religious studies today and a significant contribution if successful. Precisely because of raised consciousness about the imperialism of earlier comparisons and theories of comparison, theoretical approaches to religion and especially to comparison are highly suspect. Theory as such is unpopular. Our most unusual purpose, then, is to present a theory of comparison and make it work. This purpose itself has brought some serious qualifications and limitations to the project as will be indicated shortly.

The design of the project has been to assemble a working group of persons in the greater Boston area consisting of both tradition-specialists in different religious traditions and generalists of several types, along with graduate students, and then to set to work discussing the three large topics of religious ideas comparatively in structured ways, one each year, with a fourth year for editorial polishing of the three volumes mentioned.

The project's working group was selected to set in tension two contrary tendencies in thinking about the comparison of religious ideas. One is the tendency to see each religion, perhaps even each text within a religion's intellectual tradition, to be unique and special—and to be in danger of misconstrual when subjected to comparisons. For this purpose we recruited six specialists in different religions with a strong commitment to historical specificity: Francis X. Clooney, S.J., expert in Hinduism; Malcolm David Eckel, expert in Buddhism; Paula Fredriksen, expert in Christianity; S. Nomanul Haq, expert in Islam; Livia Kohn, expert in Chinese religion; and Anthony J. Saldarini, expert in Judaism. The list of contributors page in each volume gives the particulars of their affiliations. Of course, each of these scholars specializes in only some strands of his or her tradition and in only some periods, usually the ancient or medieval. Moreover, to emphasize the difference between scholarly comparative purpose and the worthy though different purpose of interfaith dialogue, these scholars were selected because their tradition of expertise is different from the tradition with which they primarily identify, with only one exception (Haq).

Each of these scholars was helped by a graduate assistant, sometimes to the extent of co-authorship of their papers; working with the scholars as listed above were Hugh Nicholson (with Clooney), John Thatamanil (with Eckel), Tina Shepardson the first year and Christopher Allen the next two (with Fredriksen), Celeste Sullivan (with Haq), James Miller (with Kohn), and Joseph Kanofsky (with Saldarini). The purpose of including the graduate students as full partners in the working group was not only to facilitate the research and writing but also to develop ways of teaching collaborative research in religious studies at the doctoral level. Whereas the natural sciences sponsor collaborative projects in which experts from very different fields come together on a common problem, the custom in religious studies, especially its humanistic side as involved in textual research, has been to gather like-minded and similarly trained scholars. Inspired by the sciences, our project explicitly seeks diversity.

The other tendency we sought for the working group was integration, synthesis, and generalization, a drive to raise new questions for each of the traditions that we bring into comparative perspective. Four of us represented this move, each in different ways: Peter Berger, a sociologist; John H. Berthrong, an historian of religions; Wesley J. Wildman, an historical and constructive theologian and philosopher; and myself, a philosopher, theologian, and theorist about comparison. In the first year of our study, we thought of this second group as the "comparativists" and the first group as "specialists." Quickly it became clear, however, that the specialists compared in their own ways and that the generalists had specialized religious perspectives behind their integrative work. We are pleased to find now that all of us engage in comparison, each in ways reflecting our beginning tendencies but even more what we have learned from one another in the collaboration. Moreover, as the group became conscious of itself as having an integrated identity, with habits of language and thought developed through time invested together, we came to think of our project in terms of the comparisons to which we all contribute rather than merely the comparisons each of us makes as influenced by the others. This process is by no means complete, but it is discernible and in fact described in each of the volumes in Wildman's appendices, "On the Process of the Project." In the original formulation of the project we were clear that the ways the group worked together would have to develop over time. What we had not anticipated in the original formulation of the project is the importance of the reporter, Wildman, who produced the seminar minutes and who called us continually to assess what we had accomplished, how stable our comparative hypotheses are on the one hand and how tentative on the other.

In addition to the working group the project had a board of senior advisors who reviewed the initial design and met with the working group at the end of the first year and in the concluding conference. These include Julia Ching, Jordan Pearlson, Max Stackhouse, and Tu Weiming. The outside advisors helped to bring our shared work into new and critical perspectives.

The thought was that, though both specialists and generalists are comparativists in one sense or other, the specialists would prevent too-easy generalized comparisons while the generalists would keep the specialists in comparative conversation with one another. There have been some discouraging times when we realized just how hard it is to learn to think together without dropping to a lowest common denominator, or giving in to pressures for consensus, or quickly agreeing to disagree without pushing the arguments as far as possible. The labor of joining these two kinds of approach is apparent in the progress through the three volumes. In *The Human Condition* the specialists discuss what their separate texts or traditions say about the topic, and the generalists' "conclusion" maps these and other points onto a comparative grid. In *Religious Truth*, the last volume, the comparisons take place within the specialists' chapters and the generalists' "conclusions" are indeed summaries and then reflections on important topics that emerged from the comparisons. The middle volume, *Ultimate Realities*, is truly transitional with the grid gone but the conclusions heavily formed up by the generalists. After much discussion, and with the encouragement of the outside experts at the concluding conference, it was decided to leave the form of the progressive collaboration as it was in fact, and indeed to gloss it more explicitly in appendices to each volume. These volumes thus reflect the learning process of the working group.

Why study the human condition, ultimate realities, and religious truth instead of other topics? Although each is explained and its importance outlined in the respective volumes, in a sense the selection is arbitrary. Our initial grant proposals put forward six topics of which these are only three. Salvation, food and diet, ritual, religious journeys, religious cosmologies, religious communities, illness and health, goodness and evil, the nature of religious practices such as meditation, the roles of women, social stratification, religious violence, religious beliefs as social constructions—these and many more major topics were suggested at various points and could just as well have been chosen. Most of these receive some discussion in one or more of the volumes, but each could have been treated as a major category.

In another sense the choice of topics is not arbitrary because these three lend themselves very well to investigation while laboring to develop effective collaborative strategies and to test our theory of comparison. The great religious traditions each have a literature about these topics, variously construed. These topics also have been under discussion in the Western academy for over two centuries, and there is a growing body of literature here, too. Therefore we could limit our work to examining texts, and doing so within academic traditions of interpreting these or like texts. We know, of course, that there are many non-textual expressions of ideas, but we simplified our work so as not to have to deal with them here.

To the question whether these topics and the categories that spell them out are *justified*, the answer is more complex. They certainly are justified in that they have a trajectory of scholarly analysis into which we have stepped with three volumes of further reflection that go a long way toward refining them. But have we shown that reality is such that the human condition, ultimate realities, and religious truth identify very important elements? In *Ultimate Realities*, chapter 7.1, and again in chapter 8.6, Wildman and I say that at least four tasks are required for justifying our kind of categories. First is to identify relevant plausible possibilities for comparison; second is to explore the logical or conceptual structures of the categories and to justify this conceptual or philosophical work; third is to provide a genetic analysis of the religious symbols compared and to relate this to the comparing categories, including within the genetic analysis accounts of historical, social, psychological, neurophysiological, and environmental evolution; and fourth is appropriate analysis of the circumstances that accompany the key shifts in symbolic representation during the history of the religious ideas. The Comparative Religious Ideas Project focused almost entirely on the first step in justification; nearly all of our debates were about the plausibility and relative importance of these categories. *Ultimate Realities* introduces a theory of contingency in chapter 8, and *Religious Truth* presents a theory of religious truth in chapter 8, both of which begin to address the approach to justification through logical and philosophical analysis; but these do not go far enough to justify our categories. The third and fourth steps are almost entirely absent except for an occasional genetic account of the history of ideas. The entire field of religious studies is decades away from a thorough justification of any categories in this rich sense. From time to time we have drawn close enough to see what real justification of our categories would mean, and have drawn back before the enormity of the project. Our contribution here is rather simple and fragmentary.

Why did we choose these six "traditions," and how do we study them? The religious traditions studied and compared in this project are, in alphabetical order, Buddhism, Chinese religion, Christianity, Hinduism, Islam, and Judaism. The obvious anomaly in this list is Chinese religion, because we might expect a distinction between Daoism and Confucianism, and maybe Chinese Buddhism. After all, contemporary scholars divide their expertise, intellectual styles, and professional loyalties into Daoist, Confucian, and Chinese Buddhist studies respectively. In our group, Livia Kohn is a specialist in Daoism and John H. Berthrong in Confucianism, so the temptation to distinguish Chinese religion into subtraditions is genuine. On the other hand, both Kohn and Berthrong take a stronger interest in Chinese Buddhism than David Eckel, our Buddhist specialist whose language expertise is in Indian and Tibetan tongues, suggesting that Chinese Buddhism is at least as Chinese as it is Buddhist. Moreover, Confucianism and Daoism share an ancient Chinese cosmology that is also vital to Chinese folk religions and an important influence on Chinese Buddhism. Thus, it seemed to us that the major literate traditions within Chinese religion should be considered together.

For the sake of comparison of the religions' ideas about our topics it is highly advantageous to be able to analyze some particular texts in detail. Yet these texts are meaningful as representative of the religions only when we also have in place some more general characterizations of the religions. And then of course the texts represent the religion of which they are a part in only one way, and other texts might develop the religion in quite different directions: Augustine, some of whose texts we discuss, interprets the Christian view of the human condition differently from Origen, for instance, or Mary Baker Eddy. So our strategy is as follows.

For the general characterizations of the religious traditions we go to their core texts and motifs. These are ancient scriptures and classics, events illustrated in them such as the Exodus and the Confucian revolt against disorder, or thought patterns such as yin-yang complementarity and the search for underlying unity. Religious traditions form around and take their initial identity from these core texts and motifs in such a way that all subsequent developments in each tradition have to come to terms with them. Religious traditions, as we know, are extremely diverse internally, often in contradictory, sometimes warring, ways. Yet all the kinds of Hinduism accept the importance, if not authority, of the Vedas, which are their core texts. Buddhism, a religion originating in the same South Asian environment, does not. Rather, its core texts and motifs have to do with the sermons and other teachings of the Buddha, early tales of his life, and the understanding of authority in terms of the Buddha, Dharma, and Saṃgha. Both Daoism and Confucianism base themselves on the ancient Chinese yin-yang cosmology and the classic texts of the Spring and Autumn and the Warring States periods; the *Yijing* is as Confucian as Daoist, and plays crucial roles in both throughout their histories. Sunni and Shi'ite Muslims war with one another but still define themselves as Islamic based on the core text of the Qur'ān. Orthodox, Roman Catholic, Protestant, and Radical Reformation Christians, as well as the Independent Christian Churches of Africa, identify themselves through the ways they interpret the Christian Bible, however different those ways are. Orthodox, Conservative, Reform, and Reconstructionist Jews take very different stances toward the Torah and the rest of the Hebrew Bible, but they are all forms of Judaism because that is their core text, especially in virtue of its motif of the Exodus and formation of the people of Israel.

Our strategy is to consider the six religious traditions on the one hand in terms of their core texts and motifs, and on the other hand in terms of some one or few texts that can be analyzed in detail for comparative purposes, especially in terms of how they relate to the core texts and motifs. Thus we avoid the pitfalls of attempting to describe the "essence" of a religious tradition and can still make general characterizations based on the core texts and motifs and the diverse ways they have been interpreted.[1] We also honor the nervousness of our specialists about making comparisons without specific texts to work on and their careful circumscription of the comparisons to the content of those texts.

There are two further advantages to this strategy of specific texts plus core classic texts and motifs. The first is that it invites other scholars to treat yet other texts as different representatives of religious ideas within a religion, and to make comparisons among different authors. The limitation of the texts we actually discuss here is an example of the fragmentariness of our enterprise, in the face of which our model invites supplementation. The second is that it makes our arguments vulnerable to correction by inviting criticism of our representations of the core texts and motifs, of our interpretations of how the specific texts relate to them, and of our comparisons.

It should be clearer now why we have chosen to examine six religions that have long intellectual traditions. Each has a rich mine of core texts and motifs and long, complicated histories of diverse interpretations of them. By contrast, we do not have core texts for Native American religions that have been supplemented by long traditions of diverse interpretation, although we do have core motifs for those religions that, with advancing scholarly interpretation, might soon make those religions candidates for our kind of comparison of religious ideas. Within the limits of the six traditions represented, therefore, the religious ideas we want to compare can be understood in terms of their histories and their polysemous qualities.

The experts in our group are all specialists in the ancient or medieval periods of their traditions, first millennium CE developments at the latest. We have depended on the specialists to emphasize historical and textual details. The generalists, by contrast, tend to have more philosophical interests and a higher tolerance for generalizations. Thus a healthy tension is induced in our work between the historian's concern for ancient identifications of the religions and the philosophically or sociologically minded generalist's concern for what about them is really important to compare in our late-modern historical situation.

The heart of our conception of the comparative enterprise is that it is an ongoing process, always proceeding from comparative assumptions, formulating comparisons as hypotheses, making the hypotheses vulnerable to correction and modification until they seem steady and properly qualified, and then presenting them for further correction while accepting them as the new comparative assumptions. This pragmatic approach to inquiry structured the design of the project, the actual course of our discussions, and the editorial composition of our books.

Closely related to this pragmatic emphasis on process and vulnerability is a particular conception of how a comparison is made, namely, by means of a vague category such as the human condition that is variously specified by different conceptions of the human condition. The different specifications are translated into the language of the vague category, with three resulting moments or elements: the vague category as such, the multitude of different specifications, and the restatement of the vague category as now enriched with specifications. Comparison and its problems are closely allied with translation and its problems. These issues of process and theory in comparison are discussed somewhat informally in *The Human Condition*, chapter 1, which is all the methodology a reader needs to get into the specific comparative chapters of that book or of *Ultimate Realities* or *Religious Truth*. But for those interested in a more explicit elaboration and defense of this approach, see *Ultimate Realities*, chapter 8, "On Comparing Religious Ideas," chapter 9, "How Our Approach to Comparison Relates to Others," and chapter 10, "The Idea of Categories in Historical Comparative Perspective." For how these methodological considerations relate to a theory of religion, see *Religious Truth*, chapter 9, "On the Nature of Religion: Lessons We Have Learned."

The structure of the three volumes of The Comparative Religious Ideas Project is the following. Each is written to be read by itself, providing an extended multidisciplinary and comparative essay on its topic, the human condition, ultimate realities, or religious truth, and situated with a self-conscious methodology. Each has an introduction to the topic that also explains the specific structure of the book. Each book has six chapters by the specialists, with each of these chapters giving part of one tradition's perspective on the topic, followed by one or more chapters of conclusions and essays on topics related to comparison or the topics studied. Each volume has an appendix describing the process of the project and one or more annotated lists of suggestions for further reading.

Authorship is a complicated matter for a collaborative project. Nothing in any of the volumes is unaffected by the collaborative discussions of the working group and usually it is not possible to cite the origins of the ideas and influences. Nevertheless, each chapter is the primary if not sole responsibility of some one author. The six specialists had different working relationships with their graduate research assistants, and in several cases the assistants contributed texts to the chapters as secondary authors. These are indicated in the tables of contents with the formula "X with Y," where X is the primary specialist author and Y the contributing research assistant. The collaboration between Wildman and myself grew dramatically throughout the project. I was the first author of the methodological and summary chapters. He believes himself not to have made sufficient contribution to the second summary chapter in *The Human Condition* to be listed as a secondary author, although I myself know the influence of his ideas. He is a strong secondary author in all the others, and indeed those written later show his hand nearly as much as mine. The two chapters of which he is primary author and I secondary, *Ultimate Realities*, chapter 9, and *Religious Truth*, chapter 9, are strongly his own and are oriented to relating our project to larger ongoing comparative work. Because of this full collaboration, we list outselves as joint authors in *Ultimate Realities* and *Religious Truth,* despite the fact Wildman or I wrote the first draft. We have made no attempt to disguise the differences in temperament, approach, or conviction among our authors.

Important limitations of this project need to be discussed because they derive from the choices made about the project design itself. (These are in addition to limitations that come from our incompetence or plain foolishness, which we are not prepared to admit.)

Limiting our sources to literate traditions among the "world religions" means that we have cut ourselves off from the ideas of other traditions on our topics of the human condition, ultimate realities, and religious truth. We are limited to the Axial Age religions, for instance, and some scholars are now saying that the study of religion needs to move beyond the dominance of those religions and properly seek wisdom from Native People, traditional religions, or New Age religions. This is particularly important in light of ecological concerns, for instance. Although we are not attempting to compare contemporary religious ideas, particularly, our focus makes us vulnerable to the charge that the non-literate traditions may have been far more important for our topics than we indicate. We admit that this might turn out to be the case.

Limiting our sources to six literate world religions means also that we cut ourselves off from the methods and kinds of understanding that come from disciplines that deal with mainly non-literate religion, for instance, anthropology and other social sciences, ritual studies, art-and-religion, studies of popular religion, folk culture, and the rest. We focus on the old-fashioned approaches of textual studies, literary analysis, historical research, philosophy, and methodology itself. This was a deliberate choice on our part in order to work out effective collaboration. If collaboration has seemed difficult and occasionally baffling to us, think what it would have been if it had to include the vast array of other approaches to religious studies. That we do not include them does not mean that we reject them nor deprecate their importance. Rather, it means that our approach to the religious ideas of the traditions we cover is fragmentary. Moreover, it means that our analyses and conclusions are vulnerable to being greatly qualified or overthrown when those other approaches are finally brought into collaborative connection. The strength of our approach in this matter, however, is precisely here: we are clear about the limits of what our literary methods can do, and it will be a great advance when our comparisons are corrected by what arises from outside those limits.

Limiting our discussion of the relations among different religions' ideas on our topics to *comparison* does not do justice to the problem of *translation*. The extensive literature on translation, and the history of European translations of religious texts in the nineteenth century, come at many of our problems from another angle. By no means is translation identical with comparison, but there are many analogies and overlapping concerns. One difference is that, at least according to our theory of comparison, a vague comparative category has a moment of quasi-neutrality relative to the specific things compared, and can be assessed in that regard, whereas translation does not employ a third language to mediate between the two being related. Translation indeed exhibits what Jonathan Z. Smith calls "magic" when a speaker of two languages "just knows" how to say in one language what the other says and how that sometimes cannot be said. In our theory, as developed in *Ultimate Realities*, chapter 8, translation is a proper part of comparison but set within a larger process of checks.

The limitation of our project to comparing "basic ideas" such as the human condition, ultimate reality, and religious truth, makes it very difficult sensitively to register many of the points made by the "hermeneutics of suspicion." Most writers of our religious texts have been men and reflect the male point of view. Feminists have rightly argued that a text-based approach such as ours thus is cut off from what the women around the men were thinking, and the women's thinking might have been very important for shaping the religious realities. Feminists also have rightly pointed out that our approach reinforces the general patriarchal assumption that what is important in religion is the men's opinions, expressed in texts, and that this reinforcement is worse the more effective our approach is. Other liberation perspectives, speaking on behalf of marginalized voices and religious movements, rightly can criticize our choice to deal only with the "central" world religions. Our answer to these forms of the hermeneutics of suspicion is two-fold.

First, we plead for mercy in light of the difficulty of the task of comparison. We need to begin with the most elementary and direct expositions and comparisons that we can in order to get started. Unless we can bring some greater self-consciousness and a self-correcting procedure to comparison, comparative judgments will remain at the level of anecdote and prejudice.

The second answer follows from the first. The only way to make progress in comparison, from the standpoint of the hermeneutics of suspicion, is to have steady and well-formulated hypotheses to criticize. Does the hermeneutics of suspicion overturn these comparisons? Supplement them by comparisons on behalf of women and the marginalized? Reconstruct the intellectual causal boundaries? To respond Yes to any of these questions and to justify the affirmative answer would be to make solid and important progress. Our comparisons are aimed to be in a form vulnerable to precisely these corrections. (The forms of the hermeneutics of suspicion that consist in scientific reductionism and anti-colonial theory are spoken to throughout the texts of all volumes.)

One of the subtlest limitations of this project was pointed out at the concluding conference by Jose Cabezon. The very structure of the project, with a director, co-directors, senior scholars, and graduate students, with authorship shared as primary and secondary, reflects what he called a hierarchical Cartesian approach. He meant not only the obvious hierarchical organization but also the supposition of the importance of clarity, order, and classification. A Buddhist would not have done it this way. Others in the project earlier had pointed out what they called the Confucian orientation of the project itself as well as in the expressions of conclusions; I am a Boston Confucian and this complaint was made in good humor, but much to the point of Cabezon's remark. Cabezon focused on what he took to be our attempt to reduce comparison to filling in a comparative grid. He believes our procedure claims that a comparative hypothesis works by fitting things into their Cartesian places.

To this I admit first that the project is indeed organized hierarchically, that I do not know how else to get grants from funding agencies who want someone to be responsible, and that as a Confucian I believe it is the responsibility of those with age and power to foster those down the line, step by step. Moreover, it should be reported that a fairly constant refrain through the four years of the project was that I should be more directive and not let the seminar flow under the guidance of its format alone. Though perhaps embarrassed to admit it, most of the participants believed the academic process could benefit from a Confucian Daddy.

But Cabezon was right that all this nudges the process toward order and definiteness. In defense of this arrangement, we believe this is the way to make progress. If our hypotheses have a definiteness that is false to reality, that can be pointed out. An hypothesis without definiteness cannot be criticized. If the very process itself cooks its conclusions, then that can be pointed out by showing another possible process. This was a recurrent theme of our discussions from the first year, when it was proposed that we relate narratives rather than compare in our way, or that we suspend definiteness in favor of indirection. But we could never quite organize the alternatives. This means that our procedure is vulnerable, and possibly misguided, but that someone else needs to say just how this is so and to do better. For us, at least most of us, our procedure has advanced comparison and we offer these volumes for use and criticism.

Note

1. See M. David Eckel's argument in "The Ghost at the Table," *Journal of the American Academy of Religion* 63 (1995): 1085–1110, to the effect that it is possible to talk about what is essential in the sense of *necessary* to a religious tradition without presupposing an *essence*.

Acknowledgments

The Cross-Cultural Comparative Religious Ideas Project has been supported by generous grants from the National Endowment for the Humanities and the Henry Luce Foundation, Inc., as well as cost sharing on the part of Boston University. We are deeply grateful to these sponsors without which the Project would have been impossible.

We are also grateful to Dr. Susan Only, who was the Project Administrator for the four years of its duration and who superintended finances and arrangements with great skill. We thank Ms. Shirley Budden, Financial Officer of the Boston University School of Theology, and the Boston University Office of Sponsored Programs, especially Ms. Phyllis Cohen, for their careful work on behalf of the Project. At various times, Christopher Allen, Raymond Bouchard, Mark Grear Mann (who as editorial assistant superintended the proofreading, brought order to the styles of representing foreign words, and prepared the name indices of all three volumes and the subject index of this volume), and James E. Miller performed valuable editorial services in the preparation of our publications, and they deserve great thanks.

Several people outside the Project read some or all of drafts of the three volumes that report its findings, and we thank them all for very helpful advice that has guided revisions. They include Anne Birdwhistell, Jose Cabezon, Julia Ching, Jordan Pearlson, Arvind Sharma, Jonathan Z. Smith, Max Stackhouse, Tu Weiming, and Lee Yearley. Ching, Pearlson, Stackhouse, and Tu were senior advisors to the Project from the beginning.

Our colleagues at the State University of New York Press have been extraordinary in bringing our publications to light, beginning with our acquisitions editor, Ms. Nancy Ellegate. We also thank our production editor, Ms. Marilyn Semerad, and the marketing manager, Dana E. Yanulavich. We dedicate these volumes to William Eastman, whose daring in the publication of religious studies made projects such as this possible.

Introduction

Robert Cummings Neville
and Wesley J. Wildman

Religious Truth is the third and concluding volume of the Comparative Religious Ideas Project, following *The Human Condition* and *Ultimate Realities*. Although this volume can stand alone as a treatment of its topic and a commentary on our comparative project, its most exciting contribution lies in its conjunction with the other volumes. The three volumes together constitute a trajectory of the development of comparative understanding and habits of mind. Together they record a diversity of approaches to comparison that we have integrated in the project, sometimes unwittingly.

Moreover, the chapters by each of the specialists in the three volumes—chapters 1–6 here—can be read as something like continuous essays or monographs extending from one volume to the next; this was not the initial intention, but it is manifest in the back-references in so many of the specialist essays here. The result is an extended treatment of a central Chinese approach to comparing religious ideas in the three essays by Livia Kohn with James Miller, an analogous treatment of Hindu approaches in the essays by Francis Clooney, S.J., Buddhist approaches in the essays by David Eckel, and so forth with the rest.

This volume, then, read in conjunction with its predecessors, *The Human Condition* and *Ultimate Realities*, is far richer than had been imagined at the outset of the project. The original intent, ambitious enough, was to present comparative studies of some central ideas from six religious traditions on three successive topics (namely, the human condition, ultimate realities, and religious truth). We had hoped that increasing erudition in one another's subjects, mutual adaptation of comparative habits of thought, and steadily enhanced comparative lore would arise from successive treatments of these topics, and that hope has been fulfilled. It became apparent early on, however, that formulating the comparisons itself expresses a point of view, and the summary chapters in *The Human Condition* were labeled "Confucian" in only partial jest. Subsequent volumes, especially this one, have been much more explicit about the perspective from which summary comparisons are made. Now it is clear that the specialist essays, looking retrospectively to their antecedents by the same authors, constitute other perspectives for comparison. They interweave the woof of the summary comparisons across the topics with six kinds of warp for comparisons developed through from other perspectives. The warp is not systematic, but perhaps is all the richer for that.

The topic of religious truth from the beginning took shape in our minds under the following two interpretations. On the one hand we asked what representatives of each of the traditions said about religious truth, and indeed each tradition has many different representatives. This interpretation takes religious truth to be a topic within each tradition. Our approach worked by analogy with our approaches to the human condition and ultimate realities, asking how representative ideas or texts from each tradition specify the vague topic.

On the other hand we asked in what senses the affirmations or suppositions of the various traditions might be true, which of course means that we have in mind a theory about various senses of truth that has contemporary viability. Recognition of this side of the ambiguity forced us to take responsibility for some of the philosophical suppositions and leading ideas of our comparative inquiry, a recognition previously forced upon us in chapter 8 of *Ultimate Realities*. These two interpretations of the topic of religious truth are distinguished here in the separate treatments in chapters 7 and 8, the first of which treats religious truth as a topic within our traditions and the second of which treats truth as a topic for thinking about the traditions.

The lesson about the need for explicit philosophy is worth dwelling on. We had begun the project with the unspoken assumption that, because comparative hypotheses ought to arise empirically and dialectically out of the data, contemporary philosophical considerations could only add an unwanted bias. We are as sensitive as anyone to the charges that philosophy cooks classifications and comparisons, charges that have been leveled by "scientific historians" at phenomenologists of religion from Hegel to Eliade. Yet our wariness of philosophy was strange: all the project participants are philosophically sophisticated, several (Clooney, Eckel, and Haq) focus particularly on philosophical elements in their traditions of specialty, and Wildman and Neville are plain philosophers of religion (well, as plain as one can be after participating in a project such as this). Only when we came to draw out comparative hypotheses in *Ultimate Realities*, chapter 8, did it become clear that the integration required for explicit comparison demands something not contained in the data alone (assuming that the data could ever be received pure, which they cannot). Merely to show how the different traditions say different things about the topic is not yet to make comparisons. Genuine comparison requires saying explicitly how religious ideas differ and how they are the same, where they overlap and where they are mutually irrelevant, in what their importance lies, and what connections among them are trivial. Precisely because the traditional texts and thinkers have usually not already made those comparisons, the comparisons involve adding something new. "Reading the texts together" is often something new, as Clooney points out. Within our project, however, and within the larger dynamic of recent comparative studies of which our project is a part, much of what is new is philosophy. And where the traditions have already engaged in comparison, as in the texts discussed by Clooney (chapter 2) and Eckel (chapter 3) here, they have done so philosophically.

This is not especially surprising. Some philosophical scheme, most often an interpretation of religion or of the religious, inevitably guides the selection of religious data, categories for making comparisons, and criteria for adequacy of comparisons made. The function of philosophical interpretations of religion needs to be carefully managed to avoid ideological distortions; this is a concern that grows stronger as self-consciousness about comparative method increases. In view of this, we decided to be explicit about introducing philosophical considerations and to build our concluding comparative hypotheses around them. Hence, the discussion of a contemporary theory of religious truth, chapter 8, follows the summary of our comparative hypotheses in chapter 7. In this instance, the philosophy arises from the work of Neville and Wildman, with the others signing on in varying degrees of enthusiasm and diffidence.[1] Readers should understand that, although every chapter here has been shaped by discussions involving everyone, each is the full responsibility of the authors indicated. Great relief was expressed when we realized that the integrating summary chapters of this and the other volumes do not have to be consensus documents or the result of votes as in the Jesus Seminar; they are contributions reflecting the judgments of their authors under the influence of the group.

The previous volumes of this project detailed the philosophical conception of comparison that has guided our inquiry and which in turn has been modified and developed in the course of that inquiry. Readers interested in the short version should consult *The Human Condition*, chapter 1; a longer version is in *Ultimate Realities*, chapter 8. On the relation of our conception of comparison with others, see *Ultimate Realities*, chapter 9. For a survey of the various uses of categories, including comparative categories, see *Ultimate Realities*, chapter 10.

The shortest possible version of our conception of comparison is the following. In any comparison, the things compared are compared in some respect. The "respect of comparison" is a vague category. So, for instance, to compare religious traditions or texts in respect of what they say about the human condition is to treat the human condition as a vague category that is made specific in different ways by what the traditions or their representatives say about it. The same is true in regard to comparing traditions and their ideas with respect to what they take to be religious truth. Comparative categories, then, need to be identified in three ways: in their vague form that applies neutrally to all the things under comparison, as specified variously by the things compared, and summarily so that it is possible to see just what the category is as integrating the comparisons. In *The Human Condition* we clearly understood the first two moments of identification, distinguishing the vague categories from their various specifications. But there we did not get very far past the listing of different specifications in the direction of full-blown comparison. We attempted to remedy that in the conclusions to *Ultimate Realities* and again in this volume.

The upshot of this threefold identification of comparative categories is that our comparisons are hypothetical and vulnerable to correction in three senses. The identification of the vague category by itself is an ongoing process. So many natural and easy articulations of supposedly neutral notions of the human condition or ultimate realities turned out upon investigation to be grievously biased. Only toward the end did we arrive at relatively settled opinions about the respects in which we were making comparisons. If this is so, then the specifications themselves are only hypothetical and always subject to further refinement and revision. An ongoing problem for us has been to settle upon just how representative a given text or thinker might be for a tradition, noting the diversity within each. Finally, our comparisons are hypothetical in the forms in which they attempt to sum up what we know about the comparative topic after we have seen it variously specified.

Because comparisons have the form of hypotheses for further investigation, it is impossible to stress too much the importance of vulnerability to correction. Instead of seeking well-entrenched conclusions we seek hypotheses that are stable as a result of our inquiry but ready for correction where they are wrong, misleading, or partial without proper qualification. Comparisons do not stand alone but are part of a process. We view this project as a segment in a much larger comparative process regarding the understanding of religion.

We divided the topic of religious truth into three subcategories. One is epistemological truth, embracing such themes as how we know, the meaning of knowing, criteria for knowledge and argument, and so forth. A second is scriptural and revelational truth with attendant issues of authority and interpretation. A third subcategory is truth-in-practice where the focus is less on claims, affirmations, and suppositions, and more on realizing truth, manifesting truth, and living in the truth. All of the specialists' chapters in this volume treat these three subcategories—under the titles of "the nature of truth," "expressions of truth," and "cultivation and embodiment of truth"—and make comparisons from the standpoint of their specific texts or traditions. They are sorted more clearly in chapters 7 and 8.

Throughout our project we have been aware of many contested issues in defining our framing subject-matter, religion. This is an aspect of the role of philosophical schemes in guiding selection of data and categories, mentioned above. Is there such a thing as religion? Or only religions? If the latter, how can we tell what counts as a religion? Is Marxism a religion, as Tillich claimed? We decided early on to treat Confucianism, Daoism, and Chinese Buddhism(s) as "Chinese religion," not even "Chinese religions." Our principal reasons there were their common suppositions and their close interactions both historically and in the lives of individuals. What is at stake in all this?

On the one hand, there is nothing wrong with arbitrarily choosing to study comparatively the traditions, texts, and figures that we have—we make no pretense at all to completeness regarding comparative religious ideas, or even comprehensive representation of any of our religious traditions. On the other hand, there are normative issues that have been operative throughout the study, often unconsciously. If we compare religions in some respect, we suppose that this topic is important to all of the religions compared in that respect. Does that comparative category or respect of comparison thus constitute a defining mark of religion? Is it important or religiously defining for every tradition to determine itself with respect to the human condition, to something ultimate, and to truth? Is there a religious dimension to aspects of reality and life that also have nonreligious elements? Just what is religion, such that there are religious ideas that might be true about the human condition and ultimacy? Chapter 9 below attempts to sort some of these issues.

Note

1. Neville's theory of truth is laid out in respect of imagination, interpretation, theorizing, and practical reason in his trilogy, *Axiology of Thinking* (*Reconstruction of Thinking* [Albany: State Univeristy of New York Press, 1981], *Recovery of*

the Measure [Albany: State University of New York Press, 1989], and *Normative Cultures* [Albany: State University of New York Press, 1995]), and in respect of specifically religious truth in *The Truth of Broken Symbols* (Albany: State University of New York Press, 1996). Wildman's complementary approach has been developed most concretely with regard to the physiology of religious experience in Wildman and Brothers, "A Neuropsychological-Semiotic Theory of Religious Experience," *Neuroscience and the Human Person: Scientific Perspectives on Divine Action,* ed. Robert John Russell, et al. (Berkeley: CTNS and Vatican City: Vatican Observatory, 2000); and in Wildman's *Speaking of Ultimacy* (in progress).

1

Truth in Chinese Religion

Livia Kohn
and James Miller

1.1 General Perspectives

The concept of truth in Chinese religion does not willingly offer itself up for sacrifice upon the altar of academic inquiry.[1] Legend has it that the only reason the Old Master bequeathed to posterity the text we know as the *Daode jing* was that he was desperate to get out of the country and was, presumably, in such a hurry that he had left his passport and exit permit at home. He was therefore at the mercy of the keeper of the mountain pass who, correctly discerning that the old man was a sage, asked him the obvious question: what is the secret of the universe? The old man, however, fulfilled the request with a denial of the possibility of an ultimately satisfactory answer: "Dao? Yes, I can tell you about Dao, but it won't be true forever. Names? Yes I can name names, but names don't last forever either." We do well to beware, therefore, that truth is frequently exacted at a price, sometimes as the result of compulsion, and often is not what we are looking for in any case. It is, perhaps, the satisfaction of a craving that indicates a failure of intuition, conscience, or natural spontaneity.

To trace "religious truth" in China, we must first note that the guiding religious category is not divinity, for example, God, his being, and his attributes, but divination. We are not dealing in the first instance with abstract propositions that relate eternal Being to (corrupt) temporal phenomena, but rather with events of mediation that disclose paths of action. Truth in China is not static but dynamic, not formulated in propositions but as directions for or descriptions of performance. The Western distinction, then, between truth as proposition and truth as performance is not valid in China as it is predicated on the assumption that somehow belief and action belong to two entirely discrete domains of human being. On the contrary, proposition and performance in China often coincide, and one may even go as far as saying that truth in China is like a piece of music: one listens to it, enjoys it, is moved by it, feels enriched or cleansed or saddened by it—but one cannot name its essence nor can one tie it down and hold on to it. If you stop the CD, hold the performance, then there is either silence or just one long drawn-out note—it is not music any longer. The symphony, the reality of it is gone.

Having said all that, what is distinctive about truth in Chinese religion is that it is mediated not so much orally or through oracles, but encoded symbolically in Chinese characters. Indeed the Chinese writing system has its origin in scapulimancy: ritual acts of divination performed by the Shang priest-kings in which the marks formed by heating the scapulae of oxen or the shells of tortoises were interpreted in relation to a particular question asked of the ancestral spirits.[2] The characters in which the divine advice was recorded in themselves were reflections of the essential nature of the universe and its reality. They were ideographic representations of phenomena and concepts directly encoding the interaction of heaven, earth, and humanity analogously to the way that mathematical formulae encode the laws of physics. The grammar in which they were joined, moreover, was isolating and extremely flexible in its structure, so that even written expression continued to move and change in accordance with the cosmic patterns.

The same emphasis on movement and dynamics is also prevalent in Chinese cosmology of the Han and later dynasties. Here we see fundamental forces of the universe, such as earth, fire, and water, that seem to resemble Greek and Indian elements but are in fact not solid building blocks of the world. Instead, they characterize phases of the ongoing transformations of yin and yang, from lesser to greater, and again to lesser and greater. The truth of the cosmos, as formulated in exemplary manner by Dong Zhongshu, was moreover seen in the coordination of phases of transformation in the three fundamental dimensions of heaven, earth, and humanity, and described as an everlasting hierarchical cycle of arising and decaying.[3] This vision then led to a restructuring of the Chinese religious imagination, for it turned the supreme religious art of divination into a proto-science. The semiotic substructure remained the same but both expression and action changed. The difference between cosmological formulae and shamanistic divination lies in the fact that the former are prescriptions for cosmic-human interaction, the latter descriptions of such events. The difference between cosmological formulae and modern scientific formulae, moreover, lies in that the former are the inductions of correspondence, the latter determinations of causality.[4]

The Han cosmologists were less interested in the observation of causality between two temporally successive events in one particular situation than the observation of correspondence between two different situations that are temporally simultaneous. Synchronic correspondence rather than diachronic causation is the underlying scientific principle, and its metaphysical foundation lies in a continuous intra-related universe rather than a temporal contiguity of discrete objects.[5] The result of this type of observation was the formulation of patterns of correspondence sometimes so elaborate that they seem grotesquely fanciful:

> The feelings of men and rulers rise up to penetrate heaven. Thus executions and cruelties correspond to many whirlwinds; oppressive laws and ordinances match many insect plagues. As the innocent are put to death, so the countryside reddens with drought. As ordinances are not accepted, so there are many disastrous floods.[6]

What is disturbing about this passage from the *Huainanzi* is that the two halves of each clause seem unrelatable as a scientifically plausible causal sequence. To make sense of the text (which is the goal of the intellectual historian) requires thinking not in modern Western scientific terms, but in the terms of a cosmologically entailed correspondence. This means that we must accept a completely different taxonomy of the natural world in China.

The degree to which human knowledge is intimately connected with the methods used for its classification is the subject of the preface of Michel Foucault's *The Order of Things*. Here he presents a reminder of that great passage in Borges' *Ficciones* that cites "'a certain Chinese encyclopedia' in which it is written that 'animals are divided into: (a) belonging to the Emperor (b) embalmed (c) tame (d) sucking pigs (e) sirens (f) fabulous (g) stray dogs (h) included in the present classification (i) frenzied (j) innumerable (k) drawn with a very fine camelhair brush (l) et cetera (m) having just broken the water pitcher (n) that from a very long way off look like flies'."[7]

This humorous and exaggerated ficción had to be Chinese not because Chinese taxonomies are irrational, bizarre, and incomprehensible, but because their logic seems irrational when placed in comparative contrast with the relative familiarity of its Greek, Indian, or Arabic counterparts. This contrast Borges heightens by juxtaposing the Chinese categories with the most simple, rational, logical, Indo-European form of classification, the alphabetic sequence. Yet from the Chinese perspective it is the alphabet itself that is highly arbitrary and bizarre. Why not group together the vowels, or the sibilants, or the fricatives? Why not place the letters in descending order of frequency? Why not emulate a Chinese dictionary that orders characters according to their component parts and number of brush-strokes, starting, for example, with "l" and ending with "m"? It is superficially disturbing to realize that the *Encyclopaedia Britannica*, the most venerable English-language repository of knowledge and interpreter of truth, is itself a particularly egregious embodiment of the irrational conventions of Western civilization.

"Truth" in all these instances, of course, is not one single thing that can be talked about as a firm entity, but encompasses a number of different dimensions—theoretical, linguistic, and practical—indicating representations of reality, responses to certain objects, formulations of ideas and propositions, as well as habits of response and ritual actions. In all cases truth is a relational entity, a mediating agent between an outside reality, however perceived, and something inside the human being that registers and responds to the outside reality. The more appropriate the registering and responding, the more truth is felt to be present; its loss is perceived as a disturbance in the relational interaction. To find truth means to attain representational symbols that match reality as perceived in a given tradition and become competent in them on all levels—theoretical, linguistic, and practical.

Formulations of truth, then, are volatile, changeable, and depend on classification systems and cultural preferences for their expression and activation. Other than in concepts and language, however, this makes itself felt most clearly in experience, in the sense of goodness and oneness and harmony that comes from being at home in the world and at peace with the divine. Yet experienced truth, another key aspect of religious truth in China, is even more ephemeral and fleeting than that found in concepts or language. Part of a personal or communal event, it is only a temporary phenomenon, a constellation of circumstances and feelings that make the self and the universe be true. To expand this truth into a more permanent state, personal virtues are proposed and demands are made on society to act together in a certain truthful way. As people try to live truthfully, they experience and embody truth—a yet completely different truth from that described in the abstract propositions of the thinkers or of that found in taxonomies and language.

1.2 The Nature of Truth

From the discussion so far, it follows that the nature of truth in Chinese religion can be revealed by penetrating the layers of its expression not only in philosophical discourse, but also in religious practices, be they everyday Chinese customs or highly specialized or obscure methods for gaining immortality. So far as philosophy is concerned, the first point of investigation must be to ascertain whether there is some overall characteristic that colors the whole approach to the question of truth regardless of the particular school of inquiry. This is undertaken in the investigation into truth as static or dynamic, whether truth constitutes some underlying "status" or fixed axis relative to which all propositions take their ground, or whether truth is less a foundation than a participant in the organic processes of the universe. The next question to be raised is whether some people have a privileged grasp of the nature of truth or whether the Dao is inherently "democratic" and equally accessible to all; or, to put it another way, how it is that sages have special insight into a level of truth ordinarily inaccessible. The third question is then whether, in fact, it is possible to make a distinction between truth as formulated in philosophical propositions or truth as enacted in religious lives, and if so, what the relationship between these two expressions of truth is. By answering these three questions we hope to sketch a broad outline of the nature of truth in Chinese religion.

1.2.1 Truth as Dynamic or Static

The most fundamental statement one can make about truth in traditional China is that it is not a firm, solid, underlying "ground" or existential substance to be grasped once and for all but a process, an ongoing movement, an everlasting transformation. It is thus no accident that several key words for "truth" denote something moving and fluid. There is *dao*, the "way"; there is *li* or the "patterns." "To know" even in modern Chinese is "to know the way" (*zhidao*); "truth" is the "patterns of the way" or the "way and patterns" (*daoli*), or again *zhenli*, the "perfect patterns," the ever-changing structures or principles underlying the manifest world. It can thus be described in measurements of change, with the help of devices such as the hexagrams of the "Book of Changes," the calendar, the pitch pipes, and others.

In this respect, Chinese religion shares an affinity with insights of both modern science and ancient Buddhism, which also acknowledge the never-ceasing change at the atomic level of the universe and recognize the impossibility of finding one single firm element or basic building block of the world that can be defined as cosmic or eternal truth. Unlike in the Western traditions and certain forms of Hinduism, there is no one maker of the universe in China (except when the divine Laozi is identified with Dao as the stable force at the root of creation in religious Daoism), nor is there some form of original, cosmically produced evil as in Islam. This does not mean, however, that truth is simply relative, contextual, or ungraspable. Truth, as "way and patterns" (*daoli*), is, rather, a dynamic process that is wholly qualitative. At no point is it possible to quantify truth or value or actuality such that it could be measured absolutely. This is quite apparent in the *Zhuangzi*, which proposes that truth is (a) realized in skillful practice and cannot be communicated in words, and (b) can never be reached by logic because the latter relies on conventions.

The first point is illustrated in a number of stories that describe master craftsmen or sportsmen at the height of their skill. Wheelwright Bian, for example, says:

> If I chip at a wheel too slowly, the chisel slides and does not grip; if too fast, it jams and catches in the wood. Not too slow, not too fast. I feel it in my hand and respond from my heart, but my mouth cannot put it into words. There is a knack in it somewhere which I cannot convey to my son and which my son cannot learn from me.[8]

Similar patterns hold true for the strong swimmer who goes with the current, the bellstand maker who follows the grain of the wood, and the butcher who never needs to sharpen his knife because he cuts so skillfully along the sinews of the meat. In all cases, truth is realized because the person goes along with the patterns of the world, follows the natural flow of things, moves as the universe is moving—realizing in fact a form of being in the world that ancient Daoist texts describe as nonaction (*wuwei*), a nonintentional and noninterventive way of life.[9] It usually also goes together with an emptying of the mind of all sorts of preconceived notions and evaluations, a "fasting of the mind" as the *Zhuangzi* says (chap. 4), that renders all logic and classification obsolete.

Which brings us to the second point, the uselessness of the logical deduction of truth. This was originally aimed at the logicians who attempted to arrive at truth through a process of binary discrimination (*bian*). This process took the form of posing clearly defined questions, to which the answer could only be "it is" (*shi*) or "it is not" (*fei*), "so" (*ran*) or "not so" (*bu ran*), "admissible" (*ke*) or "inadmissible" (*bu ke*). The purpose was to arrive at absolute clarity by forcing language to address reality in these fixed binary quanta. Aside from the difficulty of dealing with instances of actual transformation in the cosmos—an ox, it turns out, is both ox and non-ox at the moments of birth and death[10]—the point of the *Zhuangzi* was that "ox" is merely a conventional designation, and that if I so chose, "ox" could refer to a horse or a telephone or a particularly bad dose of the flu.[11] If we cannot even agree on basic terminology, what hope is there for ordering those terms in a logical sequence?

Although we readily recognize in our project that the vague categories that we employ are purely conventional designations—though they always have a genealogy in a particular religious tradition—from the viewpoint of the *Zhuangzi* this would be a further compounding of the error. Not only is conventional language conventional, our inter-religious comparative language is yet one step further removed from actuality and skillful practice. Not only is it the "dregs of men of old," it is the combined dregs of many old men swilled around, then carefully distilled into vague comparative categories.

In the final analysis the fact that we have been able to construct a Daoist critique of one fragment of the theoretical foundations of this confirms two insights. One is that the readily identifiable cultural origin of this research project in fact enables openness and criticism of it, and therefore achieves a degree of transparency that is to be commended. The second insight is the fact that although Daoists are able to enter into conversation with other traditions (as they have done throughout their history), this does not mean that they regard it as necessary or even desirable. If this project proves to be an intellectual distraction from the process of attaining a natural resonance with the cosmos, then it is to be deplored. If, on the other hand, comparison has as its goal not the proliferation of confusion but the ideal of becoming clear (*mingbai*) about one's orientation in the world, then it is to be encouraged.

1.2.2 *Levels of Truth*

From the earliest philosophical and religious writings in China, there is a strong attestation that there are two levels in which people deal with truth—the conventional and the ultimate. Even the *Daode jing* begins by stating that "whatever dao may be described in words is not the perfect DAO of the universe," that names may be named but will never reach out to the formlessness at the root of creation. Ultimate truth, as ultimate reality discussed in the previous volume, is beyond the sensory apparatus of humanity and can thus only be attained by developing intuition and becoming one with the root. The more conventional level of truth, then, is the one found in divination and described in cosmology, the sense one can develop for the movement of the cosmos in its various dimensions. It is good, it is important, it is a form of truth, but it has to be adjusted constantly. It has to be learned and relearned, cultivated with care, and applied with feeling. Ultimate truth, on the other hand, once realized, endows the person with a cosmic consciousness that spontaneously moves along with all the changes yet is also constantly at one with the formless center of all movement.

The *Zhuangzi* expresses this with the image of the wheel and the hub: the axis in the center that stays solid while the spokes around it move in ever swirling circles. Similarly, the mind of the perfected is at rest in the center of all, one with the cosmic openness at the root of creation. From this position, then, he can intuit the changes as they unfold and respond to them if and when necessary—without, however, ever getting involved with them or mentally exerted in the process.

Later Chinese thinkers, especially under the influence of the Buddhist "two-truths" theory as expressed by Jizang (549–623), make the same distinction and follow it up with a consecutive movement of spiritual attainment they call "twofold forgetfulness" (*qianwang*). First one sits down and forgets the "traces," the outward manifestations and phenomenal reality of the ever changing universe; then one proceeds to forget even "that which caused the traces," the underlying dynamic of the Dao.[12] Adjusting one's consciousness to seeing the world in different ways, one becomes truer in one's vision and attains increasingly higher levels of truth.

The distinction between the two levels proposed in China can be compared to similar differences established in other religions. Conventional truth, then, is similar to "ordinary" truth in Hinduism, a way of understanding reality that relies on what is clearly apparent in the world, follows sensory perception, and can be expressed in language. Here, too, ultimate truth is not readily found in the outside world, can only be glimpsed by intuition or some other form of non-sensory perception, and does not lend itself to expression in language.

Again, a comparable distinction is found in the Jewish tradition where Maimonides distinguishes between "lower truth" that is accessible to the masses and higher truth that is found only by a special elite. In Islam the pattern can be observed in the distinction between the conventional truth that is established between the speaker and the addressee in any given dialogue, and the ultimate truth that is expressed in the holy scripture and part of a divine reality.

As regards the relation between the two types of truth, the Chinese tradition is very clear that they are quite incompatible, although enlightened beings or sages are able to switch from one to other without too much trouble. The problem is that conventional truth has to be overcome, abandoned, annihilated in one's perception for ultimate truth to emerge in one's intuition. There is no smooth transition between the two; the study of conventional truth as a way to finding access to ultimate truth, as proposed in the Hindu tradition is largely rejected—the exception being certain forms of Neo-Confucianism in which *gewu*, the examination of things, leads, sooner or later, to *geli,* the penetration of principle or the "patterns" underlying the things of this world. Here the movement from one level of truth to another is gradual, differing according to the different types of people who undertake it, leading to a oneness with the cosmos that was based on the prevalent notion that ultimate reality (*dao*) is in actuality (*shi*)—not hidden away in another realm. Contrast this with the Daoist view that attaining this unity requires a leap across ordinary perceptions.

A subcategory of these levels, moreover, is the direction of truth development, being either a recovery or a discovery of truth—going back to an originally active level of ultimate truth from which conventional truth developed in a kind of "fall," or starting from conventional truth and moving forward to a completely new dimension of cosmic truth, which is to be discovered rather than recovered. The tendency of the Daoist tradition overall is toward the former, while Confucianism can be described as a mixed type: the ideal sage government and state of virtue in the world was attained in the past and has to be recovered, but the method of attainment is not forgetfulness but learning and acquisition of new and better forms of culture and behavior.

1.2.3 *Propositions versus Enactments of Truth*

The linguist-philosopher-sinologist Chad Hansen has argued in his *A Daoist Theory of Language* (1992) that the distinction between "Being" or "Truth" and "Way" is so fundamental and so hard to grasp that classical Chinese philosophy has been profoundly misinterpreted not only by Western sinologists but, more significantly, by Neo-Confucian philosophers struggling to react to the powerful Indo-European logic of Being imported by Buddhist missionaries. These revisionist philosophers, he argues, reified the concept of Dao, turning it into a metaphysical entity and logical category that it had never been in the mind of Laozi or Confucius.

More recently, David Hall and Roger Ames have continued this line of thinking:

> The *Daode jing* does not purport to provide an adequate and compelling description of what *dao* and *de* might mean as an ontological explanation for the world around us; rather, it seeks to engage us and provide guidance in how we ought to interact with the phenomena, human and otherwise, that give us context in the world. And the *Yijing* is not a systematic cosmology

> that seeks to explain the sum of all possible situations we might encounter in order to provide revelatory insight into what to do, but is a resource providing a vocabulary of images that enable us to think through and articulate an appropriate response to the conditions of our lives.[13]

Hall and Ames locate this argument in the broader context of understanding "truth" in Chinese thought not in the Western terms of "What is truth?" but in terms of the question "How may I act truly?" In terms of drawing a broad distinction between Chinese and Western philosophy, there is much to commend in Hall and Ames's argument, but it is important to recognize that the context of comparative religions demands a different approach to the question of *dao*.

When we turn to the religious nature of logical propositions, the distinction between "what" and "how" or "truth" and "practice" is perhaps not so significant after all. The nature of Christian Trinitarian formulae, for example, though couched in the seemingly arid terms of Greek philosophy, centers precisely on the nature of God (or Being in classical Christian philosophy) as an event of mediation and relation (Christ) that certainly discloses paths of action (Spirit). As Hegel argued, even the formal structure of the syllogism is itself a process of dynamic, relational becoming. Moreover, logical truth, if we are persuaded by it, carries a force of compulsion that results in the modification of behavior. Knowledge is often more dictator than maidservant.

The distinction, for instance, that Hansen notes between Greek or Indian logic and its most obvious Chinese equivalent, the Mohist "School of Names" is that in the latter "[we] find no concepts of beliefs, concepts, ideas, thoughts, meanings or truth. Mohist thinkers create realist semantics out of the project of finding constant guiding discourse."[14] Yet although Greek or Indian logic, if we may be permitted for the sake of argument to elide them both, is constructed in terms of "beliefs, concepts, ideas, thoughts, meaning or truth," this does not mean that such a logic is necessarily morally or religiously neutral. Surely the reverse is the case: however abstract the logical terminology we use to form truth-propositions, they must, if they are interesting enough to have been formulated, be able to be cashed out in terms of a moral or religious value. Whether truth is expressed in the form of mathematics or music, in neither case is it religiously uninteresting. A sharp distinction between "truth as logic" and "truth as performance" is predicated on the belief that somehow belief and action belong to two entirely discrete domains of human being. Perhaps from the standpoint of certain forms of Western philosophy this appears so, but it is in the religious sphere that these two most nearly coincide.

The physical and mental practices that constitute the Shangqing revelations, for example, rely for their justification not only on their efficacy, but on the truth of the patterns of correspondences they invoke between the cosmic and biological dimensions of existence, and on the genuine transmission of scriptures from celestial divinities to human recipients, and from masters to initiates. The truth of Shangqing teachings, then, is a broader question than either that of true belief or true action, and may be categorized vaguely as "ordering" and more specifically as (1) ordering (or ordination) in respect of the authority of transmission (2) ordering in respect of patterns of correspondence, and (3) ordering in respect of cosmic effect. In each of these respects there is a particular *dao* whose truth consists in its correct inherence in the overall *dao* of cosmic evolution in both its historical-temporal and cosmological-spatial respects.

Shangqing transmission rituals take the form of a covenant between gods and initiates that is executed at a fundamentally ontological, rather than sociological, level.[15] This means that the adept, being initiated into a sacred document, is placed not only in a historical lineage of transmission, but also in the cosmological "space" that the scripture creates by virtue of its cosmic origination and its function as mediator between heaven and humankind.

The methods that the scriptures prescribe depend upon the coordination of different dimensions of cosmic reality through a formula of activation and response (*ganying*) that is directed toward a particular pattern of correspondence. Shangqing texts are frequently developed out of talismans that "represent the 'true form' of the paradises of immortals or the names of gods, and thereby give access to them."[16] A particular method (*fa*) or practice is therefore structured around the true representation of the disposition of things in the cosmos. As such these truths are frequently transmitted visually rather than textually, and take the form of astrological charts, calendars, talismans, maps, and diagrams. Logical sequence and historical narrative are less common forms of religious truth because (unlike Buddhism) the cosmos is not chiefly characterized as a flow of temporal phenomena, but (like *fengshui*) as a space in which events are structured to be in particular relation to each other.[17]

The third form of "ordering" is the practical effect that particular methods have upon the particular paths that human beings follow. The presupposition of all Daoist religious practice is that genuine action in accordance with the Dao (thought of as nonaction in the *Daode jing*) has practical consequences for the disposition of things. There are, therefore, subtle transformations in the Dao that are the direct result of human interaction. The advice of the *Daode jing* is that the greatest power for transformation lies in human action that coheres with the natural patterning of cosmic events. In this way human action does not hinder the natural course of the Dao, which, like water flowing downhill, always follows the path of least resistance. Later Daoist religion has more complex theories of the nature of human interaction with the cosmos, but it still draws on the basic Daoist concept that the powerful transformation of human lives or social situations is possible only by means of coordination with the cosmic—and therefore natural—order of gods, heavens, and human beings.

In contrast, therefore, to the attempts of A. C. Graham, Chad Hansen, and Hall and Ames to present an understanding of *dao* that deliberately contrasts with Western philosophical understandings of truth or being, here we are more concerned to develop an understanding of how basic forms of ordering and definitions of truth formed the roots of the Chinese religious system, how truth appears uniquely Chinese in its different levels and manifestations—comparable but not compatible with its understanding in other traditions.

1.2.4 Opposites of Truth

Western formulations of truth take as their foundation Aristotle's principle that a truthful proposition asserts of a thing what it is and denies of it what it is not. Truth, therefore, takes on a binary characteristic: a statement either corresponds to reality or it does not. Since the *Daode jing*, however, Chinese philosophy and religion have proposed an alternative approach to the nature of binary oppositions: both yin and yang are manifestations of the Dao. If someone lies, he does not, like Alice, transgress some metaphysical borderline and step into a Wonderland of fantasy and logical contradiction. Even as he lies, he is somehow continuing to manifest the continuing processes of nature. The tendency, therefore, in Chinese religious history, has been to treat intellectual disputes in their proper socio-political contexts. The opposite of religious truth, therefore, is not falsehood, but failure. Like Muḥammad, a speaker of religious truth is, by definition, successful. Moreover, the tendency toward harmony and syncretism that is demanded by the myth of the universal unity of Chinese culture meant that Daoism, in its most syncretistic, dominant and politically integrated form, was known as *Quanzhen*, which may be translated variously as Complete Perfection, Total Reality, or Perfect Truth.

Another opposite of truth, especially religious truth, is heresy, which in Daoism occurs most obviously in two aspects. One is the continued and intense Daoist condemnation of all sorts of popular cults, especially those involving spirits of the dead, blood sacrifices, and ecstatic orgies.[18] The other is the extirpation by Laozi of ninety-six different *waidao,* literally "outside ways," as part of his conversion efforts in the Western countries, including all sorts of extreme ascetic practices and other unusual activities.[19]

While there is, therefore, an awareness that certain groups practice things that might not be conducive to the realization of truth, Daoists overall tended to be tolerant toward other creeds, subscribing to the belief that all religions and all practices of the world were an expression of the Dao on earth and thus prescribed efforts toward its realization. Some of these efforts were better than others, others (such as the *waidao*) were misguided and even wrong. Still, rather than a radical opposite of truth, Daoists saw deviations from the best way of approaching it, detours, so to speak, not dead ends.

As a result, the kind of heresy typically associated with the word from the Christian context—as in the inquisition, with Galileo, the witches, and the like—where certain members of the religion take certain doctrines of the same religion and interpret them differently or place certain secondary deities (Satan) in a primary position and are judged and condemned for it, does not play a significant role in Chinese religion. On occasion, the government would persecute certain cults for political or economic reasons (such as the Buddhist persecutions in the 420s, 574, and 845), but within Chinese religious groups themselves there seems to have been little sectarian strife. Different interpretations and competing pantheons and schools of ritual within Daoism, however variable they may have been, were thought of as valid alternatives to truth, the most efficacious or distinguished of which would get the most or the most aristocratic customers and thus become dominant. There were certainly no witch trials and/or excommunications—but then to have excommunications there has to be a monolithic organization that claims sole access and representation of one single truth. This was never the case in Daoism, though a uniformity of interpretation was institutionalized in the Chinese Civil Service examinations, for which Zhu Xi's commentaries on the classics were the standard.

1.3 Expressions of Truth

Religious truth, as we have so far investigated it, presents an enormously wide scope for analysis. Having attempted to discern something of its root characteristics, we now turn our attention to its blossoming in Chinese culture. This requires us to pay special attention to the nature of the Chinese language and to the construction of sacred texts and talismans from Chinese characters. Language in general is often seen either as a source or as a major expression of truth, with words, letters, and signs being imbued with superior meaning and symbolic depth. Alphabet languages show a higher degree of abstraction and often find mystical meaning in the association of letters with numbers. Chinese with its pictograms and isolating grammar presents a unique case, showing some similar tendencies but being fundamentally different. Signs and symbols, on the other hand, have a more universal character—geometrical signs often showing the four directions and the center as a replica of cosmic or sacred space, phonetic signs often representing the "Ur"-sound of the world, the creative note of all being. All these are not just means of expressing truth, however, but—as they represent the universe in its most essential form—also convey powers over the world.

Besides language, truth may be expressed in art, architecture, gardens, and so on—in different ways of shaping the physical environment to create models of sacred space and symbols of religious truth. The classical architecture of many temples, the layout of monastic compounds, the construction of graves and stupas, the creation of religious art—they all belong in this category.

1.3.1 Words and Syntax

The Chinese language, as noted earlier, consists of characters that are essentially pictograms and thus function as a direct representation of cosmic patterns. Being dynamic in their immediacy of representation, they give a sharper focus to reality and thus have a closer access to truth than alphabetic languages might, as they have a higher degree of abstraction and are one step further removed from the reality of things.[20] Thus the character for "benevolence" fittingly shows the sign for "human being" and the numeral "two," expressing in its four simple strokes more than any word ever could, going, so to speak, directly to the heart. Similarly the pictogram for "moon," an immediate representation of a half-moon hanging in the sky, evokes feelings and memories and a sensory reality that only poetry might effect in other languages.

One result of this nature of the Chinese language is a strong religious preoccupation with cosmic truth made visual in sacred characters, cosmic charts, maps of the universe, or holy talismans. Another result is the isolating grammar of the language, which means that words—with the exception of technical particles and specific adverbs—are not defined according to function. Any given character can be a noun or verb, adjective or adverb, can signify the present or past tense, be in the indicative or subjunctive mode. How, then, can texts be read? In the same way as a musical score is activated. The role each character plays in any given sentence is determined by its position within the whole. A sentence moves and changes as it is read or written, each word determining the quality of the next—the process nature of the universe activated immediately in language—and it is no accident that those learning classical Chinese with most ease are gifted or at least active musicians.

Language and especially poetry, like music, can be in harmony with the cosmic patterns but it cannot be used to grasp them. It is part of the flow and can follow it, harmonize with it, join it, but it cannot hold it. The limit of knowledge through language, then, in China is the joining of the cosmic patterns with a suitable set of words, words, moreover, that are in themselves dynamic depictions of different aspects of reality. The ultimate reality beyond the changes is formless and cannot be reached with words but only through intuition that itself turns formless but can be aided by cosmic charts. Language in logic or in sacred historical narrative as in Hinduism and Christianity is not a valid tool for the realization of truth. On the other hand, certain comparative patterns are found in Judaism and Islam, whose languages (Hebrew and Arabic) have words that consist of a sequence of consonants whose meaning changes according to the vowels inserted. Here, too, words and sentences are flexible and changing and—as they are used to express the word of God or Allah—are direct expressions of sacred truth. In Augustine's Christianity, moreover, words are signs of truth, and the whole of creation, including language, is a sign and manifestation of God.

1.3.2 *Sounds and Signs*

Truth appears in the spoken word in various traditions—in Christianity, Islam, and Judaism as the word of God, spoken directly to prophets or other blessed beings; in Hinduism as part of conventional truth and in the logic of the thinkers; even in Buddhism in the truth-statement of Aṅgulimāla who is saved by its power. In China, we have the spoken word as truth only in the form of *dhārani* or spells that develop in medieval Daoism under Buddhist influence.

Based on sacred writings stored in the highest heavens, these spells are made of the sounds of the heavenly characters that then appear as incantations and poetic stanzas, some with meaning, some without. Like the heavenly writings they have the power to control the events of the world and govern the life and death of human beings. Primordial spells of creation, such as *Zeluo jue putai yuan daluo qian*, a string of pure sounds with no meaning whatsoever, are accordingly part of the creative structure of the cosmos and have the power to save people from destruction through cosmic disasters. Less potent ones still make trees wither or people drop dead, others again secure access to the sacred realm of the demon kings. The right word, especially that of heavenly origin, spoken at the right time and accompanied with the right ritual, thus activates the power of heaven itself.

More potent, though, and more commonly used than the sacred sound is the sacred sign, the divine ideograph copied down in its original form. Such heavenly characters, written in unintelligible "Brahma script," appear in the world in the form of talismans (*fu*), strange signs on paper or silk, shell, or stone, that represent "cloud script" writing and continue an ancient tradition of seeing magic in the written word, a tradition that has also been honored in the art of calligraphy.[21] Talismans may also contain the name of one or the other deity and a spell of protection or exorcism. Written on paper or silk, they are attached to whatever is to be protected, be it the lintel of one's door, the belt of one's pants, or the side of one's computer (see Fig. 1.1). Talismans in general are powerful in the control of demons as well as the governing of natural phenomena. In addition, they are the passports and guidelines to possible visits of the other world. Used in whatever role, they are copied carefully in cinnabar ink on golden ground and kept close to the body of the careful practitioner—never to be lost or used lightly.[22] In addition to heavenly characters or protective spells written out in talismanic "cloud script," the representation of cosmic truth in sacred signs also involved the creation of complex charts or maps that contained the essence of large segments of the world or even of the whole world. Among the most famous of these is the so-called *Hetu* or "River Chart," a divine map of the universe allegedly presented to Fu Xi, the sage ruler of old, on the back of a dragon rising from the Yellow River.[23] Its history provides an interesting insight into the development of cosmic charts and even Daoist scriptures.

First mentioned in the *Shujing* (Book of History), the "River Chart" was, as far as we can tell, a precious stone that served as part of the royal regalia of the Zhou dynasty. It was a legitimating sign from heaven, stored among other wondrous objects, such as precious gems, unusual jades, and strangely formed crystals that were found in a kingdom's area and brought to the ruling house. As time went on, the precious stones were also appreciated for their unusual markings, which were interpreted as charts or maps presented by Heaven to the ruler. These divine maps, then, contained the essence of the realm in symbolic form and gave the king celestial control over his land. From the diagram stage, the sacred sign unfolded further to include a divine message spelled out in language and thus graduated to being a sacred text or scripture—written either in explanation of the chart or as a sacred sign itself.[24]

An example of such a chart in the Daoist tradition is the "Chart of the True Shape of the Five Sacred Mountains," which gives Sanskrit-style

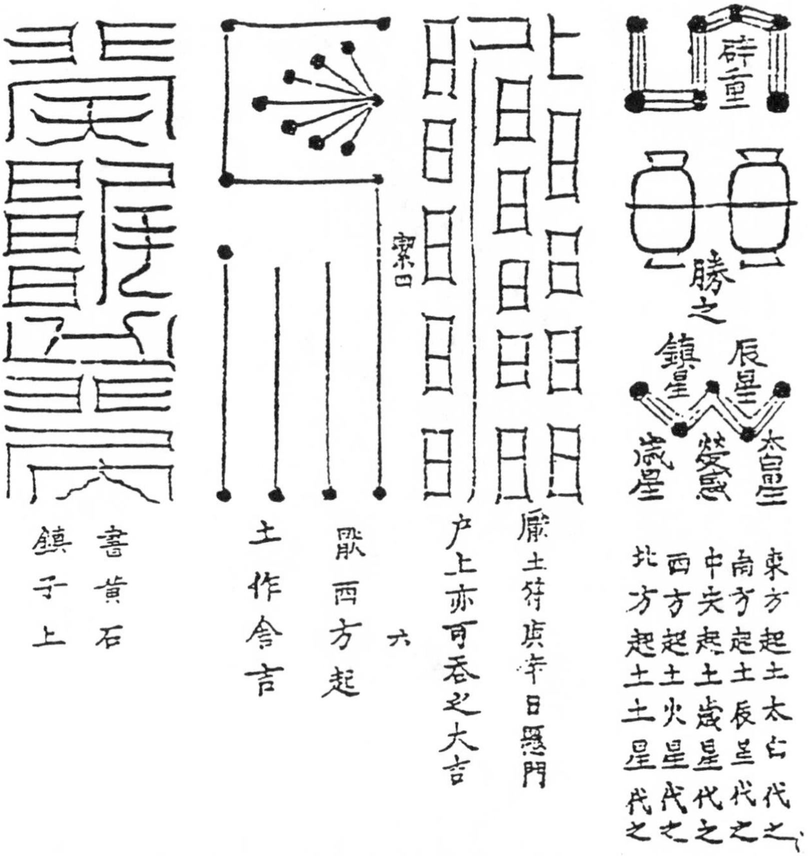

Figure 1.1. Talismans to protect house and hearth. *Source: Hunyuan sanbu fu.*

symbols for each of the five sacred peaks and thus maps out the structure of the Middle Kingdom.[25] Another is the set of the five Lingbao talismans, which contain the essential charts of the five divine emperors who rule the earth in the five directions and served to aid the mythical ruler Yu in his control of the floods.[26] In the Confucian tradition, albeit based on Daoist models, there is the famous "Diagram of the Great Ultimate" (*Taiji tu*) that was mentioned as part of the discussion of ultimate reality. Another, more recent Daoist chart is the "Chart of Inner Passages" (*Neijing tu*; Fig. 1.2), a map of the body as containing the universe, used in Daoist practice.[27] All these, in their own way, are world diagrams, comparable to the stupas and mandalas of India, which similarly rely on the division of the four direction and the center or, in some cases, on an anthropomorphic vision of the cosmos.

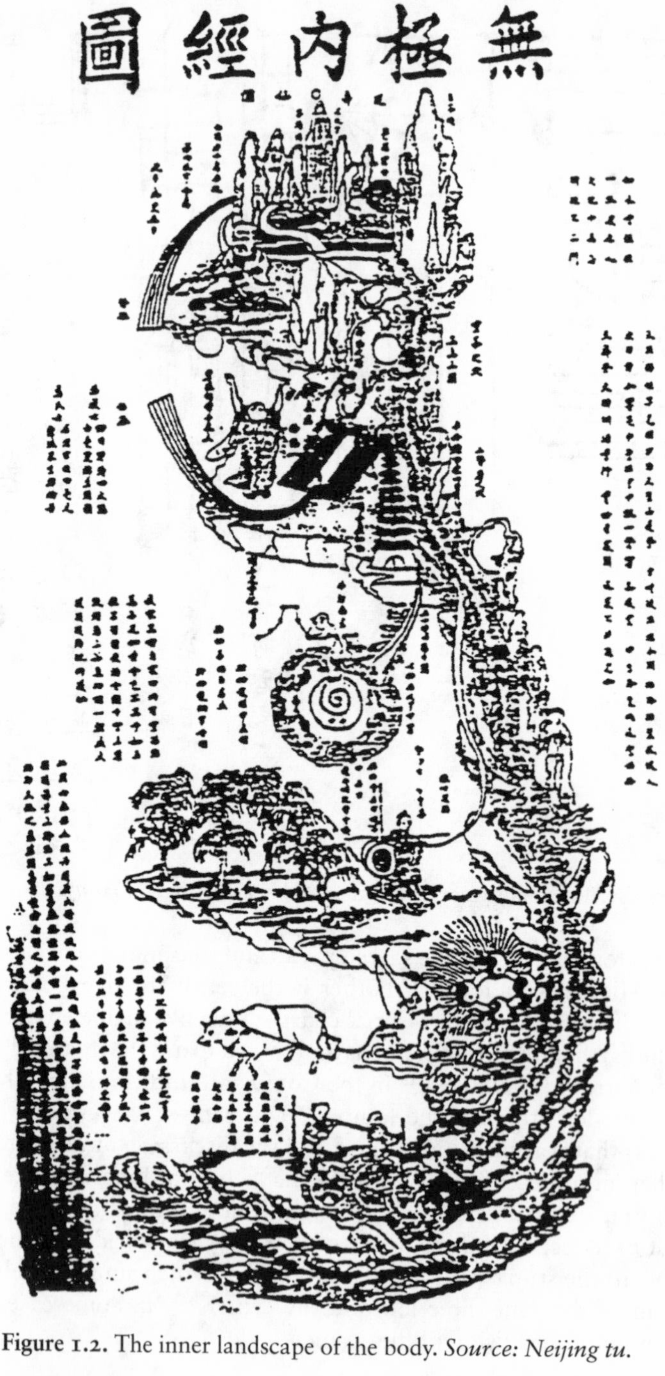

Figure 1.2. The inner landscape of the body. *Source: Neijing tu.*

1.3.3 Scriptures

The word for "scripture" in classical Chinese is *jing*. The character written with the classifying radical meaning "silk" and showing a bundle of parallel threads going vertically, originally indicated the warp of a loom, the basic threads necessary for weaving a composite fabric. From this meaning derives the connotation of a basic, underlying grid of threads and also that of a strong, continuous line that goes through even highly composite fabrics. In a more metaphysical perspective, *jing* means the inherent foundation, the underlying truth of the world, both in its cosmic and human aspects.

In ancient Confucianism, *jing* issued from the sages, who—as evident in the character *sheng*—were the masters or kings of ears and mouth, those whose senses were perfectly attuned to the movings of the cosmos, who could recognize and understand signs that others hardly noticed and who would elucidate them for others.[28] Thus the *Lüshi chunqiu* (*Spring and Autumn Annals of Mr. Lü*) has:

> The knowledge of the sage reaches for millennia into the past and the future—he is not guessing at things; he always has reasons for what he says. (20.22a)

The sage is thus one who knows, who serves the world by bringing hidden realities to the surface, revealing the supersensory, the intuitional and hidden realities of things. He does so by means of the senses and gives verbal explanations, which take shape in the *jing* associated with him. Sages can be ancient rulers or major thinkers, anyone with the right degree of intuition and insight who will recognize and translate the cosmic patterns of the world.

Confucian *jing*—commonly translated "classics" or, in translations of actual titles, "books"—then are works of cosmic import that go back to the sage rulers of mythical antiquity and were revised and edited by Confucius. There are six of them, including two historical records, such as the *Shujing*, two volumes of poetry and music, a collection of ancient rites, and the famous "Book of Changes."[29]

All these classics of the ancient Confucian tradition, then, at least according to the doctrine, go back to ancient sage rulers and present the way things were in the golden age of the past, when cosmos and humanity were interacting closely and smoothly, creating a perfect society on earth. They set the standard for later generations and were revered, recited, and memorized. However, even though there is an ideal way for humanity to interact with the cosmos, cosmic patterns change and so do the necessary human responses. As a result, the six classics have received much commentarial attention and were even supplemented by a secondary set of classics, the Four Books of Neo-Confucianism, which included the works of Confucius and Mencius together with two specially inspiring chapters from the "Book of Rites" (Great Learning; Doctrine of the Mean). Scriptural truth in this tradition, then, means a written-down explication of the workings of the cosmos and of the ideal human society, presenting the standard and measure for all times and governments to come.

In Chinese Buddhism, the word *jing* is used to translate the Indian term *sūtra*. As this indicates the sermons of the Buddha, whether on earth and in Pali or in heaven and in Sanskrit, the concept of truth is highly similar to that found in Confucianism. Here, too, a sage of superior proportions has gained insight into the workings of the cosmos and communicated his understanding to others who have written it down. The Chinese never fully realized the difference between mainstream and Mahāyāna forms of Buddhism, so to them all Buddhist sūtras issued from the sage figure, necessitating some reorganization and reinterpretation of their organization. The synthesis reached in Tiantai Buddhism of the sixth century then placed the Mahāyāna sūtras first and the mainstream sūtras second, associating them with different phases of the Buddha's life and with the different audiences he addressed. Again, the notion that the cosmos underwent changes and transformations allowed for a great variety of teachings to be considered sacred, just as the *upaya* doctrine made vastly different formulations of truth possible, and the concept of "two-truths" enabled practitioners to have significantly different visions of reality that were yet both true.

Like the classics of Confucianism and the sūtras of Chinese Buddhism, the *jing* in religious Daoism, commonly translated "scriptures," are understood as the earthly representation of a cosmic truth that is recognized by specially gifted or inspired people and put into human language to serve as a model for society and the religious community. Just as the ultimate truth in the other traditions is part of the cosmos and the realm beyond the ordinary world, so truth in Daoism is not of this world and has to be acquired with special means. Unlike the other traditions, however, Daoists propose a completely separate, celestial realm, in which the scriptures exist in an eternal, heavenly form, stored in the highest of the thirty-six heavens and accessible only to the gods, perfected, and immortals.

These scriptures "originally existed together with primordial energy, the source of all life, and were produced at the Grand Initiation of the universe," as the *Suling jing* (Scripture of Immaculate Numen, DZ 1314,

6b) has it.[30] Uncreated, direct, primordial, they are formed through the coagulation of original energy and exist before even the world comes into being. Not only powers of creation, the scriptures are also the forces of survival. When the world, as it does periodically, comes to an end, nothing but the scriptures survive. The word *jing* in this tradition thus expands the meaning of "going through" of the original graph to become the "eternally surviving" of the religion.

Stored in the highest of the thirty-six heavens, the scriptures come to earth in a translation intelligible to human beings. They are revealed by friendly deities to specially selected mediums, either by having them read the characters, then transposed into human script, on the walls of caverns (e.g., Bo Jin and the Sanhuang texts); by uttering them in a dialogue with the entranced seeker like a teacher instructing his disciple (e.g., Zhang Daoling and Kou Qianzhi receiving Celestial Masters materials from Lord Lao); by explaining them to the medium in a dialogue and having him speak them in human language (e.g., Yang Xi and the Shangqing revelations); or by guiding the hand of the medium in a form of automatic writing (e.g., later cults and the immortal Lü Dongbin). In all cases, the human replica is a copy of the celestial original, which carries power and has to be written as exactly as possible—each wrong character in copying the Lingbao scriptures meant the loss of one year of life!—but still ultimately remains a copy. The truth of the universe contained in the writings above, as much as the inner workings of the cosmos documented in the Confucian classics and Buddhist sūtras, is forever aloof, inaccessible in its original form but workable with the help of spells, talismans, and scriptures.

In a similar way the scriptures of the major Western traditions are expressions of the divinity at the center of all. Partaking in the divine, they are themselves empowered, and their contents must in all cases be true, never to conflict with anything else, be it personal experiences or objective science.

Unlike the eternally fixed and firm word of God in the West, though, the spoken and written word as well as the scriptures in their earthly manifestation all change with the flow of the cosmos, are part of this world while also representing—in a more or less direct manner—the patterns that underlie it. Expressing truth in a symbolic form, they are yet subject to change and transformation—through copying, editing, commenting, and interpreting. The dynamic nature of truth in Chinese religion is thus mirrored even in its expressions, from the eternally changing syntax through the applied charts and talismans to the editing and commenting of the scriptures. In a similar way, it also manifests in art where a preferred form is the hand scroll, unrolled a bit at a time, as opposed to manuscript pages or fixed paintings. As Laurence Sickmann says, "The hand scroll is never shown throughout its whole length, nor is it displayed in a room as decoration. It is pre-eminently art for an occasion,"[31] a onetime thing, a changing phenomenon that moves along with the patterns of the universe.

Along the same lines, religious art in China is never merely a symbol of the divine but always has a practical context, an application in people's lives. The depiction of demons, for example, is not only undertaken to show their nature and thus present a particular aspect of truth, or even to list and classify them, but very much also to give people the power of control over them.[32] Never isolated or static, the expression of truth in Chinese religion thus mediates between its conception and its experience, being a bridge that sways with the movements of the elements it connects.

1.4 Cultivation and Embodiment of Truth

One major way truth is discussed and realized is on the basis of experience. Experiential or embodied truth is the kind of truth that is validated by personal experience. One form this takes is the experience of something overwhelmingly other yet powerful and perfectly true that people have when entering some kind of mystical state. It is the "noetic" quality William James speaks about in his discussion of the mystical experience, a quality that is attested to by mystics around the world yet one that is also highly subjective and thus beyond any kind of proof.[33]

In addition, however, there is also a kind of truth that can be subjected to tests of validity through experience. "It works, so it must be true"—this is credo both of traditional Chinese religion and modern science (as opposed to that of the traditional Western religions). Experimenting with and experiencing truth directly is one of the best and most straightforward ways of dealing with the problem. Unlike modern science, though, where the truthfulness of a certain hypothesis is ascertained by the repeatability of the experiment and the inevitability of the outcome of certain constellations of circumstances, experiential truth in traditional China was measured by luck or good fortune. If a certain action or behavior was truthful in a given situation, its outcome or result would inevitably be fortunate and positive; if not, then bad fortune would result—designated by a word, incidentally, that depicts the figure of a person tumbling into a pit. Although based on different premises, a somewhat similar attitude can also be also detected in Christianity, where auspicious events, such as healing and miracles, were seen as signs of truth and appreciated accordingly.

The Chinese in general conceive of the experienced world as an ordered whole, not necessarily as a transcendent ordered whole, although for religious Daoists the root of the order is transcendent. Actions within it have immediate effects on all levels, reverberating all around the cosmos. But they are also limited by the cosmic constellation, so that the mind unlike in Buddhism does not have a strong power in and of itself. On the contrary, the more mind and personal consciousness are reduced or even eliminated, the greater the good fortune and harmony with the cosmos.

1.4.1 *Unknowing*

Religious truth, being beyond the senses, cannot be known with ordinary consciousness. To intuit it a state beyond knowledge has to be found, one that is often described as unknowing or non-knowledge. Here we have a comparable category in Śaṅkara's and Mādhyamika thought, and maybe also in Christianity where the ultimate state, a recovery of life before the Fall, is to know oneself as God knows one, without self-deceit and in a mode alien to ordinary perception.

One consequence this has in China is the tendency to express truth in stories and parables (as in the *Zhuangzi*), to force people to jump over their own consciousness by confronting strange riddles (notably the *kōans* of Zen), and by changing the meaning of the same word within a paragraph or two of religious discourse (as in the *Daode jing* and related texts).[34] The rule here is the same as that active in the maps and charts: "show, don't tell." Anything that can be made evident immediately and by pointing directly to a person's heart rather than intellect is, while not ultimate in itself, at least so much closer to ultimate truth that it is infinitely more valuable than abstract discourse and logic. Words as words, then, are condemned as mere conventional aides, designations that carry in them only as much meaning as their user, who is always a participating observer, can find, a notion contrary to that found in scriptural truth where, in the words of Augustine, "words are precious cups of meaning."

Daoist, moreover, describe a state of oblivion or forgetfulness as desirable, a kind of deep trance or intense absorption, during which no trace of ego-identity is felt and only the underlying cosmic current of the Dao is perceived as real. The classical passage describing the state occurs in the *Zhuangzi*. It says, "I smash up my limbs and body, drive out perception and intellect, cast off form, do away with understanding, and make myself identical with the Great Thoroughfare" (chap. 6). This refers to a mental state of complete unknowing, of loss of personal identity and self, a kind of total immersion in the non-being of the universe. The state, known as *zuowang* or "sitting in oblivion," developed into a key notion of later Daoism,[35] making the ideal of unknowing a central feature of the religion. Its attainment, a way of being in truth, moreover, leads to the complete freedom from fear, anger, hatred, and other afflictions—utterly unlike the attainment of knowledge or wisdom that, as proposed in the Western traditions, may increase truthfulness but still leaves the person subject to anger and fear.

1.4.2 *Truth in Practice*

Another way of overcoming conventional knowledge and the bondage of words is the teaching and acquisition of truth in practice. This means the creation of a certain type of imagination that people are shaped to or shaping themselves to with the help of specific exercises. It is strongly present in Judaism, where the Talmud consists of large numbers of rules and prescriptions for daily behavior that shape people's living in truth rather than their recognizing or understanding it. Augustine in Christianity, too, emphasizes the practical aspect when he asserts that body habits affect the soul.

Truth in practice is a strong category in China, as again it overcomes verbalization, is activated by process rather than static propositions, and is a valid way of moving along with the cosmic patterns. A good example of its activation in a religious context is the practice of Taiji quan, where a series of body movements, executed slowly and with a calm mind, are representative of the cosmic interaction patterns of yin and yang. Done regularly, the exercises transform the body into a living replica of the cosmos. The truth the practice represents, moreover, cannot be expressed in words, and even any description or depiction of the movements will not convey their reality. Here very strongly the body is the key memorizing agent, so that the truth of the universe is activated physically in a manner entirely different from and beyond verbalizations or depictions.

Embodied truth is very important in all traditions, where it appears in daily rites of prayer and purification and, most obviously, in the daily formalities of the monastic institution. Monasteries being geared toward allowing the realization of the religious ideal of a given tradition, their every aspect must conform with the ideal. As a result, all monastic traditions have strong rules for daily behavior, sanctifying ordinary physical life and creating literally bodies of divinity—often continent and free from sexual activity which, as Augustine has it, threatens the ratio and thus the pure perception of the divine. They have certain ways of walking, bowing, eating, washing, and so on—all practices that serve the transformation of an ordinary into a sacred body and thus the realization of religious truth within the moments of daily life.[36]

1.4.3 Personal Truth

Whoever has realized the mental state of complete unknowing and the physical harmony with the Dao will attain a new and perfected personality. This has been mainly described by the thinker Guo Xiang of the late third century. He formulated a doctrine of the mystical attainment of inner spontaneity (*zide*), which allowed the individual to be free from all desires and critical evaluations and thus accord with the movements of the cosmos around him or her. Guo Xiang, a Confucian official at one of the local courts of this time, is best known as the key editor and major commentator of the *Zhuangzi*. He expanded and detailed the views of the text, presenting a comprehensive theory of mind and consciousness in the process.

According to him, the human mind is originally pure and harmonious, functioning in perfect accord with the currents of the cosmos around it. It is linked to the cosmos in two ways, though cosmic share (*fen*) and principle (*li*). Cosmic share means the basic pattern inherent in the person's makeup, his or her genetic DNA, so to speak. Principle, on the other hand, is the situation in which she finds herself, the circumstances of birth, social and political situation, as well as the opportunities that come her way. These two, within the human being, are further defined as "inner nature" (*xing*) and "fate" (*ming*). According to Guo Xiang, both are utterly inescapable but have to be realized in true cosmic spontaneity, so that every human being has an ideal level of potential realization that in turn will be characterized not only by a personal sense of rightness, happiness, and fulfillment but also by outward good luck all the way around.[37]

Whereas normal people tend to be subject to social constraints and psychological limitations and develop ego instead of fulfilling their true calling, the person who manages to realize inner nature and fate to the utmost is the sage or perfected. Having attained this state, he or she can freely roam all aspects of the universe, being entirely unfettered in mind and feeling and having a sense of really "fulfilling his inborn nature" (1.1). He goes along with the changes; "using his innermost principle, he floats through he realm of spontaneous realization (*zide*)" (17.566). *Zi*, "spontaneous," here means the realized self, the natural so-being of everyone in accordance with the cosmos; it is opposed to *ji* or *wo*, the other words commonly used for "self" in classical Chinese, which Guo Xiang clearly defines as the ego of limited conscious thinking.[38] *Zi* is to be realized, *ji* or *wo* is to be forgotten, abandoned, given up completely. Thereby one follows the truth of heaven and earth. As Guo Xiang has it,

> The mind of the sage penetrates to the utmost the perfect union of yin and yang. He understands most clearly the wonderful principle inherent in all the myriad beings. Therefore he can identify with the process of change and be in utter harmony with all transformations. As a result, he will find everything all right wherever he may go. He embraces all beings and because of this nothing to him is ever not in its perfect cosmic state. . . . He has no deliberate mind of his own. (1.30)

The sage or perfected is thus one who is free from the limitations of the ordinary mind, with its various feelings and critical evaluations. He or she blends the "intramundane and the inframundane in mystical union,"[39] and, as a result, "his life becomes the course of heaven, his death the mere transformation of a being" (12.422).

Looking around himself, the perfected sees the world of dualistic thinking, desires, and emotions revolve around him in mad circles. "Taking right and wrong as a circle, the sage establishes himself in its middle. Thus he gets rid of all rights and wrongs. From such a position, he is then free to respond to right and wrong, and this responding will be just as endless as the ever ongoing circle of right and wrong itself" (2.68). In going beyond all opposites, in taking up the position in the quiet center of the tornado, the sage "realizes his aloneness" (*jiandu*). He alone is without opposite, whole in nature and self, "standing beside heaven and earth and at one with all beings."[40]

Acting in the world, the behavior of such a perfected will be like natural processes. He will not seem to be doing anything actively by himself but it will look as if he is carried fully along by the cosmos. "Free from self, free from merit, free from fame" (*Zhuangzi,* chap. 6), he leaves no tracks or traces (*Daode jing* 27). He neither changes anything in the world through the way he lives nor does he act upon others. However, he does not "experience any opposition in the world" either (2.68). He will naturally walk on dry land, never encountering the dangers of drowning; he will naturally be far away from any fire, never avoiding it, yet not coming in contact with it (6.226). The perfected will encounter useful and positive situations wherever he goes. "He will always step into good fortune" and "will never be befallen by calamities" (17.574; 1.32). At one with the cosmos, he does no harm to any living being (17.574) and is in turn never harmed by the forces of nature or society. As Guo Xiang concludes:

> Ordinary people can certainly understand warnings and avoid misfortune. But to never encounter anything inappropriate is solely the result of being at one with the workings of heaven and earth, with the processes of perfect principle. (5.219)

The truth of the cosmos is thus not only realized in the mind and actions of the perfected but it is proven to be true because of his perfect good fortune in everything he undertakes.

The personal truth realized by Guo Xiang's sage, then, has the effect of creating a kind of person who is unassuming and soft, never harming anyone or anything, yet also always stepping into good fortune and auspicious situations. In addition, the category of personal truth can be connected with two further comparative notions: sincerity and no-self. Sincerity is a key term in Neo-Confucianism, where it describes a person who engages himself in the reality of the cosmos, and also plays a role in Islam and Hinduism, as we have heard. It means being true to oneself not as an egoistic creature but as a cosmic being and as a person resting in oneness with the universe. In Neo-Confucianism it is attained by learning first about the outside world, then developing one's inner virtue, and is realized by being true both to one's social situation and to one's inner spiritual dimension. In Islam it means the match of perception, reality, and (verbal) expression; in Hinduism it is the trustworthiness of the individual. The other category of no-self means the loss of an ego-centered consciousness in favor of a more cosmic-oriented perception; it can be compared to Buddhist notions (*anātman*); to Christian ideas of a new spiritual self with spiritual flesh that is like god and unlike the ego-self; and to modern psychological ideas of what is known as the "observing self"[41] or as the state of "being" as opposed to "deficiency."[42] It indicates a state of detachment and calm, a sense of freedom and wisdom, a smooth going-along with the patterns of the cosmos.

1.4.4 *Social Truth*

Society in China is part of the overall cosmic organization and stands in an intimate relation with both the individual and the cosmos. The dominant mode of expressing the interaction between the levels is with the idea of *ganying* or "impulse and response."[43] It indicates the concept that in an utterly integrated cosmos every good and bad deed has a response in auspicious or inauspicious signs from heaven, and is thus part of universal movements that are pervasive yet usually hidden from human eyes. Vice versa, heavenly activities and natural phenomena are also the immediate expression of the state of society and human life. The concept of impulse and response reflects synchronicity, a form of thinking that is acausal and nonlinear, inductive and synthetic, and that establishes "a logical link between two effective positions at the same time in different places in space."[44] As a result, events that we would not connect with each other because they are not related in a causal sequence became indicative of the truth—showing the positive or negative impact of deeds and cosmic events.

This form of socially experienced truth understood in a synchronistic manner was by far the most common in ancient China. It found expression in a number of ways: calendar calculation and astronomy; divination with turtle shells or milfoil stalks; observation of strange phenomena, both earthly and celestial; siting houses and graves with *fengshui* or geomancy; fortune-telling with the help of dreams, body analysis, and birth dates; and philosophical theories of states of mind that would ensure perfect luck at all times. There is neither room nor need to go into all of these, so we will discuss only two: the observation of strange phenomena and the philosophical theories of states of mind.

Strange phenomena or omens were observed in Chinese history at all times. They include such well-known celestial auspices as eclipses of the sun or the moon, changes in the course of the planets, the appearance of comets, shooting stars, strange-colored clouds, and so on. In addition, earthly phenomena were also noted, including natural disasters, such as floods, droughts, locust plagues, earthquakes, and epidemics, but also other unusual events, such as the birth of strangely shaped animals or babies, the rising of a black fog, or the appearance of numinous visions of deities and the manifestation of talismans and sacred texts.

In accordance with the doctrine that dynasties alternated in the same pattern as the seasons, by following the order of the five phases and their responding colors and directions, predictions were made about the rise of a new emperor from this or that area, wearing this or that color.[45] Entire stretches of country rose in rebellion believing that a certain person dressed in yellow was the harbinger of a new dynasty—notably the Yellow Turbans in 184 CE—and once in the sixth century, when black was the supposed color of the dynasty next to arise, Buddhists with their characteristic black robes were put under mass suspicion if not actually persecuted. Visions of new dynasties, of course, would only arise when there were negative omens to begin with, earthquakes and floods, for example, that were interpreted as expressions of heaven's disfavor with the current regime. Any change in policy, the firing of an official, the execution of a prime minister, was considered right and true if and when the disasters stopped. Any alteration of court ritual was accordingly found suitable when the weather changed and the epidemic ceased. In the same vein, the Han rulers' fondness for "modern" music from the country of Chu was seen as the immediate cause for a change of course among the celestial bodies, which in turn resulted in bad harvests and other forms of natural and social disorder. Strong remonstrations admonished the emperor to abstain from his penchant for pop and go back to the sonorous sounds of old, thus righting the cosmic wrong and getting the country back on track.[46]

On the positive side, the appearance of mythical animals, such as dragons, phoenixes, and unicorns, signaled the reign of a sage king and good times ahead. Other wondrous phenomena included the manifestation of sweet dew, a kind of nourishing dew that was believed to collect only when the weather conditions were perfect, the timely rising of energy that disturbed the loosely scattered ashes on top of partially buried pieces of bamboo, the so-called pitch-pipes, the appearance of strangely shaped stones or buried talismans, as well as the presentation at court of newly revealed Daoist scriptures.

To give only one concrete example of what could be expanded endlessly, there was a series of finds under Emperor Xuanzong in the eighth century that documented the truth and heavenly approval of his reign. First, in 723, people found a half-moon-shaped piece of jade that showed a picture of a musician immortal. When struck, it made a marvelous sound. The emperor named it "Half-moon Lithophone" and had it hung in the garden of the imperial ancestral temple. Next, on the grounds of an ancient monastery another sounding jade appeared, which also was hung in the same garden. Then there was a metal fish from a distant province, found when the foundations for a new Daoist monastery were dug. It was three feet long and of purple and blue-green coloring. "It looked like nothing ever done by man" and made a spectacular sound when struck. The emperor named it "Auspicious Fish Lithophone" and put it in the Great Tenuity Temple in the eastern capital to be sounded during rituals. In 741, finally, a momentous find occurred of a celestial talisman, known as the "Heavenly Treasure." Indicated by the highest deity himself in a vision to a court official, it consisted of a stone container with a golden box and several jade plates that were inscribed with red characters in a mysterious old seal script. In response to this sign, the emperor changed his reign title to "Heavenly Treasure." Following the entire series of good omens, he also created a set of new liturgical dances, among them the famous "Dance of the Purple Culmen," which was first performed in 742. Doing so, he created a heavenly realm of the Dao on earth—both in time and space—claiming the attainment of Great Peace and celestial perfection for his reign, which indeed was the most splendid China has ever known.[47]

1.4.5 Ethical Truth

A different aspect of the social and practical side of truth is its realization in or against society. Often the religious truth a person feels deep within is contrary to the demands of society, and there are numerous stories in the Chinese and other traditions of young people being called to serve God or the Dao and being hindered and hampered by the society around them. China, being a dominantly Confucian country, has always demanded a reconciliation between the two, requiring novices to bring written permission from their parents before allowing them into religious orders and limiting the numbers of ordinations depending on the tax and conscription needs of the state.

More than that, Confucian doctrine itself focuses strongly on society and social interaction. The attainment of truth here is never a matter of sudden enlightenment or divine revelation, although that certainly is a source of deep human happiness. Realized through learning and adjusting to social conditions, being in harmony with society and living in truth coincide. They are reached through study, by gaining familiarity with the classics, which was the prerequisite for any meaningful conversation just as familiarity with cultural codes (*li*) was the prerequisite for successful social interaction, and the rectification of names (*zhengming*) was the prerequisite for good government. Truth here is experienced, for example, in the visit of friends from distant places, noted in the first section of the *Lunyu*, because at such an occasion one joins the larger human community, expands one's horizons, and has one's memories and ideas reaffirmed. It is never sought on lofty mountains or experienced in lonely isolation, but always in the society of those whose shared cultural background forms the condition for the possibility of rational discourse.

The attainment of truth or virtue in Confucianism, then, requires active participation in the established social, semiotic, and political system. It is first and foremost an ethical enterprise. Confucians do not invent truth but only discover, renew, and transmit it in discourse and conversation, learn it by heart in an ethical consciousness and by performing the proper social rituals. Unlike in Daoism, where the particularity of language and culture constitutes a permanent epistemological alienation from the truth, in Confucianism it is to be celebrated as the only means of intercourse with that which is real, true, and valuable. Human beings are always and irrevocably instituted and in a social context. Being true, correct, appropriate, or optimal is thus a matter of ethical interaction and participation in an institutional process.

1.4.6 Debated Truth

In many traditions, notably Hinduism, Judaism, and Christianity, religious truth has been the subject of debates and councils, views being contrasted, rankings established, canonical decisions made. China, too, has had debates and polemics but the issue at stake has for the most part not been religious truth as such. There has, on the contrary, tended to be a basic agreement that the world was what it was, based on a certain underlying pattern, which was the same wherever one went. Some people, then, had better intuitive access than others; some again used a different set of expressions to propose what was ultimate the same basic tendency of the world. This basic agreement is probably responsible for the relative harmony of the various traditions in China and the general trend to integrate and match concepts rather than pit them against each other.

What debates there were dealt with the issue of efficiency. In other words, the question was not what was cosmic truth but which teaching among all those that tried to express the same cosmic truth was best suited to create most good fortune for the largest number of people and thus could serve to establish the most powerful and best-run state on the planet. Debates were political in organization and outlook and did not, for the most part, ever come close to debating the kinds of issues we are interested in.

Religious truth, therefore, can be described as intrinsically political and pragmatic in character, and its expression in religious practices a form of spiritual technology that could be evaluated best in terms of its personal, social, and cosmic effects. The Chinese have generally recognized that no one can have perfect access to the absolute or, if they do, then others can do it just as well; and they have seen much value in other traditions to the point where forms of religious Daoism can be (and have been) described as the most advanced adaptation of Buddhism in China and where Neo-Confucians were happily engaging in both Buddhist and Daoist meditation practices to develop a sincerity understood in terms that create a thorough mixture of the three teachings. It was just that the Chinese, however much value they might have seen in Buddhist teachings, did not feel comfortable having Buddhists run their country; their key concern remained with the established and time-honored social truth of Confucianism. Their attitude is comparable to that found among members of other ethnic groups sharing one religion who are confronted with different beliefs among their fold: Christian Arabs in the Middle East, or Jewish Romans in antiquity. In all cases, the dominant group feels that conversion to the other religion is a betrayal of its group identity, an abandonment of Roman-ness or Chinese-ness. It is more of an ethnic and political issue than a concern with religious truth.

1.5 Conclusion

This preliminary survey has turned predominantly on the theme of truth as a dynamic relation that develops between human beings and the social, political, and cosmological environment that they in part constitute. To attain this dynamic truth, therefore, one must move along with it, trace its pattern, or pursue its roots. To get at truth by returning to the root one thus requires an explicit organic connection to it. Despite the Mencian idealism of the "Four Beginnings" as the root of sagehood within one's true nature, or Zhuangzi's wanderings free from culture, the actual historical practice of Confucianism and Daoism alike has been that such an organic connection could best be guaranteed by lineages of ordination or transmission in which cultural intelligence or religious power is not merely handed down but continuously reauthenticated.

This dialectical movement of unitive vision and interpretive performance parallels on a historical plane the organic epistemological relationship between theory and practice that is embedded in the theoretical foundation for this research project. The connection is made explicit when Robert C. Neville translates his discussion of theory in part IV of his *Axiology of Thinking* series into the concrete terms of practical responsibility (part V). He writes:

> It was argued earlier that every thing in the cosmos [*tianxia*: all under heaven] every process, substance, composite, institution, or situation [*wanwu*: the ten thousand things] is to be understood in terms of four primary cosmological categories. Every thing has a form or pattern [*li*: principle] whereby it integrates its components. Every thing has components [*xing*: nature] that are integrated. Every thing existentially actualizes its components [*xing*] and form [*li*] together with haecceity in an existential, temporal environment [*shi*: actuality] with a fixed actual past, a future structured as a field relating to other things [*ming*: destiny], and with present moments of decision. Every thing achieves [*de*: obtain] some actual value [*de*: virtue, power], a value that grows [*qi*: arise] or unfolds [*fa*: issue, manifest] through the enduring process of actualization [*shi*], and that has a cumulative worth relative to what might have been.[48]

This is, we might say, a theoretical analysis of the process of the movement from an unformed, unrealized, vague "root" to the actual flowering of a realized "branch." In these terms, therefore, this research project ought to have a particularly "Chinese" aim to it, namely, the establishment of a cross-cultural "lineage" of comparative categories whereby contemporary religious thinkers can legitimate a hermeneutical relationship with the concepts of many religious traditions, a relationship that has a thoroughly dynamic and practical aspect to it and is integrally oriented toward our cosmic environment. From a "Chinese" perspective, therefore, the creation of a cross-cultural artificial intelligence demands new practical orientations within our cosmic ecology.

Notes

1. The authors express their thanks to Anne Birdwhistell for her comments on an earlier draft of this chapter.

2. See Chang Kuang-chih, *Early Chinese Civilization: Anthropological Perspectives* (Cambridge, Mass.: Harvard-Yenching Institute Monograph Series 23, 1976).

3. See Wing-tsit Chan, *A Source Book in Chinese Philosophy* (Princeton: Princeton University Press, 1963), 271–88.

4. See Manfred Porkert, *The Theoretical Foundations of Chinese Medicine* (Cambridge, Mass.: MIT Press, 1974), 1.

5. See A. C. Graham, *Yin-Yang and the Nature of Correlative Thinking* (Singapore: The Institute for East Asian Philosophies, 1986).

6. *Huainanzi* 3:2a–2b; see John B. Henderson, *The Development and Decline of Chinese Cosmology* (New York: Columbia University Press, 1994), 25.

7. Jorges Borges' *Ficciones* (1984, xv).

8. Wheelwright Bian, chap. 13 in A. C. Graham, *Chuang-tzu: The Seven Inner Chapters and Other Writings from the Book of Chuang-tzu* (London: Allan & Unwin 1981), 140; see also Lee Yearley, "Zhuangzi's Understanding of Skillfulness, and the Ultimate Spiritual State," *Essays on Skepticism, Relativism and Ethics in the Zhuangzi*, ed. Paul Kjellberg and Philip J. Ivanhoe (Albany: State University of New York Press, 1996), 152–82.

9. See Xiaogan Liu, "*Wuwei* (Non-Action): From *Laozi* to *Huainanzi*," *Taoist Resources* 3.1 (1991): 41–56.

10. Graham, *Chuang-tzu*, 12.

11. Ibid., 48–61.

12. See Isabelle Robinet, *Les commentaires du Tao to king jusqu'au VIIe siècle* (Paris: Mémoires de l'Institut des Hautes Etudes Chinoises 5, 1977); Kohn, *Taoist Mystical Philosophy: The Scripture of Western Ascension* (Albany: State University of New York Press, 1991).

13. David Hall and Roger Ames, *Thinking from the Han* (Albany: State University of New York Press, 1998), 149–50.

14. Chad Hansen, *A Daoist Theory of Chinese Thought* (New York: Oxford University Press, 1992), 235.

15. Isabelle Robinet, "Shangqing—Highest Clarity," *Daoism Handbook*, ed. Livia Kohn (Leiden: E. Brill, 2000), 210.

16. Ibid.

17. The temporal construction of ultimate reality was, however, critical both to millenarian Daoism and in the Neo-Confucian reconstruction of historical evolution. See Kohn, *God of the Dao: Lord Lao in History and Myth* (Ann Arbor: University of Michigan Press, 1998), 305–8.

18. See Rolf A. Stein, "Religious Taoism and Popular Religion from the Second to Seventh Centuries," *Facets of Taoism*, ed. Holmes Welch and Anna Seidel (New Haven, Conn.: Yale University Press, 1979).

19. The latter is found in an eleventh-century hagiography, the *Youlong zhuan* (DZ 774) in the section on the conversion, 4.7b–8b, as well as in the *Laojun bashiyi hua tushu*. See Florian C. Reiter, *Leben und Wirken Lao-Tzu's in Schrift und Bild. Lao-chün pa-shih-i-hua t'u-shuo* (Würzburg: Königshausen & Neumann, 1990).

20. See Jonathan Chaves, "The Legacy of Ts'ang Chieh: The Written Word as Magic," *Oriental Art* 23 (1977): 200–15.

21. See Lothar Ledderose, "Some Taoist Elements in the Calligraphy of the Six Dynasties," *T'oung-pao* 70 (1984): 246–78.

22. See Monika Drexler *Daoistische Schriftmagie: Interpretationen zu den fu im Daozang* (Stuttgart: Franz Steiner, Münchener Ostasiatische Studien 68, 1994).

23. See Michael Saso, "What is the *Ho-t'u*?" *History of Religions* 17 (1978): 399–416.

24. See Anna Seidel, "Imperial Treasures and Taoist Sacraments: Taoist Roots in the Apocrypha," *Tantric and Taoist Studies*, ed. Michel Strickmann (Brussels: Institut Belge des Hautes Etudes Chinoises, 1983).

25. *Wuyu zhenxing tu*, DZ 1223.

26. *Lingbao wufu xu*, DZ 388.

27. See Catherine Despeux, *Taoïsme et corps humain: Le Xiuzhen tu* (Paris: Guy Tredaniel, 1994). Other, more abstract charts also serve to explain the nature of the world as based on the *Yijing* while detailed descriptions of the bodily organs show the cosmic network of the inner man.

28. See Kenneth J. DeWoskin, *A Song for One or Two: Music and the Concept of Art in Early China* (Ann Arbor: University of Michigan, Center for Chinese Studies, 1982), 34.

29. See James Legge, *The Chinese Classics* (Taipei: Jinwen, 1969).

30. *Scripture of Immaculate Numen*, DZ 1314, 6b. See Isabelle Robinet, *Taoist Meditation*, trans. Julian Pas and Norman Girardot (Albany: State University of New York Press, 1993), 24–28. Other discussions of the sacred scriptures in Daoism include Stephan Peter Bumbacher, "Cosmic Scripts and Heavenly Scriptures: The Holy Nature of Taoist Texts," *Cosmos* 11.2 (1995): 139–54;

Isabelle Robinet, *Taoism: Growth of a Religion* (Stanford: Stanford University Press, 1997), 125–28; Stephen R. Bokenkamp, *Early Daoist Scriptures* (Berkeley: University of California Press, 1997), 385–89.

31. Laurence Sickmann, *Eight Dynasties of Chinese Painting: Collections of the Nelson Gallery-Atkins Museum, Kansas City and the Cleveland Museum of Art* (Cleveland: Cleveland Museum of Art 1980), 23.

32. See Stephen Little, *Realm of the Immortals: Daoism in the Arts of China* (The Cleveland Museum of Art, 1988).

33. See William James, *The Varieties of Religious Experience* (New York: Penguin Classics, 1985).

34. See Kohn, *Taoist Mystical Philosophy*, 127–31.

35. See Kohn, *Seven Steps to the Tao: Sima Chengzhen's Zuowanglun* (St.Augustin/Nettetal: Monumenta Serica Monograph XX, 1987), 41–43.

36. See George Weckman, "Monasticism: An Overview," *Encyclopedia of Religion*, vol. 10, ed. Mircea Eliade (New York: Macmillan, 1987), 35–41

37. See Livia Knaul, "The Winged Life: Kuo Hsiang's Mystical Philosophy," *Journal of Chinese Studies* 2.1 (1985): 17–41.

38. See Livia Kohn, "Selfhood and Spontaneity in Ancient Chinese Thought," *Selves, People, and Persons*, ed. Leroy Rouner (South Bend, Ind.: University of Notre Dame Press, Boston University Series in Philosophy and Religion, vol. 13, 1992), 123–38.

39. Chan, op. cit., 333.

40. *Zhuangzi*, chap. 1.

41. Arthur J. Deikman, *The Observing Self: Mysticism and Psychotherapy* (Boston: Beacon Press, 1982).

42. Abraham H. Maslow, *Toward a Psychology of Being* (New York: Van Nostrand Reinhold, 1964).

43. See Charles Le Blanc, "Resonance: Une interpretation chinoise de la réalité," *Mythe et philosophie à l'aube de la Chine imperial: Etudes sur le Huainan zi*, ed. Charles Le Blanc and Rémi Mathieu (Montréal: Les Presses de l'Université de Montréal, 1992), 91–111.

44. Manfred Porkert, *The Theoretical Foundations of Chinese Medicine* (Cambridge, Mass.: MIT Press, 1974), 1.

45. See Jack Dull, *A Historical Introduction to the Apocryphal (ch'en-wei) Texts of the Han Dynasty* (Ph.D. Diss., University of Washington, Seattle, 1966).

46. See Kenneth DeWoskin, *A Song for One or Two* (Ann Arbor: University of Michigan, Center for Chinese Studies Publications, 1982).

47. See Edward H. Schafer, "The Dance of the Purple Culmen," *T'ang Studies* 5 (1987): 45–68.

48. Robert C. Neville, *Normative Cultures* (Albany: State University of New York Press, 1995), 118.

2

From Truth to Religious Truth in Hindu Philosophical Theology

Francis X. Clooney, S.J.
with Hugh Nicholson

2.1 How They Forged a Conversation on Religious Truth in Ancient India

In our preceding volume on Ultimate Reality I discussed the "Definition of the Lord" section (*Īśvarapariccheda*) of Vedānta Deśika's *Nyāyasiddhañjana*. In the course of surveying his rich array of arguments regarding God's existence and identity, I noted that although Deśika is a devout theist he argues at length against the Nyāya logical view that God's existence can be inferred.[1] The idea of inferring God's existence may be well-meant, Deśika admits, but there can never be a perfect induction; in the end, the inevitable flaws in the induction may disturb the faith of simple believers and cause them to doubt. Although it is true that God exists, this is not the kind of conclusion to which one can argue by way of an induction.

Reflection on *Deśika*'s view of the problems related to constructing a rational basis for knowledge of God has made evident to me the importance of further attention to rational discourse about God in scholarly Hindu thought. It is worthwhile to explore how Hindu intellectuals have chosen to speak about God, how they explain this speech in ways that makes sense first inside and then outside immediate believing communities, and how they defend the truth of their claims. This chapter inquires more specifically into the role of truth in that philosophical theology, that is, Hindu understandings of truth, and of religious truth as a kind of truth that functions in discourse about God. We will explore how assertions of religious truth, such as the claim that there is a God who can (or cannot) be known by reason, are located among a broader array of acts of right knowing that claim the title "truth."

Those of us contributing to this volume have agreed that religious truth has epistemological, linguistic and embodied/practical aspects—truth is to be known, expressed (revealed), lived (achieved in meditation, contemplation)—and I will keep all three aspects in mind. But my emphasis will be on truth as available in ordinary, reasoned discourse. According to the mainstream classical Hindu religious epistemology, knowing God is not entirely different from other acts of true knowledge, even the most mundane. This is why those Indian theologies that engage in arguments about God strive, in the course of their argumentation, to locate "religious truth" as a subdivision of "ordinary truth."[2]

2.2 Ordinary Truth

By "ordinary truth" I do not intend any technical definition, but only what is knowable by way of sense knowledge (*pratyakṣa*) is of course the mode of knowledge most commonly admitted by the different schools of Indian thought. To see clearly with one's eyes (*prati-akṣa*), or by one of the other senses, is to be able to ascertain the truth. Other, more complex means of knowledge, such as inference or comparison, may be distinguishable from sense knowledge, but nevertheless they come into force only in relation to sense knowledge, based upon it even when extending knowledge beyond sense data. As much as possible, truth is knowledge-like-perception, unobstructed knowing conformed to objects properly distinguished. The wager of some religious thinkers, such as the Nyāya logicians, was that careful reasoning would reveal that assertions about God and the world in relation to God can be true by standards not entirely different from those by which all kinds of ordinary things are known to be true or stated truly in ordinary life. I devote the major portion of this chapter to this broad and shared sense of truth that includes the "religious" as a subordinate category, because it is in this sense that Hindus have presented and argued for the truth of their beliefs, because it is here, if anywhere, that we can make a defensible claim to be presenting a shared *Hindu* understanding of truth, and because this is a rationally accessible truth that outsiders to the Hindu traditions can apprehend. Other important questions regarding truth—for example, the questions regarding truth as revealed and truth as lived—are, in my view, most economically and appropriately discussed subsequently, in light of the public truth of a broader rational discourse to which, after all, every person has access simply because she or he is a rational being.

2.3 Ordinary Truth as Right Knowing: *pramāṇa, prameya, pramā*

The analysis of truth as right knowing has been a technical matter in the Hindu traditions and in Western studies of this epistemology. Hindu thinkers analyzed the knowing process in a very sophisticated fashion, drawing subtle distinctions and relations among the *pramāṇa*s (henceforth, "means of right knowledge"), *prameya*s (henceforth, "objects of right knowledge"), and, *pramā* (henceforth, "right knowledge").[3] Near one end of the spectrum is Vaiśeṣika naturalism, which represents an empirical, scientific viewpoint that seeks no scriptural warrants for its views, because it wants to adhere as closely as possible to perception. Near the other end of the spectrum is Advaita Vedānta, which subordinates perception to a reliance on word, scripture, the Veda.[4]

The quest for a simple apprehension of the truth by perception is never adequately achieved in terms that are comprehensive and acceptable to all, so the means of right knowledge multiply. More ample lists of the means of right knowledge and objects of right knowledge are only reluctantly conceded, kept brief and sparing, and as close as possible to the truth of perception. The effort to forge a common ground for truth empirically known and reasoned is in part motivated by a desire to respond to Buddhist and Jain skepticism about whether the supernatural realities to which the brahmins appealed (e.g., the potency of sacrifice, self, God) could be verified or indeed needed be verified, given the adequacy and limits of perception without such postulations of unseen realities.

The goal in theorizing about the right means of knowledge was therefore to defend a firm commitment to perception as the right way of knowing, while yet being willing, albeit reluctantly, to admit other means of knowledge, particularly inference and verbal authority, in order to fill in gaps left by perception. One also has to establish a complete but minimal list of the objects of right knowledge. This quest, embodied in the natural philosophy known as Vaiśeṣika, relies as much as possible on perception alone, as an empirical endeavor to enumerate all that can be known.[5] The Vaiśeṣika project of describing material reality thoroughly according to empirical norms did eventually lead to a consideration of whether material reality was self-explanatory, explicable on its own terms, or whether an unseen cause, such as God, had to be postulated to explain what was seen. But it was only on empirical grounds that religious truth emerged, as a needed subsequent subcategory of a more general and comprehensive ordinary truth.

2.4 Religious Truth

The question of the relationship between religious truth and truth involves the differences and relations among the means of right knowledge (perception, inference, verbal testimony, and perhaps others) and those means in relation to the objects of right knowledge. The goal is to keep the two lists (which seem to have developed separately) as simple as possible, adequate to one another while yet still distinct. Truth is comprehended when the means and objects of right knowledge are fully known, in a full understanding where religious truth no longer stands apart from ordinary truth.

It was only at a later stage that Vaiśeṣika and Nyāya thinkers decided that observable reality could not be described by itself; the undeniable truth of ordinary reality raises questions that cannot be answered in an ordinary fashion. Nyāya thinkers asserted that unless a maker were introduced along with (or "behind") the component categories of ordinary reality, that reality could not be coherently explained. This maker had to be posited as an unperceived, inferred cause for the synthesis that constitutes things that can be perceived; for the world, this maker is God.[6] Even before one turns to a consideration of revelation or religious practice as categories for religious truth, an important component of religious truth is contained in this assertion that there must be a maker for the world we observe empirically.

Once God is recognized as a useful category in the project of describing and explaining the world coherently, God is used to undergird the ordering of the objects of right knowledge, making them intelligible from the viewpoint of a coherent use of the means of right knowledge. The truth about God is used to buttress ordinary truth because positing that there is a God undergirds the truth of what is seen, arguably making it plausible. Sometimes we find God among the fundamental perceptible substances (*dravya*), although occasionally God is presented as an underlying source for the substances, the maker or cause. It is this claim that paves the way for argument. We will see this position accepted in Nyāya, rejected in Mīmāṃsā, and balanced in Vedānta with verbal authority as a more authoritative means of knowledge.

As a basis for this inquiry—which represents a working hypothesis about a large body of complex material—I will refer primarily to four small, introductory manuals: the *Tarkasaṃgraha* (seventeenth century) of the Nyāya logical school; the *Mānameyodaya* (sixteenth–seventeenth centuries) of the Mīmāṃsā ritual school; the *Yatīndramatadīpikā* (sixteenth–seventeenth century) of the Viśiṣṭādvaita Vedānta school; the *Vedānta Paribhāṣā* (seventeenth century) of the Advaita Vedānta school. The advantage of such manuals, in addition to their clarity and brevity, is that they represent the schools' own summaries of their teachings for their own adherents, and therefore, their standard positions presented in a relatively simple and straightforward fashion. Other, larger texts will be referred to only occasionally, as needed.

2.5 Nyāya: God Is Like a Potmaker

The quest for an adequate description of empirical reality, made difficult and urgent by the Buddhist rejection of the need for a maker for the universe, led the logicians to focus on the fact of God's existence, giving some lesser attention to the nature of that God. The logicians claims that the truth about the world gives us access to the truth about God. The common form of the Nyāya argument is an inductive form of the cosmological argument, a position usually summarized as follows: *kṣityādikaṃ sakartṛkam kāryatvāt ghaṭavat*—"the earth, etc., has a maker, because it is an effect, like a pot."[7] If observable realities seem to be temporary and impermanent, they must be effects of something that precedes them; relatively sure claims can therefore be made that there is some appropriate precedent reality. Gerhard Oberhammer rightly stresses the *a posteriori* nature of the cosmological induction of God's existence;[8] the Nyāya induction has to do with what can and must be deduced from perceptible reality. The truth about God is a truth reluctantly acceded to, one that remains dependent on correct observation of the world and what is required to explain what is observed.

We see this reluctance clearly in the oldest Nyāya discussion, found in the *Nyāya Sūtras* 4.1.19–21. Here the question of God is raised in the midst of a longer consideration, in Books 3 and 4 of the *Nyāya Sūtras*, of the set of "twelve realities" listed in sūtra 1.1.9. The six primary realities (soul, body, sense-organs, objects of perception, apprehension, mind) are treated in Book 3, while in Book 4, the six dependent realities (activity, defect, rebirth, fruition, pain, release) are examined in detail.[9] *Nyāya*

Sūtras 4.1.11–43 discuss the topic of the origins of the six dependent realities. In 4.1.11–13 it was determined that manifest things are generated out of other manifest things, and then, in 4.1.14–43, eight alternative explanations are considered and, it seems, rejected: production from a void (sūtras 14–18), or production by God (sūtras 19–21) or due to chance (sūtras 22–24); the notions that all things are evanescent (sūtras 25–28) or eternal (sūtras 29–33); the view that there is simple, unexplained diversity (sūtras 34–36) or that nothing exists (sūtras 37–40) or that the exact number of things can actually be known (sūtras 41–43).

Sūtras 19–21 contain a terse argument about whether God is required to ensure the fruitfulness of human action:

4.1.19 The Lord is the cause, since we see that human action is fruitless.

4.1.20 This is not so since, as a matter of fact, no fruit is accomplished without human action.

4.1.21 Since that is efficacious, the reason lacks force.

In context, amid a series of proposed reasons that are rejected, the point of the obscure twenty-first sūtra is most likely to reject the need for a God who will be the guarantor of the efficacy of human activity. If there is no need for a certain kind of being, that being should not be introduced, so the suggestion made in sūtra 19, that God is the guarantor of the efficacy of human action, has no force. Since human action can be explained without positing a God, it is better to avoid this postulate. An easier empirical postulate, that the contingent arises from the contingent, suffices to account for reality. Sūtra 21 can thus be interpreted as a criticism of the postulation of theism, as is clearer in this amplified version:

4.1.21 Since that [action] is efficacious [only due to human effort], the reason [put forth in 4.1.19, regarding the need to posit a Lord] lacks force.

But the context for reading the sūtras eventually changes, perhaps due to the need to provide a more definitive account of how the perceived world began, and perhaps due to the rise of theism as a central criterion in the developing Hindu orthodoxy. The Nyāya tradition seems then to change the sūtras' apparent argument against God into a defense of God's existence, and the Nyāya commentators took the argument in the theistic direction. Sūtra 21 was then interpreted quite differently:

4.1.21 Since that [human effort] is efficacious [only with divine help], the reason [put forth in 4.1.20, regarding the idea that a Lord is superfluous] lacks force.

To defend the interconnection between the postulation of God and the practical intelligibility of the world, the Logicians had to develop increasingly complex discussions of God's existence, introducing a theistic explanatory hypothesis into a system that previously was thought to work neatly without such considerations. In some Nyāya texts the effort to infer God's existence and refute opponents of this induction is developed at great length, and becomes a goal in itself. The argument was represented in a rather complete form in Jayanta Bhaṭṭa's *Nyāyamañjari* (ninth century) and was most fully developed in Udayana's great *Nyāyakusumāñjali* (eleventh century), where a lengthy exposition of the induction shows that there must be a maker of the world, who must be eternal and omniscient, and thus, by definition, none other than "the Lord."[10]

Luckily, there are smaller texts that present the argument briefly, and here we turn to the first of the four manuals I will introduce in this essay. The *Tarkasaṃgraha* of Annaṃbhaṭṭa (seventeenth century) contains a very concise presentation of the Nyāya view of God, and we can rely on it to introduce the argument for God's existence. In an early section of the *Tarkasaṃgraha* Annaṃbhaṭṭa says simply that the supreme self, the "lord," is one of two kinds of self (*ātman*)—the other being the finite (human) self. He does not argue the point nor consider objections to it, but simply states, "The soul is the substratum of knowledge. It is twofold: the supreme soul and the individual soul. Of these, the supreme soul is omnipotent and omniscient and one only. The individual soul is different in each body, is all-pervading, and eternal."

But Annaṃbhaṭṭa does elaborate a bit in his own *Dīpikā* commentary on the *Tarkasaṃgraha*, admitting a brief but forceful set of objections to God's existence which may be summarized as follows. First, God cannot be *perceived*. God is nowhere to be seen, nor is the evidence such that we can intuit God in the way we can intuit the presence of a human consciousness "within" some human body that we do observe. Annaṃbhaṭṭa deals quickly with this first objection, since he agrees that God is not an object of perception.

A second objection is that God's existence cannot be *inferred* since there is no similar instance that corroborates the induction. Inferring the existence of a God is like no other induction in our experience. What Annaṃbhaṭṭa has in mind is the common analogy found in standard analyses of induction: where there is (visible) smoke, there is fire (visible or not). When we see smoke on a distant hill we know that there must be fire there too, since experience tells us that smoke is invariably accompanied by fire. So too, the argument goes, observation of the world we see leads us to infer the existence of a maker, God, whom we cannot see.

To this an interlocutor objects that observation of the world and its many parts does not compel us to any such conclusion, since contingent and composite realities can be explained without reference to God, in other and simpler ways. But Annaṃbhaṭṭa defends the idea that God can be inferred, since the perceptible cannot be explained in terms of the perceptible: "Sprouts, etc., are caused by an agent since they are products, like pots. Thus, the existence of the Lord is inferred by induction." Induction is the ground for a defensible claim about God, and one can then claim that it is true that God exists.[11] Thus the logicians mark out a common ground for argument with a variety of interlocutors, including Buddhists, many of whom thought that the impossibility of the induction of God's existence could be demonstrated. But even adversaries seemed to agree that there is a sufficiently shared truth independent of revelation, and this shared truth allows for heated religious arguments. Only careful reasoning is required to engage in this argument for or against God's existence, since it is true or false that God exists.

As the preceding paragraphs indicate, the Nyāya presentation of the truth about God is austere and spare, proceeding without reliance on sectarian appeal and with few clues to sectarian identity. Truth as experience is not mentioned, and the truth of revelation is appealed to only in a very auxiliary fashion. Although it is plausible to assume that the logicians could be religious Hindus, we have little information on the nature of any piety distinctive to the school. We can notice, though, the affinity of the Nyāya position with the theology of the Śaiva Siddhānta of south India, briefly introduced in my chapter in *Ultimate Reality*. Śaiva Siddhānta is an explicitly sectarian religious system, committed to a body of scriptures, and to a specific set of spiritual practices. It shares with Nyāya the view that there is a divine Maker of the world, and it names this maker Śiva. Even if it is too simple to state that the roots of the Śaiva theological positions are to be found in Nyāya or that most Nyāya logicians are Śaivas, the parallels indicate at least how the argued, epistemological, and logical truth of the Nyāya position is open to a certain kind of piety, the worship of a supreme creator God who is named in specific terms. Assertions about the rationally accessible truth of religious beliefs are not inimical to actual religious belief.

2.6 Mīmāṃsā: No Need for a World-Maker

If we look to the other Hindu schools, we can see that the Nyāya positions about the means and objects of right knowledge have much in common with the views worked out in the Mīmāṃsā school of ritual theology and in the consequent Vedānta theology. But there are differences, most important the decision of the Mīmāṃsā theorists and their Vedānta heirs to argue strictly on scriptural grounds, subordinating perception and inference to privileged sacred words. In the short run at least, God is not among the objects of knowledge, however subtle one's knowing; nor can God's existence be known inductively.

According to Jaimini, the first Mīmāṃsā author whose work has come down to us, a key presupposition is that one should appeal to any sort of unseen realities as little as possible. The world, and religion too, are best explained in terms of what is perceptible. Jaimini interpreted even the literal meaning of scripture as a kind of perception. The literal meaning of a text, often referred to as the perceived meaning, is always to be preferred unless there are factors that require one to move toward an indirect meaning. More complex modes of interpretation are considered secondary and dependent elaborations of truth. Mīmāṃsā theorists (theistic and atheistic) decided that the evidence allegedly proving the existence of God was insufficient. They also thought that there was no need to postulate a maker for the world, just as there was no need for an author to compose the Veda or an independent God to validate the Vedic rituals.

Fuller expositions of the Mīmāṃsā position on God can be found in the *Sambandhākṣepaparihāra* section of Kumārila Bhaṭṭa's *Ślokavārtika* (eighth century), a foundational text of the Bhaṭṭa school of Mīmāṃsā, and in the *Vimalāñjanam* section of the *Prakaraṇapañcikā* of Śālikanātha (ninth century), a key text of the smaller Prābhākara school. In both texts, at issue first of all is the explanation and validation of the relationship between words and their meanings, and consequently the truth of the Vedic scriptures. The topic of God is introduced as one of a number of postulates in support of that truth. Because the Mīmāṃsā theorists realize that appeals to God would move the authority of the Veda from the text to a higher source who is outside it and whose importance might possibly displace that of the Veda, they dedicate themselves to refuting the existence of such a God.

The Bhaṭṭa Mīmāṃsā position, to which we will limit our remarks, is set forth succinctly in the *Mānameyodaya*, an introductory manual begun by Nārāyaṇabhaṭṭatiri around 1590, its second part composed by Nārāyaṇasudhī a century later. In this manual the question of God arises only in the context of explaining empirical reality. The section of the *Mānameyodaya* on the objects of true knowledge begins with an analysis of divisible substances—earth, water, fire, air, darkness—but then takes up the question of their synthesis. If these substances are indeed divisible into simpler realities, how are they synthesized and held together?[12]

The Nyāya position is introduced and summarized as we saw it in the preceding section. God is the agent who synthesizes the simplest substances into more complex realities that comprise the universe, and it is God who thereafter breaks them down again. The familiar Nyāya thesis, "The earth, etc., have a maker, because it is an effect," is accepted as an adequate representation of the Nyāya position, but it is then rejected by Nārāyaṇasudhī. In his view, the attempted induction of a maker for the world does not work satisfactorily, since one would inevitably get caught in the paradox of whether such a God is embodied or not. There is no parallel instance where we see a maker without a body making embodied things, while the admission that the maker has a body would frustrate the logicians' overall intention. That body, necessarily finite and composite, would have to be explained by an appeal to some other, higher agent.

Moreover, all that we can infer from effects is that each effect has a cause, not that each separately, nor all together, has a maker. It is one thing to posit that what is not eternal must have a cause; it is quite another and more difficult task to posit a first agent, a certain kind of person who is the maker of the world. All we can say for certain is that the world has the appearance of an effect or sum of effects, and that each particular effect has a particular cause. There is no evidence to determine that the "world" as a whole holds together due to some specific intention. In any case, it does not really matter, since leaving the nature of the origins of the world indeterminate is not a flaw particular to the atheist position. Even theists, once they have stated that there is a creator, cannot explain how that creator is supposed to have created this particular world, or for what purpose. The induction about God fails: the evidence is insufficient and even optimal conclusions drawn from the induction do not add up to the God desired by the logicians.

Although Mīmāṃsā system has no place for a single supreme God, it nevertheless holds to its own religious truths, since the Vedic ritual system itself, Mīmāṃsā 's central value, is of course expressive of a particular religious worldview. Mīmāṃsā argues for a religion of ritual performance, coherent in itself, which (at least presents itself as) independent of all external factors.[13] Truth must be understood and argued in such a way as to support the coherence and coherent performance of ritual. That a Mīmāṃsā theorist would insist on the truth of the Veda as a truth entirely coherent with ordinary truth is not surprising. The key ritual realities, to which Mīmāṃsā is devoted, are integrally and deeply intertwined with the ritual words and directives found in the Veda. From this perspective, religious truth is first of all textually generated truth, since it only in that way that one knows the particular, transformative arrangements of ordinary things, actions, and persons that distinguish rituals. To a certain extent, the Mīmāṃsā theory of dharma integrates ordinary truth with religious truth by rooting the latter in a ritual re-ordering of elements of ordinary experience. What is to be known religiously is a transformation of things, persons, and actions known in ordinary life. The Mīmāṃsā theorists therefore devote great effort to showing that the Vedas are authoritative and true, not to be judged according to ordinary, empirical truth.[14]

For Mīmāṃsā, the function of the verbal expression of truth—sacred words, texts, revelations—is to fill the informative function perception cannot perfectly fill. Although this verbal truth is indeed a truth source alternative to perception, it nevertheless coheres with the data of perception and thus replicates the same "ordinary" certainty. If we cannot learn what we need to learn from perception and inference, fortunately scripture is there to inform us of the truth about the world and other important religious realities.

2.7 Knowing the God of Scripture in Viśiṣṭādvaita Vedānta

Continuities aside, though, the extension of the Mīmāṃsā discourse in Vedānta develops somewhat differently, as Vedānta adjusts the commitment to empirical truth defended in Nyāya and for the most part preferred in Mīmāṃsā. Vedānta begins instead with the authority of the Upaniṣads as the superlative form of verbal testimony, which takes precedence over perception and corrects the ordinary and inevitably flawed functioning of perception.[15] Although the Upaniṣads have strong empirical intuitions, Vedānta is skeptical about the operation and effectiveness of ordinary perception. It restricts the empiricism and experimentalism that lie near the heart of the Upaniṣads by combining some empirical observation with a great deal of emphasis on the Upaniṣads as revelatory texts. One knows that the empirical inquiry undertaken in the Upaniṣads yields true results because the inquiry is Upaniṣadic, and only consequently because the results can be verified empirically after one studies the scriptures. The Nyāya starting point in observation and reason is rejected on the grounds that it will never yield the realization of the truth of Brahman which Vedānta seeks.[16]

I restrict my comments on Vedānta to just two of the many schools. First I consider the Viśiṣṭādvaita ("nuanced non-dualist") Vedānta, which offers a complex intermingling of the views that religious truth is and isn't subordinate to ordinary truth, and then the nondualist Advaita, in which the truth of perception is more thoroughly subordinated to a scriptural truth about the world.

As for the Viśiṣṭādvaita, I begin by recalling again the position of Vedānta Deśika (fourteenth century) outlined in my chapter in *Ultimate Realities*. Deśika agrees with the Mīmāṃsā theorists in rejecting an induction about God based on observation of the contingency of empirical reality. He believes that the induction of God's existence cannot work. Observation of the world may indeed instigate us to see that it needs some kind of explanation beyond what is empirically evident, but the induction can never reach a sufficient specificity that one might conclude to the existence of a creator God. Once God is known from scripture, only then can God be reflected on reasonably.

As we shall see, this subordination of ordinary truth to religious truth is also characteristic of Advaita, nondualist, Vedānta, although the Viśiṣṭādvaita Vedānta more firmly maintains two kinds of truth, the truth of perception and the truth known by verbal authority. Although God is known from scripture, it also continues to list God among the objects of right knowing, even if God is an object to which special access is required. But there is nothing inherent in God's nature which rules out God's being an object of knowledge who can be known by an enduring, indeed eternal, human knower. Only the de facto limitations of the human capacity to know stand in the way. The object of knowledge (*prameya*) is certain, but the means of human knowing (*pramāṇa*) weak.

The Viśiṣṭādvaita position is illustrated in our third introductory manual, the *Yatīndramatadīpikā* of Śrīnivāsadāsa (16th–17th century), a theologian influenced by Vedānta Deśika.[17] According to this manual, God, who is Nārāyaṇa, is rightly listed among the objects of knowledge, and who is also the cause and foundation of empirical reality. Śrīnivāsadāsa says there are six substances: matter, time, pure matter, objective knowing (attributive consciousness), self, and God. He locates the Lord in the whole scheme of empirical realities, as shown in the figure.

The *Yatīndramatadīpikā* considers each of these realities individually and in relation to the whole, but no effort is made to derive or prove their reality. As with Vedānta Deśika, the positions regarding "Lord" are scripturally based, not argued for: Nārāyaṇa (and not Śiva or other deities) is the material and efficient cause of the world, perfect, all-pervading, present in the world in various ways including the well-known descents (*avatāra*) and in consecrated temple images (*arcā*).

God is a substance (*dravya*), one of the objects of right knowing (*prameya*). Śrīnivāsadāsa's approach combines fidelity to the empirical, skepticism about postulations of something beyond the empirical, and (in a way that is constitutive of Vedānta) respect for verbal authority as a means of right knowledge and consequently a guide to a correct and reliable power of perception. There is truth to perception, and truth to scripture. Regarding their object, the two converge (even in the short run,

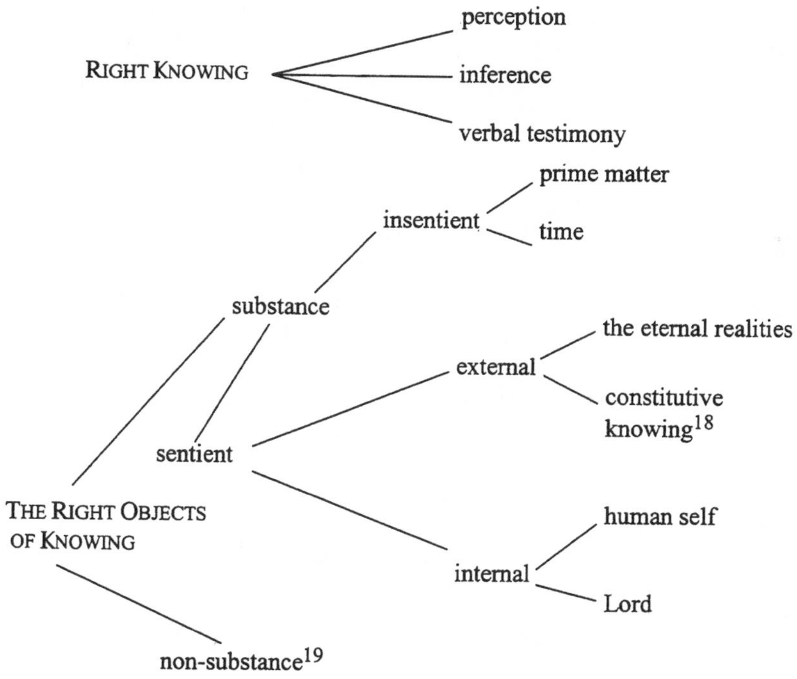

Figure 2.1. Empirical realities.

since God, who is the prime object of scripture, is also accessible in temples). God is the ultimate object of ordinary true knowing and religious true knowing. Even if God must be introduced first according to verbal testimony and not deduced from reflection on what is perceived, yet as a known entity God fits neatly into the empirical array of realities stated in the chart given above, and so is incuded in the general truth that should be accessible to all knowers. For the human knower, though, for now the two means of right knowing, perception and scripture, seem clearly extrinsic to one another, only juxtaposed. But after God's existence is known from scripture, God can then be listed among things knowable by perception and, under ideal circumstances (e.g., after death), God can be actually perceived.

2.8 Advaita Vedānta and the Scriptural Origins of Empirical Truth

The case is perhaps simpler in Advaita, the non-dualist strand of Vedānta. In the *Vedānta Paribhāṣā* by Dharmarāja Adhvarīndra (seventeenth century), a basic Advaita manual,[20] the Upaniṣadic theory of creation and description of the world (interpreted in a non-dualist fashion) is simply given precedence over other means of ascertaining the nature of the world. Ordinary perception is subordinated to scripture, corrected, and then, in a kind of eschatological climax, perception opens into a supreme, non-dual realization. Induction about ultimate reality is postponed, subordinated to scripture, always posterior, never prior. Thus, because it is not important, we do not find in the *Vedānta Paribhāṣā* the categorization of substances found in the Vaiśeṣika, Nyāya, and Mīmāṃsā, since here perception and inference are subordinated to verbal testimony and to the empiricist language used in the Upaniṣads. Nor do we find the dual language of the Viśiṣṭādvaita, whereby God can be spoken of both as revealed and as one of the objects of empirical knowledge. For these descriptions, Advaita adheres more closely to the terminology of the Upaniṣads.

The seventh chapter of the *Vedānta Paribhāṣā*, the chapter on the topics of knowledge (*viṣayapariccheda*), discusses what is knowable, without giving so ample a list of substances as is detailed in Vaiśeṣika.[21] Consider, for instance, the account of the generation of the universe, as I summarize it:

- Brahman is the source of everything, and the elements (ether, air, fire, water, earth) arise from Brahman;
- ether, characterized by sound, generates hearing, speaking, and the corresponding vital function;
- air, characterized by sound and touch, generates feeling, touching, and the corresponding vital function;
- fire, characterized by sound, touch, and color, generates seeing, moving, and the corresponding vital function;
- water, characterized by sound, touch, color, and taste, generates tasting, evacuating, and the corresponding vital function;
- earth, characterized by sound, touch, color, taste, and smell, generates smelling, sexual organs, and the corresponding vital function.

More elaborate combinations and derivations, including cosmic realities such as celestial worlds and their divinities, are likewise derived from the simpler elements listed in the Upaniṣads.

Perception is rather drastically transformed, now explained not according to the canons of Vaiśeṣika but according to those of the Upaniṣads. Ordinary truth is firmly redefined in terms of religious truth; one perceives properly when one perceives things as did the sages of the

Upaniṣads. This is a polemical and rhetorical move in Advaita that "scripturalizes" the empirical claims and energies of the Upaniṣads in order to assert the authority of the texts themselves over any and all powers of observation. Because of the insistence on Upaniṣadic priority, this approach in a sense stands at the opposite pole from the Vaiśeṣika and Nyāya understandings of truth. The empirical is firmly subordinated to the reality and realization of Brahman; perception is the final religious achievement, not a starting point.[22]

But this Advaita interpretation still has pertinence to the mundane human situation, since scripture, privileged and distinguished from ordinary knowing, tells us what we should and eventually will perceive, that toward which our knowing tends. The apparent (and dualistic) truth of ordinary life, subordinated to religious truth, is purified until it becomes really true (and non-dualistic). At the point of enlightenment scriptural truth and the truth of perception converge into one truth: in the end, one *perceives* Brahman in an act of true knowing where "ordinary truth" and "religious truth" can no longer be distinguished. It is therefore not surprising that the final, eighth section of the *Vedānta Paribhāṣā* is a section on the goal (*prayojana*), in which Dharmarāja Adhvarīndra expounds three things: immediate knowledge, the knower's identity as Brahman, and perfect bliss.[23]

2.9 The Hindu Debate about Truth

In the preceding pages I have argued that an understanding of the Hindu notion of religious truth must be rooted in the discussions about right knowledge (*pramā*), right means of right knowledge (*pramāṇa*), and the objects of right knowledge (*prameya*) in Hindu philosophical theology. Theologians in the Nyāya, Mīmāṃsā, and Vedānta traditions could talk to one another, and argue, because they shared what we might call the general "Hindu epistemology": a realist view of the world, at least three means of right knowledge (perception, inference, and verbal testimony), and either (minimally) a non-contradiction of ordinary truth and religious truth or (maximally) an ultimate identification of the two truths.

In the four introductory texts considered here, the *Tarkasaṃgraha*, *Mānameyodaya*, *Yatīndramatadīpikā*, and *Vedānta Paribhāṣā*, we find a systematic presentation of the means and objects of right knowledge. All four texts reveal a struggle to balance perception with an inevitable concession that there are other means of knowledge in harmony with perception—governed by perception or (perhaps) culminating in perception. Each seeks to maintain the unity of knowledge and the singleness of truth, keeping the number of additional sources as minimal and dependent as possible. Forms of right knowledge such as inference and verbal knowledge, and religious truth too, have public force because they are derivative and are always conceded as concessions, admitted only when ordinary realities—observable by all—could not be explained in terms of perception and its immediate implications. The same compromises and balances can be made regarding forms of worship, spiritual exercises, etc. Matters of worship and experience too could be argued, insofar as the shared Hindu epistemology was properly operative and not entirely replaced by appeals to experience or claims persuasive only within a community. One can give reasons for one's religious beliefs and practices.

All of this has been evident in the case we have considered, whether it can be shown that God exists or not. In Nyāya, empirical observation leads us to the conclusion that it is true that there is a world-maker. In *Mīmāṃsā*, it does not, and need not, indicate this truth, since God, if there is one, plays no integral role in creation or revelation or ritual (and perhaps then is only "god"). In *Viśiṣṭādvaita Vedānta*, one cannot infer that there is a God but, once one learns from scripture that God exists, one also admits that eventually one will be able to perceive God. *Advaita Vedānta* adds the vision of a final concluding point, where the truth of scripture and the truth of perception converge in a revealed-and-perceived realization of Brahman that is also the uncovering of one's own identity as Brahman.

In important ways, even the Hindu debate about God is an intellectual and religious debate about the plausibility of a coherent account of ordinary truth and reality in which truth retains a meaning irreducible to some particular community's own apprehension of the true. Each school thus participates in the shared, arguable version of truth in which religious truth can be subjected to criteria not reducible merely to sectarian interests, and each provides its own versions of the origins from which religious truth comes and where it belongs.

The debate over the means of right knowledge and objects of right knowledge has a deeply religious component because the project of describing the world empirically requires speculation about what is not empirical, and because this opens into the question of whether there is a God, and whether the revelations and practices related to claims about God can also be shown to be valid. The claim that the truths internal to the community are also true in theory and practice is a claim that can be assessed as to whether it is true for all reasoning persons. None of the communities we have considered is content to adhere to a merely private, communally circumscribed notion of truth, and each seeks to justify what it knows and believes by proving it to be true or, at least, by proving contradictory information not to be true. Real argument becomes necessary and possible because the existence of God is neither an observable fact of perception nor merely a claim made by believers; faith positions and rational assertions can never be completely sorted out, and the fuzziness of the boundary between them actually instigates a richer tradition of shared discourse about truth, religious truth included.

2.10 Public Discourse and Its Sectarian Roots

The situation described in this chapter is nonetheless only one aspect—the best beginning, I have argued—for a still fuller understanding even of the truth of revelation and the truth of experience and practice in the Hindu context. Once we understand this primary, shared understanding of truth that makes it possible for Hindu intellectuals to speak to one another and argue about the truth of their positions, one can go farther and attempt to uncover more specifically the particular religious roots of the acts of religious reasoning that appear removed from the sources of religious experience, sentiment, practice.

That larger exploration of religious truth as experienced and practiced will of course be very interesting, but if we wish to understand most fruitfully the interplay of rational inquiry, epistemological concerns, and sectarian concerns, it is better to begin, as suggested here, with the empirically weighted theory of right knowing (*pramāṇa*) and the objects of right knowing (*prameya*). By proposing a distinction between ordinary truth and religious truth, by giving priority to the former but then by tracing the interconnections between the two, we have been able to uncover the fundamental connecting thread shared by the various Hindu understandings of truth. This shared, public truth is perhaps *the* appropriate and convenient point for scholars from another culture and other religion (or none)—who do not share the same revelation, who do not live the same life—to have access to the conversation about what is religiously true in India.

Were we instead to begin our inquiry into the Hindu notion of religious truth by focusing on various scriptures and rites and meditative practices, the project of describing a shared truth certainly becomes more difficult, vague (in the bad sense), and liable to complete breakdown, a situation in which one become unable to say at all what "Hindus" mean by religious truth. Each particularity may become privileged to the extreme, Hindu rational discourse becomes a scholastic oddity somehow irrelevant for understanding how Hindus think, and the long-standing confidence of Hindu thinkers about stating and arguing their truths in public is simply ignored. Examining reasoning first gives us insight into a unified Hindu conversation and provides us with a specific way to begin considering other kinds of truth that subsequently come to the fore. By our own intellectual engagement in this public dispute about God and other topics, we position ourselves on a shared, public ground, and have an opportunity to move toward an understanding of revelation and lived truth that would otherwise be accessible only to the most determined scholarly and saintly comparativists.

Notes

1. See my "Vedānta Deśika's 'Definition of the Lord' (Īśvaraparicheda) and the Hindu Argument about Ultimate Reality," *Ultimate Reality,* ed. Robert Cummings Neville (Albany: State University of New York Press, 1999).

2. For a slightly broader discussion of fundamental Hindu theological ideas about God, see Francis X. Clooney, S.J., "The Existence of God, Reason, and Revelation in Two Classical Hindu Theologies," *Faith and Philosophy* (1999), pp. 523–43.

3. On the complexities of brāhmaṇical Hindu epistemology, see *Théorie de la Connaissance et Philosophie de la Parole* by Madeleine Biardeau (Paris: Mouton and Co., 1964), and *Śabdapramāṇa: Word and Knowledge* by Puruṣottama Bilimoria (Boston: Kluwer Academic Publishers, 1988), vol. 10.

4. As we shall see, Vedānta recasts the list of the objects of right knowledge in Upaniṣadic terms—relying more on Upaniṣadic authority and less on Upaniṣadic empiricism. For Mīmāṃsā and Vedānta thinkers, though, the words of the Veda are presented as perception: they are heard, directly known.

5. In Vaiśeṣika we find the following generally agreed on division of nine substances: earth, water, fire, air, ether (the quintessence), time, space, self, and mind. Vaiśeṣika is a realistic system: "The system starts with the postulate that all knowledge by its very nature points to an object beyond it and independent of it. These objects, it is added, are independent not only of knowledge, but also of one another, whence the doctrine may be described as pluralistic realism. . . . The *dravya*s are not all material, so that the Nyāya-Vaiśeṣika is not, like the Carvāka, materialistic. At the same time the doctrine treats all *dravya*s alike; and even the self, it regards as one object among others possessing properties, exhibiting relations, and knowable like them." M. Hiriyanna, *Outlines of Indian Philosophy* (London: George Allen & Unwin Ltd., 1964), 228–29. See also Wilhelm Halbfass, *Being and What There Is* (Albany: State University of New York Press, 1992).

6. See Johannes Bronkhorst, "God's Arrival in the Vaiśeṣika System," *Journal of Indian Philosophy* 24 (1996): 281–394. George Chemparathy points out that a key source for the Nyāya consideration of God lies in the Buddhist critique of God's existence, particularly in the *Pramāṇavārttika* of Dharmakīrti (seventh

century): "Leaving aside the other aspects of the Īśvara doctrine he centered his offensives against the NyāyaVaiśeṣika proofs for the existence of Īśvara, and this, too, from the aspect of their logical validity. . . . He argued that the proofs advanced by the Nyāya-Vaiśeṣika theists to establish the existence of Īśvara were vitiated by logical fallacies and that consequently they were incorrect or invalid. He even went further and called into question the very possibility of establishing the existence of Īśvara by arguments, since in his view the very conception of an eternal cause, as the Nyāya-Vaiśeṣika theists assume Īśvara to be, implies a contradiction." George Chemparathy, *An Indian Rational Theology: Introduction to Udayana's Nyāyakusumañjali* (Vienna: Indological Institute of the University of Vienna, 1972), 78. On the development of the argument about God in the Buddhist context, see Roger Jackson, "Dharmakīrti's refutation of theism," *Philosophy East and West* 36.4 (1985): 315–48. Dharmakīrti's critique of the argument from effects to the existence of God is also described briefly in Gerhard Oberhammer, "Der Gottesbeweis in der Indische Philosophie," *Numen* 2.1 (1965): 1–34, esp. 10–22.

7. "The earth, etc." indicates the large constituent parts of the universe, not only the earth but also the atmosphere, the stars and sun, etc.

8. See Gerhard Oberhammer, "Der Gottesbeweis in der Indische Philosophie," *Numen* XII.1 (1965), 1–34, esp. 10–22.

9. As explained in G. Jha's introductory note to Book 4, *The Nyāya Sūtras of Gautama with the Bhāṣya of Vātsyāyana and the Vārtika of Udyotakara*, trans. G. Jha (Delhi: Motilal Banarsidass, 1984), 1429.

10. George Chemparathy explains:"With the term "maker" is meant an agent that employs or directs the class of causes that are known to be able to produce the effect. The "maker" that is postulated here as the cause of "earth etc." is not just any agent, but one that can adequately account for the existence of the effect in question." *An Indian Rational Theology*, op. cit., 86. The entire *Nyāyakusumāñjali* has recently been translated by N. S. Dravid, *Nyāyakusumāñjali* of Udayanācārya (New Delhi: Indian Council of Philosophical Research, 1996). Another weighty presentation of the Nyāya position is Gaṅgeśa's "Discourse on God" (the *Īśvaravāda* section of his *Cintāmaṇi*). On the Nyāya debate in general, see the comprehensive introductory essay, "Study on the Development of Nyāya theism," in John Vattanky's *Gaṅgeśa's Philosophy of God* (Madras: The Adyar Library and Research Centre, 1984), 3–150. On the general project of the Nyāya induction of God's existence, see also Kisor K. Chakrabarti, *Classical Indian Philosophy of Mind* (Albany: State University of New York Press, 1999), 159–73; for reflection on the induction in a comparative context, see Francis X. Clooney, S.J., "The Interreligious Dimension of Reasoning about God's Existence," *International Journal of the Philosophy of Religion* (1999), and chapter 2 of *Hindu God, Christian God: Beginning to Think about God in a World of Many Religions* (New York: Oxford University Press, forthcoming, 2001).

11. Annaṃbhaṭṭa adds that there are Vedic warrants for the existence of God, e.g., the *Śvetāśvatara* text; "He who is omniscient is the knower of every thing."

In the *Nṛsiṃhaprakāśikā* commentary on the *Dīpikā*, Rāya Narasiṁha elaborates this inferential proof. He defends the idea that from the fact of an effect we can deduce purposive activity (*kṛti*) which implies an agent, and not just a cause (*kāraṇa*). Just as it is shown that purposive activity is involved in the making of the world, it can also be shown that will and knowledge are involved. Taken together, purposive action, will, and knowledge define an agent. In the required maximal measure that would describe a world-maker—infinite knowledge, perfect will, ever-successful action—such attributes constitute a definition of an original maker, and it is this maximal figure whom we intend when we speak about "God." Rāya Narasiṁha defends the use of the sprout as a specific example of the natural—even though we do not actually observe the makers of sprouts, by saying that sprouts are like pots that require a pot-maker, because sprouts too begin to exist, are complex, and require some agency to synthesize them; therefore, observation of vegetation such as sprouts can lead to a just extrapolation of a claim about the maker of everything in the world.

12. The *Mānameyodaya* has been edited and translated by C. Kunhan Raja and S. S. Suryanarayana Sastri (Madras: Theosophical Publishing House, 1933). The argument is developed in numbers 36–47 in the second major part of the *Mānameyodaya*, on the objects of right knowledge (*prameya*).

13. On the Mīmāṃsā defense of internal ritual coherence, see, for instance, my *Thinking Ritually: Rediscovering the Pūrva Mīmāṃsā of Jaimini*, vol. 17, De Nobili Research Series (Vienna: Indological Institute of the University of Vienna, 1990), esp. chap. 5.

14. Despite their systematic commitment to a nontheistic religious worldview, sometimes even the Mīmāṃsā teachers embrace theism personally. Despite his rejection of the cosmological induction, Nārāyaṇasudhī still claims to be a theist, since he concludes the section by saying that the Vedic scriptures offer sufficient and adequate evidence that there is a God, even if this God is neither the maker of the world nor author of the primal, revealed words, the Veda. Although the truth about God is asserted with an appeal to the Veda, it is not integrated with the religious truth of ritual practice, the dharma. Nārāyaṇasudhī is typical in not integrating this belief with the positions he believes to be rationally defensible. His God has no place in the system of realities, nor can one presume that a God is required to undergird the system. In traditional Mīmāṃsā such a God would have no intrinsic role in ritual performance or in regard to the authority of the Veda, either. For Nārāyaṇasudhī to confess devotion to God is therefore extrinsic to the system, admitted in such a way that it is not allowed to interfere with the objective induction. Truth and belief in God are not contradictory, but they remain extrinsic to one another. Knowledge of God remains a matter of verbal authority, several steps removed from perception, the favored means of knowledge. There are two truths, the truth of perception and the truth of the Veda; they cohere and are ranked as respectively secondary and primary, but without ever being integrated into a single model of truth. A similar separation of personal belief is admitted by Khaṇḍadeva, author of the great *Bhaṭṭa Dīpikā* commentary on Śabara's *Pūrva Mīmāṃsā Sūtra Bhāṣya*. See Francis X.

Clooney, S.J., "What's a God? The Quest for the Right Understanding of *devatā* in Brahmanical Ritual Theory (*Mīmāṃsā*)," *International Journal of Hindu Studies* 2 (August 1997): 337–85.

15. The most important discussion of Vedānta skepticism regarding reason is found at *Uttara Mīmāṃsā Sūtras* 1.1.2, where Bādarāyaṇa insists that although Brahman can be designated the source of the world, we know nothing about Brahman from the world. See my *Theology after Vedānta: An Experiment in Comparative Theology* (Albany: State University of New York Press, 1993), chap. 3.

16. See my essay "To be heard and done, but never quite seen: the human condition according to the *Vivekacuḍāmaṇi*," *The Human Condition*, ed. Robert Cummings Neville (Albany: State University of New York Press, 1999). Translated by Swami Adidevananda (Madras: R. K. Math, 1978).

17. Tr. Swami Adidevananda (Madras: R. K. Math, 1978).

18. *Dharmabhūtajñāna*: i.e., knowledge that is constitutive of the Lord, not simply a temporary attribute.

19. Non-substances include qualities and temporary, non-essential features of substances.

20. Tr. Swami Madhavananda (Calcutta: Advaita Ashrama, 1983).

21. This cosmology is spelled out in pages 152–67 of Madhavananda's translation.

22. Another version of the Advaita cosmology is found in the *Vivekacūḍāmaṇi*. See my essay in our first volume on that text, op. cit., especially the role of *māyā* as an intermediate divine power (ontological and epistemological) that is responsible for creation. In that essay I also suggested that in Advaita epistemological and ontological issues cohere and indeed are inseparable. The matter for the correction of ordinary perception, the study of scripture, and the opening into a higher, nondual perception is explained in the *Vivekacūḍāmaṇi*.

23. Dharmarāja acknowledges as his teacher's teacher Narasiṃhāśramin (sixteenth century), whose *Advaita Dīpikā* devotes its long third part to a refutation of the Nyāya inference about God and also to an Advaita reconstitution of a salvifically efficacious and nondualistic understanding of Īśvara. Truth is first of all religious truth, and the truth of ordinary experience must be seen in light of the truth that liberates its knower.

3

"With Great Noise and Mighty Whirlpools the Ganges Flowed Backwards"

Buddhist Approaches to Truth

Malcolm David Eckel
with John J. Thatamanil

3.1 Introduction

Indian philosophers (including Hindus, Buddhists, and Jains of various philosophical persuasions) developed a distinctive system of "comparative religious ideas" to allow dialogue and controversy across sectarian boundaries. This scheme consists of six *pramāṇa*s or "means of valid knowledge." To enter into public debate with a representative of another school, an Indian thinker had to be able to articulate a theory of valid knowledge to support the assertions of his own school, and he had to know the theories of his opponents well enough to defend himself against their attacks. Frank Clooney has presented a Hindu version of the *pramāṇa*s. This chapter will focus on Buddhist *pramāṇa* theory, as it was outlined in the sixth and seventh centuries by the Buddhist logicians Dignāga and Dharmakīrti and criticized by the Mādhyamikas

Bhāvaviveka, Candrakīrti, and Jñānagarbha. We hope that the combination of these two chapters will allow us not merely to encounter two separate religious visions of truth but to consider the way Indian philosophers used a common set of categories to cross religious boundaries and enter into dialogue with members of other religious traditions.

At the beginning of this year, Robert Neville reminded us that we agreed to discuss three aspects of truth—"embodied truth-in-practice," "epistemological truth," and "scriptural or revelatory truth." Following his suggestion, I have supplemented my discussion of the *pramāṇas* with a discussion of "truth-in-practice" and Buddhist approaches to scriptural interpretation. I will begin with "truth-in-practice," move on to "epistemological truth," and finish with a discussion of "scriptural or revelatory truth."

3.2 Embodied Truth-in-Practice

Wilfred Cantwell Smith once argued that American universities had gone awry not, as some believed, because they needed to be "restructured" by a redistribution of power, but because they had become captive to the idea that truth resides only in propositions.[1] The year was 1970, and the student unrest of 1968–69 was still burning in his mind. He felt that the moral integrity of the university had been challenged, and he responded, as sometimes was his custom, by spinning an argument out of Qur'ānic exegesis. His argument focused on the word *ṣadaqa*. Smith said that the word named a quality of "honesty," "integrity," and "trustworthiness" that presupposed a "human view of truth." The noun *ṣidq* named the "quality by which a man speaks or acts with a combination of inner integrity and objective or overt appropriateness. It involves saying or doing the objectively right thing out of a genuine personal recognition of its rightness."[2] To make a long story short, Smith felt that American university life had lost a sense that truth belonged as much to the integrity of the speaker as it did to the words that a speaker spoke. To write an article or carry out academic research without being convinced of the truthfulness (or the reality) of the project was like playing a basketball game with a predetermined result. The players could go through the motions and make it look like basketball, but the game would be a fake. A true game is one that involves real competition, and the truth of the game does not reside in the actions of the players but in the players themselves. Smith ended his argument by saying that "[a] university unconcerned with personal truth is untrue [*sic*] to the academic tradition, historically, as well as, I submit, sadly partial in its apprehension of intellectual rigour today."[3]

The historical situation has changed. Authenticity in academic discourse does not seem (perhaps lamentably) to be the hot issue it once was. But Smith's argument still carries weight as an introduction to the idea of truth in a religious setting, especially in the religious traditions of India. Indian traditions have a great deal to say about epistemological truth, and they have evolved a complex procedure to identify and dispute the truth of scriptural phrases, but they also have a sense that truth involves an element of personal integrity. They preserve an ancient notion that an "act of truth" (Sanskrit, *satya-kriyā*; Pali, *sacca-kiriyā*) can affect the karmic process in a real way, not just for the one who performs the action, but for others as well.[4] It can function in other words as a "piece of reality" in both a moral and a physical sense. The best way to understand what Buddhists have meant by an act of truth is to observe the way it works in a Buddhist story. One of my favorites is the Pali story of the conversion of the mass murderer Aṅgulimāla ("Garland of Fingers").[5]

The Aṅgulimāla story is a strange, almost diabolical inversion of the story of the Buddha's own renunciation. Aṅgulimāla was a diligent student whose teacher demanded that he pay for his teaching by collecting the fingers of a hundred victims. Aṅgulimāla fled to the forest and attacked travelers to collect the fingers. To keep the fingers of his victims together, he tied them on a string and wore them around his neck, hence the name "Garland of Fingers." Through a series of events too long to narrate, Aṅgulimāla was converted by the Buddha and became a member of the Saṃgha. He prospered in his discipline and became an elder of the monastic community, but it was hard for him to go back to the villages he once had terrorized and beg for alms. The villagers remembered his past and attacked him whenever he approached. One particular day he was out on his begging rounds and saw a woman struggling in childbirth. He wanted to help ease her pain, but the woman was so terrified that she would not let him approach her. Back in the monastery, he asked the Buddha for help. The Buddha told him to go to the village and perform an act of truth (*sacca-kiriyā*) by saying: "As I have never willfully taken the life of any creature since the day I was born, thereby may peace be unto thee and to thy womb!" Aṅgulimāla said that this would be impossible, because the words were untrue. The Buddha told him that the words carried the force of truth if Aṅgulimāla measured his life "from the moment of his birth as a member of the Elect." Aṅgulimāla went back to the village, made his act of truth, and the pain of the woman's childbirth was relieved. In the Sinhalese communities where this story is told, the force of Aṅgulimāla act of truth did not end with the relief of this one woman's suffering. The words are still used as a charm to ward off the dangers of childbirth. The point of the story is that truth has power, and its power can be invoked even when the person who first set the truth in motion has left the scene.

It is this issue of cause and effect that seems to concern the longest systematic discussion of an act of truth in the canonical (or semicanonical) Pali tradition. In *The Questions of King Milinda*, King Milinda challenged the monk Nāgasena to explain how King Sivi, in one of the stories of the Buddha's previous births, could give his eyes to a beggar and then have his sight restored. According to King Milinda, the restoration of King Sivi's eyes violated the strict causal principle that nothing can arise when its cause or "basis" has been destroyed. Nāgasena answered by asking the king about the causal force of an act of truth: "Is there in the world such a thing as Truth, by the asseveration of which true believers can perform the Act of Truth?"[6] The king agreed that there is, and Nāgasena explained that it was the power of Truth that restored King Sivi's eyes. What kind of truth has this power? The text's examples are quite revealing. When he answered Nāgasena's question, King Milinda said that truth makes it possible for "true believers" to bring rain, put out fires, cure poison, and "accomplish many other things that they want to do." Siddhas (accomplished saints) can intone "charms" to bring rain, put out fires, and cure poison. Here the act of truth is like the intoning of a Vedic mantra: the words themselves have the power to bring about real events.

The most intriguing example, however, has to do with a courtesan in the city of Pāṭaliputta. Nāgasena told King Milinda a story about King Asoka asking his officers whether there is anyone in the city who can cause the Ganges to flow upstream. The officers said no, but a courtesan by the name of Bindumatī stepped forward and performed an act of truth. With great noise and mighty whirlpools the Ganges flowed backwards. What was Bindumatī's "truth"? She said that, as a prostitute, she showed no favoritism to any of her customers: she treated all of them alike. As strange as it may seem, this is the classic yogic virtue of *samatā* or "equanimity." As a moral quality it is highly prized in the *Bhagavad Gītā* where Kṛṣṇa says: "Learned men see with an equal eye a scholarly sage and dignified priest, a cow, an elephant, a dog, and even an outcaste scavenger" (5.18). It would be tempting to say that the proposition "As I have never willfully taken the life of any creature . . ." is the locus of the power in Aṅgulimāla's act of truth. The same could be said of the charms that saints use to bring rain or cure poison. But in the story of Bindumatī the courtesan, the words of the act of truth are not even mentioned. Her power lies in her moral integrity rather than in the propositional content of any of her words.

With Bindumatī in mind, it seems that Aṅgulimāla's words function simply as a device to distill the power of his moral transformation and make it available to the others who need it. Certainly this is the pattern we observe elsewhere in the tradition where words are used to bring the force of a great bodhisattva's moral discipline to bear for others. The Pure Land tradition, beginning in India at a time not far removed from the date of *The Questions of King Milinda*, traces the compassion of the Buddha Amitābha to the vows of the bodhisattva Dharmākara: "May I not gain possession of perfect awakening if, once I have attained buddhahood, any among the throng of living beings in the ten regions of the universe should single-mindedly desire to be reborn in my land with joy, with confidence, and gladness, and if they should bring to mind this aspiration for even ten moments of thought and yet not gain rebirth there."[7] Once these words are pronounced, they gain an inescapable karmic force and can be invoked by devotees of Amitābha in the same way that Sinhalese Buddhists invoke the words of Aṅgulimāla. The power of the words rests on the "honesty," "integrity," and "trustworthiness" (in Wilfred Cantwell Smith's words) of the speakers as much as it does on anything that the speakers say. It is sometimes said that Mahatma Gandhi's concept of nonviolent resistance as a form of "truth-force" (*satyagraha*) rests on this ancient Indian idea of the act of truth. The connection would certainly be worth exploring, if only to see more clearly how the Indian understanding of "embodied truth" manifests itself not merely in what Stephen Beyer called the "ritualization of moral attitudes" in the practice of the bodhisattva vow but also in acts of political courage.

3.3 Epistemological Truth

Indian Buddhist philosophers share the pan-Indian system of the *pramāṇa*s, the "means of valid knowledge." Nāgārjuna wrote an analysis of the *pramāṇa* system as early as the second century of the Common Era, and by the sixth century Buddhists had developed one of the most forceful and influential accounts of the *pramāṇa* system in Indian philosophy. This account of the *pramāṇa*s is known as "Buddhist Logic" (*bauddha-nyāya*) and is associated particularly with the figures of Dignāga and Dharmakīrti. I will not attempt to give a complete description of this complex system but will simply outline its most important features so that we can identify areas that need further exploration in our discussion.

Buddhist logic starts with a strict internal symmetry. It recognizes the validity of two *pramāṇa*s: perception (*pratyakṣa*) and inference (*anumāna*). Perception is nonconceptual (*nirvikalpa*) and nonverbal and amounts to a direct awareness of the "particular" (*svalakṣaṇa*) moments in the flow of experience. (Buddhist logic is deliberately framed so that "particulars" can be interpreted as an external reality separate from the mind or as the moments of experience within the mind itself.) Inference involves judgment about "universals" (*sāmānya-lakṣaṇa*). It is conceptual and is capable of being expressed in words. Finally, the two *pramāṇa*s give access to two different levels of reality. The particulars that function as the object of perception are ultimately real (*paramārtha-sat*), while the universals are real only in a relative sense (*saṃvṛti-sat*). The different parts of this system can be organized in the displayed scheme.

	Perception	*Inference*
Objects	Particulars (*sva-lakṣaṇa*)	Universals (*sāmānya-lakṣaṇa*)
Concepts	Nonconceptual and nonverbal	Conceptual and verbal
Reality	Ultimately real (or true)	Relatively real (or true)

Buddhist logic seems, on the face of it, to be quite persuasive. The logicians picture experience as a flow of moments, each of which is different from the last. The moments of the flow are the only "ultimate reality." On top of this flow, the mind superimposes judgments about the "similarity" of one moment to another. This "similarity" (*sāmānya*) is a mental construct, like the mental construct "cow" (to choose the typical Indian example) that is used to synthesize a jumble of individual sensations of "black," "white, "brown," and so forth. The mental construct of "sameness" is called a "universal" (*sāmānya-lakṣaṇa*). These concepts of "sameness" are extremely useful. In certain situations they can lead to ultimate reality, as they do, for example, when someone uses the universal "smoke" to infer the presence of "fire" and uses the fire to cook a pot of rice. But universals themselves are not ultimately real. Their reality is merely "relative," or, to express the nuances of the Buddhist word *saṃvṛti* more accurately, they are a "concealment" or "covering" of reality. Words and conceptual constructs mislead us about the nature of things: they point to a continuity or similarity that ultimately is not there. To perceive things accurately, as they really are, a person needs to strip away or remove words and concepts to get back to the bare particulars of perception. From the ultimate point of view, epistemological truth belongs to perception. Inference depends on words and concepts and is "true," at best, in only a derivative sense. It is not uncommon for Buddhist philosophers, especially in the Madhyamaka school, to say that *saṃvṛti* is just another word for illusion. If so, the claim that words express "relative truths" has the quality of an oxymoron: it means that words create illusory "truths," which in the end are not truths at all.

It is plausible to connect the logicians' vision of the *pramāṇas* to the practice of yoga. Dignāga and Dharmakīrti both stand in the larger lineage of the Yogācāra ("Yoga Practice") school of Buddhist philosophy. In my presentation about Buddhist views of reality for last year's seminar, I said that the Yogācāra school pictured reality in three categories. Here Imagined Nature corresponds to the world of words and concepts or "universals," while Perfected Nature belongs to the world of "particulars." The Imagination is a combination of direct sensations and concepts and constitutes the world of ordinary experience. The job of a yogī is to strip away the words and concepts of Imagined Nature (including the distinction between subject and object) to experience the nonduality of Perfected Nature. This non-dual awareness is what the Yogācāra tradition calls "Emptiness." These ideas are expressed in a technical idiom and have an aura of impenetrability, but they are not inaccessible to ordinary experience. Even if you have never studied Buddhist philosophy you probably have had the experience of standing in front of a statue of the seated Buddha and feeling the calm that seems to flow from the Buddha's form. You sense that the Buddha is in a state in which words and concepts have ceased, and you feel your own thoughts beginning to melt into an experience of quiet and peace. This peace is a taste of ultimate truth.

Imagined Nature	Duality
Dependent Nature	Imagination
Perfected Nature	Emptiness

In the system of Buddhist logic, perception is not confined to the five senses. Buddhist logicians recognize four kinds of perception, of which only the first is perception by the senses. The second is "mental" perception. The logicians explain that each moment of sense perception is followed immediately by a moment of perception in the mind. The actual cognitive function of this category has been debated. Masatoshi Nagatomi has argued that it only has a place in the system of the Buddhist logicians out of reverence for an earlier system of categories that, by the time of the logicians, had been almost entirely superseded.[8] The third form of perception is "self-awareness" (*svasaṃvedana*). The logicians argued that every perceptual cognition has three aspects: the object, the subject, and the awareness of itself. In a negative sense, the category of self-awareness was meant to avoid a problem of infinite regress, in other words, to answer the question: "If you know something, how do you know that you know?" Viewed more positively, it named the irreducible cognitive nature of the mind itself. As in the Upaniṣadic image of Brahman as a "mass of consciousness," the logicians viewed the mind as fundamentally self-aware, even when all images of the object and the subject had been stripped away. The fourth form of perception is the perception of a yogī (*yogī-pratyakṣa*). This is the direct awareness of the Four Noble Truths that comes to yogīs after they have understood the Truths intellectually and then deepened their understanding through repeated practice (*bhāvanā*).

As important as it came to be, the *pramāṇa* theory of the Buddhist logicians did not lack for critics. At the very beginning of the chapter on perception in Dharmakīrti's *Pramāṇa-vārttika* (*The Commentary on the Pramāṇas*), his own *magnum opus* and the most authoritative text in the tradition of Buddhist logic, Dharmakīrti quotes a critic as saying that "particulars" are nothing more than relative truths. Dharmakīrti's answer, surprisingly, is: "So be it" (*astu yathā tathā*).[9] This short exchange is one of the few indications in Dharmakīrti's writings of a controversy between the two great schools of the Mahāyāna—the Yogācāra and the Madhyamaka—about the status of perception as a *pramāṇa*. You will recall from last year's discussion that the Mādhyamikas do not recognize that anything has ultimate reality. This judgment applies not just to the "universals" that function as the objects of inference but also to the "particulars" that are known by perception. You can imagine a Mādhyamika and a Yogācāra arguing about whether the moment of "red" that they see when they perceive the color of an apple is an ultimate or a relative truth. You might even be tempted to yawn and say *astu yathā tathā* ("So be it!"). But the discussion takes on a critical edge when you consider the category of "self-awareness." Yogācāra philosophers argued that you can doubt any of the discrete elements of consciousness, any of the elements that presupposed a distinction between subject and object, but you cannot doubt the reality of consciousness itself. You can doubt anything that you know, but you cannot doubt the act of knowing itself. This functioned as a guarantee not only of the reality of the mind but of the reality of the Buddha's awakening, the reality that all their philosophical efforts and meditative labors were intended to seek. The Mādhyamikas applied their critique to the reality of the mind itself.

Mādhyamikas agreed that the job of a yogī was to strip away false images of reality and see reality clearly, but they took the process farther than the Yogācāra. They applied it to the mind and to the act of understanding itself. For Bhāvaviveka, the final "arising" or occurrence of awareness that constituted the Buddha's enlightenment was simply a "no-arising" (*anutpāda*) and a "no-cognition" (*anupalabdhi*).[10] In other words, the event of enlightenment was a non-event. From the Mādhyamikas we would expect nothing less.

This extension of the Madhyamaka approach to the distinction between relative and ultimate truths had important consequences for their evaluation of the *pramāṇas*. The Mādhyamikas who wrote after Dharmakīrti had no trouble accepting the authority of perception. They agreed that perception showed an object that was capable, in Dharmakīrti's words, of "effective action" (*artha-kriyā*), but they did not accept that the perception was ultimate. They considered it to be "correct relative truth" (*tathya-saṃvṛti-satya*) and defined correct relative truth as "dependently produced" (*pratītya-samutpanna*), "capable of effective action" (*artha-kriyā-samartha-vat*), and "satisfying only when it is not analyzed" (*avicāra-ramaṇīya*).[11] The first part of this formula is a standard Buddhist term for the network of causes and conditions that makes up the flux of reality. The second part of the formula is Dharmakīrti's word for the pragmatic effectiveness of perception: effective action is the taste of rice cooked over a fire. The third part of the formula seems to be a distinctive Madhyamaka innovation. It seems to appear first in the works of Candrakīrti (assuming that Candrakīrti himself appeared before the eighth century, which is by no means certain). Technically, it means that you can only be satisfied with claims about the validity of conventional judgments if you do not insist that the reference of the words be specified. To ask what words *really* refer to is to ask an ultimate question, and ultimate questions get negative answers.

Mādhyamikas express this third aspect of correct relative truth by adding the Sanskrit word *mātra* to the end of whatever term they are using in the conventional sense. Jñānagarbha (eighth century) said that a correct relative reality (or truth) is a *vastu-mātra*: "only a thing," "a mere thing," or "just a thing."[12] At the end of my chapter last year, I told the story of the Dalai Lama's lecture on the nature of the self in Sanders Theater at Harvard. He started in English saying that you can know the self by being compassionate to your neighbor. Then he shifted to Tibetan for a long account of the reasons why there is no self. Finally he stopped and asked, if there is no self, who is speaking? His answer in Tibetan was *bdag tsam*. The Sanskrit would have been *ātma-mātra*. The translator translated it as the "mere I." Blessed with the benefit of hindsight, I would translate the Dalai Lama's words as "just me," as if to say, "Who just told this to you? Just the little old Dalai Lama." I have asked Tibetan lamas how they use the word *tsam* when they get to this level in their study of Madhyamaka. One person said, "What is this *tsam tsam*?" and started to laugh. No doubt, the laughter is part of the meaning. There is a lightness in this laughter but also great seriousness, especially when it is used to convey a serious point about the limitations of certain types of thinking. E. B. White said that humor "plays, like an active child, next to the big hot fire which is Truth."[13] Observers of Buddhism should listen carefully when someone begins to punctuate phrases with the words "mere" or "just" (as in the Zen masters' use of the phrase "just sitting") and try to hear what is being conveyed not just by the speaker's words but by the speaker's smile.

To say that perception is "merely" correct relative truth has an unsettling effect on the understanding of the *pramāṇas*. It is not just that the Mādhyamikas challenge the *definition* of perception; they challenge the *placement* of perception in the framework of the *pramāṇas* as a whole. The logicians claimed that perception gave access to ultimate truth while inference dealt with relative truth. If perception is considered relative, what does this do to inference? Does inference become even more relative than perception? Strangely, it turns the relationship with perception upside down. The Mādhyamikas of the eighth century (the Mādhyamikas who had the chance to absorb the influence of Dharmakīrti) claimed that inference, or reason (*yukti*), is *ultimate*: "Because it cannot be contradicted, reason is ultimate and is not relative."[14] I say "strangely" because this is still the tradition that reveres the Buddha's direct, intuitive understanding of the Four Noble Truths and says explicitly that ultimate truth cannot be "an object of inference" (*anumeya*). How can the Mādhyamikas justify such a peculiar claim? The answer lies in the word "contradicted" (*bādhita*). This word is sometimes translated as "sublated," as if it were an Indian version of *Aufhebung*, the word that names the relationship between the synthesis and the other members of a dialectic. But the comparison may be misleading. In Vedānta, as well as among the Buddhists, the process of "sublation" is compared to the relationship between a dream and the consciousness of being awake. When a person wakes up, waking consciousness "sublates" the dream. For Mādhyamikas, "reason" has this power over perception: it demonstrates that the naive perception of the reality of things has no validity when it is considered from the ultimate point of view.

Does this mean that the Mādhyamikas have turned ultimate truth into an "object of inference"? The Mādhyamikas themselves were aware of this danger and raised it as an objection to their position. Their answer gives a wonderful glimpse of their vision of reality. It is true, they say, that inference is the ultimate arbiter of what can be considered real and what cannot. But this does not mean that ultimate truth is an object *to be grasped* by inference. The truth is that there is no ultimate object, and inference is the final authoritative means to make that position clear. In the end inference has to be used against itself to show that inference too is merely a reflection of relative truth. Jñānagarbha makes this point by saying: "From the standpoint of reason, the meaning of the words 'ultimately [things] do not arise' also does not arise. Other [such statements] should be interpreted the same way." He goes on to say: "[The Buddha] considers the relative and the ultimate to be identical in nature because there [ultimately] is no difference between them and because reason also is based on appearances."[15]

At this point the argument can go in two directions. One is to distinguish between two kinds of ultimate truth: a relative ultimate and an ultimate ultimate. The relative ultimate is inference or reason: it is based on words and concepts, and the words and concepts are based on the appearance of perception. The ultimate ultimate has no words and concepts: it is simply the silence of the Buddha and the great Buddhist saints, exemplified in the Indian Mahāyāna tradition by the story of Vimalakīrti's silence in the *Vimalakīrtinirdeśa Sūtra*.[16] For those who are not content to rest in the silence of the saints, there is the satisfaction of "no analysis." Jñānagarbha's next step in his own text, after pointing out that there is no difference between the ultimate (reason) and the relative (perception), is to introduce the concept of "no analysis," as if to say that language, from that point on, can only be based on the modest presumptions of correct relative truth.

This would normally be enough to introduce the formal discussion of *pramāṇa* theory in the Indian Mahāyāna tradition. It is the Buddhist mirror to the material that Frank Clooney has presented to us from the Hindu tradition and should give us a precise tool to make comparisons in the Indian tradition as a whole. There is one more topic, however, that can help us understand the ambiguous relationship between Buddhist views of truth and the theory of the *pramāṇa*s. The most complete and authoritative list of *pramāṇas* in the Hindu tradition gives six possibilities. The last of these is the most puzzling of all. Some Hindu schools took the position that absences (*abhāva*) were real and could be known by a separate and distinct form of valid cognition. They called this the *pramāṇa* of "no-cognition" (*anupalabdhi*).[17] In time the concept of "absence" grew in importance until it became the foundation of logical procedure in the Navya-Nyāya or "new logic" that appeared in the thirteenth century. Buddhists did not recognize it as a separate means of cognition. They had enough problems with real entities, let alone with the reality of absences. But the concept of *anupalabdhi* has an important connection with Buddhist expressions of ultimate truth.

It is common, in the sūtras of the Mahāyāna, to read that bodhisattvas know things "by the discipline of no-cognition" (*anupalambha-yogena*). "No-cognition" also plays a central role in Yogācāra accounts of correct cognition: "Based on cognition there arises no-cognition; based on no-cognition, there arises no-cognition."[18] Yogācāra commentators explain this verse by saying that the *cognition* of mind-only as an objective doctrine leads to the *no-cognition* of external objects, and the *no-cognition* of external objects leads to the *no-cognition* of the subject as a separate entity, and to the loss of the distinction between subject and object. The Yogācāra interprets the final "no-cognition" as the state of awareness in which all distinctions of subject and object have been overcome. When the Buddhist logicians were asked to provide a formal account of no-cognition, they explained that it was a combination of perception and inference. (What else could they say?) To perceive the "absence" of a pot on a table, a person had to *perceive* a place on the top of the table and *infer* the absence of the pot at that place.[19]

This might seem to be nothing but philosophical hair-splitting, but not when it is drawn into the cognitive world of the Mādhyamikas. The goal of Madhyamaka philosophy is to produce an awareness of Emptiness: this is the "ultimate truth" that the tradition seeks. But what kind of cognition is the awareness of Emptiness? Strictly speaking, Emptiness is an "absence." As Jñānagarbha says, it is the absence of the idea that anything really comes into being (literally, "the negation of the concept of real arising"). How would a person cognize such an absence? According to the technical use of the concept of "no-cognition" (as the distinctive mode of cognition that cognizes an absence), it can only be cognized by combining the perception of a place and an inference about an absence. What is the place? The answer can only be that it is correct conventional truth, perceived as "mere thing" without the imposition of any imagined reality. This is what Jñānagarbha meant when he said: "The negation of the real arising of a thing is no different from the thing itself (*bhāva-svabhāva*)" and "the negation of arising is consistent with the truth (*tattva*), so it is considered ultimate."[20] Tibetans had trouble with this idea and criticized Jñānagarbha's formulation of it, but I doubt that it would trouble a Zen master. When someone asks "What is the meaning of the Buddha Dharma?" and is told "The cypress tree out front," the point does not seem to be far removed from what Jñānagarbha said in the more complex but perhaps no more "true" language of the Indian *pramāṇa*s.

3.4 Scriptural and Revelatory Truth

It is clear from the *pramāṇa* theory of the Buddhist logicians that classical Indian Buddhist philosophers did not treat their scriptural texts as *pramāṇa*s. In this respect they were quite different from their Hindu counterparts. They not only denied the authority of the Vedas, but they denied that their own texts have absolute validity. As the proponents of modern Buddhism never tire of saying, the Buddha did not ask anyone to take anything on faith, but to test all of the claims of the Buddhist Dharma in their own experience until they understand its validity for themselves.[21] If they do not find that the Dharma works for them, they should discard it. Buddhist logicians elevated this critical principle to epistemic status when they argued that, in the end, only two *pramāṇa*s could be trusted: perception and reason. But this does not mean that texts have not been important for Buddhists or that Buddhists have not had problems determining which texts they should trust or how they could use even the most trustworthy texts to extract a truth that would be effective in their own experience.

One of the most important "interpretive" acts in the Buddhist tradition is simply to collect significant texts together and group them in a way that allows them to be applied differently to different aspects of life. Buddhist tradition tells us that one of the first acts of the Saṃgha, after the cremation of the Buddha and the distribution of his remains, was to call a council to recite the Buddha's teaching and create an incipient Buddhist "canon." The canonical impulse has continued throughout Buddhist history and has led to authoritative collections of Buddhist scripture in many different parts of the Buddhist world. Southeast Asia (with the exception of Vietnam) respects the authority of the Pali canon. The northern countries in Asia have created large, amorphous collections of Mahāyāna (and other) literature that play the same role in their traditions. Within individual schools, there also are different systems for the ranking and grouping of texts. The T'ien-t'ai school in China, for example, developed an influential system for the ranking of Mahāyāna literature in which the concept of "one vehicle" in the *Lotus Sūtra* represented the Buddha's final teaching and served as the interpretive key for understanding the rest of the Mahāyāna corpus.[22] To some extent, these ranking systems made use of indigenous Indian categories. The Mahāyāna began, for example, with the notion that there were two separate turnings of the wheel of the Dharma, one in the Deer Park in Sarnath and the other on the Vulture Peak in Rājagṛha. The first produced the vehicle of the Śrāvakas or disciples (of which the modern Theravāda is an example), and the second produced the Great Vehicle (*mahāyāna*) of the bodhisattvas. The assumption, of course, was that the second superseded the first and provided the key by which all of it could be interpreted. The Yogācāra school developed a concept of a third turning of the wheel and associated it with the doctrine of mind-only, the key doctrine of the Yogācāra sūtras. It is worth noting, however, that the Indian tradition never produced a Mahāyāna "canon" but seemed to be content to the end with quite a fluid concept of scriptural authority.

For our purposes it seems more helpful to focus not on how the tradition collected texts but on what they did with them once they had them; in other words, how they went about interpreting their texts and applying the texts to their own experience. To answer this question Buddhists have used a formula known as the "Four Refuges":

> O monks, there are four refuges (*pratisaraṇa*). What are these four? The Dharma is the refuge, not a human being. The meaning (*artha*) is the refuge, not the letter (*vyañjana*). A sūtra that is definitive in meaning (*nītārtha*) is the refuge, not one that requires further interpretation (*neyārtha*). Knowledge (*jñāna*) is the refuge, not discursive awareness (*vijñāna*).[23]

This formula is found in some of the earliest Buddhist literature and comes as close as we are likely to get to a common Buddhist understanding of textual interpretation.

A few points in this passage stand out as worthy of note. First, the distinction between the Dharma and a "human being" follows the distinction between the two "bodies" of the Buddha (the Dharma Body and the Form Body). As Ronald Eyre says, in *The Long Search* video on Theravāda Buddhism, Buddhists seem to "prefer live teaching to a dead relic."[24] To understand what is important about the Buddha (or about any human teacher), a person has to focus on the Dharma. The rest of the "four refuges" simply dig deeper into Buddhist understanding of the Dharma itself. The Dharma is meaning (*artha*) rather than letter (*vyañjana*), belongs to the most definitive texts rather than to the ones that are intended to be superseded, and corresponds to a direct form of awareness rather than to one that is based on words and concepts. Of the four refuges, the one that most occupied the attention of the Tibetan tradition was the third. Tsong-kha-pa's *Draṅ-ṅes-legs-bśad-sñiṅ-po*, the text that I used for last year's chapter on "ultimate reality," has to do with "the essence of all that is well spoken in texts that are definitive in meaning (*nītārtha*) and texts that require further interpretation." In other words, it is a work on ultimate reality in the guise of a work of interpretation. The final criterion of judgment about questions of reality and interpretation, however, is "reason," the second of the *pramaṇas*, and reason, for Tsong-kha-pa, is interpreted by the logical tradition of the Mādhyamikas, informed by the broad stream of *pramāṇa* theory that made its way into Tibet through the works of Dharmakīrti.

Notes

1. Wilfred Cantwell Smith, "A Human View of Truth," in John Hick, ed., *Truth & Dialogue In World Religions: Conflicting Truth Claims* (Philadelphia: Westminster Press, 1974), 20–44.

2. Ibid., 25.

3. Ibid., 38.

4. It is well known that the Sanskrit word for "truth" (*satya*) can also be translated as "reality." Wilfred Cantwell Smith notes that this is so common in other languages (as in the Latin *verus*) that the English distinction between "truth" and "reality" begins to seem anomalous. It is less well known that "truth" (*satya*) can be treated as a synonym for *dharma* in the sense of duty, law, or righteousness. *Bṛhadāraṇyaka Upaniṣad* 1.4.14 says: "[Brahman] created the Law (*dharma*), a form superior to and surpassing itself. And the Law is here the ruling power standing above the ruling power. Hence there is nothing higher than the Law [*tasmāt dharmāt paraṃ nāsti*]. Therefore, a weaker man makes demands on a stronger man by appealing to the Law, just as one does by appealing to a king. Now the Law is nothing but the truth [*yo vai sa dharmaḥ satyaṃ vai*]. Therefore, when a man speaks the truth, people say that he speaks the Law; and when a man speaks the Law, people say that he speaks the truth. They are really the same thing." Quoted from Patrick Olivelle, trans., *Upaniṣads* (Oxford: Oxford University Press, 1996), 16.

5. For a more extensive commentary on this story and its traditional sources, see Malcolm David Eckel, "A Buddhist Approach to Repentance," *Repentance: A Comparative Perspective*, ed. Amitai Etzioni (Lanham, Md.: Rowman and Littlefield, 1997), 122–42; and Richard F. Gombrich, *How Buddhism Began: The Conditioned Genesis of the Early Teachings* (London: Athlone, 1996), 135–64.

6. *The Questions of King Milinda*, vol. 1, T. W. Rhys Davids, trans., *Sacred Books of the East*, vol. 35 (Oxford: Clarendon Press, 1890; reprint, New York: Dover Publications, 1963), 180ff.

7. *The Land of Bliss: The Paradise of the Buddha of Measureless Light*, trans. Luis O. Gomez (Honolulu: University of Hawaii Press, 1996), 167.

8. Masatoshi Nagatomi, "*Mānasa-Pratyakṣa*: A Conundrum in the Buddhist *Pramāṇa* System," *Sanskrit and Indian Studies: Essays in Honour of Daniel H. H. Ingalls*, ed. M. Nagatomi, et al. (Dordrecht: D. Reidel, 1980), 243–60.

9. *Pramāṇa-vārttika* 2.3–4: "Here, [the object] that is capable of effective action is said to be ultimate reality and the other [is said to be] relative reality. [A Mādhyamika] might say that nothing is capable [of effective action]. But we see that seeds and so forth have the ability to produce sprouts and so forth. If you consider this [ability] to be relative, so be it."

10. Bhāvaviveka defined the Buddha as "the no-arising of cognition" and as "the understanding that is no-understanding." See Malcolm David Eckel, *To See the Buddha: A Philosopher's Quest for the Meaning of Emptiness* (San Francisco: HarperCollins, 1992; reprint ed. Princeton: Princeton University Press, 1994),

158. The most important discussion of this point in Bhāvaviveka's work comes in his account of the Yogācāra concept of "absolute nature" (*parinişpanna-svabhāva*), as in Malcolm David Eckel, "Bhāvaviveka's Critique of Yogācāra Philosophy in chapter XXV of the *Prajñāpradīpa*," in *Miscellanea Buddhica*, ed. Chr. Lindtner, *Indiske Studier* 5 (Copenhagen: Akademisk Forlag, 1985), 72–74.

11. This three-part formula is discussed in Malcolm David Eckel, *Jñānagarbha's Commentary on the Distinction Between the Two Truths* (Albany: State University of New York Press, 1987), 137–39.

12. Ibid., 75.

13. *A Subtreasury of American Humor*, ed. E. B. White and Katherine S. White (New York: Coward McCann, 1941), xviii.

14. Eckel, op. cit., 71.

15. Ibid., 87.

16. Etienne Lamotte, trans., *The Teaching of Vimalakīrti*, trans. from the French by Sara Boin (London: Pali Text Society, 1976).

17. The two positions are separable. The Nyāya tradition accepted the reality of absences but did not agree that they were known by a separate *pramāṇa*. The view that they require a separate *pramāṇa* belongs to Kumarila Bhaṭṭa (ca. 625). He was followed by some Advaita Vedāntins. See D. M. Datta, *The Six Ways of Knowing: A Critical Study of the Advaita Theory of Knowledge* (Calcutta: University of Calcutta, 1972), 161–64; and Bimal Krishna Matilal, *The Navya-Nyāya Doctrine of Negation: The Semantics and Ontology of Negative Statements in Navya-Nyāya Philosophy*, Harvard Oriental Series 46 (Cambridge, Mass.: Harvard University Press, 1968), 100–2.

18. *Madhyāntavibhāga* 1.7: *upalabhiṃ samāśritya nopalabdhiḥ prajāyate/ nopalabhiṃ samāśritya nopalabdhiḥ prajāyate.*

19. Yuichi Kajiyama, *An Introduction to Buddhist Philosophy: An Annotated Translation of the Tarkabhāṣā of Mokṣākaragupta, Memoirs of the Faculty of Letters*, Kyoto University, 10 (1966), 78–86.

20. Eckel, *Jñānagarbha*, op. cit., 76. Jñānagarbha's terminology apparently is quite close to the account of *anupalabdhi* found in the Prābhākara school of Mīmāṃsā and in the Sāṃkhya. Datta (*Six Ways of Knowing*, 162) quotes the Prābhākaras as saying that the absence of a pot on the ground is identical to the "mere surface of the ground" (*bhū-tala-mātra*) and says that for both the Prābhākaras and the Sāṃkhyas the absence of a thing in a particular place is "nothing but the existence of the bare locus or the *locus per se* (*adhiṣṭhāna-mātram* or *adhiṣṭhāna-svarūpam*)." The term *adhiṣṭhāna-svarūpa* is close to Jñānagarbha's *bhāva-svabhāva*, "the thing itself." Could this be where the later Mādhyamikas got their vocabulary for talking about the relative reality of the "identity" of things?

21. For example, Walpola Rahula, *What the Buddha Taught*, revised edition (New York: Grove Weidenfeld, 1974), chap. 1.

22. Kenneth Ch'en, *Buddhism in China: A Historical Survey* (Princeton: Princeton University Press, 1964), 305–11.

23. Sanskrit quoted from the *Abhidharmakośavyākhyā* by Etienne Lamotte, "La critique d'interprétation dans le bouddhisme," *Annuaire de l'Institut de Philologie et d'Histoire Orientales et Slaves* (Université Libre de Bruxelles), 9 (1949), 341–361. The translation is mine.

24. "The Footprint of the Buddha," episode 3 of *The Long Search* (New York: Ambrose Video Publishing).

4

"To Practice Together Truth and Humility, Justice and Law, Love of Merciful Kindness and Modest Behavior"

Anthony J. Saldarini
with Joseph Kanofsky

4.1 Introduction

When the Jewish tradition addresses the substance of the topic "truth," it usually does so indirectly, with an emphasis on "truth in practice" that closely associates truth with wise or good behavior.[1] The biblical tradition identifies wisdom and foolishness with goodness and wickedness because wisdom involves both knowing and doing what is good and foolishness entails a culpable rejection of wisdom and a willful practice of evil. But wisdom literature also assumes and sometimes poetically articulates wisdom's origin and foundation in God and the divine creation of an orderly world. In this tradition the content of wisdom is roughly equivalent to truth in the western tradition. Post-biblical writings (c. 300 BCE–100 CE) continue the emphasis on practice, but also wrestle with human methods for knowing Scripture accurately in debates over the meaning of laws and verses. Serious and detailed interpretations often imply and occasionally discuss explicitly the correct ways of interpreting the text. Rabbinic literature (c. 200–700 CE) accepts and assumes the foundational authority of Scripture (Torah) as a necessary and nonnegotiable given of the Jewish worldview and as the sum of all wisdom that is important and real. Classical Jewish writings seldom find it necessary to defend Scriptural authority, unlike modern religious and philosophical writing which thematically defends Scripture in the face of the Enlightenment rejection of revelation and authoritative tradition. Explicit epistemological analyses of truth entered Jewish thought in the medieval period through Arabic philosophy, which itself mediated Greek philosophy. Discussions of how to argue logically and reach the truth function apologetically or polemically to convince Jews not fully committed to their tradition and to refute Gentiles who reject Jewish thought.

"Truth" is not a major, indigenous category in much of Jewish thought, in contrast to the Greek and Western philosophical traditions. The editors of a recent history of Jewish philosophy do not include "truth" in their index and register knowledge only as "Knowledge of God" with three page references.[2] Truth and knowledge are at stake in the literature surveyed in the essays, but do not emerge as independent topics for discussion. The editors do not stand alone. Few Jewish reference works or compendia include a systematic discussion of truth. However, a few generalizations, qualified by the usual cautions, may provide orientation concerning what is at stake about the Jewish tradition when we discuss topics related to the Western category truth.

God, the biblical texts, wisdom, Torah in the broad sense, and Rabbinic literature communicate truth in several senses. All branches of the Jewish tradition presume ontological and cosmological truth. In wisdom literature and wisdom passages in the prophets and Psalms God created the world in an orderly and intelligible way that is at least partially available to humans. God's dynamic, creative power generates a stable physical, intellectual, moral, and spiritual world that supports human life. The created world in the Bible is always peopled with humans and oriented toward humans proximately and God ultimately. Talmudic literature assumes this foundation, but seldom discusses it because truth in practice fills its agenda. The medieval philosophical tradition links logic, categories, argument, and reason to the biblical and Talmudic traditions in order to present a systematic, rationally defensible account of Jewish thought. Modern Jewish philosophers in the West, along with everyone else, have turned strongly to epistemology.

The Jewish tradition expresses truth preeminently in writing, that is, in the Torah and all that follows from it. The liturgy enshrines the Torah in a ritual drama rich in blessings and affirmations of God, the subject and goal of Torah. The mystical tradition finds knowledge of and contact with God through Torah and even the Hebrew letters in which Torah is written. Art (often found in illuminated manuscripts), architecture, and poetry have all contributed to the communication of the Jewish tradition.

The core of the Talmudic tradition seeks to embody truth in practice. The paramount topic for discussion is law (Torah) and the dominant activity is interpretation of the law. From the Talmud in the third century to contemporary responsa, Jewish scholars seek to accurately and correctly *decide* the exact requirements of the law in a multitude of concrete cases. Study of the law provides a foundation for the ultimate goal of the tradition, Jewish life lived in obedience to Torah, which is the expression of God's will par excellence. From this dedication to embodied truth or truth in practice all else follows. Interpretation of the Torah (the Pentateuch), the study of the Rabbinic tradition (Torah in the wider sense), the principles for deciding the meaning and application of laws in particular cases, the master-disciple relationship, and a Torah-observant life cohere and reinforce one another. Even mystical experience proceeds from Torah for there truth is sought in esoteric interpretations of Scripture, revelatory visions, journeys and ascents to heaven, and an inner transformation of the soul. Perhaps the medieval mystical text, the Zohar, summarizes the situation most succinctly by positing an absolutist, unified view of divine truth: "The Torah, Israel and God are all One."[3]

This exploratory study will briefly survey the biblical tradition, especially its use of words from the root *'mn*, which refers to reliability, durability, faithfulness and later faith and truth. The noun for truth and faithfulness, (*'emet* from the same root) emerges as an important and independent polemical theme in several of the Dead Sea Scrolls, so we shall examine the role of *'emet* in the Community Rule (1QS), a foundational text for the Qumran community (c. 150 BCE–68 CE). The Talmud gathers together a wide variety of traditions, stories, exegeses, arguments, and analyses. It puts them to work determining truth in practice, that is, what the Law (Torah) requires of Israel. Implicitly the Talmud and its commentaries struggle with epistemological truth, seeking to determine the meaning of the law and the significance of Scripture and other materials for Jewish life and thought. They sometimes discusses explicitly the exegetical procedures for legitimately interpreting the tradition.

Epistemological truth enters Jewish literature as a formal, explicit topic in the tenth-century writings of Saadia Gaon who taught in Islamic Mesopotamia. His Arabic *Book of Beliefs and Opinions (Kitab al-'Amanat wal-I'tikadat)* is the first systematic presentation of Jewish thought and belief as a rational whole. It was addressed to his contemporary Jews who wavered between fideism and rejection of the Jewish tradition. His introductory treatise on "Doubt and Certainty" discusses explicitly some of the problems of knowledge, truth, and error. The discussion continued in the writings of numerous medieval Jewish thinkers, preeminently Maimonides (Rabbi Moses ben Maimon, also referred to by the acronym Rambam).

During the last three centuries the European and American Jewish communities have confronted the Enlightenment with its emphasis on reason and science and its suspicion of tradition and religion. In the eighteenth century Moses Mendelssohn sought to utilize the Enlightenment political and philosophical affirmation of human liberty and its reliance on human reason in support of revealed religion. He abandoned universal ontological, cosmological truth to Enlightenment reason and carved out a place for the Jewish tradition and its way of life in the arena of truth in practice. In the next century Samson Raphael Hirsch, the founder of German Jewish "neo-orthodoxy," adopted the opposite procedure by affirming the authenticity of the Jewish tradition and the centrality of Torah. He then incorporated some aspects of secular studies into Jewish education and culture, while attributing their truth ultimately to Torah. The approaches of both thinkers still influence opposing streams of contemporary Judaism.

4.2 The Biblical Tradition

The root *'mn* refers to duration, and thus to stability and reliability.[4] The range of meanings associated with this root includes faithfulness, faith, trustworthiness, and truth. Derivatives most often refer to relationships among people or between humans and God, in regard to actions and attitudes related to honesty, integrity, and truthful communication. The Septuagint, the Greek translation of the Hebrew Bible, uses *alētheia*, "truth," most frequently to translate the Hebrew noun *'ᵉmet*. But since the Hebrew word refers to behavior and faithfulness as well, *pistis* (faith) and *dikaiosynē* (justice, righteousness; *ṣedeq* in Hebrew) are also employed. The Jewish and Christian liturgical response "Amen," which is found in the Bible (Numbers 5:22; Deuteronomy 27:15–17; 1 Kings 1:36), comes from this root. Earlier Semitic literature (Akkadian, Ugaritic, Phoenician) does not attest to this root, but it occurs in Aramaic, a language closely related to and contemporaneous with Hebrew, and in later Arabic, but not as a word for truth. Arabic uses *ṣidq* (=Hebrew *ṣedeq*), the root for "justice, righteousness," as part of a realistic epistemology in which the thing itself, the thought of the knower and the verbal communication of thought, all agree. *Ṣidq* is focused on truthfulness and truthful, just behavior. Arabic also uses the root *ḥaqq* to refer to the ontologically real.[5] In contrast, the equivalent Hebrew root, *ḥqq* refers exclusively to law and truth in practice. It denotes that which is "cut, inscribed," and thus connotes "something decreed or prescribed," that is, "statutes." Along with commandments (*miṣwōt*) and ordinances (*mišpā ṭîm*), it is one of the words used for biblical laws. The Community Rule from the Dead Sea Scrolls (see below) refers in a polemical context to the "truth of God's statutes" and the "statutes of God's truth," a usage that suggests a close relationship between divine law and truth.

In the Bible the noun *'ᵉmet* (truth) is not spread across the biblical books but appears most often in Psalms (37 times), Proverbs, Isaiah and Jeremiah (about a dozen times each) and in the later books Zechariah and Daniel, a half dozen times each. It is linked to justice, wisdom, and steadfast love (*ḥesed*) in a number of passages (cf. Proverbs 3:3; 23:23; Psalm 85:10–11; Hosea 4:1). A related noun, *'ᵉmûnah*, is often translated as faith (*pistis*) in the Septuagint, but in the Hebrew Bible it is often contrasted with falsehood, lying, and deceit (*šeger*) and thus identified with truth and faithfulness; for example, "Whoever speaks the truth gives honest evidence, but a false witness speaks deceitfully" (Proverbs 12:17). In a verse made famous by Paul (Romans 1:17; Galatians 3:11; cf Hebrews 10:38), the prophet Habakkuk contrasts the arrogance of the proud with the faith or faithfulness or perhaps trust in God of the just: "Look at the proud! His spirit is not upright in them, but the righteous lives by his faithfulness/faith (*'ᵉmûnah* in Habakkuk 2:4). In many contexts, like this, nouns from the root *'mn* can be translated as either faithfulness, faith, trust or truth.

A few more examples will concretize and contextualize the biblical understanding of reliability, faithfulness, and truth. Moses is called a faithful servant (Numbers 12:7). Messengers and witnesses are praised for being trustworthy (Proverbs 25:13; Isaiah 8:2). "A gossip goes about revealing a secret; one trustworthy of spirit conceals a matter (Proverbs 11: 13). Israel's spirit and heart are often unfaithful to God (Psalm 78:8) or the covenant (Psalm 78:37). God promises that David's house (dynasty) will endure (i.e., be *ne'ᵉm n*—2 Samuel 7:16). Interestingly, the verb *he'ᵉm n*, which means to trust or believe someone, connotes gullibility in human relations: "The simple person believes anything, but the clever person watches his step" (Proverbs 14:15). Thus the author of Proverbs advises: "When an enemy speaks graciously, do not believe it" (Proverbs 26:25). Of course, Israel appropriately trusts and believes in God: "Israel saw the great work that the LORD did against the Egyptians. So the people feared the LORD and believed/trusted in the LORD and in his servant Moses" (Exodus 14:31). In another example made famous by Paul (Romans 4:6; Galatians 3:6), who had a more than passing interest in faith, God promised the childless Abraham a multitude of descendants and in response Abraham "believed/trusted the LORD; and the LORD reckoned it to him as righteousness" (Genesis 15:6). In general, the verb to "believe, trust (in)" is not central to the Deuteronomic or prophetic vocabulary[6] and is not a central symbol of the biblical understanding of God, humans, or truth. The negative use of the verb manifests an acute sense of human deviousness and unreliability. Thus, in wisdom literature the opposed pair "wise" and "fool" are interchangeable with "good" and "evil" and (though the terms are less used) "true" and "false." The criterion for truth and falsehood is relational; one is faithful or true to God and one's fellow man or one is evil, devious, cunning, twisted, and so on.

In wisdom literature truth is generally aligned with righteousness and justice. In the Book of Job, the dialectic between righteousness and suffering throws doubt on God's justice, trustworthiness, and reliability. The interchanges between Job and his interlocutors often refer to appearances and human (mis)perceptions in contrast to divine knowledge and power. In fact this book seeks to understand comprehensively the inability of humans to explain the workings of the universe. Even though discussions of truth as such and epistemological analyses do not explicitly occur in the dialogues, Job's probing and protests against perceived injustice raise these questions. In the end God reveals something of his knowledge and power without directly resolving Job's concerns about the governance of the world. God calls upon Job to trust in and rely on him. In the Book of Ecclesiastes (Qoheleth) the issue of truth lies closer to the surface. The author, who pseudonymously identifies himself with Solomon, traditionally the wisest of Israel's kings and the author of wisdom writings, ironically debunks wisdom as incapable of explaining what happens in human life, yet concedes reluctantly that wisdom is better than foolishness. He claims all through the book that all is *ḥebel*, literally, "air, vapor" and metaphorically "nothingness, vanity, meaninglessness"; but he writes a book to convince people of his understanding of life, thus giving some kind of value to understanding. In a real sense the search for wisdom in the Bible functions like the search for truth in Greek philosophy. But the Bible comprehensively subordinates the search for wisdom and truth to good behavior.

4.3 The Dead Sea Scrolls

Many of the non-biblical Second Temple manuscripts found in the caves near Wadi Qumran by the Dead Sea use biblical themes, images, expressions, and rhetoric in prayers, exegeses, the retelling of biblical stories, and reinterpretations of biblical laws and practices. In several documents that were written by community members the word *'emet*, meaning truth and faithfulness, appears more prominently than it did in the Bible, usually in conjunction with a cluster of other words such as righteousness (*ṣ^e^dāqāh*), foundation (*sôd*) of truth, community (*yaḥad*) of truth, men (*'anšê*) of truth, ways (*darkê*) of truth, and spirit (*ruaḥ*) of truth. In many of these cases *'emet* might also mean faithfulness, so that the Second Temple Jewish ear probably heard both meanings. Since Hebrew of this period lacks adjectives, words like *'emet* and righteousness may be appended in the genitive case to other nouns so that they function like adjectives. Thus the well-known "teacher of righteousness" (objective genitive) to whom the scrolls refer may actually be "the righteous teacher" and the "community of truth" above may be the "faithful" or "authentic community." *'emet* is frequently contrasted with various negative words, such as deceit, injustice, evil, and so on. Translations of these words, which each have a range of meanings, differ, so the connotations of *'emet*, whether as truth or faithfulness or integrity, can only become clear in context, and even then only with difficulty. The Qumran group in many of its documents disputes interpretations of Jewish law and thought with the authorities in Jerusalem ("the wicked priest" and the "last priests") and with other groups that had opposed them, such as the "seekers after smooth things" (often identified with the Pharisees), "Ephraim" and "Manasseh" (the Pharisees and Sadducees?) and the "House of Absalom" (another priestly faction?). The issue of truth vs. culpable error, deception, and corruption lies at the heart of their polemics and stimulates their use of a "truth, faithfulness" vocabulary. Clearly the group at Qumran had rethought and adapted biblical terms into a new symbolic system.

The Community Rule (1QS) contains a collection of exhortations, instructions, laws, and hymns that articulate the Qumran community's principles and practices. A review of some of the uses of *'emet* (approximately forty instances) and related words will elucidate the community's view of truth. The opening instruction of the Community Rule aptly communicates the group's purpose and illustrates its modified biblical rhetoric. The members enter the community:

> that they may seek God with a whole heart and soul,
>   and do what is *good and right* before Him
> as He commanded by the hand of Moses
>   and all His servants the Prophets;

that they may love all that He has chosen
and hate all that he has rejected;
that they may abstain from all *evil*
and hold fast to all *good*;
that they may practice truth, righteousness, and justice upon earth
and no longer stubbornly follow a sinful heart and lustful eyes
committing all manner of *evil*.

(1QS 1:7)

Note that the reference to truth is embedded in an exhortation promoting goodness. Thus truth is immediately linked with two words related to justice and law. The first, *ṣ*^{e}*dāqāh*, refers to behavior in accordance with God's will and justice. The second, *mišpâṭ*, refers to Near Eastern case law, that is, to judgments of what is just. Note also that truth is to be practiced and that its practice is part of a whole program of seeking God and doing good.

Those who are to enter the Qumran community are characterized as "those who freely devote themselves to God's *truth*" and they are to

bring all their knowledge (*da'at*), powers,
and possessions into the Community of God,
that they may purify (clarify, strengthen) their knowledge
in the *truth* of God's statutes (*ḥûgā*)
and order their powers according to His ways of perfection
and all their possessions according to His righteous counsel
in order not to deviate from any single one
of all the words of God in their (appropriate) times . . .
and in order not to turn aside to the right or left
from the *statutes* of God's truth.

(1QS 1:11–15)

"God's truth," the "truth of God's statute's" and "the statutes of God's truth" all refer to biblical laws as authentically interpreted and practiced by the Qumran community, in contrast to the misinterpretations and lack of observance in Jewish society at large. The vocabulary and setting of these instructions indicate that "truth" is a polemical symbol related to interpreting and observing biblical law accurately and faithfully. Practically speaking, this means living the way of life and adopting the outlook of the Qumran community and that choice in turn requires that "all those who come into the rule of the community shall cross over into the covenant before God in order to act according to all God has commanded" (1QS 1:16–17). The religious truth promoted in this preliminary instruction concerns truth in practice, that is, a life lived in a specific community according to that community's understanding of God's law. In the background of these exhortations lie a commitment to God and Israel's covenant with God, an awareness of the cosmic conflict between good and evil, and a conviction that all will end with a divine judgment of good and evil.

The clustering of truth with other nouns continues throughout the rule. The Qumran community is a "community of truth and of virtuous humility, of love of kindness and of just intent, one towards the other, in a council of holiness and of members of an eternal assembly" (1QS 2:24–25). Members of the community atone for their sins and contemplate the light of life "by the spirit of the counsel of the truth of God" (1QS 3:6–7). The references to the community as a council and to counsel coming from God's truth highlight the importance of correctly interpreting and faithfully observing God's law. God, the community, holiness, justice, and truth along with an array of other virtues, all based on the law of God, characterize and enliven the new, reformed covenant community established by this rule. Columns five and eight, which are further instructions in the Community Rule, also invoke truth as a significant theme.

The instruction that the guardian of the community gives to the members concerning good and evil (1QS 3:15–4:26) refers most strikingly to truth and falsehood in a cosmic context. "Truth" appears fourteen times in this instruction, which teaches that all humans live according to the spirit of truth or of falsehood (cf. 3:17–19; 4:23–24). The word for falsehood (*ʿāwel*) in the instruction is generally used for evil and injustice in the Bible, with the connotation of deviating (off a path) and thus cheating, being false, etc.[7] For example, it is associated with rendering unjust judgments in court (Leviticus 19:15, 35) and using false weights and measures (Leviticus 19:35; Deuteronomy 25:16). It is also contrasted more generally with righteousness/justice (*ṣᵉdāqāh*) (Ezekiel 3:20; 18:24, 26). In later Rabbinic literature *ʿāwel* denotes faults and perversion. The particular Qumran usage associates *ʿāwel*, meaning evil, with falsehood because falsehood is the root of all evil according to the teaching and experience of the Qumran community. The priests and Israelites who withdrew from Jerusalem to the shore of the Dead Sea condemned the interpretation of biblical law and the behavior of the powerful priestly and aristocratic families in Jerusalem. In their conflict with them they accused them of willful, culpable denial of the truth and contrasted themselves with the Jerusalem leadership because they, the Qumran community, followed the truth. Their position resembles and is an intensification of the teaching in the biblical Book of Proverbs that ties truth and falsehood closely to good and evil. This Qumran instruction on the two spirits in the community rule (1QS 3:15–4:26) contrasts the "prince of lights" and "angel of darkness," the "sons of light" and "sons of darkness," the "angel of truth," "sons of truth," and the "sons of righteousness" with "sons of deceit," all of whom take part in an eschatological drama. At the end of the world the truth will go forth forever in the world (4:19). The power of this truth can be seen in God's sprinkling the spirit of truth on humans like water that purifies from all abominations of lying (*šeker*, which also means falsehood in 1QS 4:21). Most important, a person's spirit, true or false, good or evil, will be the criterion for judgment at the end.

> Until now the *spirits of truth and falsehood struggle* in the hearts of men and they walk in both wisdom and folly. According to his *portion of truth* so does a man *hate falsehood*, and according to his inheritance in the realm of falsehood so is he wicked and so hates truth. For God has established the two spirits in equal measure until the determined end, and until the Renewal, and He knows the reward of their deeds from all eternity. He has allotted them to the children of men that they may know good [and evil, and] that the destiny of all the living may be according to the spirit within [them at the time] of the visitation. (1QS 4:23–25)

The category "truth," which was peripheral in the Bible, has moved to the center of both the moral and cosmic world of the Qumran community. It is intimately related to good and evil, human behavior and God's commandments, as it was in the Bible, but now it distinguishes humans one from the other, determines their ultimate status before God, and stands as a counterforce to evil in the world. Thus, truth in the Qumran Community Rule is fundamentally embodied, lived truth, but it depends on the reliability and validity of the Bible, which reveals the commandments of God. The polemical rhetoric of truth and falsehood points to an implicit epistemology that involves the authority and veracity of the interpreting community and, in other texts, its founding teacher, the Teacher of Righteousness. The relationship of truth to God's commandments and their correct interpretation in opposition to falsehood points to a fundamental assumption of the whole rule and its polemics: the authority, authenticity, and truth of Scripture. Truth's role in the cosmic struggle between good and evil, which will culminate in the final judgment and the triumph of truth and goodness, gives a depth and power to truth that transcends the written Scriptural text and its embodiment in the Qumran community.

4.4 The Talmud

The Talmud seeks to discern all the implications of Jewish law for communal and individual behavior and to work out clear decisions concerning the practical observance of the law. At its core is the Mishnah, a group of sixty-three tractates discussing a series of topics found in biblical law. The Mishnah preserves the views of a multitude of sages (*ḥakamîm*, who were addressed by the title "Rabbi") as they debated fine points of laws and their implications. The Talmud, which is arranged as a commentary on the Mishnah, continues the process, but in greater detail. Frequently the Talmudic discussions debate multiple legal positions and hypothetical cases, using lengthy and subtle rational analyses, exegeses of words and phrases, and analogies among similar laws, cases, or hermeneutical principles. The authors of the Talmud seek to work out all possible implications of the biblical law and its Mishnaic interpretation. In addition, the Talmud contains stories, exegeses of Scripture, customs, folklore, and anything that might help to elucidate God's Torah (instruction) for Israel. Since the sages composed the Talmud over several centuries (the third to the seventh or eighth), their views and arguments testify to a variety of situations and eras, as well as differing social, economic, and political circumstances for men and women, learned and uneducated, rural and urban. Thus, the rabbis reach legal decisions to guide their communities in the observance of Torah with great sensitivity to needs and circumstances as well as fierce fidelity to divinely revealed law (Torah). For concomitant with this complex epistemological endeavor, the sages of the Talmud approached all aspects of their tradition as divinely revealed commandments that were to be interpreted according to a divinely revealed oral tradition that in turn had been faithfully preserved by the sages in the Talmud, its commentaries and the Jewish tradition as a whole.[8]

Despite, or perhaps because of, all the analyses and arguments in the Talmud, not every problem can be resolved with intellectual certainty nor can every commandment receive a definitive interpretation. A brief Talmudic story affirms this view. In response to an unspecified disagreement between the schools of Hillel and Shammai, a heavenly voice first affirms the truth in both positions: "These and these are the words of the Living God" (b. Erubin 13b). This means that both views are true, correct, and just. The sages respected both and preserved and discussed both in the Talmud. However, while the discussion continues from generation to generation and the teachers instruct new students in the subtleties and principles of Jewish law, the Jewish community requires a decision that can guide life. Thus, the Talmud continues by proposing a further principle that "the law (*h^{a}lākāh*) follows Hillel." Even those who disagree with the position of Hillel must follow his view in practice.

The highly authoritative Talmudic tradition maintains its flexibility and creativity by means of a sophisticated hermeneutical system that encourages discussion, disagreement, debate, and multiple interpretations of laws and texts. The tradition's polyvalence and openness to interpretation extends to the most sacred text, the Torah (Pentateuch), whose words and letters contain inexhaustible meanings. One familiar Rabbinic trope assigns four meanings to Scripture: the simple or literal (*p^{e}āšt*); allegorical (*remez*); homiletical (*d^{e}r*); and mystical or secret (*sôd*).[9] In a sense the central texts of the Rabbinic tradition serve as a focus for all knowledge, human and divine, and arbitrate directly or indirectly all the problems and potentialities associated with the search for truth.

Significantly, the Talmudic method of discussion, commentary, and controversy has continued until the present. The Talmud provides a foundation and theoretical backbone to the entire tradition studied by thousands of Jews. However, its role as an authoritative guide to contemporary orthodox practice has been superseded by later law codes compiled by Maimonides (the *Mishneh Torah*) and Joseph Karo (the *Shulḥan Aruch*) and subsequently by numerous responses (*responsa*) to particular questions by authoritative Rabbis. These codes and responsa frequently reach back to the Talmudic texts to justify their rulings, but they energetically and creatively address technological and social problems unimagined in antiquity.

4.5 Saadia Gaon and Philosophical Truth

Saadia ben Joseph (d. 942 CE), called Saadia Gaon (a title that means "Excellency" and was used for the heads of Jewish schools), was born in Egypt and taught in the Jewish academic city of Sura in southern Mesopotamia. He wrote the *Book of Beliefs and Opinions* in 933 CE to shore up the wavering commitment of many Jews and to demonstrate that the Jewish tradition was rational and true to students of the classical Arabic philosophical tradition.[10] The ten treatises of the book cover creation, God, commands and prohibitions, divine justice, merits and demerits, the soul and death, resurrection of the dead, redemption, reward and punishment, and finally human conduct. *An Introductory Treatise on Doubt and Certainty* addresses questions concerning knowledge, truth and error. The opening prayer of praise to God who endowed humankind with the ability to know the truth contains a capsule of the author's view of humans and God.

> Blessed be God, the God of Israel,
>   who is alone deserving of being regarded
> as the Evident Truth,
> who verifies with certainty unto rational beings
>   the existence of their souls,
> by means of which they assess accurately
>   what they perceive with their senses
> and apprehend correctly the objects of their knowledge.
> Uncertainties are thereby removed from them
>   and doubts disappear,
> so that demonstrations become lucid for them
>   and proofs become clear.

In the second chapter the author addresses the obstacles that prevent people from knowing the truth and methods for resolving uncertainties. Knowledge begins with the senses in the Aristotelian mode and then involves use of the intellect. However, people become confused because they are unfamiliar with the relevant sense objects or with methods of rational argument; they don't know what they are seeking, they take shortcuts by failing to investigate thoroughly and by leaping to conclusions without careful thought. As a result some people find the truth but are in doubt about it, some flit from one conclusion to another, and some affirm falsehood as the truth. The author composed this book to help Jews who are confused in these ways and to refute those who deny the faith. Doubters should have their doubts lifted and find certainty and those who believe "by sheer authority will come to believe out of insight and understanding."[11] Although Saadia is acutely aware of human failings, he has much more confidence in the potentialities of human reason in this world than did Augustine and much less confidence in the utility of appealing to authoritative, traditional teachings.[12] He follows Aristotle's turn to the empirical rather than Plato and Augustine's reaching for the spiritual.[13]

The third chapter sketches the process of human knowing as a series of phases or tasks that must be completed to create a proof by which we arrive at truth.[14] Humans "cannot acquire knowledge except by the mediation of a cause; that is, by the process of research and analysis, the performance of which requires certain measures of time."[15] Error and controversy result from failing to complete the process of knowing. To insist on recognizing the truth instantaneously is tantamount to demanding equality with the Creator.

The fourth chapter of the introductory treatise explains the meaning of the word "belief" that is used in the title. The Arabic word for belief, *'Amana*, comes from the same root (*'mn*) as the Hebrew words for truth, faith, and so on. For Saadia, however, belief is a kind of rational knowledge reached by investigation and thought. It is "a notion that arises in the soul in regard to the actual character of anything that is apprehended. . . . When the cream of the investigation emerges, is embraced and enfolded by the minds and, through them, acquired and digested by the souls, then the person becomes convinced of the truth of the notion he has thus acquired."[16] The wise man makes reality the criterion for his beliefs. He relies on evidence deserving of trust and is cautious when necessary. That evidence is usually gathered by the senses, but may be revealed or based on reliable authority also. The fool who has false beliefs "sets up his personal conviction as his guiding principle, assuming that reality follows his belief."[17] False beliefs are opinions.[18] The Arabic word for opinion, *I'tikad*, which is also found in the title, comes from the root meaning bind (*'qd*—found in Hebrew as well as Arabic). "Opinion" has a pejorative meaning as a kind of unsubstantiated knowing, a state of "being bound" by ignorance or one's own presuppositions.

The fifth chapter of the treatise distinguishes three sources of human knowing: observation with the senses, intellectual intuition, and logically necessary inference. In addition, Israel ("the community of monotheists") has a fourth source of knowledge, authentic tradition, which Saadia says they derive from the other three sources of knowledge. For him the revelation that is found in the Bible and interpreted in Jewish literature is based upon the knowledge of the senses as well as reason and at the same time corroborates the validity of the senses and reason. Saadia defines an intuition of the intellect as "a notion that springs up solely in the mind of a human being, such as approbation of truthfulness and disapproval of mendacity."[19] An intellectual intuition is not directly based on sense data, but is anything conceived rationally in the human mind in complete freedom from accidents. It is to be regarded "as true knowledge about which no doubt [is to be entertained]" on the assumption that a person knows how to reason, carries out the reasoning process to its conclusion, and distinguishes reason from imagination and dreams.[20] Logical necessity refers to statements the denial of which would entail the denial of reason or the senses themselves or conclusions reached by them. Most simply, if a statement contradicts observed reality, logic will conclude that the statement is false. More complexly, logic can work out the unobserved or unobservable realities presumed by a sensed reality (the sound of a human voice presumes a human speaking) or the postulates of geometry.[21] Logical conclusions must be tested against further observations or examined carefully for alternative explanations.

Saadia puts the epistemological reflections of his introductory treatise to work in the individual treatises of *Beliefs and Opinions*. He appeals to logic, Scripture, and philosophical argument. A couple of examples must suffice this brief treatment. In the first treatise Saadia employs his method to prove that the world must have been created and, in contrast to Aristotle's position, could not be eternal. He begins with a Scriptural affirmation of creation (Genesis 1:1; Isaiah 44:24) and then argues from finitude, compositeness, accidents, and temporality that the world was in fact created. In the course of the arguments he assumes and argues from pre-modern cosmology. In the second treatise he argues that God is the infinite and eternal creator, using a variety of arguments. His ultimate goal emerges in the last chapter of the treatise (chap. 13) in which he argues, in summation, that God's existence is proven by the principle of non-contradiction, "in the same way in which our minds recognize the impossibility of a thing's being existent and nonexistent at one and the same time, as well as of other such mutually exclusive phenomena, although these matters have never been observed by the senses" and concludes with an appeal to Scripture: "Furthermore, Scripture says: 'But the Lord God is the truth' (Jeremiah 10:10). Later in the chapter he synthesizes his conclusions with love of God.

> Now when a person has achieved the knowledge of this lofty subject by means of rational speculation and the proof of the miracles and marvels [mentioned in Holy Writ], his soul believes it as true and it is mingled with his spirit and becomes an inmate of its innermost recesses. The result is then that, whenever the soul walks in its temple, it finds it, as the saint has said: "With my soul have I desired You in the night; yea, with my spirit within me have I sought You earnestly" (Isaiah 26:9). Moreover his soul becomes filled with completely sincere love for God, a love which is beyond all doubt, as Scripture expresses it: "And you shall love the Lord your God with all your heart, etc." (Deuteronomy 6:5).

The prayerful, contemplative, yet rational and argumentative search for God using Scripture, philosophy, and communal piety recalls Augustine's appropriation of similar traditions in his *Confessions* in his search for God and Aquinas's Aristotelian synthesis of philosophy (medieval) science and theology that culminates in the love of God.

4.6 The Response to Modernity

Moses Mendelssohn was the most prominent modern Jewish philosopher responding to the Enlightenment in the late eighteenth century. He used the Jewish emphasis on law (*hᵃlākāh*) governing behavior to solve the

Enlightenment disputes over reason and revelation and over universalism and particularity.[22] The Enlightenment privileged universal reason and undermined the predominance and authority of particular religious traditions and revelations. The rise of empirical science and of a philosophy divorced from theology pushed Scripture, traditional religious practice, and the medieval theological-philosophical synthesis to one side in the public forum. Especially in Europe where Jews were a cultural minority, the Enlightenment critique of religion threatened to undermine the authenticity of Jewish tradition. In a crucial move Mendelssohn argued that the Mosaic revelation is not concerned with revealed doctrines or metaphysical truths and thus is not a competitor of Enlightenment truth. The revealed Torah contains the laws that in the past governed the Jewish state and now govern the Jewish community and individual Jews. He sharply distinguished Torah and Jewish thought from traditional Christian theology that was built on dogma.

Mendelssohn responded to the rise of science and empirical reason by conceding that God reveals the nature of the world and human being to all humans through reason. Thus Mendelssohn, influenced by Hobbes and especially Locke, could affirm the universal natural religion of the Enlightenment based on reason while retaining the particularity of the Jewish way of life and observance of the commandments as part of a different sphere of life. In his own words, "I recognize no eternal truths other than those that are not merely comprehensible to human reason but can also be demonstrated and verified by human power."[23] Mendelssohn argues that sublime truths about God and the world must be gained by reflection and thought and cannot be coerced by legislation or a demand for faith.[24] His thesis responds to both the European religious wars among Christians and the oppression of Jews. In a thoroughly Jewish reversal of the usual Christian emphasis on revealed dogma, Mendelssohn claims that God gave humans reason sufficient to comprehend eternal truths.

Revelation is restricted to revealed legislation that pertains to the vagaries of history and diversity of human society.[25] Peoples and cultures make their way to God and fashion a moral way of life diversely at different times. The biblical revelation in particular contains

> the laws, precepts, commandments and rules of life, which were to be peculiar to this nation and through the observance of which it should arrive at national felicity, a well as personal felicity of each of it individual members. The lawgiver was God . . . as Patron and Friend by covenant of their ancestors. . . . He gave his laws the most solemn sanction, publicly and in a never heard-of, miraculous manner, by which they were imposed upon the nation and all their descendants as an unalterable duty and obligation.

These laws were *revealed*, that is, they were made known by God, through *words* and *script*.[26]

Mendelssohn affirms the traditional Jewish way of life, but subordinates it to the universal rational truths (natural religion) of the Enlightenment. He acknowledges that the Bible contains eternal truths and religious doctrines but he attributes them to reason.[27] Their appearance in the Bible does not restrict them to the particular revelation of Israel. Thus he concedes to Enlightenment reason the epistemological, cosmological, and ontological foundations of truth and reserves for tradition (in his case Jewish tradition) the particulars of revealed and embodied truth that appear in multiple forms throughout the world and its history.

Samson Raphael Hirsch (1808–1888) responded to German Jewish assimilation to modern culture and the Jewish Reform movement, which sought to adapt Jewish thought and life to enlightenment reason and European culture, with a thorough and fundamental defense of Torah as a complete and adequate revelation from God to Israel that superseded human reason. Hirsch sought to counteract the rejection of a Torah-observant life by assimilated Jews and the radical adaptation of Jewish law by the Reform movement by adapting and assimilating nineteenth-century secular knowledge to the Jewish religious tradition. His philosophy, expounded as an educational philosophy which would guide Jewish schools in creating their curricula, has been summarized with the Hebrew phrase *Torah im Derekh Eretz* [literally, Torah with the way of the land], that is, Torah accompanied by secular knowledge or modern culture. His school of thought still guides (in a general sense) the curricula of such institutions as Yeshiva University in New York and other "centrist-orthodox" institutions. Reversing Mendelssohn's priorities, Hirsch created a synthesis of Torah and secular knowledge that remained under the rubric of Torah and tradition. He wished to provide rational understanding for the Torah's 613 positive and negative commandments and their particular details of observance by showing the breadth and depth of their imperative possibilities to the modem Jew schooled in rational thought. To underscore his position on the primacy of Torah, he argued for his position using explanations from within the Rabbinic tradition, without recourse to Enlightenment systems of discourse.

Of course, Hirsch's attempt to explain Judaism rationally but on its own terms inevitably came under categories and headings influenced by Hirsch's university training and his wide reading in contemporary philosophy. The issue for Hirsch is really the classic Jewish case *in extremis*: how to reconcile the demands and opportunities of the nineteenth century with a system of symbols, hermeneutics, and values that presents itself as eternal, immutable, and unchanging. For him Torah was supreme in Jewish thought and *Derekh Eretz*, or culture, was actually in its noblest forms a divine revelation on par with Torah. Those elements in Western thought that showed shades of truth were in fact derivatives of classical Jewish thought; what was good in classical Hellenistic thought as well as in modern humanism showed those schools' commonality, if not debt, to Jewish thought. Since revelation included both Torah and science, Hirsch maintained, one could ignore neither if one intended to comprehend the Truth inherent in the created world. His system sought the kind of intellectual harmony created by medieval scholastic theology and philosophy, but was just as fragile. His endeavor assumed a fundamental unity and harmony in the universe loosely analogous to that presumed by Chinese thought.[28]

4.7 Conclusions and Comparisons

We end as we began. The weight of the Jewish tradition falls within the sphere of embodied truth or truth in practice. Traditional Jews cultivate truth by observance of the divinely given Jewish law. The Rabbinic tradition from the Talmud on has expended most of its efforts determining the requirements for correct and comprehensive obedience to Jewish law in daily life. It reveres the Torah (the first five books of the Hebrew Bible) above all because of the predominance of law revealed by God at Mount Sinai (Exodus 19 to Numbers 10, with a reprise in Deuteronomy). At the same time, the narrative of the Torah compels assent to the origin of the laws in God who revealed them to Israel through Moses on Mount Sinai. Thus the centrality and dominance of law affirms and depends upon the prior communication of law by God to humans and assumes a veracity and stability given to it by God, the creator and ruler of the world. When Second Temple Jewish groups such as the Pharisees, priestly groups, Essenes, and Sadducees argued intensely with one another over how the law was to be observed, they implicitly witnessed to the authority and truth of biblical revelation, the laws it contained and the observant way of life it demanded. The sages (Rabbis) of the post-destruction period (70 CE on) continued the devotion to law in the Mishnah and the Palestinian and Babylonian Talmuds with their extensive discussion of legal positions, biblical exegeses and other relevant Jewish tradition and custom. Yet within Judaism's singular concentration on the law as truth in practice the sages of the Babylonian Talmud also expressed the meaning of the Torah in a rich variety of literary forms, symbols, metaphor, and rituals, using discursive strategies that included exegeses of Scripture, prayers, magical incantations, recipes, fables, and exemplary stories along with the intricate legal discussions that fill the pages of the Talmud. The Torah implicitly contains all truth and so the whole Rabbinic literary world of instruction (Torah in the broad sense) serves as the basis for the production of medieval and modern mystical texts and ethical wills, poems, and philosophical tracts as well as legal commentaries and law codes.

The Jewish emphasis on embodied or lived truth does not negate an interest in other dimensions of truth. The focus on law and practical decisions leads inevitably to questions of epistemological procedure and inquiries into divine revelation that transcends the human mind. Revealed or Scriptural (biblical) truth and its later interpretations in biblical commentaries and the Talmud are fundamental to the pursuit of truth in practice. The Torah is the stable foundation on which the tradition is built. The authority of biblical, revealed teaching is assumed in all traditional Jewish texts. As is usually the case with fixed canons, the interpretations of the biblical books vary considerably according to place, time, and author. Rabbinic teachers subjected the revealed "truths" of the tradition to constant, searching, and minute analyses. Although reason may never dominate or qualify the truth of revelation, in practice Jewish interpreters applied a great variety of logical, literary, and linguistic techniques to revealed truth.

Revealed and embodied truth relate to one another dialectically in the Jewish tradition. The Rabbinic sages cling stubbornly to the intrinsic value and necessity of human thought and responsibility as a foundation for life in obedient response to Torah. But at the same time, though the Talmudic tradition values the human mind, the human mind is never more than one other divinely created thing in the world. Since humans cannot directly and adequately know truth in itself, the human mind must content itself with the search for comprehensible truth, which in the Jewish tradition is preeminently legal (halachic) discourse and practice. To accomplish this task humans must look to Scriptural truth to ground their search and bring it to completion. The dialectical interrelation of embodied truth and truth revealed in Scripture demands constant attention to both dimensions. The sacred text of the Torah symbolizes this relationship because it transmits divine revelation that transcends the human mind, but the transcendent revelation is embodied in a physically accessible form. The Torah communicates divine truth in a form substantially knowable and discernible to the human mind (though the mystical tradition seeks to transcend these limits). Scripture, practice, and ritual lead the Jewish community toward greater appreciation of and cleaving to God, but ultimately and paradoxically God says "my thoughts are not your thoughts, nor are your ways my ways" (Isaiah 55:8).

Epistemological truth has not attracted many thematically explicit treatments in the Jewish tradition and certainly not the passionate interest it has received in the modern West. However, disputes over how to interpret Scripture and observe the law have at times threatened to tear the Jewish community apart and contact with other cultures has also thrown into question accepted understandings and practices. These social conflicts have forced the Jewish community to attend implicitly or explicitly to the ways of arriving at accurate interpretations of law. The process of responding and adapting to new social and intellectual situations is common in the major religious traditions. Conflicts between the Hindu and Buddhist communities produced apologetic and polemical discussions of logic and argumentation. Christian apologetic writings of the second century and later works such as Augustine's *City of God* and Aquinas's *Summa Contra Gentiles* responded to the powerful philosophy and culture of Greco-Roman society around the Mediterranean and in Aquinas's case to Islam as well. The Jewish teachers Saadia Gaon in Babylonia and Maimonides in Egypt responded to Islam and the Greek philosophical tradition by reconceiving and relating their own tradition to Islamic culture. Most recently, the European Jewish encounter with the Enlightenment provoked heated disagreements that continue to the present. Contact with "others," that is, with other peoples or cultures, causes cognitive dissonance at the intellectual or behavioral level of life and promotes self-conscious reflection that leads to apologetic and polemic or to adaptation and assimilation.

Consequently, polemics among and within traditions raise the issue of epistemological truth. In the Hebrew Bible/Old Testament the Yahweh-only group, which eventually dominated and wrote the Bible, were constantly in conflict with an evidently rather large group of Israelites who worshipped Yahweh the God of Israel along with other Gods of the land and, according to recent inscriptions, Yahweh's female consort, Asherah. In Second Temple Judaism numerous groups argued, sometimes violently, over how biblical law and Jewish customs were to be interpreted and implemented in life (see the earlier section on the Dead Sea Scrolls). In the early medieval period the Jewish world was split by the Rabbis who taught the Babylonian Talmud and the Karaites who rejected Rabbinic tradition. In the high Middle Ages Maimonides distinguished lower truths known by the masses and higher (philosophically apprehended) truths understood only by a small elite. His systematic and philosophically oriented works were burned by some traditional leaders who gave primacy to the Babylonian Talmud and commentaries. In the last century Orthodox European Jews forbade their communities any contact with Reform Jews in worship, marriage, or commerce. The Reform Jews were treated as renegades and many orthodox Rabbis advised their congregations to treat them as non-Jews.[29] Samson Raphael Hirsch promoted absolute separation of orthodox from Reform Jews.[30]

The history of Christian dissident movements, often centered on doctrine (i.e., "heresies" such as Gnosticism and Arianism), but also on authority (schism between the Greek Orthodox and Latin West), is long and need not be reviewed here. Conflicts among schools of thought within the Hindu (dualist, non-dualist) and Buddhist (Theravāda, Mahāyāna) communities as well as between these two related traditions have a long history in South Asia. Similar conflicts have occurred between the Sunnis and Shi'ites and among Islamic teachers of law, philosophers, Sufi mystics, and teachers of Kalām.

A few comparisons with Hindu traditions may clarify some aspects of the way to and functions of truth. The Talmud subjects the laws to a detailed working out of all the possibilities and exceptions, relating laws to one another by content and analogy. It presents numerous disputes among teachers and debates the relative authority of their views until (in many but not all cases) an accepted position emerges and the others are disposed of with a variety of polemical tools. This Talmudic process is functionally equivalent to the search for correct knowledge and the reliable means to correct knowledge (*pramā* and *pramāṇa* in Hindu logical literature). The elaborate logical argumentation of Hindu texts is functionally equivalent to the sophisticated and intricate working out of all the possible meanings of laws in the Talmud. Even the literary structure of Talmudic tractates, based on a systematic unfolding of each topic, contributes to the search for an integral apprehension of reality based on Torah. The Talmudic academies of eastern Europe in the modern period carried this method to a new height with *pilpul* (from the word for pepper), a method of dialectical debate of all aspects and details of Talmud designed to sharpen students' minds so they could make acute, logical distinctions and cogent legal decisions.

The content of these two bodies of literature and the types of questions they ask are utterly different, but they resemble one another in their persistent and detailed inquiry based an unshakable confidence that a disciplined human mind can reach the truth. Their social contexts differ as much as their content. The Hindu literature arose as a means of disputing with the Buddhists, a related but distinctive tradition. Talmudic discussions and the commentaries built on them address the Jewish community and are not part of a dialogue with any related tradition, such as Christianity.

The authority of Hindu teachers in polemical debates functions in the same way as the authoritative teachings of Rabbinic teachers handed down from antiquity and the authoritative decisions of certain prominent Rabbis in Talmudic disputes over the meaning of laws. The Talmudic principle that the meaning of the law is determined by a majority view of the Rabbis seems vaguely similar to the consensus represented by the manuals of argumentation presented in the chapter by Frank Clooney.

In both traditions religious and ordinary knowledge are closely related. Many Hindu texts claim a strong continuity between ordinary knowledge and religious knowledge in order to enhance the ability of diverse groups to debate with one another on a common rational basis. However, the Jewish tradition stresses religious knowledge, based on revelation, as foundational and uses it to encompass all other realms of knowledge, including the most mundane. Thus, ordinary experience and knowledge, so important in Hindu texts concerning knowledge, appear in the Talmud in legal discussions of biblical law that treat the most minute details of commerce, sacrifice, ritual, agriculture, bodily functions, house and farm implements, criminal behavior, and criminal law and procedure.

Jewish study of the Torah as a way to know God, the nature of the universe, the place of humans and especially Israel in the world, and the way human life should be lived parallels the Hindu discussions of truth, religious topics, and so on as the way to significant and certain religious knowledge. In Judaism truth claims about the meaning of the law depend on reasonable, defensible interpretations of the Bible. Similarly, the Hindu Vedānta tradition discovers an adequate knowledge of "the Lord" in the sacred texts and Advaita Vedānta even derives accurate empirical knowledge from the Upaniṣads.[31]

Hindu patterns of devotion as a way to God(s) and a good life, treated in a previous volume, find their counterpart in the Talmudic laws about diet, Sabbath, festival, and ethical behavior as well as in stories about the Rabbis and pastoral interpretations of Scriptural passages. Although not treated in this chapter, the traditional Jewish prayer book, the Siddur, along with the festival prayer books (Maḥzor), transmit the core of Jewish piety.

Although less capacious and varied than the Hindu traditions of South Asia, the Jewish tradition encompasses many of the same concerns for truth. More consistently and single-mindedly the Jewish community has looked to revealed Scripture as the core of its way of life and thought. Other groups may also possess truth and do good, yet they do so only insofar as their ways of thought and practice accord with the fundamental principles of Torah. Torah comes from God who created and governs the whole world and revealed his mind most adequately through Torah. Although many cultures have influenced Jewish teaching and customs over the centuries, all must be referred to and authenticated by Torah. The rational systematic scientific knowledge in the West and the cosmic harmony of the universe in Chinese thought function in their spheres much as Torah within Judaism.

Although the core of the Jewish tradition, expounded above, turns strongly toward embodied, epistemological, and Scriptural truth, another dimension of truth neglected here, but treated in the chapter on ultimate realities in the previous volume, demands brief mention. Cosmological truth, based on mystical speculation and experience of the divine, seeks detailed knowledge of God and the heavenly realm as well as the "right," absolutely certain answers to halakic questions. Many Rabbinic authorities oppose this kind of search for truth as beyond human powers; others caution against its dangers and permit such teachings to the intellectual and spiritual elite. However, in some Qumran texts, early Rabbinic mystical traditions, and the fully developed medieval mystical schools, preeminently Kabbalism, Jewish scholars and mystics speculated on the divine form, creation, God's holy dwelling, and so on. These and similar attempts to know the truth "beyond" revelation, the secrets of the universe, the divine self-knowledge, are a meta-truth that is not contained within the parameters of rabbinic, or halachic discourse.

In summary, the Rabbinic tradition consists of a polyvalent, tightly woven, self-referential, intellectual, emotional, and faith world that encompasses God, humanity, Israel, the Torah, and the world. The very nature of this Rabbinic world testifies to its autonomous claim to the truth. Study under Rabbinic teachers using Talmudic modes of argument on authoritative biblical, Mishnaic, and Talmudic texts will guide the inquiring student securely to a correct interpretation of the law and to faithful observance of the commandments that God gave to Israel. This process of study, decision, and observance includes concern for revealed truth, epistemological truth, and preeminently truth embodied in practice.

Notes

1. The quotation in the title is from the Dead Sea Scrolls, Community Rule (1QS) 5.3–4. The Community Rule drew some of its phrases from Micah 6:8: "He has told you, o mortal, what is good; and what does the LORD require of you but to do justice, and to love kindness, and to walk humbly with your God?"

2. Daniel H. Frank and Oliver Leaman, *History of Jewish Philosophy, Routledge History of World Philosophies*, vol. 2 (London and New York: Routledge, 1997).

3. *Zohar* III 62b.

4. See the entry "man" by A. Jepsen in the *Theological Dictionary of the Old Testament*, vol. 1, ed. G. J. Botterweck and H. Ringgren (Grand Rapids, Eerdmans, 1974), 292–323 for a discussion of usages.

5. See S. Nomanul Haq, "The Taxonomy of Truth in the Islamic Religious Doctrine and Tradition," chapter 6 in this volume.

6. Jepsen, op. cit., 308.

7. Other expressions from the same root are also used such as *ʿalîlôt* and *ʿawlāh,* which seems to mean "doings of wickedness/injustice" or "circumventions of injustice" (1QS 4:17).

8. For a description of the process of commentary and of the claims for revelation, see Gershom Scholem, "Revelation and Tradition As Religious Categories," *The Messianic Idea in Judaism* (New York: Schocken, 1971), 282–303, esp. 289–90.

9. In Christianity John Cassian's fourfold senses of Scripture guided much of medieval Christian: literal or historical; allegorical or Christological; tropological or moral; and anagogical or eschatological. Jewish and Christian exegetes mutually influence one another from antiquity on.

10. Saadia Gaon, *The Book of Beliefs and Opinions*, trans. Samuel Rosenblatt (Yale Judaica Series 1; New Haven/ London: Yale University Press, 1948).

11. Ibid., p. 9.

12. See Paula Fredriksen, "Patristic Pramā and Pramāṇa: Augustine and the Quest for Truth," chapter 5 in this volume.

13. Ibid.

14. Saadia, op. cit., 10–12.

15. Ibid., 13

16. Ibid., 14.

17. Ibid., 15.

18. Cf. the *Treatise on Creation*, p. 78.

19. Saadia, op. cit., 16.

20. Ibid., 20.

21. Ibid., 21–23.

22. See Mendelssohn's *Jerusalem, or On Religious Power and Judaism*, trans. A. Arkush (Hanover, N.H.: University Press of New England, 1983) with an introduction and a lengthy, detailed commentary in the form of notes by Alexander Altmann. David Sorkin, *Moses Mendelssohn and the Religious Enlightenment* (Berkeley: University of California, 1996) is also helpful in contextualizing Mendelssohn's project.

23. Mendelssohn, *Jerusalem*, 89. Cf. pp. 94, 97.

24. Ibid., 99.

25. Ibid., 90–98, 127–28.

26. Ibid., 127.

27. Ibid., 99.

28. See Livia Kohn and James Miller, "Truth in Chinese Religion," chapter 1 in this volume.

29. See David Ellenson, "Traditional Reactions to Modern Jewish Reform: The Paradigm of German Orthodoxy," 732–58.

30. Ibid., 752.

31. Francis X. Clooney, "Making Room for God," 10–14.

5

Patristic Pramā and Pramāṇa

Augustine and the Quest for Truth

Paula Fredriksen

5.1 Introduction

Our work on the idea of truth across religious cultures has revealed, once again, a wide-ranging variety of concepts, practices, and presuppositions together with certain resonances in the conceptualization of truth between different combinations of cultures brought into comparison. Thus, both Hinduism and Buddhism share a highly developed epistemological tradition (truth, *pramā*, embedded in an articulate theory of what constitutes valid knowledge, *pramāṇa*); Chinese and Jewish religion, an emphasis on doing and practice (divination of the dao; *hªlākāh*); Christianity and Islam, an embrace of revelation and consequent deemphasis, in their mystical manifestations, on intellection. These pairings could be reconfigured and other commonalities named: *sharīʿa* (Islam) and *hªlākāh* (Judaism) both foreground practice, how one lives, as part and parcel of seeking after truth/*the* Truth (God); Hinduism and Christianity, the ways that embodiment impedes perception and reception of truth; Buddhism and Daoism, a sense that the true, deep-structure of Reality is fluid, ever-changing.

For this chapter on the idea of Truth in Christianity I have chosen to focus on Augustine. Augustine commends himself to our attention not only because of his authority and influence on the subsequent Western tradition, but also because he himself viewed his own Christianity as his commitment to the quest for Truth. Standing as he does at the tumultuous confluence of post-classical notions of knowledge, intra-Christian debates on the nature of God, cosmos, and humanity, and huge changes in Roman imperial power, he was compelled to articulate his own religious epistemology as a means of expressing his definitions of religious truth and its significance for church and society. And while we see his own construction of his quest for truth in the *Confessions*, we have as well his application of the theological points of principle given in his self-portrait to the much larger canvas of world history—pagan, Jewish, and Christian—in the *City of God*. The breadth of his vision allows us that much more opportunity for comparison with the other traditions in our purview.

I propose, then, to retrace Augustine's steps as he presents them in the *Confessions*, paying particular attention to his idea of truth, his retrospective analysis of his false starts and mistaken premises, and his imaginative psychology, spelled out particularly in Books 10 (on memory) and 11 (time as a function of soul). I will analyze these according to the three broad categories that we have worked with for this volume: practical or embodied truth (which emphasizes behavior); scriptural or revelatory truth (which foregrounds semiotics and interpretation); and epistemological truth (which emphasizes thinking, knowing, and how we think we know). I will then turn to his broader application of these ideas to history and society, finally drawing more pointed comparisons with specific aspects of cross-cultural concepts of truth as they have emerged in my colleagues' presentations.

5.2 The One, the Many, and the Problem of Evil

Truth for Augustine means above all correct knowledge about God. But because he stands within biblical tradition, correct knowledge about God for him necessarily entails, as well, correct knowledge about man (made in God's image) and the universe (God's willed creation and, thus, a medium of his revelation). Further, because his historical neighborhood was the "theological bear-garden" (Peter Brown) of late Roman antiquity, Augustine confronted at close quarters various contestants for the construction of "true Christianity": Manichees, Donatists, African and Italian Catholics. He himself had lived on both sides of several of these patrolled borders.

In light of the cognitive dissonance generated by this intense intercommunal conflict, *epistemological truth* loomed especially large for him.[1] Its *pramāṇa* always lay in conforming to the authoritative teaching of the Church. Embodied truth (truth-in-practice) and revelatory truth (truth-in-scripture) also open up onto his framing of divine, human, and cosmic *pramā*: sexual renunciation and biblical hermeneutics are two of the grand themes in Augustine's presentation of his quest for truth in the *Confessions*. But these are subsumed there to the tangled tale of his epistemological history: *How* can he know God? "*Grant me, Lord, to know and to understand* (Psalm 118) which comes first: to call upon you or to praise you, and whether knowing you precedes calling upon you. But who calls upon you when he does not know you? . . . *They will praise the Lord who seek him* (Psalm 21:27)," (*Confessions* 1.1).

The *Confessions* presents in a narrative triptych his answer to this question of how to know God. Books 1–9, a sort of intellectual history from birth up to his conversion in 386, present his different efforts at knowing truth as a series of seismic reorientations: rhetorical education (3.1.1–4.7); Cicero (3.4,8); Scripture (read, evidently and significantly, in private rather than in community, 3.5,9) and, immediately following, the Manichees (3.6,10–7.9 and passim); the Skeptics ("They taught that everything is a matter of doubt, and that an understanding of truth lies beyond human capacity," 5.10,19, through 5.14,25); the Platonists (7.9,13); Ambrose and allegorical interpretation (6.4,6).[2] Book 10, centerpiece of the work's argument, investigates thought, the role of memory in knowing, and how the mind recognizes Truth. Books 11–13, finally, ostensibly an interpretation of the first several verses of Genesis, explore the concepts of time and eternity, the types of knowing and being fitted to each, and the role of Christ, scripture, church, and sacrament in mediating divine truth to humans awash in the sea of time.[3]

What then for Augustine is Truth, and how in his view do humans find it? I propose that we begin to answer this question by following the story he tells in the *Confessions*. But to understand it, we need to be aware of the two alternative views of truth that at different times commanded his allegiance and thus affected, whether negatively or positively, his later formulation: Manichaean Christianity and Plotinian Platonism, both of which he knew only in their late Latin avatars.

5.3 Mani and Plato

Augustine wrote the *Confessions* in 397. It represents his retrospection, ten years after the fact, on the spiritual and intellectual process by which he came to convert to Catholic Christianity in 386, in Milan. The seriatim conversions shaping the first eight books—to philosophy (via

Cicero's *Hortensius*) and to Manichaeism (via the Bible), which mark his university years at Carthage; and his subsequent intellectual conversion to late Platonism in Milan—seem to stand in a developmental trajectory propelling him ever closer to (Catholic) truth. In fact, however, they each represent incommensurate models of reality—of God, man, and the universe—that hit him with the disorienting force of shifting paradigms.

The combat of their competing epistemologies shaped Augustine's ultimate position on Truth and how one grasps it. Cicero's call to Wisdom broke him away from the purely utilitarian benefits of the rhetorical education meant to train him to be a "handler of words" and, ultimately, a lawyer (so that "the less honest I was, the more famous I should be," 3.3,6). The *Hortensius* changed Augustine's priorities, redirecting his thinking (or, as he characteristically put it, his *affectum*: on this more below) about what was important, turning him from "vanity" to love of Wisdom, *philosophia*. Yet raised as he had been in a Catholic household, and by an extremely devout Catholic mother, Augustine could not rest with Cicero because "the name of Christ was not contained in the book."

> For with my mother's milk my infant heart had drunk in and still retained . . . the name of your Son, my Savior; and whatever lacked that name, no matter how *learned and excellently written and true*, could not win me wholly (3.5,8).

Accordingly, Augustine moved on to a study of the scriptures. Their prose style suffered in comparison to Cicero's; their seeming simplicity offended his pride:[4] He was repulsed. His narrative subtly introduces here several major points that he will later develop systematically: (1) that truth, tantamount to the correct reading of scripture, can be found only within and by the authority of the Church (communally and within tradition's hermeneutic, as opposed to individually, as here, through private endeavor); (2) that nothing blocks apprehension of the divine like pride (hence his description of himself here as "inflated [by] conceit," "disdaining to be a beginner," "swollen with pride"); and (3) that words obscure as well as reveal, and thus that even the words of Holy Scripture itself, though uniquely and divinely sanctioned conduits of truth, are themselves only contingently related to that truth. In 373, however, the moment he describes here, his quest for Truth necessarily linked with the "name of Christ" led him to give himself over, for almost a decade, to a church that forever after stood for him as the embodiment of falsehood, religious perversion, and pride:

> I fell in with a sect of men talking high-sounding nonsense, carnal and wordy men. The snares of the devil were in their mouths, to trap souls with an arrangement of the syllables of the names of God the Father and of the Lord Jesus Christ and of the Paraclete. . . . These names were never absent from their lips; but it was no more than sound and noise with their tongue. Otherwise their hearts were empty of truth. They cried out, 'Truth! Truth!' and they were forever uttering the word to me; but there was never any truth in them. They uttered false statements not only about You, who really are the Truth, but also about the elements of the world, your creation. . . . O Truth, Truth: how inwardly did the very marrow of my soul pant after you, whenever I heard them sound your name. But it was all words—spoken words, words written in huge tomes . . . Emptiness (3.6,10).

Augustine became a Manichee.

Like their spiritual ancestors the Gnostics, Western Manichees based their rejection of the Old Testament on their highly polarized reading of the apostle Paul, with his rhetorically charged pairing of Law and Gospel, Works and Grace. They focused especially on the problem of evil as a standing challenge to any monotheist construction of Christianity: no single, all-good, all-powerful deity, they urged, could be the ultimate source of such a morally damaged humanity, or such a flawed universe. Appealing to the ethos of physical (and particularly sexual) asceticism abroad in late antique culture generally, the Manichees preached a stern, mystical ethic of renunciation enacted by the men and women of their elite stratum, the *electi*, admired by the broader support-stratum, the *auditores* ("hearers"). Finally, against a fundamentalist Catholicism that both they and even the newly Catholic Augustine characterized as *superstitio*,[5] the Manichees renounced arguments from authority, claiming that they could persuade others of the religious truth of their claims through an appeal to reason alone. It was the appeal of this promise—that the exercise of reason would lead to apprehension of Truth—that struck the older Augustine as their chief attraction to his younger, philosophically charged self: "I fell among these people for no other reason than that they declared that . . . they would by pure and simple reason bring to God those who were willing to listen to them."[6]

Their own sacred writings, the five books of Mani, together with copies of the letters of Paul purged of what they held to be later judaizing interpolations, served as the literary foundations of Manichaean truth claims. The Old Testament they subjected to a withering literalist and ascetic critique: If man is in God's image, does God also have fingernails and hair? Would a moral God order the destruction even of babies in Sodom? Insist upon blood offerings? Condone and even encourage sexual intercourse and procreation?[7] The truth about God, they urged, the truth about man and about the universe revealed through their own esoteric wisdom, was that two moral powers, Good and Evil, instantiated in two material forces, Light and Darkness, stood locked in combat.[8] Their battleground ranged from the astral planes of the upper cosmos (evinced in such phenomena as the waxing and waning of the moon, and solar and lunar eclipses) to the two souls contesting for moral control within man. This dualism spoke to both the ethical and the cosmic dimensions of the problem of evil, while preserving God/Good/Light from any compromising causal involvement. Evil was its own independent force.

Augustine stayed with this sect throughout his early adulthood, roughly from the ages of nineteen to twenty-nine. Increasingly suspicious of their reconstruction of Paul (5.11,21), alienated by their elaborate mythology and their scientific fundamentalism (which emerged in the comparison of their celestial mythology with the star charts of the more scientific pagan philosophers, 5.3,4–6), flirting briefly—perhaps out of spiritual fatigue—with the radical skepticism of the New Academy (5.10,19), Augustine did not radically change his way of thinking until he encountered, in translation, some works of Porphyry and Plotinus once he was in Milan.

For Augustine, as for many Catholic intellectuals of his age, the Platonists represented the next closest thing to themselves: in them, "God and his Word [i.e., Christ] are everywhere implied" (8.2,1). They broke him out of his philosophical materialism, teaching him to conceive of evil not as some sort of malevolent substance, but rather as the privation of Good. This fundamental reorientation changed everything of Augustine's former views on God, man, and the universe. Material reality, for example, once seen as evil because of its corruptibility, Augustine could now see, for the same reason, as good: that it could be corrupted attested to its essential or natural goodness (since if it had not begun as good, it would not have been capable of corruption, 7.12,18). No moral complications stood in the way, then, of the Good God's authorship of material reality. And God himself was nonmaterial, spiritual, just as the process of thought itself. Manichaean jibes about God's fingernails and hair lost their power, since the text of Genesis, understood correctly, showed that the divine image was in the mind, a spiritual function rather than a physical resemblance: God's image resided in the intellectual powers of the soul (cf. 3.7,12).

This intellectualist construction of the fundamental relationship between God and man will always remain determinative in Augustine's theology, his ultimate dissatisfactions with Neoplatonism notwithstanding. Knowing Truth, knowing God, believing: all have to do, profoundly, with *thinking*. To believe, he later writes, is to "think with assent," for while "not all thinking is believing . . . all believing is thinking (*cogitare*)."[9]

To apprehend the truth, for Augustine, is always and primarily to *know* it. But—true again to the Platonic tradition in which his Christianity stands—this knowing has an erotic quality. We know by loving; in knowing the truth, we love it. Hence Augustine's report of his early encounter with Cicero's *Hortensius* as altering his *affectum*: we could equally well translate "it changed my way of thinking" and "it changed my way of feeling." And this erotic dimension of knowledge will likewise affect Augustine's formulation of the relation of knowing and doing, especially knowing and doing good—and, more pointedly, knowing the good but doing evil. Our moral choices, he will argue, depend less on what we know than on how we feel; and what we do not love we can neither know nor do.

With this historical preamble behind us, let us examine Augustine's views on the nature of knowledge, particularly true knowledge of God.

5.4 The Knower, Knowing, and the Known

Manichaean anthropology posited man as a bicameral creature, an individual instance of the intercosmic battle between light and darkness, good and evil.[10] Man was at once the object, the stage, and the agent of this battle. Accordingly, knowledge of the cosmos, especially the celestial cosmos, as well as mastery of elaborate food and other physical disciplines, situated the believer more securely in his immediate (i.e., corporeal) environment: all the elements of the universe came into play. Neo-Platonic anthropology also posited man as a sort of double creature, having a contingent, historical, individual soul (the mean term between mind or spirit and the historical, contingent, fleshly body), and an interior, transcendent true self, the Higher Soul, which exists, impersonal and eternal, close to the divine Intellect (*Nous*). The goal of philosophy was finally to "know God" by effecting a union with the One: the philosopher, turning inward and upward away from the distractions of sense and the time-bound self, would merge with the true divine Self.[11]

Elements of these two systems, whether negatively or positively, reappear in Augustine's anthropology and epistemology too. Augustine defines the human being as "a rational animal subject to death" (*de ordine*) or as "a rational soul using a mortal and earthly body" (*de mor. eccles.)*. Flesh and soul, though united in one person (and in a way more immediate and essential than pagan Platonists could countenance), are of two different substances, one material and fleshly (in both senses of *carnale*), the other immaterial and spiritual. Against both Manichaeism and Neoplatonism, Augustine insists that man's soul is not itself divine, nor does it participate substantially in the divine. And while the "inner man" (a Pauline locution), the highest part of the soul, man's *ratio*, is said to be in the image of God, it is also the site of an inherited disability, the divided will, that affects man's ability both to know and to love. On account of this divided will with its consequently misdirected loves, man's soul is also properly said to be "carnal."

This divided nature of the human knower in turn affects the nature of knowledge. Higher and lower knowledge are determined not only by their objects, but also by the orientation of the knower's desire or *amor*. Love of self (*amor sui*) leads to *cupiditas*; knowing (*scientia*) motivated by such love is often about and because of vanity: it is *curiositas*. Properly oriented love, *amor dei*, leads to knowledge of Truth (a synonym for God), appropriate love for God's creatures (*caritas*), and true wisdom (*sapientia*, also a name for Christ). Knowledge of the intelligible world is not available through the senses, though sense knowledge can be a valuable step along the path to knowledge of and love of God through Creation (the argument of *Confessions* 10.6). This higher knowledge is available rather through the divine illumination of the mind through the mind's participation in the Word of God, God's interior presence in the mind.[12] Hence rational knowledge does not enter the mind from outside, but somehow is already present to it.[13]

The keystone of the self and the site of the mind's illumination, for Augustine, lies in the memory, the subject of Book 10 of the *Confessions*. Memory for us means something like the recollection of the past. But for Augustine, *memoria* serves as the interior capacity of the mind by which he can know Truth, know God.

> Let me know You, You who know me, let me know You even as I am known. O You, power of my soul, enter into it and fit it for yourself. . . . For behold, You have loved the truth, and he that does the truth comes to the light. I want to do the truth, in my heart, before You, in confession; in my writing, before many witnesses (10.1,1).

Mounting beyond sense knowledge and "all the things that throng about the gateway of the senses" (6,9), Augustine turns in toward himself, acknowledging the inner man, his reason, who knows things "through the ministry of the outer man." But since God is incorporeal, things of sense that, because created by God, provide the readiest analogies, cannot, by their very nature, finally reveal or contain Truth. Moving from there beyond "the topmost part of my soul," past even that presiding part of the soul that judges sense perceptions, Augustine at last enters "the fields and vast palaces of my memory" where immaterial images of recollected experience are stored—where, indeed, Augustine meets himself. The vastness and power of memory—"a spreading limitless room within me"—overwhelms Augustine: it is the seat of self-transcendence, despite being exactly that part of the soul where the individual is most deeply his or her individual self. "Who can reach memory's utmost depth? Yet it is a faculty of my soul and belongs to my nature. In fact, I cannot totally grasp all that I am. The mind is not large enough to contain itself" (8,15).[14]

More than a warehouse of images and past feelings, *memoria* also serves an essential cognitive function: it is the seat of *a priori* knowledge.[15] The mind, through memory, *re*cognizes truth. When such truths were formulated for him, asks Augustine, "how did I recognize them and say, 'Yes, that is true'? The answer must be that they were already in my memory, but remote and pushed back . . . as if in most secret caverns" (10,17). Through memory, too, language is processed, because the sounds of words only signify the things to which they point—in this particular case, ideas without sense-referents—yet Augustine had understood them. The Augustinian *memoria* thus functions much as does the Platonic *anamnesis*, though whereas in the pagan system this capacity points toward the life of the soul prior to its existence in the body, for Augustine it points to a preconscious intuition of the mind, implanted through Christ, on account of which the soul instinctively yearns to know God, the ultimate object of its love.[16] In this last sense, memoria provides the readiest analogy to the sort of unmediated apprehension by which God knows us, and with which humans, eschatologically, will know both themselves and God: "When I remember memory, my memory is present to itself by itself" (16,24).

Yet even animals have memory. Human knowledge of God calls for something even greater. Accordingly, Augustine urges himself onward, inward, upward:

> What am I to do now, O my true life, my God? I shall mount beyond this power of memory, I shall mount beyond it, and come to you, O lovely light. . . . I shall pass beyond memory to find you: but where will I find you? If I find you beyond my memory, then I shall be without memory of you. And how will I find you if I am without memory of you? (10.17,26)

This indwelling memory of God, through which the soul's innate desire for happiness orients it toward God, may go back, Augustine conjectures, to humanity's primal parents (20,29). With this allusion to Adam Augustine invokes, as well, the Fall, for he characterizes Adam as "that man who first sinned, in whom we all died" (cf. 1 Corinthians 15:22). From this point on, Augustine's meditation grows increasingly elegiac: themes of the ubiquity and subtlety of sin, of the moral ambiguity of sexual desire experienced in sleep, of the dangerous manyness into which the soul, slipping into love of creature rather than Creator, can dissipate itself, sound increasingly. Hence, argues Augustine, the necessity of sexual continence that God commands, "for by continence we are collected and bound up into unity within ourselves, whereas we had been scattered abroad in multiplicity" (29,40).

In the last three books of his *Confessions*, Augustine strains against the fraught disunity of man's existence, distended in time. The nature of time itself underscores and feeds this distension. Time, he maintains, is a psychological function: it exists only within the soul, in the infinitely ungraspable, elusive *punctum* of the present. Man's consciousness, his memory, his entire ability to grasp truth exists within and is described by this razor-thin slice of reality, suspended between two infinitely receding types of non-being, the Past (which has no existence, since it no longer is) and the Future (which has no existence, since it has not yet come to be).

> Not even one day is entirely present. All the hours of the day add up to twenty-four. The first of them has the others in the future, the last has them in the past. . . . A single hour is itself constituted of fugitive moments. . . . If we can think of some bit of time which cannot be divided into even the smallest instantaneous moments, that alone is what we call "present." And this time flies so quickly from the future into past that it is an interval with no duration. Any duration is divisible into past and future: the present occupies no space (11.15,23).

This distension in time constitutes the great measure of difference and distance between our mode of consciousness and that of God in eternity. God knows all things instantaneously, as do the angels who dwell in the heaven of heavens, "the intellectual, non-physical heaven where the intelligence's knowing is a matter of simultaneity—not in part, not in an enigma, not through a glass, but complete total openness, 'face to face' (1 Corinthians 13:12) . . . concurrent, without any temporal successiveness" (12.13,16). Man's existence in time distends apprehension, complicating his search for truth because meaning must be mediated—through memory (the means of the soul's contact with time, since memory, to function, functions only in the present), images, signs, words. And just as time is not the same as the units we measure it by, so meaning is not the same as those words we use in our attempts to convey it. Even the words or "signs" in Scripture, God's mode of revelation, are infinitely interpretable (12.23,32), capable of sustaining a diversity of truths whose validity cannot be limited by the historically contingent intentions of their original authors (12.23,32–30,41). The only rock of certainty to which man can anchor himself is the Church, divinely established and authorized to mediate God's word through "the ministry of mortal men" (13.15,16).

Can man, then, in this life, know Truth? In any unambiguous way, no. His soul "is like a waterless wasteland before You (Psalm 142:6)," without power to illuminate itself. The knowledge of Truth that man is built to crave, the love of Truth intrinsic to the human soul, are frustrated by man's existential, historical circumstances—circumstances that, though ameliorated by God's grace, were brought about by the fall of Adam. Until such time as God brings time to an end, this disorientation and distension are man's lot. At the end, restlessness will give way to peace. Man will rest, finally, in God (cf. the book's opening, 1.1,1); "there also will you rest in us" (13.37,52).

5.5 Some Comparisons

5.5.1 Embodied Truth-in-Practice

Every tradition we have examined has a set of physical enactments or disciplines by which the participant lives out the truth of the tradition—yoga, food disciplines, scripted prayer practices, and so on. The measure of the tradition's overachievers—holy men, saints, bodhisattvas—can be glimpsed in their embodied expertise.

Christianity too has this dimension, that truth is measured and even perceived in somatic phenomena. Thus, true sanctity frees the martyr from feeling pain when persecuted; holy men and women fast for enormous periods of time without ill effect; in saints' legends, holy infants refuse to nurse during Lent (thus presaging their adult careers); and the flesh of the holy dead—particularly the flesh of virgins—remains miraculously incorruptible, attesting to their moral and physical integrity.

Certain physical practices also embody truth and in a sense enable it. Augustine, as we have seen, advocates the practice of sexual continence as a way to shore up the soul against the distractions of living in time. He, too, practiced various food abstentions. But both his social context and the personal context of his own theology attenuate the import of such disciplines. Sexual renunciation and prolonged fasting were ubiquitous expressions of piety in virtually all forms of Western fourth-century Christianity. Indeed, in much of his polemic against other churches Augustine immediately concedes the existence of "their" virgins, "their" martyrs, "their" religious elites. The situation drives him to emphasize internal orientation against external appearance. By definition, only a member of the True Church (i.e., for Augustine, the Catholic church[17]) can be a true Christian, thus a true virgin, and so on.

This is not to say—to come to my second point, his own theology—that all Catholic virgins were "true" virgins. Here we see the full import of Augustine's emphasis on interiority, on the individual as receptor of grace given, from our point of view mysteriously, solely at divine initiative. Practice guaranteed nothing. For example, if one were rigorously ascetic and self-disciplined, the credit (so Augustine) was God's, who enabled that person to act in that way. And so unstable and shifting is the interior world of habit, impulse, desire, memory, love, that the person can change in the twinkling of an eye; or, indeed, be enmeshed in more subtle versions of the sins he ostensibly, through practice, avoids.[18]

The only absolutely secure embodiment of truth, for Augustine, is the Catholic Church itself, abstractly or eschatologically conceived. While not everyone inside the Church is holy, no one outside the Church can be. As she exists in time, the Church must be, therefore, a *corpus permixtum*, containing both sinner and saint. Only at the endtime, when God has redeemed his people, will she be *sine macula*, without spot or wrinkle, the pure bride of Christ.

5.5.2 Scripture, Authority, Interpretation

This question of the Church leads us immediately into questions of authority; of canonicity (text as a particular embodiment of truth) and authoritative interpretation; and of ultimate meaning, the unmediated apprehension of Truth.

Authority for Augustine is always exercised through *disciplina*, a word that has both instructional and coercive connotations (connotations in fact drawn from the late Latin schoolroom). Discipline is less a category of internal or personal character (cf. the sage of Eastern traditions) than an external corrective for the perennially errant human heart. Parents and teachers discipline; the Church—after 399 and again after 405 enabled through the power of the Roman state—disciplines, especially schismatics and heretics; and those doing the disciplining model themselves on humanity's ultimate disciplinarian, God, who "breaks bones asunder with the rod of [his] discipline."[19] As with "true virgins" or "true ascetics," so also with discipline: it is the interior moral orientation of the agent (Moses, say, or Pharaoh) that determines the actual truth status of the action or activity. (Both coerced Israel, but Moses did it out of love, therefore only his actions were truly disciplinary; Pharaoh's were merely abusive.) So too, Augustine argues, with the Donatists, whose situation was not the same as that of those Christians who suffered the Empire's coercion before Constantine. Now, the State coerces at the behest of Church unity; and the church directs the effort out of love for the sinner, not love of power.

Canonical scripture—those books sanctioned by the authority of the Church—is the physical expression, thus embodiment, of the Word of God.[20] But again, Augustine's awareness and interpretation of time and its effects on human apprehension complicate his approach to the biblical text. The Bible is mediated through and made up of words; and words have as their context particular, historically contingent languages. To recall Augustine's famous abreaction to Scripture the first time he tried to read it, between his inspiration by Cicero and his seduction by the Manichees: the unloveliness of translation compromised his ability to see, to hear the truths that Scripture contained (3.5,9). Two linguistic removes from the original (in the case of the Latin OT); ad hoc, local, anonymous; current in "innumerable varieties" (*de doctrina christiana* 2.11,16), the Latin biblical text, in Augustine's day, was a mess. And by the fourth century, the discrepancies between the Septuagint translation and the Hebrew original were well known.

Augustine's response to this predicament both relativizes the text of Scripture and absolutizes revelation. His semiotics and epistemology link up here: words point toward their referent meaning, but a gap between word and meaning always exists, and in that space interpretation does its work. Various interpretations can all be, variously, true, provided they do not contradict the teaching of the Church; and as we have seen, even authorial intention cannot legitimately limit scriptural interpretation (*Confessions* Bk. 13).

Biblical multiplicity and multivocality do not in the end perturb Augustine, because any text, even the original, is by his terms already, itself, a translation, from the eternal timelessness of God's existence to the mediated, temporally linear world of men. Words point to but cannot contain truth: their very existence is evidence of the dislocation of our consciousness, of the ways in which our consciousness is divided up in time. Yet Augustine's stance also allows for a surprising dimension of continuous revelation. Explaining the differences between the Hebrew and Greek texts of the Bible, he posits *God* as the author of the consequent changes in meaning. The Hebrew revealed what it was supposed to reveal in its own time to Israel; the Septuagint (LXX) prepared the biblical text for the Gentiles by reformulating (in Greek) revelation appropriate to that much later time period (*de civ. Dei* 18.43).[21] Augustine's sense of the fluidity of both text and revealed truth thus seems to contrast sharply with the posture toward sacred texts which we have seen in other traditions—rabbinic Judaism's story, for instance, that among the other things he was doing while Israel wandered in the desert, Moses wrote out individual *sifrei torah* so that all the tribes would have identical copies; or Daoism's and Islam's, that earthly Scriptures have a cosmic counterpart in the heavens.

5.5.3 Science, Government, Healing, and the Disenchantment of the Universe

God's truth utterly transcends human truths; yet, Augustine argues, religious claims cannot be true if they are contradicted by scientific, empirical truths. The Manichees' inability to negotiate the gap between their revealed cosmic knowledge and the eclipse tables of Graeco-Roman science considerably diminished their hold on the young Augustine. Thus though religious truths might vary between each other and yet all still be true, they *cannot* vary from science and still be true. For Augustine, the laws governing the physical operation of the universe stem from the same source as true revelation—God—and thus these two cannot contradict each other.

If the Church is the sole location of God's people in time on earth, does the government's allegiance to that church in turn give the government itself any particular religious status? Eusebius, enamoured of the Constantinian revolution, said yes: the *Pax Romana Christiana* was the messianic peace foretold by Isaiah; Constantine, rebuilder of Jerusalem, was God's viceroy, his *christos* on earth. Augustine, in the days of much more greatly involved imperial government with Theodosius II and after, said no. If ideas can have opposites, then the Daoist idea that, with government in harmony with heaven, peace and prosperity result for the kingdom, is utterly opposed to Augustine's. His thought here is unsentimentally secular.[22] Kingdoms whether pagan or Catholic are simply large robber bands, built on a system of exploitation and power; robber bands are simply small kingdoms. The opacity of man's experience in time accordingly carries over to his experience of government, which can never correspond to Heaven. The Kingdom of God, for Augustine, always remains an austerely eschatological concept.

So too healing. Scientific medicine (such as it was in his day) may or may not ameliorate sickness and suffering; but true healing is always a miracle, an intrusion or explosion of heaven into the earthly realm. Unlike the Daoist tradition, where correct ritual and the right word at the right time can activate the powers of heaven, for Augustine such healings are utterly unorchestrated explosions of grace, historical anticipations in the present of the final reintegration of spirit and flesh awaited at the End-time resurrection.[23] Miracles are not magic.

5.5.4 *Flesh, Bodies, and the Reception of Truth*

Augustine's acute awareness of the drag mortal flesh imposes on the soul, the ways in which it cooperates in the soul's defection from higher to lower goods, bears some superficial resemblance to Hinduism. There, the superimposition of the body through the process of reincarnation limits the persons' sense of who he is, hobbling him with a congenital desire reinforced in each birth. In this sense, fleshly embodiment compromises knowing.

Augustine would agree up to a point. For him, humanity after Adam is born carnal both in its flesh and in its soul. But reading Genesis as he does *ad litteram*, interpreting as he does the significance of Christ's incarnation and resurrection, Augustine holds that at the final redemption, when the saints enjoy the unmediated apprehension of the divine, they will do so in their fleshly bodies. Since God is the author of flesh, since he created bodies and souls joined together when he made Adam and Eve and pronounced them good, then souls and bodies belong together. It is Sin, not Flesh, that compromises man's capacity for Truth.

What, finally, of the relationship between Truth, knowledge, and reason? We have seen how their appeal to reason without authority attracted the young Augustine to the Manichees; later, Platonism freed him from them by providing him with a better way to think about God, spirit vs. matter, and evil. In the writings done immediately after his conversion, Augustine still champions the independence of the mind if it would know truth. Thus, at Cassiciacum he designates authority and reason as two separate and distinguishable ways to God or Wisdom: "In point of time, authority is first; in order of reality, reason is prior."[24] To sin, he argues early on, is fundamentally "to stray from education."[25] *Solus igitur sapiens non peccat*—only the wise man, he argues, does not sin; the wise man does not fear but even welcomes death as the liberation of the soul from the mortal body.[26]

In his mature writings, from the period of the *Confessions* on through the *City of God*, Augustine executes a full reversal on these issues. Identifying what man loves, not what he knows, as the reason why man does or does not sin, Augustine derides his own earlier enthusiasm for education as a way to know the truth: such a position would require that the man "who had a keen mind, or who was cultivated in the liberal arts" have the best chance at salvation. "But if I set up this standard of judgment, *he will laugh me to scorn* who has chosen the weak things of the world to confound the strong, the foolish to confound the wise."[27] The unlettered Monica moves throughout his autobiography as a prime exemplum of the good and faithful Christian who is awarded—no less than her intellectual, well-educated son—a glimpse of divine being through mystical experience (9.10,23–24). Finally, arguing late in his life against the Pelagians, Augustine holds that even those most excellent servants and conduits of Truth, the apostles themselves, were no more free of the troubling solicitations of concupiscence and the fear of death than the most abject sinner or—his old measure of excellence—the most educated wise man.[28]

We conclude then that for Augustine, human reality after Adam's sin is so constituted that the individual—even the individual believer within the sole legitimate (i.e., true) church; even the heroic, most excellent believers as exemplified by the apostles themselves—can have only a very attenuated grasp of truth. Even once truth is in some sense known, or received, fear, its opposite, always remains. His insistence on this point—remarkable within a tradition emphasizing the degree to which it embodies revelation—gives his theology its poignancy. Truth is absolutely necessary for the soul's happiness; nevertheless, in this life, it remains systematically elusive. It is belief in the promise of one day knowing the truth, seeing Truth, hearing Truth "not through the tongue of flesh, nor through the voice of an angel, nor through the sound of thunder, nor through the obscurity of symbolic utterance" (9.10,24) but immediately, that constitutes, for Augustine, the essence of faith.

Notes

1. So Peter Berger in seminar, 11 October 1997.

2. P. Courcelle attempts to reconstruct which of Ambrose's sermons can be dated to Augustine's stay in Milan, *Recherches sur les Confessions de S. Augustin* (Paris: Editions E. de Boccard, 1968), 93–138.

3. For the English I draw on two translations: Frank W. Sheed, *The Confessions of Saint Augustine* (London: Sheed and Ward, 1944); and Henry Chadwick, *Saint Augustine, Confessions* (Oxford: Oxford University Press, 1991). The Latin text is James J. O'Donnell, *Augustine: Confessions* (Oxford: The Clarendon Press, 1992), vol. 1.

4. His critique of his own pride, he says frankly here, stems only from his later perspective. "What I am now saying did not then enter my mind when I gave my attention to the scripture. It seemed [then] to me unworthy in comparison with the dignity of Cicero," (3.5,9). Copies of scripture were hard to come by, and in antiquity rarely was the entire collection of books bound together (cf. 7.21,27 and 8.6,14: Paul's letters are in their own volume): we do not know what Augustine, age 18, read in this first encounter.

5. By the Manichees, *de utilitate credendi* i,2; by Augustine, newly associated with the erudite, platonizing Catholicism of Ambrose's Milan, in *de beata vita* 4, one of his first writings after his conversion in 386.

6. *ut. cred.* 1,2; on their claim to superior rationality more generally, *de moribus ecclesiae* 2.2,3; *beata vita* 1.4; *c. Faustum* 20.3; *c. epistulam Fund.* 13; 15.

7. *Confessions* 3.7,12. Later, in Rome and Milan, though skeptical of much of their mythology and their theory of interpolations, Augustine was still held by the force of their criticism of OT anthropomorphism (5.10–11).

8. "When I wanted to think of my God, I knew of no way of doing so except as a physical mass. Nor did I think anything existed which is not material. . . . And for the same reason, I also believed that evil is a kind of material substance with its own foul and misshapen mass . . . a malignant mind creeping through the earth" (5.10,19–20).

9. *de praedestinatione sanctorum* (2.5).

10. See, most recently, G. G. Stroumsa and Paula Fredriksen, "The Two Souls and the Divided Will," *Self, Soul and Body in Religious Experience*, ed. A. I. Baumgarten (Leiden: E. J. Brill, 1998), 198–217, esp. 198–208.

11. See, for an excellent overview of these ideas, chapters 14–16 on Plotinus by A. H. Armstrong in *The Cambridge History of Later Greek and Early Medieval Philosophy*, ed. idem (Cambridge: Cambridge University Press, 1970), 222–63.

12. Hence Augustine's lament to God in *Confessions* when describing his quest for Truth that "I was without and You were within." The idea of Christ as the interior teacher dwelling in the mind (developed in his early post-conversion writing *de magistro*, "The Teacher") has obvious similarities with the Plotinian idea of the interior divine Higher Self through which one can participate in the One.

13. See esp. R. A. Markus, "Augustine: Reason and Illumination," *Cambridge History of Philosophy*, 362–73.

14. Cf. 4.14,22: *grande profundum est ipse homo:* "Man is a vast deep. The hairs of his head are more easily numbered than are his feelings and the movements of his heart."

15. Such as mathematical principles and other kinds of abstract thought, 10,17–11,19.

16. Again, the thought is similar to that of Plotinus, *Ennead* 6.7.23.4, who speaks of the soul's rest in the One; cf. *Confessions* 1.1,1, "You have made us for Yourself, and our hearts are restless until they rest in You."

17. That is, the Catholic Church *as he construes it*: Pelagius, Julian of Eclanum, and other anti-Augustinians during the Pelagian controversy (411–430) were equally members of the same Catholic church (Julian was a bishop): but Augustine argued that their theology in effect disenfranchised them.

18. Cf. Augustine's own admission, in the *Confessions*, that his watching a fly struggle in a spider's web, or a dog chasing a hare across a field, touches upon the same perverted enjoyment of the pain of another as fuels the *habitués* of gladiatorial fights.

19. These images, through which Augustine retrospectively describes his depressions and spiritual aridity in his youth and early adulthood, run throughout the *Confessions*.

20. Cf. his discussion in 13.15,16 of the Bible: "Who but You, O God, has made for us a solid firmament of authority over us in your divine scripture? For 'heaven will fold up like a book' (Isa 43:4) and now 'like a skin it is stretched out' above us (Psalm 103:2)."

21. "Anything in the Hebrew text that is not found in that of the seventy translators (=LXX) is something which the Spirit of God decided not to say through the translators but through the prophets. Conversely, anything in the LXX that is not in the Hebrew text is something which that same Spirit preferred to say through the translators."

22. The burden of R. A. Markus's classic study *Saeculum: History and Society in the Thought of Saint Augustine* (Cambridge: Cambridge University Press, 1970).

23. This is one of the closing discussions of *de civ. Dei* 22.

24. *de ordine* 2.9,26, written the summer following his conversion in 386. In the background of this claim must lie not only Augustine's enthusiasm for the Neoplatonic philosophy by which he had finally come round to Catholicism, but also his sensitivity to the Manichaean critique of the orthodox *superstitio* that had little use for reason whatsoever.

25. *de libero arbitrio* 1.1,2, written c. 388.

26. *de utilitate credendi* 12,27.

27. From the finale of the *ad Simplicianum* 1.2,22, just before he examines God's strong-arming of Saul as an example of the exercise of sovereign divine authority.

28. On Paul's still suffering the ill effects of concupiscence even after his conversion—the point of Augustine's reading Romans 7 as Paul's autobiographical statement as a "wretched man" even after the reception of grace—*c. ii epp. Pelagianorum* 1.8,13–14.

6

The Taxonomy of Truth in the Islamic Religious Doctrine and Tradition

S. Nomanul Haq

6.1 Introduction

It should be recognized at the outset that the threefold categorical scheme collaboratively identified for discussing truth in various religious systems—namely, the nature of truth in its epistemological, ontological, and cosmological dimensions; expressions and representations of truth; and cultivation and embodiment of truth—is vague enough to provide a fairly fruitful analytical framework when employed for the treatment of Islamic religious data. Of course, an analysis of this kind might frequently become highly problematic in that it may isolate elements that would break down upon isolation. Also, this analysis, as it stands in its neat conception, may sometimes appear to be a *post hoc* exercise, something which the tradition itself will not recognize. It would be noted as we proceed that all this happens to be true in the case of Islam; and yet what is also true is that the analysis in terms of the threefold scheme illuminates and explains a great deal, and does cast the treated data in a perspective that renders them amenable to a comparative examination.

A very good case that illustrates the efficacy of our analytical tools is that of the grand Muslim Sufi sage ʿAlī al-Hujwīrī's pithy locutions about truth. Popularly known as Dātā Ganj Bakhsh (d. ca. 1071), Hujwīrī was the first author to write a Sufi treatise in Persian, the *Kashf al-Maḥjūb* (The Uncovering of the Veiled), a text that has become an integral part of the spirit of traditional Islamic religious ethos.[1] In the *Kashf*, our Sufi quotes an older *shaykh* Dhu'l-Nūn al-Miṣrī (d. 850) as saying:

> Truth (*ṣidq*) is the sword of God on the earth: it cuts everything that it touches.

Just a little earlier in the text, Hujwīrī had elucidated the point:

> The sign of the truth (*ḥaqīqa*)[2] of knowledge (*maʿrifa*) is the truth (*ṣidq*) of [seeker's] will, and a true will cuts off all secondary causes . . . so that nothing remains except God.

And a little later:

> Now truth (*ṣidq*) regards the Causer (*al-Musabbib*), and does not consist in the affirmation of secondary causes (*sabab*).[3]

It is readily clear that Hujwīrī is here using the notion of truth with conceptual pluralism, and we note that his assertions submit to our analysis without much resistance: thus, we have here ontological truth (the sword of God, cutting by its sharp edge every secondary existence, so that nothing remains except God Himself); epistemological truth (truth of knowledge, at once engendered and corroborated by the truth of the seeker's will); and, finally, embodied truth-in-practice (affirming ultimately the Causer rather than the cause). Further, there is here an appellative pluralism too: we find two different words for truth—*ṣidq* (root, *Ṣ^aD^aQ^a*) and *ḥaqīqa* (root, *Ḥ^aQQ^a*).[4]

To be sure, this kind of multilateral conception of truth is indeed characteristically Islamic, a conception that has, at once, a cosmic-metaphysical dimension, a moral-personalistic dimension, and a logical-linguistic dimension; and all these can in principle be cast in the framework of our analytical scheme. But let us also note: all these dimensions are fully integrated so that any one of them, when considered in isolation from the others, is fragmentary and therefore, strictly speaking, religiously meaningless.

6.2 Explication of the Notion of *Ṣidq*

According to classical Arabic lexicons, the root *Ṣ^aD^aQ^a* that yields the verbal noun *ṣidq* means: to speak, say, utter, or tell, truth or truly, or veraciously; it is the contrary of $K^aDH^aB^a$, to lie, to utter, speak, tell, falsehood.[5] The verbal root and its derivatives, as well as various verbal nouns and participles they form, abound in the Qur'ān and are particularly instructive. The eleventh-century philologist al-Rāghib al-Iṣfahānī, articulating the standard Muslim understanding, tells us that

> Truth (*ṣidq*) and falsehood (*kadhib*) are primarily in what is said, whether relating to the past or to the future, and [in the latter case] whether it be a promise or other than a promise; and only in what is said in the way of information.
>
> But sometimes truth and falsehood are in other modes of speech, such as asking a question, and commanding, and supplicating; as when one says, "Is Zaid in the house?" for this implies information of his being ignorant of the state of Zaid; and when one says, "Make me to share with thee, or to be equal with thee," for this implies his requiring to be made to share with the other, or to be made equal with him; and when one says, "Do not thou hurt me," for this implies that the other is hurting him.

And then comes the classic explication of Arabic philologists:

> *Ṣidq* is . . . the agreeing of (1) what is said with (2) what is conceived in the mind, and with (3) the thing told of; *all together*. Otherwise, it is not complete *ṣidq*, but may be described either as *ṣidq*, or sometimes as *ṣidq* and sometimes as *kadhib* (falsehood) according to two different points of view; as when one says *without believing it*, 'Muhammad is the Apostle of God', for this may be termed *ṣidq* because what is told *is such*, and it may be termed *kadhib* because it *is at variance* with what the speaker conceives in his mind.[6]

It is this analysis of al-Iṣfahānī that constituted the basis of Wilfred Cantwell Smith's fascinating exposition of the Islamic notion of *ṣidq* in an essay to which he gave the rather provocative title, "A Human View of Truth."[7] Indeed, this essay is written with such conviction, coherence, and clarity that it can hardly be improved upon and I would urge the reader to pay very close attention to it. Smith begins by pointing out that the Islamic understanding of *ṣidq* is fundamentally unlike our contemporary Western notion of truth—the notion that truth is a quality that lies, exhaustively and uniquely, in propositions. The locus of *ṣidq*, in contrast, is the human being, the proposer of the proposition, the speaker of the speech. *Ṣidq* is a personalist notion of truth.

The analysis of al-Iṣfahānī also makes it explicit that the Islamic concept of *ṣidq* has been developed in what Smith calls trilateral terms. *Ṣidq* arises upon the coincidence or harmony or mutual corroboration of three factors—One: the utterance carrying the information (the logical-linguistic dimension that involves questions of syntax and what we would today call formal logic). Two: the sincere belief of the utterer in what is uttered (the moral-personalistic dimension). And three: the correspondence of the utterance with objective facts (the cosmic-metaphysical dimension, much like Alfred Tarski's correspondence theory of truth: "The statement . . . 'Snow is white' is true if, and only if, snow is, indeed, white"[8]).

All this has been nicely elaborated upon by Wilfred Cantwell Smith. Remaining within the philological domain, Smith further points out that the root *Ṣ ᵃDᵃQᵃ* is a transitive verb and therefore takes a direct object of the person addressed, the person doing the addressing being the subject of the verb; the verb thus creates a subject-object relationship between two persons (or two groups of persons), and this means that in this sense *ṣidq* is a matter of personal interrelations. "'He lied to him' or 'P spoke the truth to Q', indicates that the truth and falsity under consideration here are attributes of a statement in its role of establishing or constituting communication between or among human beings."[9] Of course, our primary sources also tell us that sometimes the direct object of the verb is God, and this means that *ṣidq* is also a matter of God-human relationship.

But *Ṣ ᵃDᵃQᵃ* is not such as to be inapplicable to non-linguistic domains of human action. Smith has noted that the primary sources cite expressions such as *ṣadaqahu al-naṣīḥa*[10]: here the verb is doubly transitive, taking two direct objects, meaning "he rendered to him truly good advice" (the two objects of the verb being (1) the receiver of the advice and (2) the advice itself). This implies, says Smith, that the counsel was both sincere and effectively wise. Two other standard examples that our veteran scholar quotes from the sources[11] are: *ṣadaqahu al-ikhā'*, "He rendered to him truly brotherly affection," or "behaved toward him with true brotherhood"; and: *ṣadaqūhum al-qitāl*, "They were true against them in battle."[12] Again, Smith points out that this latter means that they fought against them "both with genuine zeal and with good effect." Thus,

> *Ṣidq* is that quality by which a man speaks or acts with a combination of inner integrity and objective overt appropriateness. It involves saying or doing the objectively right thing out of a genuine personal recognition of its rightness, an inner alignment with it.[13]

We may call this embodied truth-in-practice. But in fact the practical embodiment of *ṣidq* takes a very concrete form. When one utters truth one believes sincerely in what is uttered, and then it becomes a duty engendered by this very sincere belief to realize *in practice* the truth of the utterance, to *make* it true, to *cause* it to be true: to truify it, so to speak. This is expressed in language simply by doubling the middle radical of the root *Ṣ*^{a}*D*^{a}*Q*^{a} so that it becomes *Ṣ*^{a}*DD*^{a}*Q*^{a} (note that the two words still remain orthographically identical), and such morphological gemination gives the root an intensive or causative form. The verbal noun of the intensive form is *taṣdīq*, and it is a commonplace among Muslims that faith consists in the *taṣdīq* of the formula "There is no God but. . . ." Smith provides a very sensitive and learned disquisition on *taṣdīq*, saying that "if I give *taṣdīq* to some statement, I not merely recognize its truth in the world outside me, and subscribe to it, but also incorporate it into my own moral integrity as a person."[14] In more practical terms, this applies to matters relating to the future: if I make a promise, it becomes my duty to take steps to *make* it come true (literally, *Ṣ* ^{a}*DD*^{a}*Q*^{a}). Thus, *ṣidq* signifies, *inter alia*, a commitment to act, "a personal making of what is cosmically true." In sum:

> Truth as a relation to the world, is seen as existing also in relation to man; and man is seen as acting in relation to truth.[15]

It is now clear what al-Hujwīrī means when he says that truth "cuts off all secondary causes . . . so that nothing remains except God." He is giving *taṣdīq* to the belief in one and only one God, other than Whom there is no god; the Sufi sage is realizing in the depth of his being the truth of this affirmed belief, a *ṣidq,* so that all false gods are negated and annihilated; in the end all idols of worldly greed and desires and attachments are cut by *ṣidq,* the "sword of God," and are replaced by an eternal longing whose sole object is He *(Huwa).* Then, nothing remains for the Sufi save the "face of Allah."[16] This is the dynamic of *taṣdīq*: al-Hujwīrī is truifying *tauḥīd,* giving *taṣdīq* to *tauḥīd.*

6.3 Abū Ḥāmid al-Ghazālī's Hierarchy of *Ṣidq*

One of the most original and formidable thinkers of Islam is Abū Ḥāmid al-Ghazālī (d. 1111) who has often been called the greatest Muslim after none other than the Prophet himself. In the Islamic literature he is typically referred to as the Ornament of Religion, Scholar of Scholars, Heir of Apostles, Proof of Islam, Grace of Times—and, indeed, the Guide to the True Faith.[17] This last epithet is hardly an exaggeration, for in terms of his influence Ghazālī is the father of latter-day normative Islamic religious tradition: a large majority of present-day Muslims still lives in a Ghazālian twilight. And, to be sure, the question of *ṣidq* constitutes one of the central issues in the *magnum opus* of this Persian sage, the famous *Iḥyā' al-'Ulūm al-Dīn* (Revival of the Religious Sciences).

The *Iḥyā'* contains a chapter entitled, "On *Ṣidq*: Its Virtue and Its Essential Reality (*Ḥaqīqa*)." Beginning here with a discourse on the merits of *ṣidq*, providing copious citations from the Qur'ān and Ḥadīth, Ghazālī proceeds to construct a subsection: "Elucidation of the Essential Reality (*Ḥaqīqa*) of *Ṣidq*, Its Meaning, Its Grades." Thus we read that "The utterance '*ṣidq*' is employed in six different meanings: (i) *ṣidq* in word; (ii) *ṣidq* in intention and volition; (iii) *ṣidq* in determination [to carry out a certain act]; (iv) *ṣidq* in faithfulness to one's determination; (v) *ṣidq* in deed; and (vi) *ṣidq* in realizing *(taḥqīq*, root *Ḥ^{a}QQ^a)* all [mystical] stations of religion. The one to whom *ṣidq* is attributed in all of these ways, so he is *ṣiddīq*, having fully attained *ṣidq*."[18]

Then comes the elaboration. The first kind of *ṣidq*, that in word, had to do with reporting something:

> Now reports relate either to the past or to the future, and included in this is the honoring and dishonoring of promises. It is the duty (*ḥaqq*)[19] of everybody to keep an eye on what he has uttered, and not to speak anything other than the truth. . . . Thus the one who protects his tongue against reporting what does not correspond to things as they are, so he is to be called *true*.

Here two perfections are involved, says Ghazālī: First, refraining from uttering obscurities, for an obscure truth practically functions as falsehood. Second, attending to the meaning of the words uttered; thus, when one says, "Lord, Thee only do we worship," then one also ought to possess the quiddity of the worshipper, otherwise on Doomsday one's truthfulness will not be established.

In this discussion of *ṣidq* in word, Ghazālī takes up the question as to whether one ought to speak truth solely for the sake of truth. What if severe harm results when one reports a particular matter as it really is, such as divulging to an enemy the secrets of one's country? *Ṣidq* is not intended as an end unto itself, says Ghazālī, it is intended as that which leads to *ḥaqq* and that which invites to *ḥaqq*. How do we translate *ḥaqq* here? While I shall be looking at this appellation presently, we can in the meantime translate it as "proper," "appropriate," "real," "rightful," "fitting," "legitimate." Thus one ought to look at the ultimate aim of *ṣidq* and not only at its correspondence to things as they are. But then, if one must make a report that lacks this correspondence, it is necessary to remain within the limits imposed by God and concretely elucidated by the Prophet, and to do so only insofar as such report is meant for common good; and even here one must as much as possible speak in figurative terms so that the utterance does not become a blatant lie.

In this connection, Ghazālī presents an anecdote that is reminiscent of the Buddhist Aṅgulimāla story we read in M. David Eckel's chapter. Recall that prior to his conversion by the Buddha, Aṅgulimāla went around killing travelers, collecting their fingers, and wearing them as a garland around his neck. When he is instructed by the Buddha to perform the "act of truth," Aṅgulimāla says that he could not do this because the act involves declaring that he has never willfully taken the life of any creature, and this was not true. The Buddha eases Aṅgulimāla's moral anguish and tells him that these words would carry the force of truth if he were to measure his life from the moment of his birth as a member of the Elect. Our Persian sage has a parallel anecdote. He narrates the story of a man who became the potential target of a violent attacker, and this attacker would come to his house looking for him. "Is your husband home?" he would ask the wife. What should the woman say if, indeed, the man happens to be in the house? The man resolves the wife's moral anguish by asking her to draw a circle, place her finger inside the circle, and to cry out: "No, my husband is not *here!*" This way, the wife was saved from lying and the husband was saved from the attacker. Indeed, the words uttered carried the force of *ṣidq,* and this despite the fact that the man was in the house and the understanding of the culprit was to the contrary.

As for the second type, *ṣidq* in intention and volition, Ghazālī equates it to *ikhlāṣ*, total sincerity—that is, he tells us, doing everything for the sake of God. Thus an action may be overtly praiseworthy, but may not have been carried out with sincere intention, and for this reason it will not constitute *ṣidq*. Ghazālī refers to a Ḥadīth that speaks of a man who is asked on Doomsday, "To what use did you put your knowledge?" and he claims, "I did this and I did that . . ." "You are a liar," God would judge, "your aim was only to gain a reputation, that people call you learned!" Ghazālī points out that here the overt action is not being dismissed, but only the intention, the lack of sincerity (*ikhlāṣ*). "Thus one meaning of *ṣidq* is purity of intention, and this is *ikhlāṣ*; hence, one who is true (*ṣādiq*) is necessarily one who is sincere (*mukhliṣ*)"[20]

Ṣidq in determination to do something, the third type, is characterized as "fullness and firmness." Thus, when a man makes a determination (such as making a determination to give all his wealth to the poor should he gain wealth) and becomes weak or partial in his determination when the moment arises (not giving all his wealth to poor when he, indeed, becomes wealthy), then this was contrary to *ṣidq*. Evidently the *Iḥyā'* is here directly based on Qur'ān, 9: 75–76:

> Amongst them are people who made a Covenant with Allah that if He bestowed on them of His bounty, they would give in charity and be truly amongst those who are righteous. But when He did bestow of his bounty, they became Covetous, and turned back. . . .

Ghazālī's fourth *ṣidq*, *which is ṣidq* in faithfulness to one's determination, is a process of actualizing of truth in one's being and externally in the world around. We have already discussed this in connection with the concept of *taṣdīq*. Again, without specifying his primary sources, Cantwell Smith effectively expounds the Ghazālian position most eloquently: "[It is] the process of making or finding true in actual human life, in one's own personal spirit and overt behavior, what God—or reality—intends for man."[21] Here Ghazālī quotes several Qur'ānic verses; one of them he severally quotes more than once, namely: "There are people who have been true to their Covenant with Allah." More fully:

> Among the believers are men who have been true to their Covenant with Allah: Of them some have completed their vow in its fullness. And some (still) wait: But they have never changed their determination in the least—that Allah may reward the people of Truth for their Truth.[22]

Ṣidq in deed was the fifth kind: "This consists in striving to prevent overt acts (*ẓāhir*) from signifying something that is, in fact, absent from one's inner heart (*bāṭin*). This is to be achieved not by abandoning overt acts but by bringing what is latent in the heart into harmony with what is outwardly manifest in acts."[23] Ghazālī here speaks about worshippers who develop pious faces by which others are easily deceived: for the onlooker would indeed consider them "as if they are standing before God" even though "latently they stand before some worldly greed!" Then he identifies four paradigms: (1) If the latent is worse than the manifest, and the lack of harmony between them is intentional, then this would constitute a case of lying, loss of sincerity, and hypocrisy. (2) If the latent is worse than the manifest, and the lack of harmony between them is unintentional, then this is an instance of loss of *ṣidq*, but not that of loss of sincerity nor an instance of hypocrisy. (3) If the latent is truly reflected in the manifest and the two are in perfect harmony, then this is a case of *ṣidq*. (4) If the latent is better than the manifest, then this too would embody *ṣidq*, and this would in addition embody humility.

It is typical of Ghazālī to lead his audience ultimately to a point that lies in the realm of Sufi discourse, transcending rational and systematic considerations of a purely theological kind. Thus, his final category of *ṣidq* is both formulated and characterized in unmistakably Sufi terms.

This was *ṣidq* in realizing all mystical stations, a category naming the supreme *ṣidq*, occupying the highest grade among all other categories of *ṣidq*, and being most rare. We are told that this *ṣidq* concerns the truth of spiritual stations such as Fear and Hope, Glorification and Renunciation, Contentment and Trust, Love, and other stations along the Path—all these, we note, are standard Sufi terms. These stations, writes Ghazālī, have their earlier indications, and the tendency is to identify them prematurely by their appellations as soon as these first indications make a manifestation—but then comes their perfection and their true reality (*ḥaqīqa*), and one who reaches this reality is the true one, the one who gives *taḥqīq* to these stations. Note that the word *taḥqīq is* morphologically identical and semantically analogous to *taṣdīq*; and just as *taṣdīq* means to *make* true, to *cause* to be true, to 'truify', to *actualize* truth, the verbal noun *taḥqīq* means to *make* real, to *cause* to become real, to realize, to *actualize* reality, and so on. "When an attribute governs over and becomes complete in the one who is attributed, the attributed is called 'true' (*ṣādiq*)." Again, all this is inspired by the Qur'ān, which Ghazālī quotes:

> Only those are Believers who have believed in Allah and His Messengers, and have never since doubted, but have striven with their belongings and their persons in the Cause of Allah: Such are the True Ones.[24]

And:

> It is righteousness—to believe in Allah and the Last Day, and the Angels, and the Book, and the Messengers; to spend of your substance out of love for Him, for your kin, for orphans, for the needy, for the wayfarer, for those who ask, and for the ransom of slaves; to be steadfast in prayer, and render regular charity, to fulfill regular contracts which ye have made; and to be firm and patient, in pain (or suffering) and adversity, and throughout all periods of panic. Such are the people of Truth.[25]

6.4 The Ontological Equivalence of Truth and Reality: *al-Ḥaqq* and *al-Ḥaqīqa*

It is evident from the foregoing discussion that even though the religious notion of *ṣidq* has an integral cosmic-metaphysical dimension, the conceptual focus of this notion is moral and practical. In explicating *ṣidq*, Ghazālī's fundamental purpose, for example, is not to develop a theoretical discourse for a rational grasp of the concept of truth, or to investigate philosophically the nature of truth as such, this investigation being an end in itself: Ghazālī is here concerned rather with moral conduct; he is teaching not theology but an Islamic way of life. Thus, it is the case typically with religious discussions of *ṣidq*; they are generally carried out in a moral framework with a view to works rather than to achieve an intellectual understanding for its own sake.[26]

On the other hand, the term *al-ḥaqq* (root, *Ḥ*[a]*QQ*[a]), which we have already come across, is employed to serve a different purpose, given its characteristic and compelling ontological connotations. Indeed, the very primary meaning of the word *ḥaqq* is "established fact," and therefore "real"; whereas "correspondence to facts," and therefore "truth" is its secondary meaning.[27] With the definite article, the word *al-Ḥaqq* is in its primary signification a divine Name and occurs frequently in the Qur'ān as the opposite of *bāṭil* (see below). But the primary and secondary meanings of the word, however, have become semantically equivalent in the tradition, rendering the two concepts it designates ontologically equivalent—*ḥaqq* was both that which was true and that which was real. Given this subsequent equivalence, lexicographers sometimes start from the secondary meaning, considering it to be primary. Thus, Lane says that the "primary signification [of *ḥaqq*] is *Suitableness to the requirements of wisdom, justice, right, or rightness, truth, reality or fact*" And then a little later that *ḥaqq* is "the *state*, or *quality*, or *property*, *of being just*, *proper*, *right*, *correct*, or *true*; *justness*, *propriety*, *rightness*, *correctness*, or *truth*; *reality* or *fact*."[28]

As compared to *ṣidq*, then, *ḥaqq* characteristically designates ontological truth and is employed in discussions of a metaphysical rather than moral kind. *Ṣidq,* we noted, is the contrary of *kadhib* (lie); *ḥaqq*'s contrary is *bāṭil*, nonexistent, unreal, untrue, negated, epistemologically false, improper, empty, vacuous. As Cantwell Smith says, "Behind . . . [*ḥaqq*] is metaphysical power, while the other [sc., *bāṭil*] in strident dichotomy from it is ludicrously vain and vacuous."[29] In the context of *ḥaqq*, therefore: Whatever is true is real, and whatever is real is true; and, further, whatever is real, exists. Ultimately, God is the Real, He is the Reality, He is the Truth.[30]

The abstract substantive noun derived from the root, namely, the noun *ḥaqīqa*, has predominantly acquired the meaning of ultimate reality or essential reality, rather than truth; indeed, *al-Ḥaqīqa* has become a standard Sufi term, designating God Himself.[31] What is most interesting both philologically and conceptually, expressions such as "*ḥaqīqa of ḥaqq*" *also* occur in Islamic religious literature[32]—and this expression lends itself to several legitimate renderings, "the essential/ultimate truth of the Real," or, "the essential/ultimate reality of the Truth," and so on. Once again, Smith:

> *ḥaqq*, like *satyam* and *veritas* refers to what is real, genuine, authentic, what is true in and of itself by dint of metaphysical or cosmic status. It is a term par excellence of God. In act, it refers absolutely to him, and indeed - *al-Ḥaqq* is a name of God not merely in the sense of an attribute but of a denotation. *Huwa al-Ḥaqq*: He is reality as such. Yet every other thing that *is* genuine is also *ḥaqq*. . . . Yet the words means reality first, and then God, for those who equate him with reality.[33]

6.5 The Epistemological Question

It is a characteristic feature of the Islamic religious tradition that despite the availability of the term *ḥaqq*, the analytical question of truth as such—that is, truth as an analytically *isolated* notion—hardly figures in it. There exist no long discourses on the doctrine of *ḥaqq* and its precise nature, unlike the case with *ḥaqīqa* on which Sufism has left a rich legacy of literature. But, to be sure, it does not mean that Islam has been unconcerned with the articulation of the notion of truth. What it does mean is that the Islamic tradition takes both the concept and substance of *ḥaqq* as a given; something that does not need to be built up from first principles. The Qur᾽ān embodied the truth; the cosmos was a created entity carrying God's signs, and was true to its purpose, its *amr*; and of course God was the Truth. And so questions about *ḥaqq* appear as epistemological questions. What is the nature of the knowledge of truth? How does one attain this knowledge? How can this knowledge be validated? And added to this is the question, Why should one seek truth? This last question, it will be noted, can be classified under the last category of the threefold scheme, namely, cultivation and embodiment of truth.

In the process of the formation of the normative Islamic tradition concerning the articulation of the notion of truth, we find a multiplicity of disciplines making epistemological claims—there were the Hellenized philosophers (*falāsifa*); and there were the *kalām* theologians; then, vying with the rest were the Sufis; and, finally, there were the legal scholars (*fuqahā*'). From among these we can disregard the *falāsifa* for they remained peripheral to a consciously cultivated Islamic religious outlook of the rest. The legal scholars, *fuqahā*', formed a formidable group of thinkers; and as for the rest, they all live in the grand Ghazālian synthesis. It should be noted that many later *fuqahā*' agree with Ghazālī in their theory of knowledge, but as a rule they have a different metaphysical thrust; and it is due to this difference that Ghazālī undermines them as we shall see.

In general, then, we can speak of two approaches to the articulation and cultivation of truth in the Islamic tradition: (1) A *functional* approach, which seeks to discover systematically the truth revealed to man by God through his last Prophet, thereby articulating the whole of Islam as a *function*—that is, as an all-embracing code of private and public conduct, generating the grand body of Islamic law, so that to embody truth and put it into practice becomes the whole purpose of the discovery of truth. And (2) A *rational-mystical* approach, represented by Ghazālī—an approach whose ultimate aim is to seek the revelation of the essential reality (*ḥaqīqa*) of the Truth (*al-ḥaqq*), both cognitively and experientially, in the depth of one's being.

6.6 The Functional Approach: *Fiqh* and *Sharīʿa* Recalled

The basic premise of the whole program of legal scholars, we recall, is the following: Allah sent humanity to this world charged with the obligation to create a moral order, and this moral order will come about only if God's commands are followed. Now these commands, as we know, constituted Sharīʿa which is embodied in the Qurʾān, the Word of God. In concrete terms, Sharīʿa was the sum total of God's judgments on human acts, expressed in terms of a categorization of these acts into classes of permitted, forbidden, obligatory, and so on. Given the fundamental human moral onus, then, a knowledge of Sharīʿa is a knowledge of the *whole* of Islam as a *function*. The articulation of Sharīʿa by a human agent—a process known as *fiqh* (literally "understanding")—thus becomes the articulation of *ḥaqq* revealed by Allah; the seeker after Sharīʿa is then a seeker after truth, and a concern with Sharīʿa—a fundamental Islamic concern—is a concern with truth.

Note that the subject of Sharīʿa is God, the subject of *fiqh* is the human being, and the object of *fiqh* is Sharīʿa.[34] Sharīʿa, therefore, is eternal and true, while *fiqh* is fallible and does not enjoy epistemological finality. Furthermore, Sharīʿa is not precisely spelled out for the benefit of humankind. When one searches through the repositories of divine revelation, one finds, not statement of rules, but legally imprecise and highly interpretable words and phrases that must serve as indicators (*adilla*) of divine rules. God in His Wisdom has chosen to engage human beings in the toilsome task of ferreting out truth from these indicators, of articulating God's law.[35] These articulations are not to be identified with Sharīʿa; rather they constitute *fiqh*, a human effort to discover Sharīʿa. But though every *fiqh* can always be replaced by a better one, and every *fiqh* is limited by the limits of human competence, it nonetheless remains *legally* binding until such a time as a superseding *fiqh* is developed.

Herein lies one powerful and highly productive trend in the Muslim engagement with truth.

6.7 The Rational-Mystical Approach: The Ghazālian Synthesis

In his *Iḥyā'*, Ghazālī surveys all the various disciplines that make epistemological claims.[36] Philosophy of the Hellenistic kind he rejects, but admits formal logic; *fiqh* for him was essential to the life of the individual and the community, but he considers this science by no means the ultimate aim of the seeker after truth; the science of *fiqh* was only propaedeutic to the soul's achievement of higher perfection; and as for *kalām* theology, while it may be necessary for the community, its utility was restricted and many *mutakallimūn* attached themselves to false opinions that became an impediment to the acquisition of the knowledge of truth. Regarding Sufism, Ghazālī says that Sufis attain knowledge by inspiration (*ilhām*)—that is, by direct apprehension of the angel that bestows knowledge on the heart. This is achieved by purification through ascetic exercises. But again Ghazālī seems to imply that such spiritual discipline is beyond the competence of most people and so Sufi approaches have a limited scope. Indeed, the most noble of the sciences was what he calls the "science of the states of the soul (*aḥwāl al-qalb*)," a kind of a higher theology, higher in status than all other disciplines.

Thus in the *Iḥyā'*, Ghazālī provides two detailed and distinctly different classification of the sciences, the first in the *Book of Knowledge,* and second in the *Book of the Wonders of the Heart* [or *Soul*].[37] In the former treatise, speaking of sciences whose acquisition is the duty of the community (*farḍ kifāya*),[38] he distinguishes nonreligious sciences from the religious sciences and, within the latter class, those whose aim is the good of this life from those whose aim is the good of the next life.

Ghazālī, who himself wrote a *fiqh* work, places that discipline in the category of those sciences whose aim is the good of this life. And as for the category of those whose aim is the good of next, everlasting life, in that he places "the science of the states of the soul and its moral characteristics, good and bad." Although dealing in part with moral actions, the science of the soul does not fall under *fiqh* since this latter has access only to external conduct and overt action and cannot grasp the inner states of one's being. Subsequently, in offering a detailed account of the sciences whose aim is the good of next life, he names two—*al-Mukāshafa* and *al-Mu'āmala*. The latter—a standard Sufi term denoting the idea of the fulfillment of moral duties, literally meaning "the science of mutual dealings"—he identifies with the science of the states of the soul; it was the higher ethical science through which the soul seeks its ultimate perfection.

6.8 Essential Reality of the Truth

On the other hand, the science of *al-Mukāshafa* was the higher theology that embraced the knowledge of the celestial realm, its governance of the material, sublunary world and its role in accomplishing the perfection of the human soul—it was the ultimate of the sciences. To have this science is to have authentic knowledge of God's uniqueness as creator, the highest *tauḥīd*—that is, to have a knowledge of the Truth. As Frank points out, *al-Mukāshafa* was effectively higher metaphysics with its integrated psychology and cosmology.[39] Through this science "one achieves the true knowledge of God's being, and of His enduring and perfect attributes."

In the *Wonders of the Heart,* Ghazālī distinguishes between rational sciences and religious sciences. The latter were those whose foundation and source lay in the revelation; whereas the rational sciences were those that could not be acquired on the sole basis of authority or transmitted reports. And here the science of the states of the soul was classified under the rational sciences. In the *Wonders* Ghazālī explains how the heart is the locus of cognition. Using the metaphor of the mirror, he says:

> Every intelligible has an essential reality (*ḥaqīqa*), and this reality has a form (*ṣūra*) which is impressed upon the mirror of the heart.

And then to steer clear of pantheism, he points out that here we have an ontological plurality:

> Just as the mirror is one thing, and the forms of individual objects is another thing, and the image obtained is yet another thing, so we have here three entities (*umūr*), and likewise [with regard to cognition] we have three entities too: the heart, the essential realities of things, and the obtaining in the heart of essential realities in themselves and the presence of these realities in the heart.[40]

Ghazālī goes on to point out that just as a mirror *by its nature* is ready to have manifested in it the essential reality of Truth in all things (*ḥaqīqat al-ḥaqq*), so is the mind by its nature ready to receive the knowledge of the truth. But this does not always happen due to five impediments: (1)

Inadequacy of mind—for example, immaturity such as that found in youngsters; (2) Impurity of heart due to immoderate appetites; (3) Failure to seek knowledge; (4) Attachment to false opinions; and (5) Ignorance as to how to go about seeking knowledge. It is the fifth point here that effectively provides the scope for Ghazālī to admit in his synthesis the rules of logical inference—what he calls *ṭuruq al-iʿtibār*, "ways of systematic reflection"—even though he vehemently dismisses Hellenized Muslim philosophers. He says that one who seeks to know cannot achieve knowledge of what is unknown "except by reflection on the things he does know, which are directly related to that which he seeks to know." Now when one follows the *ṭuruq al-iʿtibār* (method of formal logic), "the essential reality of what he seeks to know is revealed to his mind."[41]

> The fact is that the mind is ready to have the essential reality of the Truth in all beings revealed to it, and something interferes only on account of the five causes we have spoken of; they are, so to speak, a veil which comes between the mirror of the mind and the Well Guarded Tablet on which is engraved everything which God has enacted until the day of resurrection.[42]

Two things are to be noted here. First, Ghazālī makes it very clear that while knowledge ultimately comes from God, it comes only when certain conditions of its reception are met. Thus, when Ghazālī says that God gives "the light of mind" to certain individuals, what he means is that it is given immediately by a secondary cause upon the fulfillment of the conditions of its reception by the individual soul, and the observance of the rules of logic are part of these conditions. Indeed, this reception is impossible if these conditions are violated or not complied with—God has the power to create only that the conditions of whose coming to be are fulfilled. And given that God was the Truth, the other thing to note, following Frank,[43] is that when Ghazālī talks about the heart receiving "the essential reality of Truth in all things," he means that in addition to the knowledge of the essential nature of things, this higher knowledge includes, or, as Frank says, comes to include, insights into the presence of God as the primary cause of the events that take place in the world, and so an insight into the cosmic system as the manifestation of God's originating "Determination (*taqdīr*)" and His "Accomplishment (*al-qaḍā'*)."

Finally, a word about the "Well Guarded Tablet": the expression occurs in the Qur'ān, 85 where verses 21-22 read, "Nay, this is a Glorious Qur'ān, inscribed in a Well Guarded Tablet." This Tablet is considered to be the eternal determining plan of God for the universe. In Ghazālī it designates the angel that is associated with the outermost celestial sphere.

"The essential realities of all things are spread upon the Well Guarded Tablet," which is also referred to as "the hearts of the angels that stand nearest." The Tablet is explained by an illustrative example:

> Just as an architect puts on paper the plan of the construction of a house, and then according to this plan brings the house into real being, so the Creator of the cosmos wrote on the Well Guarded Tablet the blueprint of the world from its beginning to its end, and then brought the world into real being according to it.[44]

Ghazālī stands as the supreme representative of what has become the latter day nonnative Muslim ethos—an ethos in which all elements identified in our threefold analytical scheme run together, integrated in a characteristically Islamic way.

Notes

1. The famous poet-philosopher Muhammad Iqbal has written a whole poem in honor of Hujwīrī and has paid him resounding tribute, saying, incidentally, that "His word makes Truth (*ḥaqq*) speak louder." *Kulliyāt-i-Iqbāl* (Lahore: Shakh Ghulām 'Alī and Sons, 1973), 52.

2. The word *ḥaqīqa* can also be translated as "essential reality" or "ultimate reality." For a detailed discussion of this term see my chapter on ultimate reality in the previous volume.

3. I have given here my emended version of the classic translation of R. A. Nicholson, *The "Kashf al-Maḥjūb," the Oldest Persian Treatise on Sufism by al-Hujwīrī*, Gibb Memorial Series, No. 17, 1911, repr. Karachi: Darul-Ishaat, 1990, 101. All insertions in parentheses (except the first) and in brackets are mine; note particularly that Nicholson with good justification translates *ṣidq* as "sincerity."

4. See below and also note 2 above.

5. See E. W. Lane, *Arabic-English Lexicon*, ed. S. Lane-Poole (London: Williams and Norgate, 1877), s.v.

6. al-Rāghib al-Iṣfahānī is quoted in Lane, ibid. I have rearranged Lane's text, taking some other minor liberties too; all emphases are mine.

7. In *Truth and Dialogue in World Religions: Conflicting Truth Claims*, ed. John Hick (Philadelphia: Westminster Press, 1974), 20–44. Note, however, that Smith does not make any reference to al Iṣfahānī.

8. K. R. Popper's elucidation of Tarski's ideas in the former's "Truth, Rationality, and the Growth of Scientific Knowledge" in idem, *Conjectures and Refutations* (London: Routledge and Kegan Paul, 1984). Popper argues that Tarski's correspondence theory is also applicable to natural languages rather than to formalized systems only.

9. Smith, op. cit., 25.

10. See Lane, op. cit.

11. All these examples are in ibid., which identifies all primary sources that Smith draws upon. But note, again, that Smith does not refer to these sources.

12. Note that I have not always imitated Smith's translations.

13. Smith, op. cit., 25.

14. Ibid., 27.

15. Ibid., 29.

16. Qur'ān, 28:88

17. See, for example 'Idrūs, 'Abd al-Qādir, *Ta'rīf al-Iḥyā'* (Cairo: al-Maktabat al-Tijāriyya, n. d.). Cf. Smith, M. *al-Ghazālī the Mystic* (London: Luzac & Co., 1944).

18. *Iḥyā'*, v. 4, Cairo ed. (1965), 386–93. My translation.

19. Note this translation of the word *ḥaqq*. For the lexical and conceptual range of the word see below.

20. *Iḥyā'*, loc. cit.

21. Smith, op. cit., 28.

22. Qur'ān, 33: 23–24.

23. *Iḥyā'*, loc. cit.

24. Qur'ān, 49: 15.

25. Qur'ān, 2: 177.

26. It should be noted that the term *ṣidq* is used by Hellenized philosophers of Islam to denote the notion of logical truth. It is for this reason that I have specified that we speak here of *religious* discussions, not all kinds of discussions.

27. Cf. Macdonald [Claverley], "Ḥaqq," *Encyclopaedia of Islam, New Edition, s. v.* The authors speak on the authority of the *Ta'rīfāt* of Jurjānī.

28. Lane, op. cit. Italics in the original.

29. Smith, op. cit., 23.

30. It is clear that the question of (ultimate) reality in Islam is intimately bound up with the question of truth. See my chapter on ultimate reality in the previous volume.

31. For a detailed discussion of the term *al-ḥaqīqa* see my chapter on ultimate reality in the previous volume.

32. For example in Ghazālī's *Iḥyā'*, "Wonders of the Heart," op. cit.

33. Smith, op. cit., 22–23.

34. This has already been discussed at some length in my chapter on the human condition in *The Human Condition*. It is for this reason that I intend to keep this section brief.

35. These expressions are largely those of B. Weiss in his *The Search for God's Laws* (Salt Lake City: University of Utah Press, 1992).

36. In the following section I have used as my main guide the excellent monograph of Richard Frank, *al-Ghazālī and the Ashʿarite School* (Durham: Duke University Press, 1994).

37. *Iḥyā' al-ʿulūm*, 1:13–123; 3: 2–48 (Cairo: 1965).

38. This is a standard term of Islamic law.

39. Frank, op. cit., 22–27.

40. Ghazālī, *Iḥyā'*, *Wonders of the Heart*, 3:13.

41. Ibid., 14.

42. Ibid., 18–19.

43. Frank, loc. cit.

44. Ghazālī, *Iḥyā'*, *Wonders of the Heart*, 3:20–21.

7

Religious Truth in the Six Traditions

A Summary

Robert Cummings Neville and Wesley J. Wildman

7.1 Religious Truth: Our Categories and Their Justification

In this chapter, attention shifts from making sense of first-order religious ideas and what it means to speak of their epistemological and performative truth to the second-order accounts of religious truth that we encountered in the religious traditions we studied. Anticipating our (contemporary) theory of religious truth in chapter 8, a conversation between it and what the various traditions have to say about religious truth ought to be possible. In this conversation the extent to which our theory takes account of the various traditions' insights into religious truth should be evident and adjustments and improvements should follow. Such a conversation does not simply begin, however, thereupon to be instantly effective. On the contrary, a precondition for success in such a conversation, according to our method, is self-consciousness about the manner of our appropriation of the data from the religions we have studied. This self-consciousness is expressed especially in the flexible organization of the data from the religious traditions by comparative categories—categories hard won in the exhausting if not rigorous process of mutual torment that we have come fondly to think of as comparison. With the usual debates and worries, therefore, by the end of our third year we had tentatively settled on a richly nuanced set of subcategories for spelling out various dimensions of the general category of religious truth. The three categories are the nature of truth as an epistemological problem; the expression of truth in scripture and other forms, considering issues of revelation and authority; and the cultivation or embodiment of truth.

As Haq showed in chapter 6, the three subcategories are not easily kept apart, and in fact are interwoven in such a way that, at least in Islam, little of significance can be said in regard to one without also making reference to the others. So, for instance, the classical epistemological or lexical explication of truth (*Ṣidq*) requires that for a claim to be true it must not only correspond to its object but be sincerely intended by the claimant (6.2). The sincerity of the claimant in making the claim true is deeply involved in moral and religious embodiment of truth, as Haq points out (6.3). In the language of our theory in 8.1, making truth claims in this context is a speech act that typically includes among its felicity conditions both the epistemological truth of the interpretation expressed in the claim and the performative truth (especially as sincere and appropriate intentions) of the act itself. Islam is relatively unusual in the lengths to which it goes to spell out felicity conditions for truth speaking and truth doing, distinguishing while entangling epistemological and performative truth. We take this to be a result of a sophisticated philosophical tradition with an emphatic legal emphasis whereby felicity conditions were naturally conceived at multiple levels and simple propositions were thought of as extreme abstractions potentially masking ill-will. Other traditions we studied exhibit the merging without the same degree of explicit philosophical framing. Despite this widespread entanglement, their distinction in various ways—rarely at the level of definition, as in the case of Islam—makes it possible to organize our comparisons according to the three subcategories.

In chapters 8 and 9 of *Ultimate Realities*, we discussed in detail what is meant by the justification of such categories. We noted the importance of not relying solely on the "what seems obvious to us after a long while" approach to justification. That works better in a mixed group like ours than with an individual theorist, to be sure, because the degree of cross-checking and the chances of noticing parochial readings—leaving aside the compassionate yet colorful ways we have discovered to point such lapses out to each other—are much greater. Nevertheless, that essentially phenomenological criterion for the adequacy of comparative categories is still vulnerable to bias; even groups have blind spots corresponding to shared assumptions about what is obvious and we did not have the luxury or problem of an even larger and more diverse group. As important as it is, therefore, phenomenological reasons for categories need to be supplemented with other lines of justification.

There are at least four other ways of justifying comparative categories.[1] Two of these are more conceptual in character and correspond to insights registered in philosophical and archetypal approaches to comparison. They are: (1) accounts of what is conceptually feasible that are capable of explaining why some ideas recur and others don't show up at all; and (2) accounts of the structured relationships among ideas that are capable of explaining why some transformations of ideas occur with more frequency than others. With regard to these two lines of justification, we claim with the philosophers, mystics, and archetypal theorists that there are genuine limits on what ideas tend to work for religious traditions and that no amount of historical analysis can help to explain the preponderance of ideas of that sort. The other two ways are more historical and contextual in nature and express the wisdom garnered over the years from the historical approaches to the study of religions. They are: (3) accounts of social, biological, and historical circumstances that are capable of explaining why certain religious ideas originated when and how they did; and (4) accounts of origins of social, biological, and historical circumstances that are capable of explaining why certain religious ideas transform in the flux of events in some ways and not others. With regard to these types of warrant for our comparative categories, we claim with the historians and sociologists that knowing the range of the conceptually feasible from the first two kinds of accounts does not begin to settle the question of why a religious tradition realizes particular possibilities and not others. An answer to that question requires an understanding of specific features of the relevant contexts within the blessed rage that is the history of cultures and religions.

This chapter makes use of these lines of justification in a variety of ways. In all our treatment is rather uneven, with a bias toward the conceptual rather than the historical, reflecting the competencies and limitations of the authors, though this bias does not reflect our interests because all four lines of justification strike us as vital. With regard to the first, the main conceptual justification for our threefold set of subcategories is the theory of truth presented in the following chapter. It is there that we distinguish between epistemological truth and performative truth, noticing how various are the felicity conditions that apply in any given case. Epistemological truth corresponds directly to our first category; performative truth is parsed into two categories in this chapter with important variations in felicity conditions due to the differences between sacred texts and personal or communal forms of piety. With regard to the second line of justification, our analysis in chapter 8 of the connections between epistemological and performative truth explains why it is that our three categories are entangled yet distinguishable, as rehearsed above. It also explains why a tradition giving one dimension of religious truth special prominence is likely to find itself trying to find ways to make more room for the others, too, perhaps in very different ways. With regard to the third and fourth lines of justification, we freely acknowledge our weakness in this area. We will be content if the reader notices our use of them as this chapter unfolds, beginning with our appeal to the legal style of Islamic philosophy as a key historical condition for its peculiarly integrated theory of religious language.

The purpose of this summary chapter is not to enumerate the various ways by which our traditions and the texts studies specify the nature of religious truth, although some of that will be found here. The specialists' chapters do that admirably themselves. The purpose rather is say in some cumulative sense what religious truth is, as that might be found from our traditions, making explicit the comparisons among them and with our own theory in chapter 8. We shall focus on the three subcategories in turn, beginning in section 7.2 with consideration of the nature of truth as an epistemological problem, which is also involved with ontological and cosmological matters as illustrated in chapters 1, 3, and 6 especially. Subsequently we shall turn to religious truth in texts (7.3) and religious truth as a matter of cultivation or embodiment (7.4). Finally, section 7.5 deals with a theme turned up by all of our specialists: religious truth as contrasted with error, deceit, and failure. This gives us a convenient way to become more specific about some of the felicity conditions that apply to various kinds of religious truth.

Reflecting on the specialists' chapters in this volume, it becomes clear how fortuitous was the choice of the earlier two topics, namely, the human condition and ultimate realities. What one takes the human condition to be makes a great difference in how one relates to reference, meaning, and interpretation. Significant differences are registered if you think that human life, and hence its truth claims, are constantly changing and relating to similarly changing things; or that human life is fundamentally unified and stable so that the appearances of changing consciousness and objects is only illusion; or that life needs to escape suffering by abandoning identification with things that appear stable but are not, including oneself. So also with differences among conceptions of ultimate realities, both ontological and anthropological (oriented toward some religious quest). The specialists' chapters in this volume have been written with many back-references to their treatments of the human condition and ultimate realities in the earlier volumes.

7.2 Religious Truth as an Epistemological Problem

With these goals and this plan in mind, we shall consider several spectra of positions on the nature of truth as an epistemological problem. One concerns reference, and its poles are static reference on one end and dynamic on the other. A second concerns meaning, and its poles are that religious truth is close to ordinary truth on one end and on the other that religious truth is extraordinary or esoteric. A third concerns how interpreters treat the religious claims with which they engage reality, as propositions at one pole or as holistic enactments at the other. It is already clear from these spectra that discussion of religious truth as an epistemological problem will lead naturally into other dimensions of religious truth. Reference, meaning, and interpretation are thematized in chapter 8.

Consider first the spectrum regarding reference. Kohn and Miller (1.2.1) emphasize a strong contrast between static and dynamic theories of truth. Although there are not many candidates for static theories as they depict them, their emphasis on dynamic truth is powerful because they conceive both the object of truth and the interpreting claims of truth to be dynamic. The cosmos and the Dao are in flux, and therefore the ways to refer to them need also to be in flux. Thus, they reject the views that there are stable ultimate realities such as the Dao or stable goals for human religious perfection. In order to keep track of these ultimates, cognition itself needs to play from one form to another, working indirectly. Because the form of true religious interpretation in China, according to Kohn and Miller, is skillful practice, not the assertion of a logically formed proposition (1.2.1), mastery of indirect speech is part of skilled practice for religious thinkers and writers.

Even in the Chinese case, however, there are limits to the double-duty dynamism. Factoring in the higher levels of truth, Kohn and Miller point out that one who knows ultimate truth is like the hub of a spinning wheel, itself "at rest in the center of all, one with the cosmic openness at the root of creation" (1.2.2). This being "at rest in the center of all" is at least a relativizing of dynamism. The Confucian emphasis on the rectification of names also needs treatment before the Chinese case is settled with respect to dynamism and static elements of truth.

But at the opposite end of this spectrum are the religions of India that assume a double-duty theory of static truth, at least in religion at the higher levels. As Clooney has argued throughout the seminar, supported by Eckel, what is really real is supposed to be beyond change, and if something can be shown to change, that is an argument against its full reality. Moreover, the way to know the static reality is with a static mental act like a perception or intuition. Inference and some other forms of knowing might be unavoidable, as chapter 3 indicates; but perception, even intuitive perception, is what is most adequate to a static really real reality.

The two religions of India we studied, Hinduism and Buddhism, draw different morals from this. The former defends the reality of static ultimates and the validity of intuitive perception or realization. The latter claims that there are no ontologically ultimate static realities and that suffering arises from people's clinging convictions that there are. Buddhism itself has a spectrum of opinions on this point. Eckel in chapter 3 has nicely contrasted the Yogācāra view that only the intuitive perception of the moment is real and, being static, is swept away with time, with the Madhyamaka view that there is not even that much static reality or realistic perceptive cognition.

Between these poles are the monotheistic faiths that do not allow univocal stasis or univocal dynamism in either objects or truth claims that refer to them: the eternal is also temporal. In various historically related ways, Judaism, Christianity, and Islam affirm that God is somehow eternal and beyond change, and yet related dynamically to human beings in revealing, judging, and eschatological ways. By the same token, each of those faiths claims that there are laws, or doctrines, or revealed commandments that are stably true, even if subject to interpretation. Yet all would claim that our understanding of these is finite and ready for revision, as in ongoing commentary, understanding awaiting heavenly vision, or human law (*fiqh*).

All the positions across the spectrum of reference illustrate the three forms of reference (8.3): iconicity, indexicality, and convention, with some limiting cases. The very idea of contrasting the static and dynamic with regard to religious theories of truth supposes that at least some ideas, if not the very form of assertion or claim, is iconic with reality. Kohn and Miller, in fact, argue that because reality is dynamic, proper claims about it should be dynamic too, and therefore it is a good thing that Hansen has shown that Daoism,[2] and Chinese language more broadly, provides a dynamic way of referring with claims of deference and skillful practice. Claims in Advaita Vedānta, and perhaps other forms of non-dual Hinduism and Buddhism, and in some monotheistic mystical traditions, are thought to be wholly iconic to the exclusion of indexicality or convention, with no difference whatsoever between the reality and the intuitive cognition of it.

Similarly, to the extent that religious claims become nearly exclusively performative, matters of skillful practice that are completely ethical and not theoretical, their reference comes close to being wholly indexical.

When this is carried to an extreme, as in Zhuangzi, the conventional elements in truth are denigrated and used only indirectly to point to the appropriate action. In those strands of monotheistic faiths that stress the paradigm of the Word of God and view that Word as incomprehensible by ordinary human rationality, the emphasis on the conventionality of religious claims can be extreme.

Consider now the spectrum regarding meaning. At one end is the view that religious truth is rather like ordinary truth. Clooney in chapter 2 develops this at great length for certain positions within Hinduism. Perception is the most reliable means to ordinary truth, even though it needs to be supplemented by other forms of knowing. What distinguishes religious from other truth is the object, not the knowing. This position is not characteristic of all forms of Hinduism, obviously, certainly not the non-dual forms in which the non-dual perceptive intuition (if that is how one characterizes realization of the non-dual) is extraordinary and is contrasted with the māyā of ordinary perception.

Moving along this spectrum we come to various positions that suppose that the religiously important truth requires some special development in the interpreter so that it is truth at a higher level. Eckel, in chapter 3 and in *Ultimate Realities*, chapter 6, as well as *The Human Condition*, chapter 3, elaborates a subtle interpretation of several versions of the Buddhist "two truths" doctrine that distinguishes conventional from enlightened truth. The distinctive contribution of some forms of Mahāyāna Buddhism is the distinction of these two truths from the conventional standpoint and their identification from the enlightened standpoint. Kohn and Miller (chapter 1) discuss the improved knowledge of "perfected" people, noting that there are many different schools in China that encourage somewhat different senses of perfection. Saldarini (chapter 4, and also chapter 2 in *Ultimate Realities*) notes the special skills developed by rabbis in the Talmudic tradition, and also the esoteric knowledge both of philosophers such as Maimonides and Kabbalists. Fredriksen explores the movement in Augustine from unlettered faith (Monica) to rhetoric, from there to bad philosophy (the Manichees), to good philosophy (Platonists and Neo-Platonists), and to the Christian philosophy, which affirms that true wisdom has more to do with what you love than what you know in the other philosophic senses. As a result, unlettered Monica turns out to have the higher truth of love rather than the mere lower truth of sophisticated cognition. This is something like a Mahāyāna Buddhist identification of the most sophisticated with the least, though also something different from that insofar as Christian movement to the higher truth is a refocusing and intensification of love and attachment, whereas the Buddhist trajectory is opposite. Fredriksen also significantly notes

Augustine's conviction that true knowing of the highest sort requires a heavenly vision with a heavenly body, and that all finite earthly philosophical or theological expressions of truth, no matter how well-guided by love, are fallible and at best proleptic. All of this shows what has appeared frequently in our work, namely, that felicity conditions for epistemological truth in religious matters forcefully draw other dimensions of religious truth into the picture.

Consider finally the spectrum of means of engagement, that is, the things that might be true of reality when interpreted. The spectrum runs from propositions to holistic enactments. Several of our authors insist that religious truth is not propositional. Kohn and Miller do so from the standpoint of their interpretation of Chinese language, to the effect that it is not subject-predicate propositional and is instead to be understood in terms of performance. But the significance of this is not always clear. After all, it can be said in Chinese that the cat is on the mat. Can anything religiously important be said in Chinese propositions? One way of identifying a proposition is by asking whether it has a negation, for example, "the cat is *not* on the mat." Kohn and Miller cite the beginning of the *Daode jing*, a negative proposition: "The Tao (Way) that can be told of is not the eternal Tao." The meanings of some of the terms in this phrase are controversial, but a claim is made nonetheless, even if in propositional form different from the subject-object propositional form of Indo-European languages. Or consider the claim made by some Neo-Confucians that Dao is Li (Principle), not an easy proposition but a proposition nevertheless with direct religious significance.

Others of our authors are quite comfortable with a propositional form for religious truth claims. Clooney in chapter 2 and even more in *Ultimate Realities,* chapter 5, discusses religious truth claims in scholastically formed, precise propositions, understood across competing schools. Eckel also emphasizes debates among schools in propositional form, especially in the work of Bhāvaviveka, beginning in *The Human Condition* chapter 3. Augustine, the subject of Fredriksen's chapter, argued philosophy propositionally, and is regarded by many to be the founding forerunner of Medieval Christian scholasticism. Saldarini discusses religiously important propositions in both rabbinic disputations over the law and in Jewish philosophy. Haq discusses law, Islamic Aristotelianism, and the creative Islamic philosophy of al-Ghazālī, all of which involve propositional assertions of religious importance.

We conclude that all of our traditions are friendly to the propositional form for religious claims *in certain circumstances*. The circumstances have to do with the existence of a sufficiently public and universally accepted context that the myriad qualifications of the propositional form in interpretation, noted in 8.2, can be taken for granted. This flexibility of felicity conditions with regard to the truth of religious claims in propositional form appeared in all of the traditions we studied. In the scholastic Hindu-Buddhist debates, the contexts of formal argumentation and a history of interaction make the religiously significant propositions, for instance, that "God (the Lord, Īśvara, Nārāyaṇa) exists" rather like "the cat is on the mat." Medieval Jewish-Christian-Muslim scholasticism is similar. Legal and commentarial traditions can also reach such contextualized stability. Kohn and Miller represent the Chinese religious tradition as being unfriendly to such stable contexts, with its insistence that thought like the rest of reality is on the move. They are right (1.2.1) that the Chinese school of logicians, with its attempt to formulate propositions so that yes or no affirmations can be made of them, was never popular with either Daoists or Confucians. Perhaps they underplay the Confucian conviction that proper harmony with the Dao requires the rectification of names, although they would be correct to say that rectified names rectify use rather than automatically give rise to rectified propositions. Their fascinating discussion of the Chinese sense of connectivity established through the replication of patterns in different parts of reality, and macro-microcosmically, seems to stand at odds with verbal propositions; but what they say of the use of those patterns has an uncanny analogy to the early Wittgenstein's theory of facts and propositions. Admitting that there are few scholastic contexts in China outside of Neo-Confucianism for the widespread agreement on univocal meanings for religiously important propositions, it still can be said that, where those contexts exist (for instance, in Han or Song Confucianism), religious truth has happily been claimed by means of propositions.

The reference here to scholastic contexts, however, underscores the central point in our own theory of religious truth as far as epistemological matters are concerned. Truth claims are made in interpretations and the qualifications of reference, meaning, and the various contexts of interpretation are all part of the felicity conditions for truth claims. Where those qualifications can be taken for granted, the truth claim can be treated as a proposition, that is, as a syntactical assertion whose terms and structure are defined by a semiotic system. Where those qualifications cannot be taken for granted, the very identification of the truth claim itself must make reference to more than its propositional form, even if a proposition is used in expressing it.

The other end of this spectrum, then, is the situation in which the religious truth claim consists in the entire interpretive act, including the registration in the interpreter of what is important in the object as represented by the ideas involved. If something is claimed truly, then the interpreter is different from what would be the case if the claim were not true but false, or if the claim were not made. The difference is the actual carryover of what is valuable or important into the interpreter in the intentional respects. The result of having the truth about the religious object is to be rightly oriented and related to that object, at least in the respects in question. In this sense, any religious truth is "enacted in religious lives" (1.2), namely those of the interpreters.

We insist in 8.2 that interpretation is an intentional engagement of reality, with give and take, including the carryover of something important from reality into the interpreters. Enactment of truth, or "embodiment" as some of our authors put it, thus has to do with the differential ways that true ideas shape the dynamics of engagement. Moreover, one of the most obvious felicity conditions of whether something is true is whether acting upon it integrates one better with reality, discriminating real distinctions of fact and importance. A religiously learned person ought to have poise and adeptness in dealing with life in its religious aspects. Pragmatic tests of this sort can be simple or complex. If Chinese culture is as dynamic as Kohn and Miller say, and we agree with them, then religious adeptness can be tested in many ways large and small. If the religious object is a ritual, a true knowledge of it will be displayed in its performance. If the religious object is a divine ground or creator who transcends subject-object distinctions and with which human beings cannot obviously interact, the pragmatic tests of dynamic engagement are far more complicated. Still, as Fredriksen reminds us for Augustine, a true knowledge of God proves itself in shaping the devotee to love God aright. We believe that all the religions we studied would agree with something like our thesis that religious truth is the carryover of what is important in the religious object into the interpreter so that this registers in and rightly relates the interpreter to the object.[3] Identifying the religious "claim" which is said to be true depends on whether some or all of that larger dynamic interpretive engagement can be bracketed as assumed. So we suggest that all of our traditions occupy all the positions along the spectrum from religious truth as proposition to religious truth as skillful action or performance. It should be noted that this spectrum is different from the one to be discussed below concerning the degree to which interpreters need to be perfected in higher learning in order to enact or embody certain truths.

7.3 Religious Truth as Expressed in Sacred Texts and Objects

Kohn and Miller (1.3) give the most fulsome catalogue of expressions of truth, distinguishing words, syntax, sounds, signs, talismans, and charts, as well as scriptures. All of these have analogues in most of the religions we studied, though few were focused on by the other authors. Many fascinating questions arise about the senses in which mantras, music, mudras, and maps might be true. For instance, in what respects are they iconic, indexical, or purely conventional? How can they be wrong? Most of us would agree that there are religiously important ideas in music. Clooney has written an important book on Mīmāmsā ritual.[4] By stating the subject matter of this project to be the comparison of religious *ideas*, however, we discouraged thorough pursuit of these questions, taking for granted that ideas are something like words and are expressed in texts rather than scores. What is most fruitful to interpret here, therefore, is the problematic of scriptures, their alternatives, and their authority.

Our discussions demonstrated that each religious tradition we studied has a multitude of approaches to scripture. This is not to say that every tradition has some expression of every possible approach. But it is to acknowledge that few if any approaches are the exclusive preserve of any one tradition.

In *Ultimate Realities*, chapters 2 and 4, it was pointed out that for some elements of Judaism and some elements of Islam, the Torah and Qur'ān respectively are ultimate realities, part of or definitive of divinity. Christians have generally thought that the New Testament is a human testimony to divine revelation in Christ, perhaps guaranteed in its accuracy by God; but "God in Christ" and not the Bible is usually taken to be the Logos, the true Word. The inclusion of scripture, or a scripture-archetype, within divinity is a complication for the theologies of these monotheistic faiths that like to think of their divinities as pure and simple. Nevertheless, that extreme approach to scripture has been part of reflective piety in those traditions, and perhaps also in some Hindu attitudes toward the Vedas and in some medieval Daoist construals of the heavenly origin of their scripture.

A more common approach has been to take scriptures to be authoritative because they are related to the foundations of things or are themselves cosmically founding. Thus, it is more common in Judaism and Islam to regard scriptures as dictated by God than to see them as themselves as aspects of divinity. As Fredriksen points out, the earliest Christians were Jews and followed the Jewish belief in this respect, however much they interpreted the Septuagint differently from other Second Temple Jewish groups. Because of their origin, scriptures according to these approaches have an absolutely trumping authority over other sources of religious knowledge. Without being regularly assumed to be of divine origin, some Hindu schools give all of the Vedas that absolutely trumping authority, and some, for instance, Śaṅkara's Advaita Vedānta, accord only the Upaniṣads that authority.

The problem with trumping authority of course is that it has to be interpreted, and the interpretations themselves are rarely held to have that same trumping authority, especially when they conflict with one another in diverging commentarial traditions. Nevertheless, there are strong as well as weak claims made for the authority of the interpretations. Fundamentalisms in all the traditions assume that their interpretations are literally true of the scriptures. Most traditions also recognize, however, that interpretation itself is ampliative. Some go so far as to say that God guides the interpretation with greater or lesser control and hence certainty; this is frequently asserted by Christians regarding the Holy Spirit. Others say that some finite and fallible yet authoritative institution, for instance the rabbis, the Christian bishops in council, or the legal scholars in Islam, provide decisive interpretations. Most of our traditions recognize that specific commentators become authoritative because their intelligence, wit, penetration, clarity of expression, or personal piety make them charismatic in some sense, and attractive to followers who treat their commentaries as founding or advancing a school.

For Buddhism, Confucianism, and at least classical Daoism, there are no scriptures with absolute authority of the sort attributed to the Qur'ān. Buddhism is explicit in rejecting the Vedas and Upaniṣads. Yet the Buddhist sūtras became authoritative in a less absolute way as defining interpretations of the Way upon which schools are based. The Buddhist "canon" of several hundred books is too long for anyone to study completely and the sense of its authority, as well as its content, varies from school to school. Buddhist sūtras function in liturgical practice and as intellectual centers of gravity, calling forth commentaries, much like West Asian scriptures for which more authority is claimed. There are West Asian theologians, especially since the European Enlightenment, who regard the Bible and Qur'ān to be authoritative in non-absolute senses, one among many sources of religious knowledge.

The classics and Four Books of Confucianism, and the *Daode jing* and *Zhuangzi* of Daoism, have a great though not absolute authority; they are not always treated as trumping authorities. Rather they are treated as sources of insight and enlightenment, guidance and inspiration. They are frequently cited to bolster a position, and when used in refutation, are used indirectly. Taken to be classic repositories of wisdom, they are the subjects of many commentaries, and the origins of diverse commentarial traditions. The notorious split within Neo-Confucianism between the Cheng-Zhu and Lu-Wang schools is symbolically centered over the interpretation of the Great Learning, one of the Four Books. But the competition is over how best to edit and interpret the ancient scripture, not over whether the opponent is wrong because in contradiction to scripture.[5] Although our conversations frequently mentioned scripture, and the question of the authority of scripture was mentioned, especially in conjunction with Śaṅkara's argument for Advaita Vedānta, scripture was not as important a topic for our discussions of truth as might be expected. Issues of authority, particular scriptural authority, have been important for most of our traditions, indeed for all if one counts criticism and rejection of authority. Yet our discussions, perhaps affected by European Enlightenment impulses about what counts for truth, sought out appeals to reason and experience more than appeals to scripture. Perhaps our comparative conversations were more in sync with Saldarini's reflections on Judaism in modernity (4.6) than we would have liked, had we been more aware of the texture of discussion at the time. All this was true for our group, despite our tendency to focus on premodern texts.

One more issue needs to be raised about expressions of truth. Both in this volume and in the previous ones a wide variety of genres of religious writing have been discussed. These reflect at least the current research interests of our specialists, if not their abiding preferences regarding expressions of religious truth. Kohn and Miller love parables, pictures, and how-to manuals. Clooney loves theological digests and student guidebooks. Fredriksen loves theologians who twist in the winds of disputation. Saldarini and Haq are intent on synoptic visions of diverse genres connected through time. Eckel loves stories. These genres are manifested in all our traditions. All involve propositions of some sort or other and all suppose existential affects on those who participate in them. But a special mention needs to be made of story.

Eckel from the beginning of the project has been sensitive to the difference between religious truth contained in metaphorically potent stories and that expressed in more philosophic forms. The construction of the entire project has had a philosophic, systematic metaphoric base. That is part of the reason that the organizing principles of *The Human Condition* and its summary chapters presenting hypotheses for further study were called "Confucian." His own expositions of Buddhism have included not only philosophical analyses and diagrams but also many stories. He argued that the entire approach to the human condition ought to be framed around the story-form of the search for a soteriological goal, such as the release from suffering. In the present volume he not only tells the marvelous story of Aṅgulimāla, which is cited by several other authors, but also the story of how he told a story in *Ultimate Realities* about translating the Dalai Lama. What is it that makes good stories so powerful? What are the felicity conditions for such stories? When, why, and how are they true?

The narrative form of understanding is intriguing. It is also awkward because it usually involves an allegorical translation of the story into a moral for hearers; yet allegory is unpopular these days among hermeneutical thinkers. Narratives stand at the cusp of mere particularity and universality.[6] On the one hand, narratives particularize their participants and call attention to the particularity of situations and meanings. They give particular directions or templates for how to act and that makes their interpretation a matter of particular, actual, response. This accords with several Buddhist senses of "suchness" and is illustrated by Eckel's chapter for this volume that emphasizes the rejection of universal conventional meanings in favor of the particularity of dharmas arising in consciousness (Yogācāra), if even that (Madhyamaka). On the other hand, important stories have applicability far beyond their apparently historical form. "Once upon a time" means "and for you too, perhaps." Narratives provide frames in terms of which others think of their own lives as having something like that narrative form.

In shaping responsiveness, narrative both presupposes broad applicability and drives its hearers toward particular responses. Thus, the felicity conditions for narratives—the conditions under which they are true—blend universal and particular elements. One way of breaking this down further is to say that narrative conjoins the typological with the personal, and then to parse felicity conditions into those two categories.

On the one hand, then, to be true at the typological level, stories must be representative. They achieve this especially by focusing their themes on universal human experiences such as birth, death, friendship, family, sickness, adventure, suffering, or war. Their faithful recounting of the feelings associated with and consequences of decisions taken in such contexts make up one sort of felicity condition; the hearers of stories need to recognize themselves in the story in one way or another. Identification is one precondition for the story to have potency for personal change. There is an obvious downside here: human beings are fully particular, "thises" as Duns Scotus, the Christian medieval realist, called them. Sometimes what is religiously important to a person is what is absolutely particular and unique, or a typical event in its absolutely unique aspect of being "mine"; consider birth and death.

On the other hand, to be true at the individual level, stories must evoke more than constrain response, through making space for the hearer to identify with and interpret the narrative in his or her own, unique way. Even though a person's true story might not be generalizable, stories retain their effectiveness through allowing each individual hearer to read their own true story into the narrative structure. This is one kind of felicity condition that balances the felicity conditions for the typological, universal side. Another kind of felicity condition on the individual side bears on the concreteness of stories. Particular and interesting characters are the best way to do this; they make for the best stories. There is a downside here, too, and it is the confusion that can be induced by the narratives eschewal of abstractions, even if abstractions are truer in respect of descriptive accuracy. For instance, God in narrative has a finite role, and all of our religions that refer to an ultimate as God either assert that God is beyond finite roles or is not to be understood in narrative form. People can undo such suggestions, juxtaposing contradictory stories then depending on a communal context within which such narrative tensions can become thoroughly absorbed.

7.4 Religious Truth as Cultivation and Embodiment

We have met with claims about the cultivation and embodiment of truth several times in this chapter. Let us now distinguish more precisely between two problematics that might have reference here. One is the point we have noticed for all or most religious truth claims, indeed for any interpretation affirming something to be true or false, namely, that the interpreter is affected by having the truth. The effect might be minimal, such as filling in information of the sort the interpreter expects to deal with; or it might be profound, learning something that transforms thinking theoretically or transforms life practically. We have argued so far that because interpretation is engagement, it develops and perhaps alters how the interpreters are oriented toward the world. In religious matters, religious truths alter how the interpreter is oriented to ultimate realities in respects in which the truth claim stands for them.

The other sense of cultivation and embodiment supposes the first but has to do with how the interpreter's character is enriched, elevated, and transformed by some means or other so that it is possible for higher level truths to be registered. This is, a person's spiritual character needs to be developed in certain ways if reality is to be interpreted in certain higher level respects. The discussion of the spectrum of meaning ranging from ordinary to esoteric truths in 7.2 marks out some of the issues about the different levels of meaning. The topic here is the transformations of character required for the extraordinary levels to be accessed. Our topic is sageliness, or saintliness in regard to the attainment of truth.[7] In some traditions it is said that the yogis *actualize* or *realize* the truth.

Kohn and Miller use the locution "the perfected" to describe any number of models of spiritual growth. In Chinese religion, the human condition is conceived to be in full continuity with the rest of the cosmos.[8]

Spiritual growth, then, is seen as tapping into the ultimate elements of the universe, the Dao, which are already part of human nature but ordinarily obscured. China has different models of what the ultimate is, and how to access it, including Daoist unknowing, Confucian ritual creation, and medieval Daoist esoteric practices to connect with the Dao both outwardly and inwardly.[9] Birdwhistell reminds us that these models are coded for gender and ethnic identification. Neither the means chosen nor the conception of the ultimate that needs to be accessed in the perfected truth are agreed upon by the various Chinese schools. The Daoists and Confucians are largely opposed to one another on the roles of conventions in both method and goal. But both would agree, under different interpretations, with the Confucian statement of the goal, "to be one body with the world."[10] The achievement of that goal allows for effective action on the one hand, moving with the joints of the Dao, and also stillness and centeredness like the hub of a turning wheel. Thus, the Chinese case illustrates both that every interpretation claiming to be true in religious matters needs to be understood in terms of the performatory difference the claim makes to the interpreters, and that adepts need to work hard to be good at accessing the subtle and most powerful elements of the cosmos. That labor might be in disciplined, even esoteric, paths. See chapter 1 for comparisons with other traditions on this point.

None of the other religions has quite the cosmological continuity in its conception of the human condition that Chinese religion has.[11] The Mahāyāna Buddhist position, both Yogācāra and Madhyamaka, is closest with regard to continuity, although it asserts a continuity of mind rather than cosmic stuff (*qi*). For the Buddhists of both sorts treated in chapter 3, the transformations needed to embody the religious truth (of ultimate emptiness) are all within the contours of mind, regardless of the dynamics of ontological realities. Whereas in the case of Chinese religion the yoga is to open the mental part of the *qi* to the grosser, and finally the finer, foundations of the *qi*, in the case of our forms of Mahāyāna Buddhism the yoga is so to alter the functions of mind that its references involve no attachments. This is a shift wholly within intentionality, from an intentionality of specific hope for objective things to one of acceptance of things *in their samsāric appearance* as all that is real and worthy. The Buddhist schools differ over what survives as "reality."

Hinduisms, as one might expect by now in light of their dialectical rejection of Buddhism, take the transformation of soul in the cultivation of communion with the divine to be a move over an infinite divide between finite things whose particulars and limitations are nothing except those limitations, and enlightenment or participation in the freedom of attaching to form voluntarily. As Clooney argues here (chapter 2) and argued in

Ultimate Realities, chapter 5, not all apprehensions of religious truth claims need to involve more than learning or appreciating arguments. In this sense not all transformations involved in truth claims are very great, nor does the transformation require a reorientation from the finite to the infinite. However, his discussions of Advaita Vedānta in *The Human Condition* and in this volume indicate that a transformation of soul of vast proportion is required to enter into (or discover its) non-dual relation to the rest of things. Clooney has argued that the act of reading texts, which might seem to be minimally transforming existentially, in fact can lead to vast transformative changes characteristic of non-dualist experience or bhakti devotion.[12]

Judaism, Christianity, and Islam are alike in encouraging one family of transformations, namely, from ordinary shortsightedness to appreciation by faith of the presence of God in some finite Word, for instance, in the Torah, Jesus Christ, or the Qur'ān. Perhaps it is fair to say schematically that this transformation has two steps. The first step is to come to appreciate the word or its representation as being authoritative. The second is to be able to see (feel, hear, understand) the divine to be present in the Word. Although there are many paths through these transformations, they do not seem to be distinguished according to religious tradition. All the traditions acknowledge that acceptance of authority might simply be a matter of growing up in the traditional culture, or a conversion from a different attitude toward the authority. All have some version of priority of will to knowledge, as in "faith seeking understanding." All also acknowledge that faith in the authority of the Word can be built up through argument and incremental understanding. Each of the traditions urges that practice with the symbols recognizing authority can lead to increasing adeptness with them in engaging the Word in question as authoritative. They also agree that the transformation to the point of recognizing the authority can be effected by something quite different from the symbols of the authority itself, a shock, or even sudden insight about something else entirely.

The second step, taking the divine to be present in the authoritative Word, differs among Judaism, Christianity, and Islam according to their different conceptions of the divine. On this, see *The Human Condition*, chapter 7, and chapters 1–6 of *Ultimate Realities*. The transformations of soul required to see the authoritative Word as the dwelling of God might be differently described in the three traditions, but they all involve enhancing aptitude with the symbols of the Word and God so as to experience them as characterizing the same reality. This is not a matter of logic alone, for the logical assertion of the presence of the divine in the Word is not difficult. What is difficult, a matter of great skill and spiritual maturity, is to experience them as characterizing the same thing. Such a transformation is more likely to be called an intensification and purification of piety than an advance in learning, though it is still the acquisition of a higher level of truth.

Judaism, Christianity, and Islam are also alike in having mystical traditions that advocate transforming the soul so as to be able to glimpse infinite divinity. We mean "infinite" here in a vague sense simply to denote religious objects characterized as transcending candidate finite determinations. The mysticisms are apophatic. The three traditions differ within themselves as well as among themselves in modeling the infinite. The Neo-Platonic model is perhaps most common, especially as it has been elaborated in the "perennial philosophy." It provides a clear way of thinking about the infinite and how it might relate to finite things that emanate from it. Creation models are common to the three traditions, though there are several of these. In the mystical path, the required transformation of soul is that the mind must somehow become able to apprehend the infinite with both the kataphatic structure of the path and the apophatic denial of final determination at once. This is done for some by using complicated metaphysical theories as interpretive signs, by others using highly metaphoric conventional signs as in Kabbalah, and by yet others by transforming the cognitive intentionality to something like devotion or love that takes an infinite object. This last is what Fredriksen ascribes to Augustine, for whom final knowledge is not possible in this body but is required to be in some (celestial) body.

Bearing in mind the Chinese case particularly, the perfected "vision" is not only a cognitive truth claim but also an existential one. That is, the sage lives in greater attunement with all things bearing on the ultimate, with greater powers of accomplishment in ordinary affairs as well as heroic engagements of the ultimate. As Kohn and Miller point out, there are different schools concerning what the content of these powers and their objects are.

7.5 Religious Truth as Opposed to Error, Deceit, and Failure

This survey of various dimensions of religious truth as we encountered them in our study has involved distinguishing between the sorts of things that can be true (e.g., claims, texts, transformations) and also specifying the sense that truth has in each case by describing the applicable felicity conditions. In concluding this chapter, we revisit the question of felicity questions from another angle, namely, explicit discussions of them provided by the religious traditions themselves. One way that felicity conditions for the various dimensions of religious truth are often registered in the religious traditions we studied is in terms of its opposite or lack. All the specialist chapters, in one way or another, characterize religious truth in such terms. Kohn and Miller (1.2.4) make the strong claim that the opposite is not error so much as failure to attain the mark, the inability to develop an appropriate level of performance. "Failure to attain the mark" is one of the Christian words for sin (*hamartia*). This comes from the view, prevalent in several traditions, that the most important religious truth is the one in which the person or community is transformed so as to "be in the truth," or, as in the case of Chinese religion, to behave truthfully in religious matters.

In this section we shall distinguish three generic opposites to truth, corresponding to our major subcategories of religious truth. The opposite of epistemological truth is error, of truth in expressions deceit, and of truth in embodiment failure.

In epistemological truth, an interpretive idea is supposed to carry over what is important in the object into the interpreter in the respect in which the idea represents the object. If it does carry over the value, it is true, and if it does not, it is false. Truth is thus a dyadic value: either true or false. To use the Aristotelian language, a claim is true if it says of what is that it is and of what is not that it is not.

Immediately upon saying this we must admit qualifications. Given the complexity of most religious truth claims, the best we can hope for is that the interpreted claim is partially true, true in some ways but not others, in some contexts but not others, limited by apparently countertruths, and so forth. Fortunately the theory of religious truth in chapter 8 gives us a precise way of specifying these qualifications. It is helpful to list the kinds of qualifications that apply in principle, although chapter 8 will have to be consulted for the explanations of the qualifications:

- A claim might be true in one context but not in a slightly different context because all truth claims are concretely contextualized in interpretations.
- A claim might be true in its intellectual but not in its practical interpretation.
- A claim might be true in its practical but not its intellectual interpretation.
- A claim might be true in the abstract context of theory but not in broader contexts.
- A claim might be true insofar as it shapes a community but false in theory and unimportant in devotions.
- A claim might be true for a specific devotional use but dangerous for the broader community and absurd in theory.
- A claim might be true for the right referent but false for a slightly different referent that is easily mistaken for the right one.

- A claim might be true for some secondary referents but inexpressive for others.
- A claim might be true on one level of meaning but not on others.
- A claim might be true within its own symbol system in isolation but false when overlaid on or resonating with other systems.
- A claim might be true in some respect but not in others, and these might be confused.
- A claim might be true in a limited domain of application but not when generalized.
- A claim might be true generally or vaguely, but not specifically in ways that carry over what is important.

If one were to sort through all these qualifications and still be able to ask the yes-no question, then the truth claim is simply either true or false. The opposite of truth is to be in error. One of the purposes of theological inquiry in all religious traditions is to sort the special confusions in these qualifications and to be able to frame genuinely determinable theological questions. The beauty of scholastic traditions is that they confront these qualifications head-on. The faintness of their beauty is that, after all the qualifications are specified and the truth question asked, the resultant expression is likely to be so complex and pallid that nobody gives a damn and many people suspect they fail to contain the living waters.

Islam is particularly meticulous in distinguishing between heretics and infidels. A heretic is someone who presumably had access to the true interpretations, perhaps even in their existential complexity and intensity, and nevertheless declares some true idea false or a false idea true. The heretic is in a genuinely dyadic situation, though all the qualifications mentioned above might provide mitigating circumstances. An infidel is one whose religious ideas either are not up to interpreting the religious object in the relevant important respects or are so alien as to fail to affirm what is true (according to the tradition) because the ideas that would carry over what is true are missing in that person. The infidel thus is in a triadic situation of not having the right meanings at hand; of course, the reason for this might be voluntary rejection of the preferred ideas, and so on.

In expressive truth, the failure to be true is to deceive, that is, to mislead the interpreter. The ideas appear to be true when used to interpret the object, but in fact carry over the wrong thing. This is an extremely complicated issue when considering different genres of theological ideas and different kinds of religious expression. We did not spend much time on this except to discuss narrative, philosophical, and metaphoric expressions. Each can be deceitful or misleading. Deceit suggests an intent to mislead, which might not lie behind every wrong expression. But even if there is no personal intent, a person misled by an expression will think himself or herself deceived, if only by their own gullibility.

The question of authority for expressions is particularly intertwined with deception. In a foundational sense, a misplaced authority has the deliberate element that transforms an innocently misleading word to a deceptive one. This is why, in traditions that lay great stock in the authority of scriptures, disagreements about authority so easily become vitriolic: a scripture that turns out to have no authority after all has been a deceiver in claiming authority, and those deceived sense themselves also to have been betrayed. Whoever persuaded the interpreter to accept the authority in the first place has been a deceiver, even if that person as interpreter is also deceived. The transformations of mind previously discussed involved with accepting authority are also subject to being revealed to be deceptive.

In the long run, deceit in expression is primarily a function of error in epistemological truth. But not entirely so. If expressions are inadequate to carry over what is important, that might not be a function of a choice between expressions (dyadic error) but a failure of imagination. It is imagination that provides the meanings that allow people to engage reality in various respects,[13] and if imagination is pale or puny, the available expressions are deceitful about what they claim to carry over. Strangely, the failure of imagination was rarely discussed explicitly in our seminar. Rather, we generally assumed the posture of defending the imaginative constructs typical of our texts or figures, which invariably tended to be every bit as rich as one would expect of traditional classics.

The opposite of cultivating or embodying truth is neither error nor deceit but failure to attain to the interpretive form and activity required to access the religious object in the relevant respect. In one sense, this is a simple point. The religious object is what it is (our traditions disagree about what that is) and the religious ideas, symbols, theories, and other signs are adequate to carry that across to an interpreter who is ready. But the interpreter in question is not ready. The partner is there, the music is playing, but the person cannot dance. In the technical language of our theory of religious truth, the interpreter in question is not a secondary referent of the relevant ideas, so the applicable felicity questions are not met.

In another sense, of course, the point is not simple at all when we ask how and why the interpreter is unready and what our traditions say about this. Persons unconnected with the religion might be unready for any number of obvious reasons. Here we are concerned with people intending to engage the religious object in respect of a perfected level of truth, and who fail. There are two general sources of the failure noted in our religions, and they might be combined. One, characteristic of theistic religions whose cultic practices include petitionary prayer, is that the religious object has not yet revealed itself to the interpreter. Grace is needed, and the interpreter simply has to wait. Something like this is always involved when the interpreter prays for vision or success in relating to the ultimate. The other source of the failure is some fault in the interpreter. Such faults also can be of two general types, the negative limitations of being stuck in the ordinary unenlightened world and the positive but still limited failure to advance far enough in the religion's yoga of spiritual perfection. Roughly this corresponds to the distinction between those who have not committed themselves to the religion's path and those who have.

For our purposes, investigating the failure of the intention to achieve a high level of truth, the second group is the more interesting. All the cultic apparatus of a religion—its worship, spiritual practices, studies, and religiously organized family and community life—are aimed to enhance religious virtuosity. This is the center of gravity of George Lindbeck's interpretation of religions as cultural-linguistic systems: life within those systems is shaped and intensified so that the symbols and ideas become more and more meaningful and effective, increasing the capacities of the people to engage the world in their terms.[14] For our present interest, it is perhaps necessary to distinguish those elements of a religion's cultural-linguistic system that are for everybody—ordinary Daoists, Buddhists, Brahmins, Jews, Christians, Muslims—and those for adepts. All the traditions we studied have both kinds, often in multiple versions not coincident with one another. Within a cultural-linguistic system there are many elements the practice of which is aimed to foster spiritual perfection, including diet, exercise, travel, meditation, study, rituals, and prayers of many kinds. Among these are elements that involve interpreting the ultimate and religiously related matters with the ideas of the faith that are claimed to be true. Focusing on cognitive perfection, as we are here in our concern for religious truth, readiness to engage reality at the higher levels of truth requires practice with the ideas for doing so. Unreadiness in this context means that the interpreter has not achieved sufficient competence with the ideas that might carry over what is important in the respects they engage the object.

In many instances, failure to attain the spiritual competence to engage reality at the level of the higher truths is a combination of both sources, the gracious and the personal. In *Ultimate Realities*, chapter 3, Fredriksen detailed the problematic of impurity disqualifying persons from approaching the divine, and construed the dynamics of early Christianity to be the purification of those persons through Jesus Christ, who was the purifying sacrifice. Once purified and made acceptable, Christian devotees still need to practice holiness and go on to perfection. Although her discussion focused on the purification and making holy of all believers rather than the spiritual perfection of saints, her point expresses the complex interaction of the two sources. Her particular example is Christian, indeed Jewish, in its emphasis on ritual purity. Something like that interaction takes place in some forms of Buddhism, however, when the gracious giving of the Dharma is combined with the monastic search for enlightenment. Medieval Daoists celebrate their scriptures that introduce the esoteric way; even Confucians construe purity to be very important, and emphasize the presence of Heaven in human nature as the ground of the human connection with the Dao, a heavenly nature the pursuit of which is education.[15]

The fact that the opposite of truth in embodiment is failure to attain to interpretations at the higher levels of truth emphasizes the dynamic quality of interpretive engagement of reality. To be rightly related to ultimate realities, ontological and anthropological, is to be oriented a certain way, to be able to do certain things, to be in touch with reality in rarely interpreted but important respects, and to comport oneself appropriately. Although our studies stress this most in regard to Chinese religion, it is true for all the traditions we studied in different ways.[16] What this means for religious ideas, in terms of our theory of truth (8.3), is that there are important indexical references in their interpretation, references that connect with and point the interpreter's behavior to the religious realities. The proper connections and the appropriate pointings correspond to the various felicity conditions for religious truth in all its manifestations.

Notes

1. In chapter 9 of *Ultimate Realities*, the second volume of our series, we argued that all four lines of justification taken together with phenomenological insights and the prizing of vulnerability to correction jointly constitute a comparative method that profits from and overcomes the weaknesses of existing approaches. In several chapters of the first volume, *The Human Condition*, we argued for a particular conception of comparative categories and for a particular way of understanding their relation to one another and to the tentative results of comparison in terms of a dialectic of vagueness and specificity. In all three volumes we tried to put this method into action with, we think, varying degrees of success. The first volume's comparative efforts emphasized mainly the dialectic of vagueness and specificity and the ability of a mixed group of experts to get the phenomenological description correct. There we distinguished various sites of phenomenological importance by which we were able to achieve a kind of fairness of description without having to resort to all of the philosophically

problematic intricacies of phenomenological methods such as Husserl's. While that discipline became an ongoing feature of our group practice, the second volume stressed more the justification of our comparative categories along lines other than faithful phenomenological description, intimating theories of ultimate realities in the process. Now, in the third volume, an explicit attempt is being made to make use of the comparative material for building a theory of religious truth, even while the awareness of phenomenological considerations and lines of justification for our operating categories remains high.

2. Chad Hansen, "Term Belief in Action: Sentences and Terms in Early Chinese Philosophy," *Epistemological Issues in Classical Chinese Philosophy*, ed. Hans Lenk and Gregor Paul (Albany: State University of New York Press, 1993).

3. We say they *would* agree with something like our theory if they had in fact engaged our theory. But they have not. Most Western interpreters of religious truth suppose, for instance, that the kind of "thing" that can be true is an intentional object of the sort Frege analyzed. Our naturalistic theory of truth, emphasizing causation, rejects the entire Fregean project, and instead accounts for intentionality as a high level kind of interpretation associated with consciousness. The claim so common in many religions, that truth is in behavior, attitude, passion, and other forms of embodiment, is not at all paradoxical on our theory, though it seems merely metaphorical on Frege's.

4. Clooney has written an important book on Mīmāṃsā ritual in *Thinking Ritually: Rediscovering the Pūrva Mīmāṃsā of Jaimini*, Volume 17, De Nobili Research Series (Vienna: Indological Institute of the University of Vienna, 1990).

5. John H. Berthrong, *Transformations of the Confucian Way* (Boulder, Col.: Westview Press, 1998), chaps. 4–5.

6. Although we did not explore it much, the question of nominalism (only particulars are real and stories are the only good way to generalize beyond them without falling into arbitrary convention) versus realism (universals or common natures or patterns are also real and can be ingredient in individuals) is of great importance for understanding expressions of religious truth.

7. Robert C. Neville, *Soldier, Sage, Saint* (New York: Fordham University Press, 1978), chap. 3.

8. See *The Human Condition*, chap. 2

9. See Kohn and Miller in *Ultimate Realities*, chap. 1.

10. For instance, in Wang Yang-ming's commentary on the Great Learning, Wing-tsit Chan, *A Source Book in Chinese Philosophy* (Princeton: Princeton University Press, 1963), 659.

11. See Kohn and Miller's chapter in *The Human Condition*, chap. 3.

12. Clooney, *Theology after Vedānta: An Experiment in Comparative Theology* (Albany: State University of New York Press, 1993); idem, *Seeing through Texts: Doing Theology among the Śrīvaiṣṇavas of South India* (Albany: State University of New York Press, 1996).

13. Robert C. Neville, *Reconstruction of Thinking* (Albany: State University of New York Press, 1981), part 2.

14. George Lindbeck, *The Nature of Doctrine: Religion and Theology in a Postliberal Age* (Philadelphia: Westminster, 1984).

15. See the beginning of *The Doctrine of the Mean*, in Chan, op. cit., 98.

16. This having been said, we must stress the enormous diversity within and among our traditions regarding their construals of ultimate realities about which high level truth claims might be made, and their construals of the ways the human condition is defined by these ultimate realities. The first we studied at length in *Ultimate Realities*. The second we studied systematically in *The Human Condition*, chapter 8 especially.

8

A Contemporary Understanding of Religious Truth

Robert Cummings Neville
and Wesley J. Wildman

8.1 Truths in Religion

Contemporary understandings of religious truth have come a long way from the eighteenth-century European philosophy of religion that regarded the problem merely as a matter of the epistemological justification of beliefs. To be sure, that problem remains; much contemporary philosophy of religion in the mode of analytic philosophy continues the eighteenth-century discussion.[1] Moreover, the discussions in the first six chapters include treatments of religious truth in this epistemological sense, albeit from a fascinating range of perspectives at times alien to analytic philosophy of religion. It follows that the tradition of the study of epistemological truth in religion, though somewhat dissociated, is alive and well.

Twentieth-century developments in the philosophy of language have complicated the question of religious truth, however. There is widespread recognition now that religions use language in expressive, exhortative, and performative ways, as well as in fact-asserting ways that intend to be true in the epistemological sense. Not surprisingly, then, religions have developed diverse understandings of truth that express standards of adequacy or felicity for these kinds of language use. The recitation of a sūtra, narrative, or creed might have little or no descriptive content and yet be highly functional as an act of mental focusing, as a community's affirmation of its identity, or as an influential reminder of group values. And those tasks can be done better or worse, they can be "true" or "false" in special senses, quite apart from the epistemological truth of the descriptive or fact-asserting content.

The recognition of expressive, exhortative, performative, and a range of other rule-governed uses of language has come from two philosophical traditions in the twentieth century. On the one hand, there is the Anglo-American tradition of philosophy of language, beginning especially from the work of J. L. Austin.[2] Austin's insights proved fruitful in subsequent decades as a large number of philosophers turned their attention to the study of language. The most important works from this period are those of Wittgenstein and Searle.[3] On the other hand, a rich integration of descriptive and cognitively shaped action was also and earlier developed by the American pragmatists Charles Peirce and John Dewey, and to some extent by William James and George Herbert Mead.[4] Behind the application to religious language of both of those philosophic traditions in the West lies the Romantic criticism of theology as propositional truth. This Romantic complaint is famously expressed in Schleiermacher and Hegel, for both of whom "feeling" and "consciousness" were categories of morality as well as cognition.

Our concern here is not with any particular usage of religious language—whether assertative, expressive, exhortative, performative, or something else—but with any and all such uses insofar as they can be "true" or "felicitous" in some sense. This concern leads us to distinguish and pursue (often simultaneously) several specific interests. First, in the background of our work in all three volumes of this project is an attempt to understand *first-order religious language and activity*. Most religious acting and speaking is highly structured, which is both a familiar fact and an unsurprising one in view of the successful philosophical tracing out of the rules governing a wide variety of spheres of discourse and behavior. Second, we are interested in *the conditions of adequacy* that apply to the rich usages of religious language. This is one way to find out about the structure of first-order religious language and practice, of course, but it is also crucial for our focus in this volume on religious truth. Third, we are especially interested in *the religious ideas that express, cultivate, and regulate those conditions of adequacy* of religious language and practice. This is to be distinguished carefully from the second interest: the ideas of religious truth that exist within religious traditions can themselves be second-order attempts within a religious tradition to describe or modify its own first-order structures of religious language and action. Our study focuses on the ways those potentially second-order ideas about the truth and felicity of first-order religious speaking and doing are similar or different. Fourth, we are interested in *what can be done to develop a theory of religious truth* with such comparisons as we make about religious ideas of truth. That is, we are interested in bringing the data flexibly organized by our comparative categories to bear on a positive theory of religious truth. This is a constructive philosophical task that involves making simultaneous use of contemporary theories of religious truth and the implications for theories of truth that can be derived from the data of religious studies, ideally well organized by careful comparison.

As pointed out repeatedly in all three volumes of this project, and especially in chapter 9 of *Ultimate Realities*, the comparative categories organizing the data pertaining to ideas of religious truth are designed to be flexible and responsive to criticism. They are not at all like an immovable foundation for a building but more like the flexible scaffolding that is placed around it and that can be changed whenever needed. The group process we have gone through has involved repeatedly correcting or abandoning previous insights about religious truth in the traditions we have studied—we hope in the direction of improved categories for our comparative efforts.

It is worth pausing to offer a different analogy for the flexibility of the categories we use for making comparisons about religious truth. Consider the dynamic cytoskeleton of many cells whereby the cell is given particular shape in a mind-bogglingly complex environment. The cell is responsive to its environment in part through specific enzymes that alter the shape of the proteins making up the cytoskeleton, enabling global shape changes as needed. Those enzymes are contextually activated, as when a red corpuscle changes from its flat, indented disk-like shape to a rolled-up tube when it needs to pass through tiny capillaries. This analogy should not suggest overly convenient flexibility, as if comparative categories can be changed to serve whatever need presses most urgently for attention, ignoring data. Rather, it is intended to indicate how the vastly complex data of religious phenomena can be seen as a structured environment within which comparativists may travel, genuinely engaging and responding to that environment. Now, drawing in the perspective of evolution in the analogy, it is precisely through the adaptiveness of those engagements that the red blood cell develops the capacities it has; the proteins and enzymes necessary for a flexible cytoskeleton are encoded in its DNA. In the same way, the comparative project, if responsive to data and properly concerned with justification of provisional conclusions,[5] allows the comparativist's ways of understanding to adapt and introduces selective pressure for more adequate formulations. The result is comparative categories that express the character of the religious environment even as the red blood cell's cytoskeleton expresses the character (the DNA) of its host organism. We (Neville and Wildman) claim that the least apt aspect of this analogy has to do not with complexity but with the length of time involved. As difficult as it is, the comparative project can be pursued on the time scale of generations, much like the natural and social sciences, rather than the millennia of cultural evolution or the billions of years of biological evolution.

From what has been said to this point, it follows that some religious practices might very well involve making descriptive claims, affirmative or negative, as discussed particularly in chapter 2. The question of the truth of such practices comes close to being the question of what we are calling the "epistemic" truth of the claims made in them. Other religious practices such as liturgies, prayers, and meditations, or the construction and decoration of symbolically rich garments, buildings, or political constitutions, may also be true, but in a different sense. Each of these practices has its own distinctive felicity conditions, the conditions according to which it is deemed appropriate, acceptable, correct, and so on. This is what we shall call "performative" truth.

"Felicity" may be a better general category than "truth" for embracing both epistemological and performative truth. It has the advantages of surmounting the strictly logical conditions for truth that have been much emphasized in Western philosophical epistemology and of being responsive to recent non-Western critiques of the epistemologization of religious language.[6] The felicity of "felicity" has two important limitations for our context, however. One is that it might be construed to suggest that a happy result is brought about by a religious practice or expression entirely adventitiously. On the contrary, felicity in our sense should be connected with conditions of adequacy regarding the kind of practice at hand; the following sections in this chapter indicate how complicated, and yet logically connected, these conditions might be. Second, religious traditions tend not to make such a sharp distinction between epistemological and performative truth, even though most traditions do notice the distinction. Our project has been inclined to register the blurring of this distinction by retaining the name "religious truth" for the general category of religious ideas to be investigated in this volume. Kohn and Miller argue (1.1) that the distinction between epistemological truth and performative truth is not valid in China. This is a good reminder that the blurring of the distinction happens in different ways and to different degrees. But at least the distinction needs to be registered, in China as elsewhere, and its nature explained, even as the distinction between belief and action is registered even if blurred in practice. So we remain with "truth" as the more general category and use "felicity" to name the conditions under which truth obtains in this broad sense, especially when both performative and epistemological aspects of truth are in view.

The reasons for this blurring in our religious traditions are important. First, religious practices typically are shaped by religious symbols that suppose (assume, imply, celebrate, or proclaim) something to be true that is religiously important. Indeed, the effectiveness with which a religious practice makes these suppositions (assumptions, implications, celebrations, or proclamations) is usually one of the felicity conditions applied to it. Too sharp a distinction between the performative truth of the practice and the epistemological truth of the associated suppositions would tend artificially to separate what religious traditions have usually—and often deliberately and self-consciously—kept together. Second, felicity conditions are enormously diverse. Just as apologies should be sincere, descriptions true, condemnations just, exhortations effective, and testimonies beautifully expressive, so religious practices have a wealth of felicity conditions, often active simultaneously. In such a context, sharply distinguishing epistemological truth from performative truth is a bit like distinguishing one otherwise unremarkable piece of straw in a pile of hay. You can do it but you can't get too carried away with it. Religious practices are subject to the most complex felicity conditions of anything that human beings do, by far, and there is no sense in getting too excited just because epistemological truth shows up in the mix.

That said, it is still possible to make the distinction between epistemological and performative truth, and then to ask about the epistemological truth of both explicit religious claims and claims implicit in religious practices. It is to that topic that we turn in sections 8.2 and 8.3. Then in sections 8.4 and 8.5 the focus shifts back to performative truth. Despite this division, we mean to be speaking of different aspects of a single, complex phenomenon in religion, namely, the fact that the diverse felicity conditions of religious phenomena are conceived in quite specific ways by religious traditions.

Throughout this chapter and the next, it is important to distinguish between the two levels of religious ideas with which we are working because our task is different in relation to each. On the one hand, religious traditions contain second-order ideas about what truth means and about how to realize truth in practice. Comparison draws attention to the similarities and differences between these traditional ideas of truth; that material is discussed most directly in chapters 1–7. The contemporary theory of religious truth presented in this chapter aims to make sense of those second-order ideas in their delicious variety. On the other hand, religious people have beliefs and practices that express or presuppose first-order ideas. Traditions differ in the extent to which they make resources available for adherents to assure themselves that these presupposed ideas are true; some traditions facilitate obsession over the issue while others promote near-obliviousness to it. All traditions register the issue, however, and an adequate contemporary theory of religious truth needs both to address this question of justification of the first-order ideas expressed in beliefs and practices and to explain how the variation of religious attitudes toward it expresses second-order ideas about religious truth. We present a contemporary theory of religious truth in this chapter in the hope that chapter 7 will then have served both to demonstrate how we have taken account of the comparative results from chapters 1–6 and to make the weaknesses of the theory of truth more evident.

Many factors condition religious beliefs and practices, including first-order religious ideas. Even when the ideas are not the most important conditioning factors, which is often the case with ritual practices, ideas are still present, conveyed in, and mediated by religious symbols. A convenient way to present a theory of religious truth is therefore to address the question of what it means to say that religious symbols are true. This is an extremely complex question, as the previous discussion of the multifarious felicity conditions for religious beliefs and practices suggests. Specifically, the truth of a religious symbol involves issues in at least four dimensions: (1) how the symbol interprets its object to those interpreters engaged in the practice; (2) whether what the symbol purports to refer to is as the symbol says it is; (3) just what the symbol means itself, with all its resonances, ambiguities, double-plays, and implications; and (4) how the interpreters are adequately transformed through practice so as to be able to grasp this meaning. Thus, interpretation, reference, meaning, and transformation are the topics of a theory of religious truth, and of the sections of this chapter.

8.2 Truth in Interpretation

Interpretation is (1) the taking of reality (2) by an interpreter (3) to be the way an idea (a sign, symbol, etc.) says it is in the respect in which the idea is taken to represent the reality as an object. This formula will be explicated in the remainder of this section.[7] But first some things need to be said to locate the problem of religious truth as a matter of interpretation.

Interpretation need not be conscious or deliberate. It simply is the differential taking of reality to be a certain way by means of representing it in ideas. An automobile driver interprets the road in vast and complicated ways, as much with kinesthetic signs of body-feels as with perceptions that isolate objects clearly against backgrounds. Religious life is densely shaped by symbols in many ways. Although sophisticated theologians might know the verbal meanings of the symbols, most religious practitioners are not sophisticated theologians. Yet their religiously shaped lives take reality to be the way their religious symbols diversely represent it. The verbal accounts they give indeed might be contrary or irrelevant to the ways the symbols in fact represent reality within their lives. The question of religious truth in the context of interpretation is about whether the ways interpreters actually take reality to be, insofar as that taking is shaped by the ideas, are the ways reality is.

Simple descriptive propositions might seem to be far less complicated than fancy religious symbolic claims. Consider the favorite of analytic philosophers, "the cat is on the mat," the truth of which can be checked by looking at what, if anything, is on the mat. This example seems to make no reference to actual interpreters of the cat-mat reality who employ the propositional-sign "the cat is on the mat." But that is because we can assume that any English-speakers who know their way around cats and mats would be able to make the interpretation. We thus leave the interpretation in the subjunctive—"the cat is on the mat" would be true for any relevant interpreter if the cat in fact is on the mat. But the interpretive situation in religion is often far more complex and controversial. Suppose the Buddhist dharma needs an adept to be understood, and there are no adepts; then the dharmic claim is not true for anyone, or false: an uninterpreted claim is not claimed or asserted, assumed, and so on. What is true for an adept might be silly, irrelevant, incomprehensible, or even plain false (as in the two-truths doctrine) for others if non-adepts use it to interpret reality. In religion it is extremely important to be able to specify the interpretive situation, and the stage of spiritual discernment and state of soul of the interpreters. The subjunctive assumption of an ideal interpreter is problematic in religious cases.

"The cat is on the mat" seems to have unequivocal terms for English speakers (unless one wants to play philosophical games). Thus, it is easy to assume that the meanings of those terms are general and define a community of meaning, so that all statements of its ilk are public, not private. Religious symbols too are mainly conventional and hence defined by a community. But often the religious community is one of initiates, or of practitioners at different stages of initiation. Moreover, for very many people, the religious symbols have particular histories in their lives and that of their immediate neighbors; so the same symbols might mean different things on opposite sides of the hill, especially where meaning includes an emotional tone. Religious symbols also interact with one another, and take on special resonances and association. The Buddha's Four Noble Truths are more colorful in Tibet than in Sri Lanka, and the Christian cross is different for Roman Catholics who represent Jesus on it than for Protestants who see it as a bare ladder to resurrection. The meanings of religious ideas need to be contextualized very subtly, something usually not relevant to "the cat is on the mat."

The reference of "the cat is on the mat" has been somewhat complicated in the philosophical literature. Which cat? Which mat? But consider how vastly more complicated the problem of reference is with regard to many religious ideas. In nearly all the religious traditions we have studied ultimate realities are represented as if they could be named like things—God, Brahman, the Dao. Madhyamaka Buddhism says that what is ultimate involves the denial of naming things except conventionally. Yet all those same traditions take pains to point out that the ultimates are not things like other things that bear names over against namers—"the Dao that can be named is not the true Dao," begins the *Daode jing*.[8] The apophatic theologies of West Asian monotheisms have parallels in the other traditions. How can religious ideas refer to things if their referents are not things? Religious symbols for things other than ultimate realities often take their bearings from their relations to the ultimates, either ontological or practical ultimates. So they too have complicated reference. Religion, of course, is not the only area of life with complicated reference. "The global ecological problem," "the bittersweet of success," and "the beauty of Mozart's music" are all well-recognized and referred-to realities but with complicated kinds of reference. Nominalist philosophers who take physical objects as the paradigm of referents tend to declare these to be nonsense and attempt to reduce them to particulars. "A cap is on the market" refers in ways quite different from "the cat is on the mat."

All these complications mean that the truth of religious ideas even in the context of interpretation requires an extremely complex analysis, and the applications of modes of analysis apparently adequate for many other kinds of ideas are likely to be reductive. We are now in a position to spell out some of the aspects of interpretation singled out in the formula above: *Interpretation is (1) the taking of reality (2) by an interpreter (3) to be the way an idea (a sign, symbol, etc.) says it is (4) in the respect in which the idea is taken to represent the reality as an object.*

To say that interpretation is "the taking of reality" is to adopt a theory of truth based on the causal metaphors of interpreters engaging reality. This is quite different from other commonly supposed theories, and is defended at length in Neville's *Recovery of the Measure*.[9] For instance, it has no resonance with the mind-body dualism of Western enlightenment philosophy. For that dualistic position, interpretations are supposed to be mental realities that mirror extra-mental realities if they are true. For our theory, by contrast, ideas are ways or habits of responding to reality that have been shaped by eons of interaction into semiotic codes that organize responses with discernment, and that each individual comes to master more or less well. Many of these ideas can themselves be objects of conscious awareness and analysis, but many are not. Any given activity—driving a car, singing a hymn, living the life of a Buddhist monk—has many semiotically shaped responses operative at once, most of which are not matters of attention.

The causal theory of interpretation also stands in contrast to idealisms such as Yogācāra's "consciousness only" position. That theory of course is deeply causal, but the causation affects ideas only. On our theory, the engagement of interpreters with reality involves interactive causation among all things referred to and referring. Within interpreters, the causal patterns take on semiotic structures so that human behavior is directed to discern what is important and accomplish its purposes in the larger environment. This process is not foolproof and human beings often make mistakes about what is significant. Nevertheless, interpreters take up reality by means of discriminating ideas, and they take up ideas as they interact discriminatingly with reality. In the sense deriving from the continuities and connections of different kinds of causal processes, this theory of interpretation is naturalistic, although naturalism in this sense does not entail any mechanistic or physicalist theory of nature.[10]

An idea is true, on our theory, when it carries across into the interpreter whatever is important in the referent or reality interpreted, in the respects in which the idea is taken to stand for the referent. Aristotle, and much of the Western philosophic tradition, assumed that what is important to get from the object to the knower is the object's form. That might be the case in some instances, and it is what gives rise to conceptions of knowledge based in mirroring or isomorphism between reality and mind. The more basic point, however, is that it is the value in the object that needs to be carried across. In crude pragmatic circumstances it is the force and cold of the wind or the danger of the tiger that need to be noticed. As Peirce pointed out, however, once interpreters develop complex semiotic systems that allow them to question reality, the really important things to know are what the ideals of life are, what is worth striving for, what character is desirable, what social arrangements are just, how to find and make beauty.[11] When interpretation includes query, it seeks out what is valuable, and develops symbolic forms for discerning and dealing with that.

A religious idea is true when it carries across what is important in the religious object or referent into the interpreter or the interpreter's community, in the respects in which the ideas are used to represent reality, as qualified by the material, cultural, semiotic, and purposive nature of the interpreter.[12] Suppose for the moment that an object is religious if it is, or is related to, something ultimate, either something ontologically ultimate or an ultimate quest, which we referred to in *Ultimate Realities* as an anthropological ultimate. A religious idea is true, then, if what is important in or about the ultimate is carried over into the interpreter, or the interpreter's community, in the respects in which the idea represents the ultimate.

Following Peirce, we can call what becomes interpretively resident in the interpreter an "interpretant." Two kinds of interpretants need to be distinguished, if only to be shown to be overlapping. One, which can be called an "intellectual interpretant," consists of the rendition of what is carried over in a network or system of symbols. If all symbols were verbal ones, we could say that the intellectual interpretant is the verbalization of what is important in the object. But there are many other kinds of symbols, signs, or ideas, including gestures, pictures, music, and the like. Intellectual interpretants are ways of embodying what is important in the object in the terms of a semiotic system. The other kind of interpretant is "practical," by which is meant how the interpreter's habits and behavior, including habits of mind, are modified so as to register what is important in the religious object. Except for intellectuals, the payoff of religious truth is mainly practical, and religious intellectuals hope that even for them the truth is at least practical.

The distinction between intellectual and practical interpretants allows us to acknowledge that some intellectuals understand their religion but do not live it and that some non-intellectual people are paradigms of authentic piety without being able to understand that intellectually. The connection between the intellectual and practical interpretants is crucial, however, when critical questions arise about how to understand or live out the bearing of the ultimate on life. Intellectual analysis gives people a critical purchase on what appear to be practical consequences of religious interpretations; practical engagement with ultimate reality in life gives another kind of critical purchase on the intellectual analysis. All of the religions we studied are complex ways of life, practically shaped by ideas, which have been thought through in many ways for each of them.

Interpretation always takes place within a larger context, and in every context it is relevant to distinguish the intellectual from the practical line of interpretants. Consider but three major contexts, the theoretical, the communal, and the devotional.

In a theoretical context, say a debate between theologians before an authority, or a theological classroom, the practical interpretants are aimed to maximize agreement on meaning and sharpen the readiness of the claims to be shown mistaken or well taken. Much religious language is highly metaphorical and, in theoretical contexts, universality of meaning presses toward developing more nearly literal language that does not have to be qualified from one context of usage to another. Perhaps no theological language is completely literal, but theoretical contexts press in that direction. Hence, the intellectual interpretants are likely to be abstract, universal, and relatively flat in emotional tone. Regarding the theoretical concern for truth, there is a recursive layering of definitions of truth and discussions of criteria such as illustrated in chapter 2 and elsewhere.[13] All this is to say that in theoretical contexts, the terms for intellectual interpretants are shaped by the pressures for universal agreement on meaning and critical vulnerability for being corrected. The practical interpretants in turn are made possible by theoretically framed intellectual ones.

In a communal context, a religious object is truly interpreted by intellectual symbols that make sense of how the community is religiously shaped and by practical interpretants that shape the community in the relevant respects. Consider a liturgy. It has intellectual symbols nested in systems that are more or less coherent and that depict in organized fashion central imaginative structures that epitomize elements of the religion's practice. These might be quite different from theoretical intellectual symbols. A ritual worshiping Guanyin (Avalokiteśvara) with petitions for healing uses personalizing symbols that are a far cry from the austere Madhyamaka or Yogācāra metaphysics discussed in chapter 3. A Christian eucharistic liturgy compacts symbols of suffering, death, resurrection, nourishment, participation, communal solidarity, historical identity, religious authority, and cannibalism that are vastly more vivid than the theoretical notions of divine creation, Trinitarian unity, or a logos Christology that might explain the liturgy theoretically. The practical interpretants of the liturgy are the effects the liturgy has on the worshipping community, and they are true or false depending on the practical implications of the religious object for that community, as represented in the respects in which the liturgical symbols and acts stand for the object.

For a devotional context, consider, for instance, a retreat practicing St. Ignatius's spiritual exercises. On one of the days the devotee would concentrate on visualizing Jesus carrying the cross from the Jerusalem court to the hill of crucifixion. The intellectual interpretants of the visualization would not at all have to do with whether Jesus and the crowd dressed as the devotee imagines, or whether the streets look the way imagined. They rather have to do with what Jesus's "way through the streets" means for the devotee's life of suffering, of "bearing crosses." The practical interpretants have to do with how the devotee's life is changed so as to become more Christlike with respect to bearing suffering, which depends in part on the particulars of the devotee's pains that might be quite alien to anything in Jesus's particular experience. This point will be expanded in 8.5.

This section has discussed at some length the notions of truth involved in interpretation as "taking a reality" "by an interpreter." We have yet to discuss how that taking is by means of the idea that stands for the reality in some respect. A theory of truth in reference is required for the next step.

8.3 Truth in Reference

Reference was a confusing notion in our discussions in several ways. Eckel frequently represented Madhyamaka Buddhism to say that there is no reference, that ideas do not refer and that it is the illusion of ignorance to think they do; enlightenment among other things means that there is no objective reality to which ideas might refer. Kohn sometimes argued, as appears in 1.2.1, that reference seems to imply that reality has to remain fixed as referred to, and that because reality is processive and not fixed it can be referred to, if at all, only elliptically. But both Mādhyamikas and elliptical Daoists would say that it is a mistake to claim that reality is filled (really and not merely conventionally) with stable, self-contained, unchanging entities. It is a mistake, they would say, because reality in fact does not have such substances, but is something else. The Mādhyamikas and Daoists take different turns here, the former focusing on the nature of knowing and the latter on tuning up with process. But they both refer to reality as lacking real substantiality (especially as having to do with religious concerns). What funny kind of reference is this?

Peirce distinguished three kinds of reference: iconic, indexical, and conventional.[14] Iconic reference refers to its object or referent as being like the iconic idea or sign, at least in some respect. Indexical reference points to the object by means of the idea. Conventional reference, which Peirce called "symbolic," refers to the object by the meanings involved in the idea, as framed in a semiotic system. Ideas can refer in more than one way. Indeed, any idea we can talk about has to be at least conventional so as to be expressible in language, and might also be both iconic and indexical. Illustrations of the three kinds of reference can explain some of the confusions about reference that characterized our discussions.

Iconic reference has many levels of generality. At perhaps the most general level, people take their culture as a whole, a rough collection of semiotic systems, to be iconic of reality; that is, reality is like what *can be* noticed about it, expressed, and addressed in the culture's forms. Those cultures not conscious of the conventionality of ideas or of cultural relativity would not distinguish reality from the cultural forms, the strongest possible assertion of iconicity. Those cultures that are aware of cultural forms still take their culture to be potentially iconic. Among the latter, many cultures are aware of the problematic character of at least some cultural forms, particularly those involved in religion. All of the axial age religions we studied are of this last sort, with some kind of apophatic sensibility about basic religious reference.

Less general than whole cultures, religious myths are taken to be iconic of reality, at least in some respects; again, there is a distinction between those mythopoeic cultures that do not distinguish reality from the myth and those that recognize the mythic character of their myths. "Grand narratives" are myths in this latter sense for cultures whose members believe themselves to be beyond mere myth. Paralleling the grand narratives of West Asian religions is the "cosmic physics and geography" of East Asian religions, which are also iconic (see *The Human Condition*, chapter 2). Of course there are much more specific iconic references within religions.

Special notice should be taken of a particular iconic reference, namely, the claim made by many in West and South Asian cultures that reality is like the *structure* of *language*. Indo-European (and some other) languages have a subject-predicate structure, which some philosophers, such as Aristotle, take to be iconic of reality, with the philosophic result that reality is construed to be made of substances with properties or attributes. Aristotle's metaphysics of substance is quite subtle, and modern European philosophers such as Descartes, Spinoza, and Leibniz developed brilliant variations on it to comprehend the findings of modern science. The early Wittgenstein proposed that the formal structure of an ideal language is iconic of reality, or at least of reality's facts.[15] Some of the same substance thinking characterized Sanskrit-based cultures that assume that real things (substances) do not change whereas their properties or attributes might change. Every culture, however, recognizes that at least some things do change, and that we experience the world as extremely processive. Therefore, the iconicity of subject-predicate language to reality as substance-attribute in structure cannot be the whole story. Plato thoroughly understood this and criticized the iconic reference of language, claiming that it might apply to ideas alone but not to concrete reality that is in constant flux. Platonic epistemology was designed to deal cognitively and normatively with the concrete political and personal world of change; he was willing to say that only the static world of ideas has *being*, though the dynamic world of *appearance* is what is of philosophic interest and importance. Thinking has to be dialectical, Plato thought, constantly shifting perspectives and angles of vision, in order to address changing affairs.[16] By contrast, dialectic for Aristotle was a form of logical mistake. The twentieth-century philosopher Alfred North Whitehead was a Platonist who reformulated modern metaphysics from its Aristotelian substance metaphors to Platonic ones in order to understand how mathematics, the Platonic paradigm of form, might apply to a world of flux.[17] Many of the same problems and strategies evolved in South Asian philosophy, often with an exaggeration of the Platonic distinction between static reality and dynamic appearance to a distinction between static reality and the illusion of dynamism (see Clooney in *The Human Condition*, chapter 5). In some forms of Hinduism and Buddhism, the static reality was taken to be more important and interesting (at least religiously) than dynamic flux; Vedānta, for instance, affirms the unchanging reality of Brahman, and Madhyamaka denies the reality of static realities and its alleged though mischievous importance.

As Kohn and Miller point out (in 1.2.1 and in *The Human Condition*, chapter 2), the Chinese never thought that reality is full of substances. Nor is Chinese language of the subject-predicate sort. Therefore the Chinese were not tempted at least along those lines to think their language is iconic of a reality full of substances. But were the Chinese tempted to think that their different, non-subject-predicate language structure is iconic of reality, so that reality is like Chinese language? The work of Chad Hansen does not support an affirmative answer to that question. He argues that Chinese language and the culture based on it form people to be discriminating and responsive in their interactions with reality, especially with typical movements of things and special worths. Chinese language does not emphasize concepts such as truth and representation but rather mastery of attunement and particular action in accord with changing realities.[18] All this is to say that the important reference in the language itself to reality is indexical, not iconic.

Indexical reference consists in an idea or other sign pointing out something otherwise unnoticed or obscured. Peirce argued that causal connections are at the root of indexical reference, and this is particularly the case when ideas referring indexically guide behavior to recognize, address, and respond to things, as in the Chinese case according to Hansen. Although much more is involved than referring indexically in transforming personal character so as to conform more to the Dao, to be liberated from ignorance and its sufferings, or to attain a vision of God, some indexicality of ideas is surely necessarily involved. Indeed, if interpretation is the *engagement* of reality, then at least some of the interpretive ideas must be indexical. To the extent that religious ideas are practical, as has been emphasized throughout our volumes, they involve indexical reference. Chinese culture is by no means the only one to register what we here call indexicality in language. To the extent, however, that European philosophy has thought of language as names with syncategorematic connectives, and logic as a structural mirror of reality, typical European assumptions about language have been overly observant of iconic reference to the neglect of the indexical.[19]

Conventional reference consists in the employment of a system of ideas or meanings to stand for the object in some respect. To understand this, it is necessary to distinguish extensional from intentional reference.[20] *Extensional* reference is a function of the ideas or signs internal to a semiotic system, defined by the system's codes and expressing a range of possible interpretations. The totality of the semiotic system contains all the possible interpretations of reality that can be made when reality is engaged with that system, sort of like Leibniz's God's array of *compossibilities* before a definite set is chosen for actualization. Every referent of any idea within the system can be represented by another idea within that system, which is its extensional referent; extensional reference is entirely intrasystemic. *Intentional* reference is the engagement of reality by means of ideas shaped within a semiotic system. It uses configurations of ideas or signs from within a semiotic system, replete with their meanings as defined by that system, to engage reality. How those ideas intentionally engage reality, in what respects, depends on their extensional meanings within the semiotic system. The failure or refusal to distinguish extensional from intentional reference has led some postmodern thinkers to believe that signs refer only to signs, not to realities outside sign systems. Extensional reference, of course, is that way, referring only in and around the semiotic system. When asked to specify what one is referring to, one always uses other ideas or signs to say that; every referent itself can be expressed within the sign-system. But this is not to say that we do not refer to things that are external to our semiotic systems. When we say, "The light ahead is turning yellow!" we refer intentionally to the real light, even though the whole proposition is within our semiotic system, even "the light ahead." Acknowledging the difference between extension and intention, it is still possible to agree with Peirce that real things, outside of semiotic systems, have the character of signs insofar as they can be objects of other signs and themselves serve as signs at least of their causal connections.

Conventional reference, then, employs ideas or signs semiotically defined according to extensional meanings to make intentional interpretations that refer to reality so engaged. Conventional reference is far more varied than one might think if overly fixated on iconicity between semiotic structure and its objectified reality. Metaphor, indirection, paradox, and gesture, particularly ritual gesture, are important kinds of conventional reference in many kinds of cultural activities, including religion. Davvening is as referential in its conventional way as saying aloud "the Lord is One." Religions can be understood in part as complex ways of life by means of which people refer to the mystery of the ultimate so as to take up personally and culturally what is ultimately important. Such "ways of life" are vastly important conventional references to the ultimate.

The question of religious truth needs to be parsed through the complexity of reference involved. Truth, we proposed above, is the carryover of what is important from the object referred to into the interpreter in the respect in which the idea or sign stands for the object, with the "carryover" qualified by the material, culture, semiotic systems, and purposes of the interpreter. That Aristotle was enamoured of iconicity of reference explains in part why he thought the carryover is of form: the form in the matter of the object is carried over into the matter of the interpreting mind. Even if iconicity were to be completely understood as mirroring forms, that is not sufficiently general to deal with the question of truth in reference. To the extent that an interpretation involves indexical reference, the question of truth is whether the interpreter is rightly pointed to the object, rightly oriented, rightly perceptive of what is otherwise obscured, rightly triggered to be appropriately responsive. The indexicality of religious reference was extremely important in the previous chapter as we understand the performative aspects of cultivating the character to know the higher truths, or "becoming true. To the extent that an interpretation refers by means of the conventional ideas defining a religion as a way of life, the question of truth is even more complex. To go further with this point, it is necessary to look at truth in meaning.

Another dimension of reference needs to be lifted up before turning to meaning, however. Let the object of reference be called the "primary referent." Religious interpretation, and perhaps other kinds, also has a "secondary referent." Whether an idea can refer (iconically, indexically, or conventionally) depends on whether the interpreter is the right sort existentially for that idea actually to carry across what is important. Suppose that the extensional meaning system articulates a certain interpretation; it still might not be the case that a given interpreter can use that articulation or idea to engage reality. For instance, an adolescent might know the dictionary meanings of the terms but still not be able to use them as an adult might. In a religious tradition that calls God "Father," everyone might know that God is not literally a father, or even gendered; but people who in childhood have been abused by their father are less likely to be able to use that idea symbolically than those whose real father seemed godlike. Even more obvious, a person whose soul is shaped deeply by one religious tradition might learn the theology of another but be unable to engage reality with the other tradition's ideas and symbols.

The secondary referent of an idea, therefore, is the interpreter who is of the right stage in life, the right state of soul or psychological and spiritual state, and the right deep religious culture. The extensional reference of an idea, what it can refer to within the semiotic system of ideas, need not take into account secondary reference, only primary reference. But intentional reference requires both primary and secondary reference: there can be no actual engagement or interpretation of a religious reality unless the interpreters are of the right stage, state, and culture for the ideas effectively to carry over what is important.

To understand truth in the reference of religious ideas, therefore, is to grasp not only the mode of primary reference but also the conditions for secondary reference. It is in respect of the subtleties of secondary reference that Buddhists pay such attention to *upaya*, "expedient means," which seem not to be literally true but effectively true.

8.4 Truth in Achieved Meaning

The problem of truth, as it applies to the meanings of ideas, is whether a religion has ideas that can engage religious objects in the relevant respects. Two considerations make this problem difficult. On the one hand, there is the question of whether the appropriate ideas exist within the religion's semiotic or cultural system. Having a sign or idea that can stand for an object in a certain respect is what allows the interpreter to engage the object interpretively. Without an appropriate sign or idea, the object cannot be engaged in the respect in question. For instance, desert people need to distinguish more kinds of sand than Eskimos, and have the concepts and words to do so. Eskimos in deserts would need to get ideas and invent words if they were to tell good stories about desert dunes. More significantly, the evolution of the human species to civilization required the development of cultures full of signs that allow reality to be engaged in the respects necessary. Crude pragmatic ideas get people food and alert them to predators. More sophisticated ideas expressible in language make complex social life possible. Having ideas makes a difference. On the other hand, there is the question of whether religious practitioners are adept enough to access those ideas, and hence whether they are able to interpret the religious objects the way their religion should enable them to do so. This second question is the issue of transformation and will be treated in the next section. The question here is the achievement of religiously profound meaning, which includes the having of the right signs or ideas.

First, some structural things need to be said about religious ideas or symbols. An idea, say Jesus as the sacrifice for the sins of the world (see *Ultimate Realities*, chapter 3), has its meaning defined in a system of related ideas or symbols. Fredriksen analyzed this in terms of the use of sacrifice in purification so that defiled or impure persons could re-approach the Holy, as developed in the Torah and temple ritual. This, she showed, rested within a larger family of sacrifice motifs in the ancient Roman world, which made the notion intelligible when applied to Jesus in non-Jewish communities. Then there was also the system of symbols that interpreted sacrifice in terms of the Passover according to which the angel of death passed over the houses of Jews with the sacrificed blood on their doors when it slaughtered the first-born of Egypt; from this system arises the imagery of Jesus as the paschal lamb. Then again there was the Jewish-Hellenistic apocalyptic system of ideas involving the struggle between Satan and God in which Jesus was sacrificed as a ransom. Each of these symbol systems interprets sacrifice in a different way. Yet, as Fredriksen pointed out, St. Paul used them all, and other interpretive ideas, in trying to "explain" how Jesus effects salvation. He used them all in confused ways, piling one system on another. There is no single algorithm for combining all the layers of sacrifice-symbolic systems. But they resonate together. The *idea* of Jesus as an atoning sacrifice requires them all, without sorting, and it cannot be expressed by one alone, for St. Paul; perhaps later Christian thinkers have done no better. That would be because the idea at hand in fact consists in a mutual interplay, an inter-resonance, of many expressible idea-systems together.[21] This is one of the reasons religious ideas are so hard to express in words, why theology in being abstract is thought to leave out so much, and why so many clear religious ideas need to be qualified to the point of near-denial—they express only one of the idea-systems out of the many that actually function together when a religious person engages the reality, such as a Christian appropriating the atoning work of Jesus.

As if the interplay of meaning systems in religion were not complex enough, religious ideas have complicated ways of being referable to religious objects. Sometimes an idea requires a whole system of ideas beyond itself to refer to the relevant ultimate. In the above example, if Jesus is to be interpreted as effecting the purity that allows people to come into the divine presence—ultimacy as a goal—much can be discussed nevertheless about atonement ideas without mentioning purity and its role in positioning people before God, as Fredriksen describes it. So, some ideas are religious only in the sense of being parts of larger systems of ideas that holistically refer to some ultimate object. Another complication is that some ideas have what might be called metaphysical meaning and others schematic meaning. The West Asian monotheisms, for instance, generally regard God as infinite in a metaphysical sense, and hence it is hard to conceptualize the approach of finite beings to God. But they all schematize the relation of the finite to infinite with ideas of heaven that locate the infinite finitely. Thinkers in those traditions, when pressed by metaphysical questioners, would say that God is not really on a throne, or in a house, or in a garden. They would insist, however, that what is important for the human quest about God as infinite is adequately and not falsely schematized in terms of God's place in heaven. This conception of heaven as a place to meet the divine is schematization in Kant's sense; a Kantian schema-image would be how heaven is concretely imagined.[22] All these complications add to the difficulty of analyzing properly just what the meaning of a religious idea is.

Difficulties of analyzing the meaning of religious ideas aside, the question of truth regarding meaning is whether a religion has the ideas it needs. That is a paradoxical expression of course, "the ideas it needs." So often the very heart of a religion is the ideas in fact it has that give classic expression to an event (the Exodus for Judaism), a person (Buddha, Jesus), or a teaching (Confucianism, Daoism, the Vedas, Islam).[23] Yet religions are not static, and perhaps do not even have a beginning with a first idea or founder. Consider Fredriksen's acute observation in *Ultimate Realities*, chapter 3, that the first generation or two of Christians were merely a slightly deviant group of Jews, with nothing distinct from Judaism in their views about God; the distinctive Christian view of God as Trinity came generations later. What made the earliest Christians distinct from other Jewish groups was their relation to Jesus, and they (principally St. Paul, in Fredriksen's analysis) struggled to understand what Jesus meant for their traditional Jewish belief in the swinging Roman world of the first century. To put the matter most crudely, the earliest Christians took Jesus to lead them to interpret the human condition and God in new respects, and they worked overtime to adapt old ideas and invent new ones to express this. Whatever ontological act God performed in Jesus Christ, according to St. Paul and subsequent Christian thinkers, the subjective acts of Christians to understand and appropriate what Jesus could mean for them about God required the development of

Christian ideas. As with all the other traditions we studied, the development of religious ideas continues throughout the tradition's history, not just its founding moments, though with many different forms—for instance, commentaries or innovative "theologies."

At least four reasons should be noted for the continued development of religious ideas within a tradition. The one illustrated above in the case of Christianity relative to Judaism is that a significant person or event calls for a reinterpretation of previously given ideas. It took Christians several centuries to work out a completely separate identity in relation to Judaism. A second reason is that geniuses arise in the course of history and simply enrich a tradition with new ideas that grasp the religious reality in new respects, with greater clarity and depth. A third reason is that religious ideas have plausibility not only in terms of their interpretation of the ways previous ideas interpreted the religious reality but also in relation to the larger culture of the era. The Near Eastern context of the earliest Christianity had different plausibility conditions from those of Spain, Parthia, India, China, and Egypt, to which Christianity was quickly taken. The ideas fit for Christianity as a persecuted minority religion were not entirely plausible when it became a state religion. The plausibility conditions for Nestorian Christianity in Tang Dynasty China were different from those of the contemporaneous European Dark Ages. Modern science has made radical shifts in plausibility conditions.[24] With every cultural change, religious ideas need to be rethought and their meanings adapted in order to represent what they had represented in the previous age. A fourth reason for the continuous development of religious ideas is that the religious traditions themselves interact. In all, changing times require creativity in achieving meaningful religious ideas.

Bearing in mind all these qualifications and complications, the question of religious truth bears upon meaning in respect of achieving ideas that can be true or false in respects in which the religious objects should be interpreted. The very practice of a religion establishes respects in which the religious object needs to be interpreted. So, the earliest Christians, to continue that example, took Jesus to be salvific in ways other elements of their religion, for instance, temple sacrifice, were not: how could this be understood? Christians thus needed to develop ideas of the atonement. Or, to take another example, the early practice of Buddhism focused on the Middle Way as framed by the Four Noble Truths. But this was paradoxical in light of the Upaniṣadic doctrine that ātman is Brahman, a doctrine as much a part of the home culture of early Buddhism as Second Temple Judaism was of early Christianity: so Buddhism had to develop an idea of no-self. The "hard ideas" in each of the traditions have been forged to be able to interpret a religious reality in some respect that the tradition requires.

Religions enter times of intellectual crisis when they seem to lack ideas they ought to have, or when old ideas that once seemed true now seem false—that is, they either fail to carry over anything in the right respect or carry over the wrong thing. The late-modern crises of the traditional religions we studied illustrate this point, a consistent theme of Saldarini's chapters in all three volumes. No traditional religion today has good ideas properly polished to deal with the religious dimensions of the human relation to the environment, of distributive justice in global economics and politics, of human relations in the age of the internet, or even of the contemporary encounter of religious traditions. All are scrambling to catch up, repristinating old ideas and searching for new ones that faithfully extend the traditions into a new situation. Should we think it would have been much different in the historical periods we have studied?

8.5 Truth in Transformation

The opposition between religious truth claims as doctrine and the use of truth claims to effect soteriological results is difficult to overcome (see 1.1). It is decisively overcome, however, in the theory that truth (religious and otherwise) is the carryover of what is important in the object into interpreters in the respects in which ideas (signs, symbols, propositions, theories) interpret those objects. How so? In the carryover theory there is a spectrum of possible transformations of the interpreters, all of which can be "true" or "false" in the variety of senses of performative truth (i.e., depending on the relevant felicity conditions), but none of which can be taken to be truth-claims without assuming or making an analysis of the intentional shape of the carryover. The intentional shape of the carryover consists in how the conditions of interpretation (interpreter taking the object in respects determined by the ideas in theoretical and practical ways), reference (iconic, indexical and convention, extensional and intentional, primary and secondary), and meaning (coded interplaying systems, achieved as means to engage reality) obtain in the truth claim at hand. The spectrum of transformations runs from simple informing of the interpreter in terms already given to altering the interpreter's character in ways that have no immediate relevance to the descriptive content of the religious ideas. Sketching out some typical stages on this spectrum will illustrate the force of this point about religious truth.

First, the least transformative pole of the spectrum has a fully formed set of ideas and the truth claims merely make assertions and denials in those terms. If the truth claims are arguments, or offer new evidence couched in the given terms, the transformation might be learning something new in addition to learning what is asserted or denied. The ideal described by Clooney, especially in 2.2, is for such a situation in which learning and debate take place exclusively within what logicians now would call well-formed formulae. This is the safest context in which it might be valid to speak of truth as applying to propositions alone without reference to the interpretive situation with the ambiguities of reference and meaning. Transformation at this pole of the spectrum is merely being informed, or grasping logical implications. At this pole, Aristotle's claim that the carryover from object to mind is of form alone is quite plausible. Truth claims at this pole of the spectrum, and the neighboring ones, are likely to be accompanied by considerable disquiet because it is recognized or felt that the precisely defined ideas screen out or distort something that should be carried over but is not. Truth claims are always focal points within a background, and the background can give clues about distortion. The distinction between kataphatic and apophatic theology formalizes this point.

Second, next along the spectrum is the situation in which the interpreter is learning, but has not yet become adept in, a preformed scholastic language. The transformations involved are not only those of being informed and alerted to inferences but those of adopting the habits of mind determined by the scholastic system of ideas.

Third, next is the situation in which a community of interpreters is attempting to develop a univocal set of ideas with universal application that can interpret reality in whatever respects any context of interpretation might intend; or, more realistically, to develop such a set of ideas for a limited domain of reality, for instance, theological topics as in chapter 2. The transformations involved at this stage along the spectrum are not only the acquisition and exercise of a univocal set of ideas but the invention of them, moving from relative confusion and parochial limitation to terms that can be used by anyone in the conversation with generally understood meaning. Actually, there are probably many stages on the spectrum that distinguish different degrees and senses of self-consciousness about this kind of transformation. These range from the relatively simple attempt to get everyone to agree on common definitions, to explicit awareness of what is given up when this kind of idea is used for theological purposes, to grand narratives and theories of theories that understand the roles of ideas in cognition and performance (such as this very discussion). Technical discussions of univocity versus analogy, of literal versus metaphoric assertions, of description and explanation versus evocation, and the like give rise to complex self-conscious multiplex approaches to theoretical truth.

Fourth, whereas the above three stages on the spectrum have emphasized the transformations effected as intellectual interpretants, those stages also might effect practical transformations. Debate within the first stage, for instance, might convince a theist that atheism is true, with the practical consequence that the interpreter should switch school-affiliations. Learning within the second stage might transform the interpreter into an adept and teacher within a community. Learning within the third stage might make the interpreter a more humble multiculturalist. Learning what is true in any of the first three stages might have far-reaching consequences for how to live and build communities. If responsibilities are thereby incurred, their exercise is subject to appropriate felicity conditions, depending on the context. Likewise, appropriately contextual felicity conditions govern announcements of decisions to change community or school affiliations, apologies for past behavior, expressions of gratitude for kindnesses shown, and engagements in religious rituals, any of which may occur in conjunction with intellectual transformations.

Fifth, next along the spectrum of transformation come stages that are interpretations for the sake of building communities. These stages are not easily ordered among themselves. Religious ideas function normatively to shape many kinds of community, family, and religious groups, including entire societies shaped by many ideas in addition to religious ones. Intellectual interpretants are often important in community transformations, especially when there are serious questions about how to live and what to do. But equally important, and usually far more, are practical interpretants—family rituals for ancestors, meal-time prayers, the organization of community worship, institutions of handing on religious learning, religious effects on cultural ideals and social policies. Whereas we in our project have usually talked about this as embodied truth, actualized truth, or being true (personally as well as communally), the community side to it is perhaps more helpfully called *faithfulness*. This is, what is important in the religious object is carried over faithfully into the community in the respects intended by the ideas. This is a way of speaking about how the fidelity conditions for these kinds of truthfulness are importantly different from those associated more directly with individual transformations.

The work of cultural anthropologists such as Clifford Geertz and theologians such as George Lindbeck has sometimes been construed to mean that faithfulness is merely a matter of the consistency and thoroughness with which a community's life is organized according to its system of ideas or symbols, broadly construed.[25] This is, there is no truth as carryover from the real object into the belief and practice of the community. But this inference need not be drawn, and surely ought not be drawn in Lindbeck's case. The situation with respect to truth claims is that reality can indeed be engaged by a community and interpreted with its cultural-linguistic semiotic, and that interpretation is true if the community's response is faithful to what is important in its real object. The cultural-linguistic system might register the truth-claims as mere information or logical discovery; people in the religious community might learn their cultural-linguistic system better by attending to the truth claims; and the cultural-linguistic system itself might evolve, as surely all such systems have.

Sixth, beyond these stages are transformations of communities in which the practical interpretants are as before, that is, things that conform the community to what is important in the religious reality in the respects in which the ideas represent such reality, but in which the intellectual interpretants are not descriptive, strictly speaking. The intellectual interpretants rather are symbols from scriptures or liturgies or other imaginative sources that are used but not themselves much interpreted. Those symbolic interpretants are often themselves arranged in systems and given a rational order. But their context of use is more local than the more nearly universal ideas discussed earlier. Their metaphors are particular to their context. They often articulate a narrower cultural world than their interpreters in fact inhabit, as when an interpreter enters into an ancient ritual whose terms do not relate to contemporary political, social, and cognitive ideals. Such narrow symbolic systems would not be called true in a descriptive sense, an ideal to which the more philosophic literal functions previously discussed aspire. But they are true in a profound sense if the communities formed by them, for instance, as liturgies form a worshipping community, are transformed by their carrying over of what is important in the religious object. That is, the applicable felicity conditions for true transformation in such cases may be so dominantly matters of communal formation and participation that descriptive adequacy becomes negligible in importance. Of course it is difficult to tell when such a true transformation takes place. In the case of more theoretical forms of truth claims, the claims themselves and their surrounding arguments are the relevant places to look, although it is far better to find corroborating evidence from many different angles too. In the case of practical community transformations by religious ideas that are not specifically true considered in their own intent, only corroborating evidence from other sources is possible. A Buddhist would judge the appropriateness of *upaya* and a Christian would look for "fruits of the spirit," in St. Paul's phrase. In the same way, the judgment of the truth of a community's practical interpretation of a liturgy or a scripture invokes complex criteria that derive from deep within the tradition in question, having survived the test of time. Felicity conditions of this sort do not appear from out of thin air. They are forged in corporate experience and win their authority there.

The virtue of at least some of these local ideas or symbol systems is that they are able to carry over kinds of importance that the more theoretical ideas cannot. The impotent religion of the French Revolution showed the limitation of using relatively abstract and universal language for conveying religious truth important for concrete communities. The local ideas and symbol systems not only convey more vivacity than do abstractions but also those aspects of particular identity, history, and locale that are important in different ways for different religions.

There are many models for the relation of the more abstract and theoretical ideas to the more local symbol systems. In some situations, the more abstract interpret the more local in a wider context; in many religions, however, there are histories of the interpretation of the abstractions and independent histories of the interpretation of the local symbols with little reference to the abstractions. Another model is that the abstractions characterize sophisticated thought and the more local ones popular religion. Another model is that the abstractions allow communication between religious communities, as discussed in chapter 2, whereas the more local terms facilitate concrete personal and communal religious commitment and life. No simple model is helpful for long: Śaṅkara, one of the most abstract of all religious thinkers, accessible to nineteenth-century Englishwomen as well as to his own comrades, cited the local Vedas as his source and authority. In all the religions we studied, there have been complex interactions between the more theoretical intellectual interpretants and the more local intellectual interpretants.[26]

Seventh, yet farther along the spectrum, reaching now the other pole, are personal transformations in what might be called the life of the devotee in which the practical interpretants are completely separated from the intentional content of the intellectual interpretants. In the previous case, there is at least supposed to be a continuity between the local ideas and the more abstract universal ones: for Thomas Aquinas, that God is the Act of Esse which was supposed to be a conceptualization of the same God who talked and bartered with Abraham. Religions sometimes express this continuity in the form of controversial tensions, with advocates for the local ideas and their community embodiment, such as Bernard of Clairvaux in the Christian Medieval period, differing with the more abstract thinkers. In the present case of transformations on the spectrum, however, that continuity is abandoned. Ideas contemplated in devotional meditation are often wholly fantastical and exaggerated. Tibetan Buddhists who contemplate pictures of ugly armed goddesses wearing skulls are hoping to be awakened; they are not affirming that emptiness is like an ugly goddess. A Zen kōan is contemplated not for its answer but for its awakening surprise. Whether the devotional ideas function truly, carrying across what is important for the devotee, is extremely difficult to judge. In this case, the appropriate felicity conditions are embedded within the complex traditions of spiritual discernment in all the religions we studied. Moreover, the application of these felicity conditions is at least as much the task of the individual as of a community to which he or she may belong. This brings to the relevant felicity conditions the greatest possible degree of flexibility.

All along this spectrum, from theology classroom to hermit's hut, religious ideas can be understood as true if they carry across what is important in the object they interpret to the interpreter in the respects in which they stand for that object. By carrying something across, they transform the interpreter with effects as slight as transferring data to as mighty as enlightenment and holiness.

A final and crucial point about transformation needs to be made. A religious idea can be transformative only when the interpreter is ready for it. Only when the interpreter is the right secondary referent for the idea's use in referring to its real object can the transformative interpretation be made. As previously argued, this requires the interpreter to be at the right stage of life, in the right spiritual and psychological state of soul, and with the right culture (which involves having the right ideas or signs available). In the case of theoretical transformations at the beginning of the spectrum above, this might not mean much more than learning a theological vocabulary. But in the communal and personal devotional stages of the transformative spectrum, readiness is more complicated. Traditions of spiritual discernment include awareness of the proper timing of transformations, inviting patience on the part of adepts and students alike; devotional and even communal transformation has its seasons. This is a key feature of felicity conditions for transformative truth.

For all of our traditions it is probably fair to say that the deepest religious ideas have many levels of access, and that the truth applicable at any level depends on the interpreter being at that level. As Edward Conze pointed out, decades of yogic practice might be required to make a serious judgment about the validity of an important religious idea.[27] He contrasted this with graduate education in the sciences in which a few short years can suffice for learning both criteria for judgment and decent taste. As scholars, we in this project are not so modest as to assume that we have no depth of yogic insight into the profound ideas we study and compare. On the other hand, none of us pretends to be an adept at an esoteric level in any of our traditions. So our comparative judgments are complicated yet again.

Are the ideas we compare, and the senses of truth attached to them, at comparable levels of spiritually transformed understanding? We have no good way of answering that question. We have taken the methodological dodge of not raising the issue and assuming that we have the level of understanding typified in the latest scholarly literature. This sets us up for criticism by an adept in any of the traditions who tells us, "You just don't get it!" Truth to tell, each of us has been tempted to say this (and many succumbed to the temptation) to others of our group attempting to represent our favorite tradition or text; this happened more at the beginning than at the end of the project. This applies even to the theory of truth presented in the present chapter: our group is not in uniform agreement with it. Although it does connect the theoretical discussions in each tradition with the performative, which our group judges to be a virtue, various among our number would weigh the felicity conditions we have discussed differently than this chapter has. Some would place even greater stress on spiritual disciplines and discernment. Others would point out that our self-referential entanglement in these religious traditions changes the felicity conditions for our own work, drawing in spiritual dimensions that scholars tend to marginalize when it is themselves rather than others under examination. In the long run, however, we all acknowledge that first-order religious ideas are believed to be true by those who hold them, and that the traditions themselves have second-order ways of accounting for this, ways that were discussed in the previous chapter.

Notes

1. For an intriguing survey of contemporary philosophy of religion in relation to its eigthteenth-century sources, see Eugene Thomas Long, *God, Reason and Religions* (Boston: Kluwer Academic Publishers, 1995). This volume is a reprint of the twenty-fifth anniversary edition of the *International Journal for Philosophy of Religion*, vol. 38, 1995. What is astounding about the collection of essays by distinguished American philosophers of religion is that they mainly take Christianity to be the religion of analysis; in this they are no different from their eighteenth-century ancestors such as David Hume. Neville's contribution to the volume shows how the first volume of the journal, in 1970, sported studies of other religions by an international group of scholars, whereas the later volumes returned to a more Christian and epistemological orientation. The moral of this, in light of the great burgeoning of religious studies, is that philosophy of religions as such is much broader than the technical craft of philosophy of religion, as it is usually expressed in recent issues of that journal.

2. See J. L. Austin, "Other Minds," *Proceedings of the Aristotelian Society*, Supplementary Volume XX (1946): 173ff, in which he uses ideas that the preface to the famous *How to Do Things with Words* (Oxford: Oxford University Press, 1962) says were formed in 1939. Austin 1962 introduces a number of important terms, including "speech act" and "illocutionary act." Stating is a kind of illocutionary act to which considerations of truth and falsity apply but there are a great many others illocutionary acts. He tentatively lists five classes: "the verdictive is an exercise of judgment, the exercitive is an assertion of influence or exercising of power, the commissive is an assuming of an obligation or declaring of an intention, the behabitive is the adopting of an attitude, and the expositive is the clarifying of reasons, arguments, and communications" (Austin, *How to Do Things*, 163). Each has its own ways of being felicitous or infelicitous; for instance, behabitives such as apologies or expressions of sympathy may be sincere or insincere. The illocutionary force of an utterance crucially depends on context and background; different illocutionary acts can be achieved in the same utterance, depending on context.

3. These philosophers include P. Geach, P. Grice, R. M. Hare, and P. F. Strawson. Wittgenstein's *Philosophical Investigations*, trans. G. E. M. Anscombe (New York: Macmillan, 1953) also belongs to this tradition. In some respects this book continues the philosophical attitudes of his earlier *Tractatus Logico-Philosophicus* (London: Routledge & Kegan Paul, 1922), but it is a dramatic reversal in other ways. In particular, the later work abandons the earlier work's rigid approach to meaning, as well as all theories of meaning that focus on sense and reference, looking instead toward the use of language as the source of its meaning. The "meaning is use" motto characterizes the work of many of these philosophers. Searle, *Speech Acts: An Essay in the Philosophy of Language* (Cambridge: Cambridge University Press, 1969), launches an appreciative attack on the vagueness of this motto and the fallacies to which it leads. Where Austin analyzed and classified speech acts, Searle offers a relatively comprehensive theory of language as a rule-governed form of behavior, including much sophisticated and consistent analyses of the conditions of adequacy of many kinds of speech acts. The attempt to analyze the conditions of adequacy of religious speech acts defines the principal sense in which our own project is a continuation of this philosophical tradition.

4. The literature on pragmatism in this regard is equally vast and overlaps in some places with the Anglo-American philosophy of language. Perhaps the best secondary introductions are J. E. Smith, *Purpose and Thought: The Meaning of Pragmatism* (New Haven: Yale University Press, 1978); and Steve Odin, *The Social Self in Zen and American Pragmatism* (Albany: State University of New York Press, 1996). For Peirce's semiotics see Vincent M. Colapietro, *Peirce's Approach to the Self: A Semiotic Perspective on Human Subjectivity* (Albany: State University of New York Press, 1989); for more fulsome interpretations of Peirce see Douglas Anderson, *Creativity and the Philosophy of C. S. Peirce* (Boston: Martinus Nijhoff, 1987); and idem, *Strands of System: The Philosophy of Charles Peirce* (West Lafayette, Ind.: Purdue University Press, 1995). Neville's

interpretation of Peirce is in *The Highroad around Modernism* (Albany: State University of New York Press, 1992). Neville's, *Normative Cultures* (Albany: State University of New York Press, 1995) employs Peirce to distinguish action and theorizing, and his *The Truth of Broken Symbols* (Albany: State University of New York Press, 1996) expands Peirce's semiotics into a theory of religious truth.

5. See *Ultimate Realities*, chapters 7 and 9, for a discussion of precisely what is meant by justification of comparative categories.

6. See Chad Hansen, *A Daoist Theory of Chinese Thought* (New York: Oxford University Press, 1992); and idem, "Term-Belief in Action: Sentences and Terms in Early Chinese Philosophy," *Epistemological Issues in Classical Chinese Philosophy*, ed. Hans Lenk and Gregor Paul (Albany: State University of New York Press, 1993).

7. The formula is actually a paraphrase of Peirce's characterization of the triadic character of interpretation. The formula is expanded into a general theory of interpretive truth in nature in Neville, *Recovery of the Measure* (Albany: State University of New York Press, 1989), especially parts 1 and 4; it is the basis of Neville's theory of religious truth in *The Truth of Broken Symbols*. It also structures Wildman's theory of religious experience in Wildman and Brothers, "A Neuropsychological-Semiotic Model of Religious Experiences," *Neuroscience and the Person: Scientific Perspectives on Divine Action*, ed. Robert John Russell, et al. (Vatican City State and Berkeley, Cal.: Vatican Observatory and Center for Theology and the Natural Sciences, 2000).

8. Translation from *A Source Book in Chinese Philosophy*, ed. Wing-tsit Chan (Princeton: Princeton University Press, 1963).

9. Op. cit., 1989.

10. Religious naturalism is a typical position within American pragmatism. It generally means a causal continuity among things. Its objection to supernaturalism is not to transcendent deities, spirits, or paraphysic phenomena, all of which have been of great interest to Peirce, James, and others. It is rather to the claim that such religious entities can be separate from nature and still act within it. Pragmatic naturalists have usually been anxious to define natural processes in non-mechanistic ways. Peirce, for instance, modeled natural causation on interpretation. Whitehead offered a different account of natural processes that he called organicism. Neville, in *Recovery of the Measure*, develops an extensive philosophy of nature that connects semiotic causation with other kinds, and gives an account of intentionality consonant with the claim that truth is the carryover of value from the object into the interpreter in the respects in which the signs in the interpretation stand for the object. The difficulty with philosophic non-mechanistic reconstructions of natural processes is that they are difficult to coordinate with scientific representations of nature, which usually aim to be mechanistic. The importance of Wildman and Brothers, op. cit., is that it folds neurophysiological mechanism into a Peircean theory of natural process so that it is possible to speak of brain conditions being experiential and interpretive.

11. On this see Neville, *The Highroad around Modernism*, chap. 1.

12. The "qualification by material, cultural, semiotic, and purpose" is necessary to acknowledge continuities and discontinuities along the causal route of carryover. How can a holy mountain or an intangible Daoist spirit get carried over into a human being with a meat brain? By being transformed into a different material with a cultural and semiotic shape and activated by purpose. Without such qualifications, brute causality, physical or spiritual, cannot be grasped intentionally. For an analysis at length, see Neville, *Recovery of the Measure*, chaps. 3–4.

13. See the discussions of theory in Neville, *Normative Cultures*, chaps. 1–4.

14. Peirce's theory of signs is extremely complex. He developed it in many places, often as an aside in dealing with other topics. The most focused discussion is in Peirce, "Speculative Grammar," *The Collected Papers of Charles Sanders Peirce, vol.* 2, ed. Charles Hartshorne and Paul Weiss (Cambridge: Harvard University, 1932). The theoretical discussion of reference is in chapter three of that book, "The Icon, Index, and Symbol." Peirce used the word "sign" to mean all kinds of significant items, and the word "symbol" to mean signs that refer through conventional means. To preserve the specialized meanings of "symbol" in religious contexts, we use "convention" for what Peirce meant by "symbol." Moreover, though "idea" has the same technical range as Peirce's "sign" (for us as well as for Plato), we will usually use "sign" more specifically and "idea" more vaguely.

15. Wittgenstein, *Tractatus*.

16. Plato's Charmides and Euthydemos are his delightful comic discussions of language and the flow of reality. *The Republic* is the masterpiece of argument to the effect that we need to acknowledge unchanging forms in order to deal with practical politics and the ordering of personal life in a world of constant change. Plato's prime concern was with the concrete reality of "becoming" rather than the static formal world of "being." Later thinkers, beginning with Aristotle, would give pride of place to being over becoming.

17. Alfred North Whitehead, *Science and the Modern World* (New York: Macmillan, 1925); and idem, *Process and Reality: An Essay in Cosmology* (New York: Macmillan, 1929; corrected edition ed. David Ray Griffin and Donald W. Sherburne (New York: Free Press, 1978).

18. See Chad Hansen's *A Taoist Theory of Chinese Thought,* and "Term-Belief in Action," the latter of which is a compact summary of his main point.

19. This is the view Wittgenstein attributes to Augustine (falsely) at the beginning of the *Philosophical Investigations* (2) and against which he launches his theory of language games.

20. For a more complete analysis of this technical distinction, see Neville, *The Truth of Broken Symbols*, 32–47.

21. On this claim that religious ideas are often compactions or resonances of symbols participating in many symbols systems at once, systems not quite coordinated and perhaps even contradictory, see ibid., chap. 3.

22. Kant's analysis is in *The Critique of Pure Reason* (translation including both the first [1781] and second [1787] editions by Norman Kemp Smith [London: Macmillan, 1956]), the chapter on Schematism, 1787. Schematism in religious ideas in this sense is discussed at length in Neville, *The Truth of Broken Symbols*, chap. 1, and at great length as defining imagination in his *Reconstruction of Thinking* (Albany: State University of New York Press, 1981), chap. 7.

23. On this notion of "classic expression," see David Tracy, *The Analogical Imagination: Christian Theology and the Culture of Pluralism* (New York: Crossroad, 1981), chaps. 3–5; for an analysis of how "classics" are formed and work religiously, see Hart, *Unfinished Man and the Imagination* (New York: Herder, 1968), passim.

24. On the notion and role of plausibility conditions, see Wildman, *Fidelity with Plausibility: Modest Christologies in the Twentieth Century* (Albany: State University of New York Press, 1998), especially the introduction and the conclusion.

25. Clifford Geertz, *The Interpretation of Cultures* (New York: Basic Books, 1973); and George Lindbeck, *The Nature of Doctrine: Religion and Theology in a Postliberal Age* (Philadelphia: Westminster, 1984).

26. On local systems of symbols, contrasted with more abstract and universal ones, see Clooney, *Seeing through Texts: Doing Theology among the Śrīvaiṣṇavas of South India* (Albany: State University of New York Press, 1996).

27. Edward Conze, *Buddhist Thought in India* (London: George Allen and Unwin, 1962), 17–22.

9

On the Nature of Religion

Lessons We Have Learned

Wesley J. Wildman
and Robert Cummings Neville

The Comparative Religious Ideas Project has not been about religion, as such, but rather about literate religious ideas. That leaves out a lot, from religious practices to tribal religions lacking an extensive literature of ideas, as well as other cultural phenomena with a religious character yet not closely associated with religious texts. Nevertheless, there are a number of implications for the understanding of religion embedded in the project's work. The task of this chapter is to tease out these implications.

Two motivations are especially important as we consider this subject. First, to avoid misunderstanding, it is important to be clear about what can and cannot be inferred from the project's research with regard to controversial issues such as the nature or the identification of religion as such. Second, and more constructively, we (Wildman and Neville) think that the project's conclusions imply hypotheses that can be tested in future attempts to formulate theories both about particular religious ideas (such as the human condition, ultimate realities, and religious truth) and about the nature of religion as such. These hypotheses should be stated clearly as a way to expose the results of the project to discussion and correction.

Our observations are organized into four sections. First, we have a number of general comments about the nature of religion that are especially pertinent to its complex nature and the resulting complexities of its study, which is of course what we have been grappling with in this project for a number of years. Second, we shall offer some more specific comments about the nature of religion that emerge from the attempts we have made to construct (incomplete) theories about various aspects of religion. Third, we have comments on the nature of religion in respect of the relation between comparison and theory building. Finally, we make two conjectures, one concerning whether categories for comparison determine theories of various aspects of religion (such as religious truth), and the other concerning the possibility of constructing an overall theory of religion based on the results of systematic comparison.

9.1 Remarks on Our Experience of Studying Religion

Religion has been studied in many times and places, and in many ways, with an intriguing result. There is a proliferation of definitions of religion and few who have studied it are willing to fall on their swords (or knitting needles) for any one of them, even for a definition they themselves advocate. Why is this? Simply stated, religion is enormously complicated. Few generalizations survive scrutiny. Even the point of making generalizations can seem obscure after sufficient exposure to the details. As in the study of history, it seems, details are everything in the study of religion. Our project's work amply confirmed this feature of religion. In fact, it did so in several quite specific ways that bear simultaneously on the study of religion and the nature of religion.

First, if the point of generalizations in the study of religion can be rendered obscure by the masses of details relevant to testing them, then comparative generalizations about religious phenomena might wisely be avoided. This is one of the reasons so many scholars are skittish about comparison in religion. Surely they are wise to be cautious. Yet in working together our project members confirmed an impression already formed from familiarity with the literature: we frequently make comparisons about religious phenomena even when we are not explicit about doing so. Comparing is a fundamental element of human rationality, especially where making sense of a lot of context-dependent details is needed. Even the apparently innocent move to call a particular religious activity a "ritual" is actually to classify and thus to make the comparative judgments of similarity and class membership that underlie all classifications. Comparison is extremely common in the study of religion.

Being in it up to our necks, we would do well to be self-conscious about it so as to do it as fairly and competently as possible—and to avoid being swallowed up in the confusion that results from lack of awareness about scholarly procedures.

The facts that comparison is unavoidable and that religion is complicated jointly have determined the task of our project. It is precisely in recognition of the complexity of religion, not in defiance of it, that we have advanced, used, and tested a sophisticated theory of comparison. Moreover, the character of that theory of comparison reflects our unanimous impression that it is genuinely difficult to produce stable generalizations about religious phenomena. How so? The details of religious phenomena make any comparative generalization so precarious that it can only survive if it is vaguer than the phenomena compared by means of it. Details that might destroy an overly specific generalization can be regarded as specifications of carefully constructed, but vague, comparative generalizations. This is not a strategy to protect comparative judgments from immediate falsification by the data of religious studies. Rather, it is in the very nature of the case that the only kinds of comparisons that can be rendered stable in the study of religion are comparisons of this vague sort. In other words, the theory of comparison being tested in our project is a theory developed in recognition of the complexity of religious phenomena.

Second, studying the crystal structure of quartz using the tools of X-ray crystallography and analytical chemistry is usually an existentially uncomplicated matter. By contrast, religion is complicated in a special way that makes its study existentially tricky. Religion makes claims on and about people who study it in a way that quartz does not. Moreover, trying to take those claims seriously necessarily involves taking up a posture toward the fact that they are about us. For example, to study a religious text in which a disciple is portrayed as learning from a master that understanding of any sort is only possible through the cultivation of a special capacity to see reality rightly, beyond the limits of conventional seeing, is to pose an intense difficulty for the scholar of religion. How can such a text be taken as seriously as it demands when it is studied merely in the dispassionate scholarly mode? And how can such a text be meaningfully compared with other religious attitudes to spiritually enlightened knowledge unless all such texts can be taken with the seriousness demanded by the account of understanding they offer? The problem goes beyond existential self-reference of this specifically epistemological sort. Almost all religious texts invite, even demand, particular attitudes in their study and most religious ideas implicate the one who thinks about them in ways that reach far beyond the scholarly role.

Surely this conundrum is one of the reasons that it simply has not occurred to most people in most cultures through most of history to make what we now call religious phenomena the objects of study. We found instances of interest in comparing certain aspects of religions in all of the traditions we studied—least of all in Judaism but even there the divine covenant with Noah is interpreted at times as relevant to the understanding of non-Jewish people. Nonetheless, comparative religion has been of most interest in the West, specifically among Christians, and most recently a fascination of the Western academy. How is the dimension of the complexity of religion that bears on existential self-referentiality handled in our project, which is an instance of the Western academy's interest in the study of religion? This is a problem upon which we reflected several times in our project without coming to a satisfactory solution. The Western academic model for comparing religious phenomena is quite simply limited. It is conceivable that we did in fact miss out on important insights because our group did not meditate together or try to achieve the conventionality-transcending ways of understanding promised in so many texts. We were forced to rest content with the hope that our distinctively Western form of partiality—which includes the claim to impartiality and strategies for achieving it—would have special virtues that might make our project valuable in spite of everything it did not and could not achieve.

Third, the importance of complex details in religion showed up in another way in the course of our project. The first volume, *The Human Condition*, made explicit use of five phenomenological sites of importance as a rubric for describing religious phenomena that was designed to ensure that those descriptions would be properly balanced. The second and third volumes did not make explicit use of that rubric but the awareness of its importance stayed with us. The vital contribution of the phenomenological sites of importance was to help us express our awareness of the complexity of religion with respect to the various points of view from which the significance of religious phenomena can be appreciated. Phenomenological sites of importance are relevant to describing realities beyond the borders of the religious but they are especially important in religion.

The first four sites of phenomenological importance are: (1) the intrinsic, which involves expressing and analyzing ideas in their own terms; (2) the perspectival, which concerns the ways that religious ideas determine a larger perspective on life; (3) the theoretical, by which we mean the ways that the ideas lead to larger theoretical considerations; and (4) the practical, which has to do with the implications of the religious ideas for practice. Each of these sites is an important part of properly thick descriptions of religious ideas and we tried to register all of them throughout our project with varying degrees of success. The fifth site deserves special mention. It is the singularity of religious phenomena, the special qualities that cannot be analyzed or compared. The only way to get at religious ideas and practices in their singularity is to become competent in their use, which in the case of ideas superficially involves mastery of metaphor and other forms of indirection used in the special social-linguistic context within which the achievement of mastery is fostered. More profoundly it involves engaging putatively religious realities to see whether truth is quickened. It follows that not everything in religious phenomena can be brought to the discussion table and made the object of comparative generalizations. Our project has been keenly aware that our comparative efforts have been both limited by ideas considered as singular and complicated by the diversity of phenomenological sites that are relevant to expressing them.

By way of summary then, the complexity of religious phenomena has been registered in our project in a variety of ways. One sort of complexity is associated with masses of details, another with the unavoidability of vagueness in comparisons, and still another with the conundrums of existential self-reference. Then there is the complexity associated with the various dimensions of the importance of religious phenomena expressed in the phenomenological sites, and finally the singular quality of religious phenomena in respect of which they cannot be brought into the domains of analysis and comparison. Our project has grappled with each of these dimensions of the complexity of religion quite self-consciously, though with varying degrees of success.

Having admitted the complexities that limit comparison, we should not fail to stress that we have in fact articulated and explored a number of important comparisons throughout the three volumes. On the one hand, these are all hypotheses about comparison, asking for further probation. On the other, they have been made stable by the challenges we have given them. Some of our comparisons are merely vague, especially in *The Human Condition* where we specified similarities and differences according to grids that mark out the details of the sites of phenomenological importance. Others have been framed vaguely and then specified in detail through cumulative discussions; these are found primarily in the specialists' chapters when they are read sequentially through the three volumes, for instance, the three treatments of Chinese religion, the three of Islam, and so forth. Yet other comparisons combine both the vague articulations and the specific filling in of detail with analyses of how these add up to say something about the human condition, ultimate realities, and religious truth. These last are found mainly in our (Wildman and Neville) reflective chapters in each volume.

9.2 Remarks on Our Construction of Theories of Aspects of Religion

In this volume and the previous one, *Ultimate Realities*, we (Neville and Wildman) made an attempt to develop theories of aspects of religion, though not of religion as a whole. These theories remain incomplete, of course, and their elaboration was not our main concern. Nevertheless, they are important for justifying comparative categories and we gave a fair bit of thought to them. In the process, we noticed that certain well-known features of religion had to be addressed. These features are usually registered in two famously distinguished strands within the study of religion and so we have come to think of our comparison-based approach to theory building in religion as a synthesis of these existing approaches.

First, many sorts of philosophy of religion, comparative mythology, and Jungian or other archetype approaches to religion, lift up a fundamental feature of religion, and especially of religious ideas: religion is not entirely conventional. Religious ideas are many and varied, to be sure, and their meanings are strongly dependent on cultural context, but they are not arbitrary. There is something about the way the world shows up religiously to people across cultures and history that invites certain religious ideas and not others. Ultimate reality has never been thought of by any major religious tradition as seventy-three dimensional, as a beat-up yellow Volkswagen, as more blue than red, or as a lot like sliced pineapple. It is not that these ideas could never be used for ultimate reality, just that they are never likely to catch on. Moreover, there are important similarities in ideas of ultimate reality, as expressed in the comparative generalizations of *Ultimate Realities*. Likewise, there are significant similarities in ideas of the human condition and religious truth, as seen in the first volume on *The Human Condition*, and in this volume.

The givenness of religion is not, therefore, merely a matter of Durkheimian codification of ultimate social commitments that is then objectified in social processes and encountered as something capable of molding our imaginations and experiences. That process occurs, as the sociology of knowledge has amply demonstrated, but the givenness of religion also appears to involve culturally transcendent or invariant features. Another way of saying this is that there is a feedback mechanism capable of correcting ideas about religious realities in the long term. It is not much like the strong feedback mechanism relied on in scientific experimentation, nor does it seem capable of forcing adjustments in all religious ideas. Nevertheless, a weak and partial feedback mechanism does seem to be operative. How this is to be explained is a matter for philosophers, theologians, or psychologists—and many have tried in the history of the study of religion. For our purposes, the main point is not to explain it but to allow this genuine feature of religion to be registered properly in our work.

In practice, the givenness of religion has shown up in two ways in the course of the project. The first is in the comparative conclusions that we have drawn about the human condition, ultimate realities, and religious truth. Such conclusions cannot seriously be thought of merely as contingent structural similarities among utterly conventional cultural-religious ideas, though they are certainly culturally dependent and conventional. It is the patterns among these similarities that make the "merely conventional" line of explanation for them implausible. This has been noticed repeatedly in the history of the study of religion; archetype theories of religion get that much correct even if they neglect the proper roles of historical contingencies and cultural conventionality. The second way the givenness of religion shows up in our project is in the justification of comparative categories, which relies heavily not just on phenomenological considerations but also on theoretical articulations of what is possible with regard to religious ideas of any particular sort. For example, with regard to ultimate realities in the second volume, we (Neville and Wildman) argued that the possible ideas range from ontological ultimates to ultimate ways and from personal gods to impersonal principles. Moreover, we argued that certain transformations of symbolic expressions of those ideas are also inherently likely, as when an emphasis on personal symbolizations of ultimacy evokes balancing, non-personal symbolizations, and vice versa. Which of the possible ideas is realized in any given cultural context, and which transformation is sponsored by any historical circumstance, is a matter of contingent influences both external and internal to the religious tradition. But the givenness of religion is present in the structuring of possibilities for symbolization of ultimate realities.

Second, the history of religions approach has tended to explain any particular configuration of ideas in a cultural-religious setting in terms of influences and contingencies, ranging from geography to weather patterns and from trade routes to invasions. This surely reflects a genuine characteristic of religion: religious phenomena are highly dependent on every kind of context, on historical contingencies, and on raw chance. Our awareness of this feature of religion shows up as the balance side to the feature just called "givenness" above. For instance, in justifying comparative categories, the reason why any of a wide range of possible ideas is realized in any particular place and time is to be explained not by appeal to the givenness of religion but in terms of contingencies. Likewise, even if patterns of possible change can be expressed in theoretical terms independently of any particular cultural-religious context, actual changes within the matrix of the possible dynamics of religious ideas require explanation in terms of concrete circumstances and cultural contingencies. All of this is reflected in our theory of religious truth in chapter 8.

The givenness and the contingency of religious ideas are both indispensable in justifications of comparative generalizations. In this way, theories of aspects of religion based on the comparative procedure we defend synthesize the two main explanatory traditions within the study of religion: those that focus on givenness such as philosophy of religion and comparative mythology and those that stress contingency such as the history of religion. There is no need to separate these traditions within the study of religion because they complement each other, as we hope we have begun to show in this volume. Nor is there any need to oppose these approaches to the tradition of the phenomenology of religion, with its emphasis on description rather than explanation. Thick phenomenological descriptions, paying attention to the sites of importance previously discussed, are the condition for the possibility of comparative judgments even as those judgments must in the end also be supported by explanatory theories drawing on the givenness and the contingency of religious phenomena.

How might we think of givenness in religion so as to avoid the suggestion that phenomena are given in some pure or uninterpreted state, such as the logical positivists supposed about sense data? Likewise, how might we speak of contingency in religion so as to avoid the suggestion that conventions are merely contingent and arbitrary, that they are only "about" other conventions with no reference? If we might be pardoned a linguistic barbarism, the combination of attention to givenness and contingency in the reflective comparative study of religious ideas might best be called a complex analysis of religious "takenness." We study how different traditions "take" the human condition, ultimate realities, and religious truth. This supposes that the subject matters are "real," but not identified except through contingent conventions. It supposes also that the conventions are historically and contextually contingent, and yet not wholly arbitrary. Religious conventions, like those in agriculture and warfare, arise through the engagements of life, even if they do not have the strong feedback mechanisms of modern science. The critique of the "myth of the given" does not apply against our procedure of supposing that religions "take" real aspects of existence by means of their conventional signs and practices. Nor can our approach to religion be charged with epistemic solipsism just because we recognize that it is interpreted in being "taken"; religious ideas could not be said to be true or false, faithful or foolish in directing practice, unless they are supposed to refer. Once this point is appreciated, the barbarism of "takenness" can be expunged.

Our attempts to acknowledge and combine those disciplines that build upon givenness and those that emphasize contingency by construing religious ideas to take their objects to be such and so, admitting the complexity of identifying the objects, are consistent with the theory of truth defended earlier. It follows from the emphasis on engagement. It is also consistent with the theory of comparative categories detailed in *Ultimate Realities*, and with how religions frequently construe the dimensions of truth in their own affirmations and practices.

9.3 Remarks on the Relation between Comparison and Theory Building

This chapter so far has focused on general observations about how our project has expressed and taken account of certain features of religious phenomena. More specific issues are driven into the open by our contention that comparative categories are justified not only on the basis of phenomenological descriptions but also by theoretical ventures. The issues can be encapsulated in the form of a deceptively simple question: What is the relation between comparison and theory building in religion? On the face of it, this question may seem strange, perhaps bordering on a category mistake owing to the intuition that comparison and theory building are only distantly related intellectual activities. We (Wildman and Neville) believe the project has shown that there are at least two ways in which the relation between comparing and theory building is quite intimate.

First, comparative categories in our procedure are justified in the first instance by judgments of similarity or dissimilarity based on rich phenomenological descriptions. Subsequently, justification calls for theoretical ventures of four sorts: articulations of (1) what is possible with regard to religious ideas, (2) what is possible with regard to the dynamics of religious-idea change, (3) what contingencies in fact caused certain ideas to be realized rather than other possibilities, and (4) what contingencies in fact caused certain dynamics of religious-idea change to be realized rather than other possibilities. The first two derive from the feature of religion called "givenness" above, while the second two derive from the feature of religion called "contingency." Comparison can proceed without these theoretical justifications, of course; anyone can make comparisons about anything. As we argued in *Ultimate Realities*, chapter 9, however, without such theoretical forms of justification, comparative generalizations are always in danger of the arbitrariness that plagues judgments of similarity. Virtually any two things are similar in some respect. The trick in successful comparison is to find the respects of comparison that disclose what is important about the phenomena being compared. Respects of comparison are nothing other than comparative categories and the best comparative categories are those for which complex theoretical justifications of these four sorts can be offered.

The problem of arbitrariness in comparison of religious phenomena is also addressed in our approach by the way in which the dual justification of comparative categories by means of phenomenology and theory renders our comparative generalizations vulnerable to correction in specific, detailed ways. That is, the complex yet explicit justification for our comparative category of religious truth in this volume makes it clear what someone would have to do to challenge it. This is a great improvement over the all-too-familiar situation of comparative generalizations that can never be pinned down specifically enough to see what would be required to overthrow them as inadequate. Thus, the connection between comparing and theory-building in the study of religion is not only close, it is also important for overcoming one of the great weaknesses in the comparative study of religion to date.

Second, there is another kind of connection between comparing and theory building in religious studies. Because of the enormous complexity of religious phenomena, efforts to give explanations for them are immediately swamped with data, with the result that arbitrariness in constructive efforts becomes an insurmountable problem. Anyone can advance a theory that makes sense of some of the data but the hordes of exceptions and the masses of unanalyzed data lead to lame or face-saving theoretical excuses, or else are simply ignored. What is needed is a way to organize the data of religion so that what is more important for building theories of religious phenomena can be distinguished from what is less important, and so that theories can be made more clearly vulnerable to the data they intend to explain. In the natural sciences, such data-organizing theories are called theories of instrumentation. In the study of religion, the analogues of theories of instrumentation are produced in the process of comparison in the form that we have described and tested it in this project.

Comparative categories, when carefully justified from as many angles as possible, offer a flexible organization of the data of religion, as we (Wildman and Neville) argued in *Ultimate Realities*, chapter 9. This organization makes explicit the theory-laden character of the data of religion, which makes for greater accountability of both comparativists and theory builders. The flexibility of this comparison-based method of data organization follows from what has been said above about the vulnerability to correction of properly justified comparative categories. The end result remains something of a pipe dream, but it is one that we have begun to explore. Theory construction in religion is far less arbitrary and far more vulnerable to improvement when it proceeds on the basis of data organized by means of a process of comparison, in our sense. It involves the work of many people, to be sure, and corrections in data organization by comparativists might force messy changes in the work of religious theorists. The conjecture, for which we (Wildman and Neville) argued at greater length in *Ultimate Realities,* chapter 9, is that this messy process will not be utterly chaotic and uncontrolled but, in the long term, more akin to the organized chaos of the natural or perhaps the social sciences. The key to such a transformation in the study of religion is the provisional embrace of a theory of comparison—a theory that we take to be the most adequate extant offering but that stands ready to be improved by subsequent insights.

9.4 Conjectures on Comparison and Theories of Religion

Having advanced an audacious conjecture about the future of the study of religion, we conclude with two more, both bearing on the relation between comparison and theories of religion, and each an answer to a question.

First, do well-established comparative categories determine theories of aspects of religion? For example, once a significant amount of comparative work has rendered the category of religious truth stable and well justified, do we then automatically have a theory of religious truth? Our conjecture is that we do: a well-established comparative category determines at least a partial theory about the topic of that category. The reason for this is that the process of justifying the comparative category involves theories of the sort previously discussed in 9.3. A full theory of religious truth doubtless would cover more than the two basically philosophical and the two basically historical aspects of the theoretical justification of religious truth as an adequate comparative category. But the theoretical adventures involved in justifying the comparative category certainly give any more general theory of religious truth a flying start.

The more general theory also would inherit helpful structural features from the part-theory generated in the process of justifying the comparative category in question. For example, the part-theory is already structured by the dialectic of vagueness and specificity (described in numerous places in the project's publications). This allows various sorts of religious truth to be distinguished and coordinated as specifications of religious truth more generally. The result is that a hierarchy of comparative subcategories can be elaborated, beginning at the most general level with three major categories of this volume: epistemological truth, scriptural truth, and truth in practice. This is not merely a principle of organization; the justification of the general category of religious truth includes theoretical explanations for why truth in religion shows up in these three ways. Any more general theory of religious truth that intends to be based on the part-theory produced in justifying the comparative category would be structured in a similar way.

This hierarchical structure of vagueness and specificity has a number of promising virtues for a more general theory. It forces the full theory to notice more of the data than many other theories of religious truth in the past have managed to take into account. It subjects the full theory to correction more specifically by actual religious data. And it provides a natural structure for elaboration of theoretical concerns that are not immediately relevant to the justification of the comparative category. For instance, theoretical elaboration of the connection between truth and logic might be tied to the subcategory of philosophical truth whereas theoretical elaboration of the connection between truth and hermeneutics might be tied to the subcategory of textual truth. Overall, then, the process of comparison aids theory building by offering a foundation that is both structured by the dialectic of vagueness and specificity and closely related to the data to which the theory must be responsible.

Second, do well-established comparative categories determine an overall theory of religion? In this case we have an innocent looking question that is in fact capable of bringing our entire project into disrepute, for good reasons. The long-standing experience of experts in the study of religion is that religious details rudely interrupt large-scale theories of religion, catching them by their pretensions and flinging them onto the towering trash heap of grandiose speculations. We have already ventured into unpopular territory by trying to show how a properly justified comparative category offers a basis for theories of aspects of religion such as religious truth or the human condition. Has our project led us to that basest form of corruption in which depraved state we could believe that this greatest of theoretical challenges—producing a master theory of religion—can be solved, or dissolved, by our procedure for comparison? Well, in this case our answer runs in a negative direction, but with a twist.

Here is the negative part: We (Wildman and Neville) conjecture that an overall theory of religion is not determined by any amount of comparison using the approach we defend. The reason for this is, basically, that our project had little use for "religion" as a comparative category. We use the word "religious" in the name of the project and we have used "religion" and cognates denotatively in the course of the project, as when we speak of "religious truth," "religious ultimates," and "Chinese religion." On the face of it, it might well be thought of as a vague comparative category that has been specified in our various uses of it. Then an attempt could be made to justify the category "religion" in all of the usual phenomenological and theoretical ways. If successful, the result would be a partial theory of religion capable of serving as a structured foundation for a full theory of religion. As a matter of fact, however, none of us seemed to have much confidence that the category "religion" could be treated in this way.

The more general theoretical point being made here is quite important. In the course of our project, we disposed of many more candidate comparative categories than we kept. Just because we can think of a category and begin to try to organize data with it does not mean that it can be justified either phenomenologically or theoretically. The point of justification is to identify categories with special characteristics such as effective registering of patterns in the data, naturalness with regard to what we earlier called the "givenness" of religious phenomena, and convenient sorting of what we earlier called the "contingencies" of religious phenomena. The most effective categories, the ones that survive, are the ones that can be justified best in these ways. In the scope of our project, "religion" always seemed a bad candidate for justification. While useful in a hand-waving way for indicating denotatively what we mean sometimes (e.g., we are dealing with religious ideas and not just any old ideas), any attempt to specify a precise boundary between religious and nonreligious ideas is futile. Moreover, the specifications of religion—even the six we used: Hinduism, Buddhism, Chinese religion, Judaism, Christianity, and Islam—are themselves not much use as comparative subcategories in our sense; they suffer from the same problems that "religion" does. Dividing up religious phenomena into religious groups is only useful in limited ways for the historical "contingency" sorts of considerations but not useful at all for the philosophical "givenness" sorts of considerations or the phenomenological considerations, all of which must feed into the justification of categories. So our conjecture is that "religion" is not useful as a comparative category and thus that our comparative procedure is unlikely to be able to specify the theoretical basis for a general theory of religion.

So much for the negative conjecture; now for the twist. Actually, there are two twists. First, we can imagine circumstances under which religion might be a feasible comparative category in a way that seems unlikely at present. This speculative scenario would falsify our second conjecture but it would also lead to the basis for a general theory of religion. To see how this might occur, consider that the concept "religion" plays a heuristic, denotative role in our work. We have been able to articulate a host of subcategories organized under three major comparative categories—the human condition, ultimate realities, and religious truth—because we have presupposed informal and unanalyzed notions of religion as such. These notions functioned denotatively to allow us to marshal our various disciplinary contributions for the construction and exploration of sturdy comparative categories. We somehow knew what we were "taking" comparatively even if the disparate conventions of our traditions and the existential commitments of different religious practices made detailed agreement difficult. "Culture," "economics," "science," and "society" are similarly heuristic concepts in other scholarly contexts. Such larger, informal denotative contexts are crucial in human understanding. If one could be found that allowed religion to be specified more precisely—perhaps along with culture, economics, science, and society as well—then religion would at least have a chance to be a viable comparative category. Whether the comparative category "religion" could be justified under those circumstances remains an open question.

What might such a broader, unanalyzed heuristic context be? Religious studies as a field is not yet ready to treat religion responsibly as a comparative category but perhaps it might be able to serve as a broader heuristic context at some point in the future. For some thinkers, frustration with the difficulty of developing a responsible comparative theory of religion has trickled down to frustration with any and all comparisons. In this project we believe that we have taken some small and partial, but decisive steps to reverse that frustration. Comparisons can be made responsibly, subject to the limitations we have described (and perhaps others). Well-grounded comparative categories can indeed function to order something like a data-organizing theory of instrumentation for the further study of religion. Prolonged comparative work can contribute to theories of important aspects of religion. And the dialectic of vagueness, specification, theoretical hypotheses, and vulnerability to correction serves to model at least part of the structure of further studies that might undertake a full-blown theory of religion. As we have said, this is highly speculative. Under such circumstances, however, we would be glad to see our second conjecture fail.

The second twist is consistent with our second conjecture and quite realistic. There is a way that a large-scale pseudo-theory about religion can be pieced together from large-scale theories about other topics. The result would not be a systematic theory of religion but it would be a loosely coordinated conglomeration of relevant theoretical insights. That is more or less what is happening at the present time. To see what is meant here, consider an example of a large-scale theory of a stable comparative category—not religion itself, which we do not think can be made a stable category, but a category such as the human condition. The part-theory emerging from the justification of the comparative category "human condition"—a justification that we did not attempt systematically, unfortunately—forms the basis for a general theory of human beings in regard to religious concerns. That general theory of human beings as religious could then be (and in fact sometimes is) placed into conversation with other general theories of human beings, such as those from anthropology, evolutionary biology, psychology, or neuroscience. Such a process of interdisciplinary cooperation might have a chance of producing the grand theoretical narrative to trump all other grand narratives about human beings—at least for a while.

Meanwhile, the same interdisciplinary cooperation can be applied to topics such as religious truth and ultimate realities, among others. The result is a family of theories about topics that are important in religious studies. Piecing these together, we have a loosely coordinated series of ideally profound and systematic insights into religion. We do not have a master theory of religion but we have something important nonetheless—and it may well be as far as we can travel in the way of a comprehensive theory of religion. None of this can be achieved without both a serviceable theory of comparison and an extended history of comparison by means of which the data of religion are made available for the systematic formulation and correction of theoretical ventures in religious studies. Our project has aimed to take a single, sure step in the direction of that goal.

10

Director's Conclusions

Robert Cummings Neville

Publications have long careers during which what is significant in them can change greatly. The Eleventh Edition of the *Encyclopaedia Britannica* was state-of-the-art knowledge when it was published in 1910. Now nearly all its scholarship and science, especially its political geography, have long been out of date. But it has become perhaps the best compendium of materials extent of modernist thought: what better text for studying modernism in all fields than the Eleventh Edition? So will it be with our volumes, *The Human Condition*, *Ultimate Realities*, and *Religious Truth*, to the extent they are remembered at all. The strengths they have now might fade, and their weaknesses might become their long-term positive contributions.

It is fitting, indeed imperative, for me as project director to attempt some assessments of the Comparative Religious Ideas Project and these volumes. I shall do so with the above observation about changing significance in mind.

The greatest contemporary strength of the three volumes is that they are rich, multicultural, interdisciplinary, and multi-authored essays on their respective topics. Many books contain conference papers on topics such as these, and nearly always they contain a few brilliant articles; sometimes they contain a report of the conference discussion. But our volumes are far richer than this. *Religious Truth*, for instance, has chapters on how six different religious traditions have regarded at least three dimensions of the topic, the epistemological, scriptural, and the existential. It also has chapters that attempt to explain why the six traditions have the range of variations on the topic they do, and on why that simply follows from the nature of religious truth as we can best understand it in our own terms. Even if these chapters are specifically wrong in important points, their very interplay exhibits something of the texture of religious truth.

Moreover, the process of the seminar is such that each chapter is the result of at least two explicit discussions of early drafts, which is far more criticism over time than most conference papers get. Even more important, during the eight seminar meetings on the topic, the tradition specialists not only benefited from discussions of their own papers but took part in the travails of their colleagues also addressing issues of religious truth. Through this intense process the real topic became religious truth, not just the Chinese, Buddhist, Jewish, Christian, Muslim, and Hindu ideas about religious truth. The cumulative impact of each specialist working through the specific approaches to the topic in the context of the others doing the same, each contributing to the others, bridged the theoretical and existential gaps between the vague category of religious truth and the diverse religions. Thus the comparisons made in the specialists' chapters are well-honed and carefully bridge the vague-specific divide.

Reading across the three volumes, yet another great contemporary strength becomes evident. The three chapters on Chinese religion, for instance, amount to an original and rich way of looking at Chinese religion. Rarely is it studied under the aegis of its respective approaches to the human condition, ultimate realities, and religious truth. By asking these special questions, which come at Chinese religion with odd slants, new biases, angles of vision uncommon in Chinese studies, new dimensions of Chinese religion are highlighted. The same is true with respect to all the other traditions. Because the categories of the human condition, ultimate realities, and religious truth have arisen out of Christian intellectual traditions, one might expect these topics to be least creative and original as ways of probing the nature of Christianity. But in point of fact Paula Fredriksen each year forced us to see early Christianity a new way, making it strange for us; where we might expect the Christian focus on ultimate realities to be about the Trinity, she showed the focus to be on the sacrifice of Jesus in providing access for Gentiles to the ultimate. Although these cross-volume cumulative chapters on each of our traditions are not systematic new interpretations of them, they are creative and original, and should be the object of analysis and review.

These multi-part "essays" on our three topics and on each of our traditions constitute important, timely, and original contributions to scholarship. They will have abiding significance, I think, as landmark examples of the richness of collaboration over time in a process that repeatedly subjects thought to criticism and revision. But over time also their insights will become old hat. The next generation of graduate students will come upon the ideas as known and taken for granted, not as novel hard-won insights, and the generation after that will engage in overthrowing our ideas in favor of greater sophistication and the improvements of new angles of vision. In ninety years our scholarship will be as outdated as that in the Eleventh Edition of the *Encyclopaedia Britannica*. All historical and comparative scholarship suffers so from time.

How well do our volumes, and the Project as a whole, substantiate the conception of comparison on which they rest and the method that flows from that? Here, I believe, the answer is mixed.

The answer is very positive in the respects that are evident in the previous point. The method of discussion and re-discussion of papers on each tradition's specific ways of addressing the general topics thematized the philosophical distinction between vague and specific comparative categories and accomplished their integration in the comparisons in the specialists' chapters, especially in this third volume. These authors, and perhaps a number of readers, will feel premature and unprotected in future solitary scholarship that does not benefit from enduring the fires of methodic collaborative vulnerability. These volumes make evident that specific historical scholarship is already replete with comparative judgments, and needs to make those self-conscious and well grounded in comparative discussions with other specialists. They also make evident that generalists need ever more specific detail to make their comparative hypotheses stable and fruitful.

A more general point is also a positive conclusion: methodic vulnerability is a very good thing. Instead of defending interpretive positions, making them well-entrenched against all comers, the better strategy is to make them vulnerable to correction in all possible ways. When the correction comes, take it! Interpretive hypotheses of all sorts are justified, not by apriori starting points and Cartesian deductions, but by seeking out the hardest challenges and coming through. The fallibilist critical method not only gives proper shape to the hypothesis but firms up its claim to truth.

As to whether our study has justified the specific philosophical conception of comparison with which we worked, and that is detailed in chapter 8 of *Ultimate Realities*, I give a much less positive answer. The distinction between vague and specific levels of comparative categories was well understood and helpful. But the conception of comparison is more complicated than this. It involves highlighting a kind of dialectical tension between theory-construction and explanation on the one hand and phenomenological description and testing for the theory on the other. Whereas most understandings of explanatory and descriptive theory suppose that the theories provide the empirical categories in terms of which specific investigation is to be carried out, our theory here says that independent phenomenological investigation is required to confirm or correct the empirical categories derivative from the theory. Without the phenomenological investigation the theory risks becoming tyrannical, deceptive, and oppressive, rightly criticized by "critical theorists." Without explanatory and descriptive theory, phenomenological investigation never moves beyond anecdote, magic, and what Wildman calls "genius" comparisons. Both sides are needed for the comparative method to remain public and vulnerable at each stage of its development. This was all spelled out in my *Normative Cultures* with which the Project began, but in technical terms alien to the idiom of our discussions of the traditions.

Whereas the specialists learned deeply from one another, and the generalists absorbed the specialists' teachings like sponges, I suspect the specialists did not want to go very far in mastering the philosophy involved in the conception of comparison. They got the point about vague and specific categories. They also bumped against the theory hard enough to see its sharp edges and hence to recoil in favor of narrative, for instance, or swinging attacks on metaphysics. But they did not get into the philosophy enough to go the next step, to see how the theory acknowledges and attempts to answer those criticisms, and to engage more thoroughly on those levels. Objections were often left at the level of merely citing alternatives, saying that the alternatives seem more congenial to some specific texts or traditions without exploring how the theory would respond at the level of theory. Thus there was a kind of suspicion that the conception and method we employed had its status by my authority, genial as that might have seemed, rather than by actually exhibiting its worth.

This lack of real collaboration at the philosophical level is manifest in the difference between the conclusions in *The Human Condition* and those in the other volumes. In *The Human Condition*, on behalf of the group, I constructed a grid of the various categories and subcategories we had found helpful, crossed by the four angles of analysis or phenomenological sites, and attempted to say how each of the traditions would specify each node in the grid compared with others. Although these comparative hypotheses copiously cited the specialists' chapters for evidence, they did not arise out of those chapters. They often were at a different level of vagueness-specificity than the discussions in the specialists' chapters. They also did not go far enough to take the third step in comparison, which would have been to add up what the result is for the human condition. Most important, the other members of the seminar simply could not sign on to the array of comparative hypotheses because most of it went way beyond their own fields. Not only was most of it beyond the texts for which they took responsibility in that volume, it was beyond what any respectable scholar in their field would dare to speak on. Finally, of course, it is pretty boring to move from one node to another because of the structure of the grid. What would have been more interesting would have been to move from one comparison to another because of the insights in the comparisons.

So the seminar decided to emphasize primary authorship for each of the chapters, which allowed me to make such daring, speculative, and systematic comparisons as I please and the specialists to dissociate themselves from that. In *Ultimate Realities* and *Religious Truth*, the comparisons take place mainly in the specialists' chapters, though unsystematically, and the concluding chapters are frankly more philosophical, integrative, and explanatory, with close collaboration between Wildman and myself.

But this is a disappointing failure in collaboration. For all their faults, the two concluding chapters of *The Human Condition* make possible a kind of methodical objectivity and vulnerability, forcing analyses from the angles of the different phenomenological sites, and setting the comparative hypotheses next to one another so that they can be examined for congruence, consistency, and for how they handle multitudes of exceptions to their descriptive generalizations. They present a vulnerability to further discussion by their very systematic and speculative grandness that is lost in the comparisons of the later volumes. The later comparisons are all presented as hypotheses, but couched very much within the perspectives of the authors, not within the perspective of an ongoing process. For all of the collaboratively gained knowledge lauded above, the later comparisons retreat to a kind of privacy in contrast with the grand methodic plan of those in *The Human Condition*.

In what did this specific failure in collaboration lie? Certainly it was not in a failure of will or intelligence. Perhaps a bit of it lay in the threat of the guilds when the specialists would see every one of my speculative comparative hypotheses as a red flag subject to a thousand qualifications. But most of it lay, I believe, in what our method demands of the collaborators in terms of mastering the philosophy behind the method and the explanatory parts of comparison. How much philosophy does real collaboration require everyone to learn? If Frank Clooney had said that everyone had to learn Sanskrit to understand his contributions, we would have said he needs to be public in English. But then we trusted his Sanskrit. The philosophy was both met with "blank stares," as Wildman puts it in the appendix to *The Human Condition*, and resisted when perceived to run contrary to a pre-existing philosophical prejudice. Although not everyone needs to know Sanskrit, freshman class teaches that everyone has a philosophy and should study the subject to improve it. So, among us, not only is everyone a philosopher, but the comparative task itself requires everyone to function at a philosophic level. Sanskrit can be translated into English, albeit with some loss; philosophic expressions can be translated into other philosophic expressions; but philosophic ideas cannot be translated into nonphilosophic ideas without ceasing to be philosophic ideas. When the philosophy gets hard, the collaboration stumbles and people retire to expertise.

How intractable is this kind of failure in our collaboration? What does it portend for the future of collaboration? Ways forward do exist. I could have been both clearer and more forceful in demanding philosophic responses. Also it might be that the philosophy I was developing simply is not much good and that is why people did not engage it; so, an improved philosophy would be a way forward. Other participants in the seminar could have worked harder at it, even though that would have felt as if they were abandoning the territory of their authority and expertise for someone else's. Perhaps a different, or longer, collaborative process would help alleviate that worry. Surely our process did overcome a great number of obstacles to collaboration. But in the end I think it must be said that, although this particular collaborative process illustrated much of the philosophic conception of comparison and the resultant method, it did not test it thoroughly. The result is that many of the comparisons are not as daring, well tested, and vulnerable to further correction as they should be.

Nevertheless, in ninety years, when our comparisons are historical curiosities, I suspect that the ruminations about the philosophic nature of comparison and methods of collaborative critical inquiry will have an enduring place in conceptions of the field of religious studies. Among the reasons for this is the fact that the philosophic theory exhibits so precisely where the collaboration failed: it failed to keep the theorizing and phenomenology in tension, allowing them to relax apart, and thereby failed to keep the array of public checks vulnerable.

We are, of course, still very close to the Project and perhaps cannot see the forest for the trees. To the extent that our work has been enlightening and has indeed advanced both comparative understanding and put forward a lengthy lesson in collaborative process, the conception of comparison and the method flowing from it have indeed been confirmed.

Quite the opposite of this qualified assessment of the published outcome of our collaboration regarding testing comparative theory, the Project as a transformative learning process has been an unqualified success. Perhaps we did not all learn philosophy or Sanskrit, but we all did learn the value of learning with others from different disciplines. We learned a lot of what one another knew. We learned how to share our basic reference texts, our canon. We learned how to talk across disciplines without sinking to the lowest common denominator. We learned how to allow our minds to be changed through the correction of something stupid that we have said.

The graduate students perhaps learned most in this way. It would be worthwhile incorporating collaborative projects such as this into graduate programs, modeling multicultural interdisciplinary learning. Also, the scholars, both specialists and generalists, came to be adept at collaborative work, and to appreciate the strengths it gives. This will have a ripple-effect within religious studies. If scholars from genuinely different disciplines can collaborate on religious ideas, why not on religious rituals, on institutional practices, on dietary differences? If it can be done in religious studies, why cannot it be done in "human studies" with anthropology, psychology, sociology, neurobiology? This project has opened doors for a new kind of inquiry, collaborative, fallible, and subject to evaluation. We are proud.

Therefore we present not only these volumes but our work itself as a quite specific but very large and complicated hypothesis about the comparison of religious ideas. Lovers of vulnerability to correction that we are, we hope for "reviews" not only quick upon publication but periodically as our field goes far beyond these steps.

Appendix A

On the Process of the Project During the Third Year

Wesley J. Wildman

Can a diverse group of scholars with very different backgrounds and training ever agree on anything crosscultural? In religious studies, we commonly see irreconcilable disagreement to the point of rancorous chaos or appreciation of insights to the point of undiscriminating indulgence. Skepticism about the prospects for solid consensus about crosscultural comparative judgments is understandable. Moreover, any claim that agreement about comparisons had been achieved would be deeply suspect. After all, *serious* agreement presupposes a high degree of cooperation among members of a group that is representatively diverse with regard to training and approach. But we all know that highly diverse groups of any sort famously cannot work together, except perhaps in the experimental sciences, in the armed forces, or where vast sums of money are involved. It follows that the chances are slim of ever putting together a diverse group of religious studies scholars who could still work together enough even to test whether they can agree about comparisons.

One of the exciting dimensions of the Comparative Religious Ideas Project is that it was conducted by just such a group—designed with high diversity yet, despite profound disagreements about how to approach the material under discussion, able to work together well enough both to generate comparisons that are vulnerable to correction and to get somewhere with actually correcting them. While the project's objective output takes the form of three volumes, of which the present volume is the third, the corporate dimension of the project is difficult to convey in publicly digestible form. We have been tempted not even to try; but a group process of the sort we have experienced is essential to the methodology of the project and leaving out a faithful description and analysis of that process would seriously distort the account of our results offered in these volumes. In an appendix to each volume, therefore, I have tried to convey something of the character of our group process in order to illumine our method from angles other than those that dominate the rest of each volume. The three appendices can be read together but each makes sense by itself. Each is an analysis of one year in the life of the project, written from the point of view of the project's endpoint. This last installment covers the third year's meetings and the continuation of the work into the fourth year as we met in conference with our advisors and as the editing tasks proceeded. I refer to participants listed as contributors to this volume by their given names, which was our practice during seminar meetings.

At the Beginning of a Third Year

The third year's beginning was quite different from those of the previous two years of the project for a couple of reasons. On the one hand, our project meetings held few surprises after having done it sixteen times so the expectation of hard work was a larger factor in everyone's minds than curiosity about how our discussions would develop. On the other hand, we were all deeply involved in writing and rewriting the draft chapters for the first and second volumes. The pleasure at seeing each other again at the first meeting was thus complicated by the awareness of how exhausting the effort of learning so much new material and the process of mutual criticism would continue to be. The expectation of hard work in familiar circumstances brought with it a certain comfort, however, as did seeing one another again.

The group was identical to that of the second year. A new configuration of faculty leaves led us, as in year two, to select a schedule that would minimize absences at project seminar meetings. The research students were further along in their own studies, most teaching on the side, writing dissertations, and looking for jobs; each was enormously busy in just the ways that graduate students inevitably are expected to be.

The first two seminar meetings of the year were held on consecutive days at the Boston Research Institute for the Twenty-First Century, in Cambridge. There, after warm greetings and fine breakfast food, we began by discussing the future of the project. Bob gave his reasons for not applying for another three years of grant money, resolving a question that had been asked from the beginning. With regard to the testing and enhancement of the comparative method, another three years were not really needed. With regard to using the method to generate stable cross-cultural comparative categories, the work was almost infinite in scope and it was not at all clear that we ought to be the ones to press further ahead with it. Together with consideration for everyone's time and energy, these factors suggested that ending the project after three years, allowing for an advisors' conference in the fourth year, would be the most effective use of the sponsors' money and best for everyone involved. My impression is that the knowledge that there would be a firm schedule for completion of the entire project helped energize us all for the final year's effort.

The first meeting then yielded to intensive discussions of the existing drafts of the first two volumes. There was no trouble whatsoever in filling an entire day with feedback, comments, debates over organization and emphasis, and reevaluations of certain categories. In the afternoon we finally settled on the major categories that were to guide the specialists' chapters for volume two on *Ultimate Realities*, having spent the previous year discussing that theme. The care with which these decisions were conducted and the group's fidelity to the goal of discerning the primary categories from out of the swirling hours of debate and mutual correction cannot be overstressed. It is hard to imagine how we could be any more empirically grounded given the basic limitation that we were studying not chemistry in a laboratory but religious ideas in texts.

The second and subsequent meetings followed the usual pattern. Each day, two specialists would make a presentation of a draft of their papers on religious truth, aiming to describe how religious truth is thought of within their traditions. Respondents were assigned in order to focus the ensuing discussion. We also followed the same daily schedule of four ninety-minute sessions separated by two 30-minute breaks and an hour-long lunch. Our project was on the home stretch.

Religious Truth

There was an important difference between the way the categories for religious truth were arrived at and the way categories were figured out for previous years. Rather than waiting until after each year's discussions were complete before attempting to infer what categories had finally bubbled to the top of the cauldron of discussion, we began year three with a clear sense of what categories were important for the elucidation of religious truth across the traditions we were studying. Specifically, we needed to consider the three-fold distinction among philosophical truth, scriptural truth, and truth in practice, all three of which tended to recur in the ideas of our religious traditions with a colorful variety of emphases.

It is not that the empirical commitment of our proceedings had somehow been violated. On the contrary, these categories had emerged in the previous years as we grappled with the human condition and ultimate realities; the topic of religious truth just kept coming up. Each time it resurfaced, we would take care to distinguish ideas having to do with religious truth from those bearing on the topic for the current year. In this way we developed some useful distinctions for making clear what was important to our various traditions about religious truth and we also generated a strong consensus around the three-fold distinction just mentioned. This was particularly pleasing because it showed that the intertwining of the major categories for our project did not need to hinder our work but actually could make it more efficient.

The theme of justification of our categories was broached in the appendix to the second volume on *Ultimate Realities* and it was just as large a concern in the minds of the generalists in the third year. Having seen in previous years the need for openness about the role of philosophical ideas, we were determined to be clear on that point from the beginning and also to try to be as self-aware as possible of the multiple lines of argument that flow together to justify a set of categories. At the same time, our discussions of religious truth moved comfortably from questions of philosophical presuppositions and justification of categories to the detailed analyses of religious traditions, texts, and practices—and back again. The dialectic of vagueness and specificity described in a number of places in the three volumes was operating more smoothly than ever. The specialists' essays, especially the revised drafts that guided our discussions in the second half of the year, were more adventurous in the making of comparisons, on the whole, than in previous years. They were also more compatible with one another in terms of the scope of coverage of each tradition. Both changes improved the prospects of drawing meaningful conclusions from the specialists' work.

To my mind, all of these developments demonstrate that it really is possible for a diverse group of religious studies scholars to teach each other both how to think outside of the boundaries set by training and familiarity—be it learning tradition-specific details or by venturing comparisons—and how to contribute to a larger project that no one of us could have managed alone.

The Concluding Conference

As the third year drew to a close, we turned our attention to completing the drafts of all three volumes. During the fall of the fourth year, we met to discuss the evolving drafts and to make needed adjustments. During the Christmas break of the fourth year, drafts of the volumes (at various stages of refinement) finally became available. The three volumes were then sent out to a number of prominent scholars in religious studies for their comments. These scholars were invited to join the project members and advisors in a conference in the Spring of the fourth year (May, 1999). The aim of the conference was for project members to have the opportunity to take account of as diverse an array of criticisms and suggestions as possible, with a view to improving the final drafts.

Many changes were made before the volumes reached their published forms. Some of these changes were structural, some were matters of emphasis and rhetoric, and some were corrections of factual details or omissions. Most were indebted in one way or another to the discussions that took place at the concluding conference. I think it is fair to say that project members were slightly nervous prior to the conference because a project such as ours is complex enough to make it easy to misunderstand as well as politically somewhat incorrect given the skepticism about comparison that seems to abound in the religious studies academy at the present time. Scholars also get nervous when they move out of the regions of their demonstrated expertise into the strange new lands of the expertise of others—and everyone in our project had made that unsettling journey to various degrees. The drive of our project toward vulnerability and improvement was expressed perhaps most tangibly in the determination to learn as much as possible from our advisors and guest critics, despite the natural discomfort at having our adventurous attempts at scholarly collaboration scrutinized so closely. But the goal of vulnerability to correction is vain talk if it cannot be given this sort of existentially daunting translation into encounters with serious feedback.

The conference was held in the Boston University School of Management in lovely surroundings. As always, the food was wonderful, which takes me back to the importance of food in bringing and holding our motley group together, a topic on which I mused briefly in the appendix to the first volume on *The Human Condition*. Each of the visiting scholars was assigned the task of responding to various aspects of the project. Each helped us understand the project from his or her own distinctive point of view. Even though those points of view were utterly familiar from our own group discussions, there is something refreshing about being in the presence of someone who holds it and uses it to evaluate our corporate efforts. In particular, it was driven home to all of the project members how large was the gap between the rich diversity of our seminar discussions and the relatively focused presentations of our work in the three volumes. Almost everything anyone ever thought in religious studies came up in one form or another over the course of four years in those two hundred hours of seminar meetings or in the manifold discussions outside the formal seminar meeting days. Yet only a fraction of that rich awareness of the world of religious studies was registered in the volumes.

The reminder of this difference between the internal and external points of view on our project was mildly unnerving. We knew it would be difficult to communicate effectively with the ranks of religious studies scholars who are delicately attuned to issues that receive little coverage in the volumes even though we talked about them in our seminar meetings all the time—issues such as the need for power analyses of religious histories and texts, the question of fair treatment of the other in the broiling aftermath of colonialism, the critique of the quest for master narratives to guide the interpretation of religious ideas and practices, or the need for awareness of the subtle and not-so-subtle influences on our research of our own religious convictions and scholarly habits. We could not constantly apologize for not covering other important questions, however, but had to plunge ahead with the important questions that we had committed ourselves to investigate. Perhaps it is fair to say, then, that this aspect of the final conference drove home to us the impossibility of controlling the readings that the volumes would receive and so catalyzed in us a simple determination to express what we did cover as well as we possibly could.

The visiting scholars and advisors at the conference were anxious for us to convey to readers how the method we used actually worked in practice. The expositions of it in the various volumes have an abstract philosophical orientation, even when they are pared back for the sake of ready understanding. As mentioned in the appendix to the first volume on *The Human Condition*, this was an issue that our group debated back and forth almost from the beginning. On the one hand, it is pointless trying to recreate in a book the process by which the results were achieved; most readers would be bored by that anyway and likely to find the references to group process distracting and self-indulgent. On the other hand, the project is devoted in part to the implementation and refinement of a method for detecting and justifying comparative categories and the social process is so important a part of that that any reader interested in the method would be justly frustrated if no account if it were furnished. As a group, project members had eventually decided against making the attempt to convey anything about the process but we were urged to change our minds at the conference. The insistence on the importance of making the group process at least somewhat transparent was heartwarming; at least these careful readers had grasped the methodological innovations of our procedure. Yet we still had no idea how to satisfy their demand for some degree of transparency. After much hand wringing and puzzling, these appendices were deemed to be the optimal way to proceed but there is only so much they can convey and we are sharply aware of their limitations.

As to the method itself, the visiting scholars at the conference were both appreciative and ready with suggestions, of which I mention but two here. First, we were urged to consider how our own approach to comparison relates to the approaches to comparison in play in other cultural-intellectual contexts. We had set out to track this angle on comparative method right from the beginning but simply had to let it go because we had too much else to do. We returned to it now and then, as when we studied South Asian philosophy's pramāṇa theory and the Indian practice of interreligious debates before powerful benefactors, but we could not give the issue the focused attention that it deserved.

Second, we were challenged to treat the thesis of incommensurability more seriously rather than simply blocking the extreme versions of it with obvious appeals to biological continuity of humanity across cultures, thereby evading the complexities of the middle ground. Of course, in the first volume on *The Human Condition* we had taken full advantage of the so-called phenomenological sites of importance in which the complexities associated with translation and interpreting the other are thematized in powerful ways. But that way of presenting our conclusions fell away after the first volume (though not in our seminar discussions) because there was too much to manage. Nevertheless, our commentators forced a number of significant changes in the final versions of the three volumes as we attempted to register more fully the complexities of this issue.

With regard to the results of our research, our scholarly advisors and critics were again appreciative without being short on suggestions. Two issues will suffice as a representative sample of a great many comments. We were invited to consider the arbitrariness of the categories that name the three volumes. This we were happy to do; there are a number of comments in the three volumes in which this acknowledgement is clear. Yet we also wanted to push back, claiming that our own results rather strongly confirmed these categories (we called them the "big three") as applicable to all of our traditions and helpfully illuminating. Alternative "big" categories were suggested but our list of alternatives was already comically long. Perhaps the most forceful criticism under the heading of results concerned the near absence of ethical considerations in the three volumes. Of course, there is actually rather a lot about ethical matters in our work but there is no centralizing of ethical categories in the second and third volumes. I think we all wondered about that from time to time. My reading is that we had a natural way of dealing with ethics under the heading of the human condition but that too many normative questions had to begged if ethical categories were to be introduced under the encompassing categories of ultimate realities or religious truth. In other words, ethical categories would tend to be distorting, which is a sign of their not being really basic. Though I see a conclusion rather than merely an omission in this treatment of ethics, I am not confident that this conclusion would command consensus in our group as a whole were we to discuss the issue.

In all, the conference was an informative and challenging experience for project members. We were left with a wealth of insights by which our final revisions could be guided and a debt of gratitude to the men and women who spent good hours from their lives laboring over our work.

Looking toward the Future

The conference was the last time we were together as a group. There was rewriting to be done, of course, and *ad hoc* meetings in twos and threes to facilitate that. And we still regularly ran into each other at meetings or, for locals, in elevators. That said, I miss everyone. It is not that anyone wanted to continue on—heaven forefend! I suspect that we are all relieved to be done with the project; for my part, I derive considerable pleasure from the realization that I need write no more notes for project seminars and no more chapters or appendices for project books. It is rather because of interrupted habits of rhythmic discussion, writing, and eating that I miss everyone. I hazard that in this I am typical, which if correct would be a tangible reminder of the way our comparative method works: it really does forge a community of inquirers guided by habits of communication and mutual criticism, a community capable of tolerating both frustration with the process and the life changes that affect us all over time.

Such a community includes personal dimensions well as professional ones. We had tried to estimate at the beginning the odds of one of our number dying sometime during the course of the project—I believe one of our advisors, Max Stackhouse, brought this possibility to our attention. Well, nobody died but we had one departure, some nasty diseases, several traumas to limbs, at least two job placements, a tenure case, many book publications, new relationships, and two babies. All that and nineteen lives of teaching and learning parallel to everything we did in the project.

With this multi-faceted image of corporate scholarly life in place, we come to a glance forwards into the future of the study of religion. If we are right, comparative efforts will go best when diverse groups of scholars commit themselves to the complex joys and frustrations, the attachments and confusions of collaborative work. A few comparative geniuses may not need the help. For the rest of us, moving beyond the randomly associative aha! approach to comparison in the direction of producing sturdy justifications of comparative categories is possible only with collaboration. Successful collaboration permits the growth of the kind of serious dialectic of vagueness and specificity that we sought to achieve and that we contend is needed to keep the generalizations of comparative categories in touch with the details of traditions and texts. Many sorts of research in religious studies need not have this collaborative aspect but rigorous comparison probably requires it.

As an investment in this future, the project was designed from the outset as a training ground for graduate students, of which we had the honor of working with seven at various times—eight, if we include the project administrator, and another ten if we include those who worked on the bibliographies. For those working with the six specialist scholars and attending all of the meetings, the aim was to inspire or perhaps to infect them with indelible memories of collaborative work. We also wanted them to experience first hand the virtues and discomforts of trying to transcend disciplinary boundaries in the name of curiosity about complex realities that do not conform neatly to academic fields. Those graduate students already have or will soon have teaching positions and so take their experiences on to other places and people. Every bit as much as the three project volumes, these men and women represent our investment in a collaborative vision of scholarly research in religious studies.

Meanwhile, the volumes themselves will be read and discussed, praised and criticized. The attempt to make our work vulnerable to correction means first that we make our case as strongly as we possibly can, perhaps even risking the mistaken impression that we don't really want any feedback. Then we pay close attention to responses with a view to discerning how our position can be improved or perhaps even whether it needs to be abandoned. The process of correction and improvement is not just our task, however, but also the task of scholars who engage our work and attempt to improve on it or fight against it in all of the ways that these responses are played out in academic circles.

Our collaborative group is now dispersed, with vacant spaces where once stood habits of work, and with relief to be regaining the time to pursue other scholarly ventures. But our efforts are meant to change the way comparison is done, both in terms of the way comparison is conceived in the minds of individual scholars and in terms of the hoped-for emergence of other scholarly groups who value collaboration as the optimal context for rigorous comparison of religious ideas. We can only hope that these anticipated groups will enjoy the fun, frustration, and quality of food and companionship that has brought such color into our lives for the last four years.

Appendix B

Suggestions for Further Reading

Wesley J. Wildman

The Comparative Religious Ideas Project was designed to involve students both as participants in the seminar meetings and in background tasks. One of the more adventurous student projects has been the development of a set of twelve annotated bibliographies on a number of topics relevant to the project. These bibliographies are suggestions for further reading in each topic covered. I am grateful to the students involved in the annotation project: Marylu Bunting, John Darling, Greg Farr, Andrew Irvine, He Xiang, Mark Mann, Matt McLaughlin, David McMahon, Glen Messer, James Miller, and Kirk Wulf. I am also grateful for the suggestions of books to annotate that we received from Profs. Jensine Andresen, John Berthrong, Frank Clooney, Jonathan Klawans, and Frank Korom. The first bibliography in this volume contains suggestions for further reading on the topic of the volume, religious truth. Subsequently there are tradition-specific bibliographies on Judaism, Christianity, and Islam. Each contains annotations on reference works, primary texts in English translation, and secondary sources that discuss various aspects of the tradition. The next bibliography contains annotated suggestions for further reading in the area of schemes of comparative categories that have or might one day attain classical status in the academic study of religion. Then there is a bibliography containing suggestions for introductory reading in religious studies that is especially intended for those wanting to deepen their general knowledge of religion. The final bibliography contains annotated suggestions for further reading in the area of comparative method, which is intended to help those wanting to evaluate the method used in this project against other approaches to the comparison of religious ideas.

—Wesley J. Wildman

Annotated Bibliography: Religious Truth

Abraham, William J. 1998. *Canon and Criterion in Christian Theology: From the Fathers to Feminism.* New York: Oxford University Press.

Abraham introduces this book by distinguishing ecclesial canons and epistemic criteria. The former he characterizes as "means of grace and salvation," which "presuppose a complex vision of creation and redemption" (2). The latter are "crafted means of articulating the justification of one's beliefs" (ibid.). Abraham's thesis is that, while canon and criteria exhibit theological connections, modern Christian theology typically reduces the notion and role of canon to those of a criterion, with destructive consequences for any cohesive authority within the Christian tradition. The argument proceeds by a theological and philosophical history of Christian thought about canonicity, and ends with a schematic proposal for the re-examination of premodern distinctions that firmly place epistemic criteria in the role of methodical aids in the understanding of canon.

Adler, Mortimer Jerome. 1990. *Truth in Religion: The Plurality of Religions and the Unity of Truth.* New York: Macmillan.

Arguing from philosophical realism, the position that reality exists independent from human thoughts about it, Adler contends that since there is one reality there must be a unity of truth about that reality. Hence, while the diversity of reality may cause different religions to formulate different views, these views if true must be complementary. If two religions hold contradictory views concerning reality, only one view can be true since there is only one reality. Thus, Adler concludes, while pluralism of complementary views should be tolerated, a religious pluralism that tolerates contradictory views must be rejected.

Alston, William P. 1991. *Perceiving God: The Epistemology of Religious Experience.* Ithaca, N.Y.: Cornell University Press.

Alston argues, first, that a kind of religious experience he dubs "Christian mystical practice" (CMP) is genuine perceptual experience, albeit not reliant on the physical senses. Alston characterizes CMP as a social practice leading to the formation and testing of beliefs about the object of perception, and on this basis claims for it an epistemic value on a par with sense perception. He concludes that beliefs formed through CMP could be shown to be unreliable only by criteria developed in continuing CMP. A detailed theory of the truth of such beliefs is not provided. Alston concedes that the existence of vital religious communities besides Christianity challenges his account of the mode of mystical perception and its reliability.

Ariel, Yoav, Shlomo Bidermann, and Ornan Rotem. 1998. *Relativism and Beyond.* Boston: E. J. Brill.

This collection of essays seeks to overcome two shortcomings in the current literature on relativism: first, the overpolarization between relativism and absolutism and, second, the overemphasis on Western sources in the explication of relativism. The first section of essays seeks a middle path between absolutism and relativism through critiques of Rorty, Wittgenstein, and an evaluation of the logical pitfalls of a thoroughgoing relativism. The second section of essays includes topic studies of relativism and absolutism in non-Western sources including Maimonides and Jung as well as Indian Buddhist, Muslim, and Taoist traditions.

Berger, Peter. (ed.) 1981. *The Other Side of God: A Polarity in World Religions.* Garden City, N.Y.: Doubleday.

The polarity invoked in the subtitle refers all experience of religious ultimacy either to a reality external to the self or resident in the depth of (self-) consciousness. It was proposed as a heuristic device for a 1978–80 seminar, "Monotheism and the World Religions." At issue is whether and how apparently conflicting truth claims among the world's religions might be reconcilable. Part I considers the polarity in monotheistic traditions; Part II, Hinduism and Buddhism. Harvey Cox's concluding reflection points to the emerging need for a theory of truth-in-dialogue and a sensitivity to all experience as endowed with a religious dimension.

Biderman, Shlomo. 1995. *Scripture and Knowledge: An Essay on Religious Epistemology.* Studies in the history of religions; 69. New York: E. J. Brill.

Biderman argues "that scripture, by its presumed significance and uniqueness, serves a central epistemological role in religious traditions" (3). For Biderman, this means that scriptures are understood religiously as sources of true knowledge, both factual and valuational, about reality. To think about scripture in this way goes beyond two alternative theoretical approaches, the textual and functional, which Biderman reviews and criticizes in favor of the epistemological interpretation. Studies of classical and modern Midrash in Jewish tradition and the orthodox approach to

Hindu scriptures of the Mīmāṃsa school exhibit the thesis, but in contrasting perspectives. The contrasts illuminate the issue of harmony and disharmony between between empirical and scriptural knowledge.

Biderman, Shlomo, and Ben-Ami Scharfstein (eds.). 1989. *Rationality in Question: On Eastern and Western Views of Rationality*. Philosophy and Religion: A Comparative Yearbook; vol. I. New York: E. J. Brill.

The editors have gathered essays that reflect, they claim, a contemporary trend toward a "more reasonable . . . rationality" (xiv), that is, a range of accounts of rationality that are cognizant and respectful of empirical limits, cultural variance, contextual relevance, and practical "fuzziness" in the deliverances of reason. Part I contains five essays addressing the nature of rationality, in relation to logic, ethics, politics and the sciences, asceticism, and contextualization. Part II consists of seven comparative essays studying theories of rationality across the world's major religious traditions.

Brockelman, Paul T. 1992. *The Inside Story: A Narrative Approach to Religious Understanding and Truth*. Albany: State University of New York Press.

Brockelman advances a case for religious truth as a matter of transformation in accord with mythic narratives. Religions serve this mythic expression and/or disclosure of cultural life-worlds. Brockelman recommends this view as a way to overcome the "modern" split of subjective and objective knowledge that, he claims, results in the dilemma of confessional fundamentalism on the one hand and skepticism on the other. His main influences are continental phenomenology and American narrative theology.

Carnes, John Robb. 1982. *Axiomatics and Dogmatics*. Theology and scientific culture; 4. New York: Oxford University Press.

Carnes argues that the methodology of theology, and thus its formal criteria for truth, is the same as that of mathematics. This means that theology and science are theoretical enterprises on a par with each other, although the "facts" that they observe and understand are different. Science is concerned with "ordianry experience," theology with "religious experience." Since in each enterprise, observation is theory-laden, neither science nor theology is normative with respect to the field of experience it observes. Theological truth, then, is a matter of the meaningfulness—that is, the coherence and practical satisfaction that a set of religious beliefs offers (cf. 120).

Christian, William A. 1964. *Meaning and Truth in Religion*. Princeton, N.J.: Princeton University Press.

Christian takes the approach of analytic philosophy to show "how religious utterances can express genuine truth-claims" (1). By "utterances" is meant statements proposing something for belief. This is a major development (not Christian's alone) out of a philosophical tradition that, as in the case of Ayer, declared religious statements to be meaningless. The truth of religious proposals is a matter of reasonable certainty—a criterion that attempts to integrate demands for conformity to evidence and for the guidance of coherent and appropriate conduct.

Cragg, Kenneth. 1992. *Troubled by Truth: Life Studies in Inter-faith Concern*. Edinburgh: Pentland Press.

In this compassionate and incisive volume, Cragg pursues the question of how personal "inner faith" is changed and challenged in inter-faith encounter via thirteen biographical studies of people (four Muslim, four Christian, two Jewish, and two Indian) intimately and daily involved in such encounter. None among these figures is a professional theologian or mystic, for Cragg sought those whose encounter was of a necessary and experiential nature and those who thus had to come to terms with this encounter not on an academic level but on a sincere personal level that potentially 'troubled' their own faith. All but nineteenth-century English missionary Martyn Henry are twentieth-century figures and many of these latter are involved in literature or the arts including Charles Freer Andrews, Elie Wiesel, Salman Rushdie, Salah ʿAbd al-Sabur, and T. S. Eliot.

Dean, Thomas (ed.). 1994. *Religious Pluralism and Truth: Essays on Cross-Cultural Philosophy of Religion*. Albany: State University of New York Press.

The essays in this collection date from the late 1970s and 1980s. They focus largely on methodological questions about how to do cross-cultural philosophy, and how to judge whether it is being done well. A preoccupation among the essays is with whether such a thing as cross-cultural truth can be recognized, or if particular truths are necessarily sacrificed for the sake of one perspective. The volume offers the encouragement that, as a nascent discipline, cross-cultural philosophy of religion is no less pluralistic than its field of inquiry. This is especially evidenced in the persistence of the essayists in looking for concrete resources for comparative thinking already in use in religious traditions: the topical divisions of the book address "Religious pluralism and cross-cultural truth," "Criteria of cross-cultural truth in religion," "Models of cross-cultural truth in religion," and "Hermeneutics of cross-cultural truth in religion."

Deutsch, Eliot. 1979. *On Truth: An Ontological Theory*. Honolulu: University Press of Hawaii.

Deutsch develops a constructive theory of truth out of his own lengthy engagement with Western philosophy and Advaita Vedānta. Truth is the valuable achievement of "rightness," that is, something is true when it realizes its own intention. In accordance with this, Deutsch starts with the experience of truth in art and religion, and from there develops an account of truth in propositional language. In Vedāntic terms, it is a theory of truth appropriate to the plurality of conventional reality; it does not attempt to adjudicate on what is true absolutely. This truth is wordless liberation.

Dewart, Leslie. 1970. *Religion, Language and Truth*. New York: Herder and Herder.

In this overview and condensation of his larger work, *The Foundations of Belief*, Dewart argues that contemporary debates in Catholic theology are caused by a fundamental difference in the way scholars view the relationship between language and reality. He outlines the "semantic" and "syntactic" views of this relationship. The former holds that thought is prior to language and thus language is a mere means of communicating truth, while the latter holds that language is prior to thought, the condition of thought, and thus truth is a function of linguistic interrelationships and clarity. Dewart defends the syntactic view and argues that theologians should be concerned with articulating reality fully and thus truthfully.

DiCenso, James. 1990. *Hermeneutics and the Disclosure of Truth: A Study in the Work of Heidegger, Gadamer, and Ricoeur*. Studies in religion and culture. Charlottesville: University Press of Virginia.

DiCenso traces a theory of truth relevant to historical and existential (i.e., interpretative) processes. He begins his study with an overview of "Aspects of the problem of truth in the history of thought," which traces a path from correspondence theories of truth to coherence theories to a critique of coherence. This is followed by an examination of Heidegger's ontology and the view of truth as disclosure that arises from it. Next, DiCenso explicates Gadamer's historical hermeneutics as a process by which truth is disclosed before turning to Ricoeur's work on language as a "world-disclosing" medium.

Frankenberry, Nancy K., and Hans H. Penner (eds.). 1999. *Language, Truth, and Religious Belief: Studies in Twentieth-Century Theory and Method in Religion*. Texts and translations series (American Academy of Religion), no. 19. Atlanta, Ga.: Scholars Press.

This volume collects some of the most influential twentieth-century philosophical and anthropological reflections on religion, together with critical responses. The pieces are arranged in a thematic sequence from Logical Positivism to Functionalism to Relativism. The editors aim to promote critical reception of the theoretical tradition in the study of religion while showing that tradition's continuing hold upon religious studies. In a fourth section, four essays point toward an alternative, "holistic" and semantic approach to the study of religious truth and meaning. In this latter approach, "the inherent rationality of a . . . religious system consists in the relations that constitute the various elements of the system" (5). Further suggested readings are appended to each section.

Griffin, David Ray, and Huston Smith. 1989. *Primordial Thought and Postmodern Thought.* Albany: State University of New York Press.

Here, Griffin and Smith undertake an extended debate and critique of one another's views. They open their debate in the first chapter with biographical sketches and argue that they agree on a basic level with one another. They go on, however, in chapters two through five to belie that pleaded agreement. Griffin sets the debate going in chapter 2 where he sets his process view of an everlasting and relational God against Smith's perennialist view of a primordial, perfect, and wholly other God. He finds no less than six internal and seven external problems with Smith's view. In chapter three Smith replies, but in chapter four Griffin contends that at least seven problems still remain in Smiths conception. Smith again replies in chapter five. Throughout, careful attention is paid to the metaphysical differences between these two views as well as to the stakes, ontological and existential, that are involved in the adoption of either. While not a survey of either the perennialist (Smith) or the postmodern, process (Griffin) position, the book makes clear the fundamental commitments of each.

Griffiths, Paul J. 1991. *An Apology for Apologetics: A Study in the Logic of Interreligious Dialogue.* Faith Meets Faith. Maryknoll, N.Y.: Orbis Books.

Griffiths argues that frank debate over the cross-cultural truth of religious doctrines is an obligatory component of dialogue between religious traditions. Doctrine-expressing sentences that intend to state truth about reality are an essential part of religious discourse. The marks of such truth claims are: (1) comprehensibility to both insiders and outsiders; (2) a measure of commensurability with doctrinal statements in other traditions and thus; (3) capacity of being incompatible with doctrines of other traditions. Griffiths advocates for "negative" apologetics (a means to greater consistency and clarity within a tradition) and "positive" apologetics (argument for the superiority of one's own doctrines), and sets out conditions for the propriety of each mode. A final chapter conducts a case study in comparing Buddhist and Christian doctrines of the self.

Guerrière, Daniel (ed.). 1990. *Phenomenology of the Truth Proper to Religion.* Albany: State University of New York Press.

This collection of essays indicates the broad range of approaches taken in phenomenology of religion by its division into five sections: Existential, Hermeneutic, Ethical, Deconstructive, and Transcendental. Husserl, Heidegger, Levinas, Ricoeur, and Derrida are all important reference figures for the collection. Guerrière provides an introduction to phenomenology and its concerns. The most useful essays for non-specialists are Dupré's, on religious and philosophical truth, Clayton's, on religious and scientific truth, and Farley's, on the purpose of religious truth.

Gupta, Bina. 1991. *Perceiving in Advaita Vedānta: Epistemological Analysis and Interpretation.* Lewisburg: Bucknell University Press; London: Associated University Presses.

The fundamental issue in this book on Advaita epistemology is explicating the difference between delusory consciousness and the pure consciousness that sees reality as it truly is—that is, the non-duality of Ātman and Brahman. The author provides a transliteration and translation of the chapter on perception from Dharmaraja's classical work on this topic, and makes free use of its traditional commentary in her own explication and interpretation of the topic in relation to other Indian schools. A fairly technical work in twentieth century (Neo-)Vedānta.

Heim, S. Mark. 1995. *Salvations: Truth and Difference in Religion.* Faith Meets Faith. Maryknoll, N.Y.: Orbis Books.

Heim's primary thesis is that "there is a real diversity of religious ends" (6), that is, that the religions—and the "salvations" they promote—are genuinely plural. In Part I, Heim critically reviews the pluralistic hypotheses of Hick, W. C. Smith, and Knitter, arguing that their pluralism is insufficiently thoroughgoing. In Part II, he presents and tests his theory with respect to philosophical debates in epistemology, history and sociology of religion, and ethical challenges. He concludes that there are many true religions and that each is, for its adherents, the only way. Religious truth, then, is wrapped up with salvation.

Hick, John. *A Christian Theology of Religions.* Louisville: Westminster John Knox Press, 1995.

Here, Hick restates his "pluralistic hypothesis" and addresses key philosophical and theological criticism that this hypothesis has evoked. The pluralistic hypothesis states that all religious traditions are equally valid responses to the transcendent "Real." In the philosophical section, Hick addresses, among other criticisms, the criticism that his hypothesis does not account for the different and conflicting truth claims of various religions. He argues that what is different are rather the concepts, particular to each tradition, that differently structure the engagement of the one Real. While the structure of the engagement is different, the truth claim that each tradition engages the Real is fundamentally the same and thus not conflictual. In the theological section, Hick confronts the criticism that his hypothesis undermines doctrines of salvific uniqueness and religious superiority. He admits flatly that his hypothesis does do this, but that this undermining is a necessary consequence with which sincere pluralists will have to reckon. The final chapter presents Hick's vision for a much liberalized Christianity of 2056 in which worshipers will view Jesus as a moral teacher and draw their scriptural lessons from the texts of many traditions.

Hick, John. 1974. *Truth and Dialogue in World Religions.* London: Sheldon Press.

This collection of essays explores the question of the commensurability or incommensurablility of religious traditions. R. C. Zaehner argues in the opening chapter that the truths of each religion flow from the Holy Spirit. Ninian Smart, attempting to correct misperceptions of Hinduism, urges that the differences between religions ought not be glossed over. Others take up the task of comparison: Geoffrey Parrinder between the *Bhagavad Gītā* and the Christian notion of the bible as the Word of God; and Cantwell Smith between the Islamic and Christian views of truth and reality.

Hofmeister, Heimo E. M. 1990. *Truth and Belief: Interpretation and Critique of the Analytical Theory of Religion.* Studies in Philosophy of Religion. Vol. 14. Boston: Kluwer Academic Press.

Arguing from a historical perspective, Hofmeister surveys figures and schools in analytic theories of religion. He hopes to show that each subsequent figure or school moved the analytic theory forward by taking up the unresolved questions of prior figures and schools. The survey includes the Vienna Circle, A. J. Ayer, Wittgenstein, Anthony Flew's gardener parable, Hare's view of religions as unfalsifiable worldviews, Jame Fross' analysis of analogical language, and Malcolm and Hartshorne's defense of the ontological argument.

Hook, Sidney (ed.). 1961. *Religious Experience and Truth: A Symposium.* New York: New York University Press.

This collection of thirty seven essays by a roster of important philosophers and theologians stems from a 1960 meeting. An essay by Tillich,

"The Religious Symbol" (curiously placed in an appendix), is a point of departure for much of the discussion. Tillich's reply to criticisms, "The Meaning and Justification of Religious Symbols," opens the volume, providing the title for Part I. Part II concerns "The nature of religious faith," and H. Richard Niebuhr is the key participant here. Part III, "Meaning and truth in theology," leads out with an essay by linguistic philosopher Michael Ziff.

Jaki, Stanley L. 1999. *Means to Message: A Treatise on Truth*. Grand Rapids, Mich.: Eerdmans.

In this extended essay, Jaki argues that while all truth must begin with objects, the consideration of objects necessarily leads to metaphysics. In so doing, he hopes to wrest philosophy from science by showing that the quantitative measurements of objects that science provides do not exhaust the possible knowledge of objects. Most notably, Jaki argues that science cannot provide accounts of causation, change, freewill, and purpose, all of which he takes to require metaphysics. For this reason, he argues that philosophers must like science be concerned with objects but most seek the whole truth of objects including that truth that is metaphysical.

Lindbeck, George. 1984. *The Nature of Doctrine: Religion and Theology in a Postliberal Age*. Philadelphia: Westminster.

Lindbeck here asserts an analogy between religion and language. In his cultural-linguistic theory of religion, doctrines symbolize truth claims. They form a sort of grammar, which gives coherence to the belief system that comprises a faith tradition. Becoming religious means becoming skilled in the 'language' of one's own religion. The author intends to open the topic of religious doctrine to an ecumenical dialogue by means of his use of this theory.

Long, Eugene Thomas. 1995. *God, Reason and Religions*. Boston: Kluwer Academic Publishers.

This collection compiles essays written to celebrate the twenty-fifth anniversary of the *International Journal for Philosophy of Religion*. Most contributors comment on what they see as the key problems or questions presently facing philosophy of religion. William P. Alston argues that philosophy of religion still confronts the question of the factual status of religious statements. He denies the correspondence theory of truth (that linguistic truth can be adjudicated relative to its correspondence to an independence reality), assets that religious truth is dependent on mind, and defends the reality of Christian Mystical Experience (CMP), while yet acknowledging the difficulty for this latter notion in account for religious diversity. John E. Smith contends that philosophy of religion still needs theology to prevent it from becoming overly formal and professionally overspecialized, while theology needs philosophy of religion to prevent it from becoming fundamentalist and superstitious. Robert C. Neville holds that philosophy of religion must remain the critic of religion's metaphysics and that the most pressing need is for comparative categories that avoid "disciplinary nominalism" and "vicious reductionism." Other contributors include David B. Burrell, Richard Swinburne, and Phillip Quinn.

Nasr, Seyyed Hossein. 1989. *Knowledge and the Sacred.* Albany: State University of New York Press.

In these, his Gifford Lectures, Nasr argues that the Western tradition is in need of a resacralization of knowledge that his Islamic tradition can provide. In the tradition of Coomaraswamy, Schuon, and Huxley, he argues that every religious tradition is a repository for the perennial truth of God. All religions are thus unified in that they find their source "first and foremost in the Absolute, which is at once truth and reality and the origin of all revelation and of all truth." In this perspective, knowledge that is divorced from an understanding of the divine cannot be considered knowledge at all.

Netland, Harold, A. 1991. *Dissonant Voices: Religious Pluralism and the Question of Truth.* Grand Rapids, Mich.: W. B. Eerdmans; Leicester, England: Apollos.

Netland hopes to provide a "defense of Christian exclusivism—a prolegomenon to an evangelical theology of religions." He traces the development of dialogue between Christianity and other religions and outlines the three major stances (exclusivism, inclusivism, and pluralism) that Christians have adopted in these dialogues. He argues, however, that religious truth is propositional and therefore only exclusivism is a logical possibility. In the case of two conflicting propositions, only one can be the case. Nevertheless, he urges evangelicals to adopt an attitude of humility and tolerance in inevitable situations of dialogue.

Neville, Robert Cummings. 1996. *The Truth of Broken Symbols.* Albany: State University of New York Press.

Neville defends the pragmatic view that the truth of symbols is the carryover of value from the interpreted to the interpreter. Religious symbols are thus true in the degree to which they enable religious practitioners to engage the divine. Since the form of this engagement is different in different contexts, the nature of the carryover of value, the truth of the symbol, will also be different. In short, religious symbols are true in different respects depending on the context in which they are engaged, be it devotional, cultic, theological, or public. Neville illustrates this theory with a careful analysis of the truth of the Christian symbol of the Eucharist as people engage it in various contexts.

Phillips, D. Z. 1988. *Faith after Foundationalism*. London; New York: Routledge.

In these essays, Phillips assesses and critiques the recent non-foundationalist epistemologies of Plantinga, Rorty, Lindbeck, and Berger. He argues that each author remains foundational because each merely substitutes one theory of foundation for another, whether this substitute is theological, linguistic, or sociological. Moreover, in this substitution, each author neglects or denies the complexity of individual religious practices and beliefs. Phillips argues that the true non-foundationalist will not ask "what is God" but "how can humans talk about God?" The task of the theologian or philosopher is thus to illustrate the interrelationship of concepts and thereby contribute to non-foundational conceptual clarity rather than foundational, empirical certainty.

Phillips, Stephen H. 1995. *Classical Indian Metaphysics: Refutations of Realism and the Emergence of "New Logic."* Chicago: Open Court.

This readable introduction to debates between realist and idealist schools of Indian metaphysics is meant for novice students and expert scholars alike. While idealists hold that truth is a function of mind or consciousness, realists hold that knowledge is a function of reality independent of mind. Phillips provides two introductory chapters on the Upaniṣadic background of twelfth-and fourteenth- century idealist and realist exemplifiers Śrīharsa and the Navya Nyāya or New Logic school, respectively. In his third and fourth chapters, he argues that the motivations and contexts of the Advaitan idealist Śrīharsa and the realist Navya Nyāya school are more complex than scholars have usually assumed. Sriharsa, while concerned to respond to the Nyāya "Logic" school, was also a positive idealist philosopher who drew on Buddhist as well as Upaniṣadic material. Navya Nyāya, on the other hand, was not simply a realist reaction to Śrīharsa, but a true refinement and innovation of the Nyāya school's argumentation.

Randall, John Herman. 1986 (1958). *The Role of Knowledge in Western Religion*. Lanham, Md.: University Press of America.

Randall outlines three historical views of religious knowledge (that it is gained through revelation, though experience of a higher realm, or that it is primarily functional "know-how"). He defends that third view arguing that this functional "know-how" helps individuals and groups to unify, sanctify, and clarify their values and context. "Knowing God" thus refers to knowing which values orient individuals and groups. The theologian must examine these values, testing them against natural science, and thereby enabling them to more fully unify the individual's or group's experience of the world.

Rouner, Leroy S. (ed.). 1985. *Knowing Religiously*. Boston University Studies in Philosophy and Religion; vol. 7. Notre Dame, Ind.: University of Notre Dame Press.

This collection of essays addresses three themes, "The Nature of Religious Knowledge," "Religious Truth Claims Considered," and "Philosophy of Religion and Contemporary Culture." Contributors include Cornel West, Charles Hartshorne, Ninian Smart, Anthony Flew, Gordon Kaufman, and Jurgan Moltmann, among others.

Runzo, Joseph. 1986. *Reason, Relativism and God*. New York: St. Martin's Press.

Runzo examines various conceptions of relativism and argues that conceptual relativism is the only coherent form of relativism. It holds that assertions are true or false only relative to the conceptual system in which they are asserted. He describes and critiques three strategies (an appeal to experience, an appeal to metaphysics, and an appeal to kerygmatic authority) that theologians have employed to counter relativism. While Runzo finds each of these strategies inadequate, he sees faith as a fourth strategy. Following William James's definition of faith, he argues that faith is an answer to relativism since a believer's faith provides him or her with a coherent system of belief.

Santoni, Ronald E. (ed.). 1968. *Religious Language and the Problem of Religious Knowledge*. Bloomington: Indiana University Press.

This work argues through a collection of essays that the question of the possibility of religious knowledge is directly related to the question of whether religious language can be considered true or false and in what sense. McPherson and Ayer argue that religious language is non-sense because it does not refer to anything that is verifiable through sense perception. Combie delineates "logical idiosyncrasies" and "anomalous formal properties" of religious language, but argues that these allow believers to "grasp meaning" and help them to delimit the "reference range" of religious language. Tillich argues that, if taken literally, religious language is absurd, but if taken symbolically, religious language can be profoundly meaningful. Buber and Bultmann argue that religious language is true only in the experience of relational encounter with God, which encounter radically relativizes all human efforts to name God literally or definitively.

Sherry, Patrick. 1977. *Religion, Truth, and Language-Games*. New York: Barnes & Noble Books.

Sherry argues that religions are not one language game but a collection of language games. He hopes to correct the misperception that Wittgenstein's concept of language games implied a single language game for each tradition. The philosopher's job, in Sherry's view, is to locate, relate, and validate these collections of language games. Moreover, Sherry argues that religious truth no less than other categories of truth attempts to "correctly define some actual state of affairs."

Smart, Ninian. 1995. *Worldviews: Cross-Cultural Explorations of Human Beliefs*. Second edition. New York: Charles Scribner's Sons.

Smart argues that "what people believe is an important aspect of reality whether or not what they believe is true." He contends that those involved in the field of comparative religions should enlarge their preview to world view in general, since ideology, such as atheism and Marxism, functions for their adherents in much the same way as religions, making the world intelligible and meaningful to them. Worldviews share six dimensions, according to Smart, including the philosophical, the mythic, the ethical, the ritual, the experiential, and the social. He explores each of these in relation to major secular and religious worldviews.

Smart, Ninian. 1964. *Philosophers and Religious Truth*. London: SCM.

Smart explores five major issues in philosophy of religion with reference to five major philosophers. He begins with the problem of argument and truth within the context of discussion of Hume's view of miracles. Next, he explores causation and the question of human freedom with the assistance of Kant. Next, Smart discusses the question of the existence of God via a dialogue between Thomas Aquinas's "proofs" and Kant's reactions to them. Finally, he explores the issue of revelation and religious experience with reference to Rudolf Otto and the problem of evil with reference to F. R. Tennet.

Smith, Wilfred Cantwell. 1964. *Questions of Religious Truth*. New York: Scribners.

Smith argues that the question of religious truth is primarily a question of personal faith. Religious truth is particular to particular people at particular times. Therefore, the Qur'ān, as Smith contends in one chapter, is the Word of God for a Muslim in Mecca while it may not be for a Christian in New York. In this sense, religions can be more or less true given that different people will hold them to be true in different respects and degrees. Smith concludes that such a personal understanding of truth has the potential to make interfaith dialogue more possible and productive since it acknowledges the truth of each religion for its adherents.

Sölle, Dorothee. 1969. *The Truth is Concrete.* trans. Dinah Livingstone. New York: Herder and Herder.

Truth is concrete, Sölle contends, in that it is always experienced in specific contexts. Christianity itself is a religion of concrete truth since it proclaims the incarnation as the revelation of the truth of God. Sölle fears, however, that Christianity has lost its hold on truth as concrete as it has become institutional and separated from the liberation struggle of individuals. She urges reform of the church and sees the existence of people working in solidarity for liberation, a church outside the church, as a sign of hope.

Sontag, Frederick. 1995. *Uncertain Truth.* Lanham: University Press of America.

Sontag argues that a situation of cultural and intellectual uncertainty characterizes the twentieth-century context of the search for truth. He attributes this uncertainty to developments in quantum and theoretical physics as well as philosophy and linguistics. While truth may henceforth be fragile, dependent, and inexhaustive, Sontag maintains that there is still truth analogous to the truth of psychoanalytic interpretations of dreams that are true be do not exhaust the possible meaning of the dreams. He concludes such inferential and aesthetic notions of truth are more appropriate to the context of uncertainty.

Streng, Frederick J. 1967. *Emptiness: A Study in Religious Meaning.* Nashville: Abingdon.

Streng studies the the term *sunyata* ("emptiness") as it is used by the second-century Indian Buddhist philosopher, Nāgārjuna, to express the nature of ultimate reality. Nāgārjuna's thought is distinctive in its denial that ultimate truth requires a correspondingly ultimate reality, for both conventional and ultimate reality are "empty." Streng traces the relations of *śūnyatā* to other central topics in Buddhist metaphysics. He then considers the norms and rules guiding Nāgārjuna's religious dialectic. Finally, he explicates the religious meaning of emptiness and develops a theory that the truth of religious knowledge is as a means for ultimate transformation.

Thiel, John E. 1994. *Nonfoundationalism. Guides to Theological Inquiry.* Minneapolis: Fortress Press.

This work is a survey of the non-foundationalist movement in philosophy (reviewing Quine, Davidson, Rorty, Sellars, and Berstan) and theology (reviewing Frei, Thiemann, Tanner, and Lindbeck). This survey serves as a preparation for Thiel's argument that theology must be contextual and acutely aware of the "contingency and revisablity of all knowledge." Theologians should be forthright about their presuppositions and appeal to the "holistic justification" of the Bible as a witness rather than an objective authority.

Tracy, David. 1981. *The Analogical Imagination: Christian Theology and the Culture of Pluralism*. New York: Crossroad.

In this work, Tracy addresses the question of religious truth in the context of ecumenicity and pluralism. He argues for and employs his proposed method, "analogical, theological imagination." Religious truth, Tracy contends, is analogous to the truth of literary classics that articulate universal meanings as interpreted in the particular forms of a culture. The event of Jesus Christ defined as the present liberation of the believer mediated through the theological meanings of the tradition's memory if the Christian classic. Tracy argues that fruitful interfaith dialogue could take place is believers from each tradition could analogically and imaginatively step into and experience the classics of other religions while carefully attending to the similarities and the differences with their own tradition.

Troeltsch, Ernst. 1971. *The Absoluteness of Christianity and the History of Religions*.Trans. David Reid. Introduction by James Luther Adams. Richmond: John Knox Press.

Based on a lecture Troeltsch gave in 1901, this book is a classic statement of the problems that still set much of the agenda of contemporary Christian theology. What character can the "absoluteness" of Christianity possess given the evidence that Christianity, as much as any other religion, changes through history? Not only this, but the claims Christianity makes in its own behalf change, too. Troeltsch analyzes alternative conceptions of absoluteness and proposes a version based on the claim that Christianity exhibits and inculcates to a superior degree such normative religious values as can be proposed from a study of the world's religions.

Van Huyssteen, Wentzel. 1989. *Theology and the Justification of Faith: Constructing Theories in Systematic Theology*. Trans. H. F. Snijders. Grand Rapids, Mich.: Eerdmans.

Van Huyssteen argues that theology has a place in the secular university because its truth is akin to scientific truth in that it may be judged to a greater or lesser degree as experientially falsifiable. He seeks a holism whereby religious beliefs would be tested on the truth of their depiction of reality, their critical and problem-solving ability, and their constructive and progressive nature. He finds justification for this approach in the philosophy of science, particularly Thoman Kuhn. In addition, he explores how Pannenberg and Sauter have attempted to unite religion and science and argues that his own methodology is more satisfactory since it makes knowledge of science not only compatible with but also indispensable to theology. Indeed, the theologian must, in Van Huyssteens view, consult science in order to test the truthfulness of his or her theological picture to the actual world.

Vroom, Hendrick M. 1989. *Religions and the Truth: Philosophical Reflections and Perspectives*. Trans. J. W. Rebel. Grand Rapids, Mich.: Eerdmans.

On the assumption that one must understand what each religion means by truth before fruitful dialogue may occur, Vroom takes an inclusive and wholistic survey of the definitions of truth in Islam, Hinduism, Buddhism, Judaism, and Christianity. He finds that five types of definitions can be found throughout the traditions. These five types of truth include: *doctrina* or basically accepted truths, *verita* or truths understood over time, *vera religio* or lived truths, *intellectus verus* or truths resulting from momentary enlightenment, and *veritas* or the transcendent itself, which is the norm and source of all other truths. He concludes that the full understanding of a religion will only result from an experience of that religion in all five facets of its truth. Therefore a holistic and experiential dialogue is needed rather than a mere comparison of doctrines. He finally cautions that all religions have some conception of the fundamental limitations of human's ability to understand and thus urges great patience on the part of dialogue participants.

Walker, Ralph Charles Sutherland. 1989. *The Coherence Theory of Truth: Realism, Anti-realism, Idealism*. International Library of Philosophy. London; New York: Routledge.

For the sake of clarity in contemporary debates, Walker explains the coherence theory of truth with special reference to its key proponents and their motivations for promoting the theory. The coherence theory of truth states that the truth of a proposition is its coherence with a set of beliefs that the individual sees as her or her fundamental beliefs about a subject. Spinoza, Kant, Fichte, Hegel, and Wittgenstein are reviewed as expounding coherence theories and Descartes as arguing for a variant of the coherence theory. While Walker demonstrates to his own satisfaction that the coherence theory is not patently absurd as recent philosophers, such as Russell, have assumed, he still finds coherence basically untenable and opts for a provisional correspondence theory that holds that the truth of a proposition is its correspondence to reality independent of the proposition.

Watt, William Montgomery. 1995. *Religious Truth for Our Time*. Oxford: One World.

Truth is to be found in all the world religions, and is seen by the quality of life of their adherents, says Watt, a pre-eminent Islamist and himself a Christian. The diversity among the religions can be explained by the inadequacies of human thought and language to understand the world and express convictions about it. Moreover, factual differences among the religions (and factual disagreements within a tradition) are not the measure of truth, since religions aim to uncover significance in the world for the sake of changing lives. Watt then considers truth in the biblical testaments and in other religious traditions, before considering challenges all the religions face in common. A clear expression of one view for laypeople.

Watts, Fraser N., and Mark Williams. 1988. *The Psychology of Religious Knowing*. Cambridge; New York: Cambridge University Press.

The authors approach religious knowing from the perspective of cognitive psychology. They argue that religious knowing is not a different kind of knowing but analogous to aesthetic knowing and personal insight. They note that the religious person learns of God in much the same way that people undergoing psychoanalysis learn about themselves. They further argue that religious knowing is not concerned with knowing a reality other than that of the everyday world, but rather is concerned with learning to interpret the everyday world religiously.

Whittaker, John H. 1981. *Matters of Faith and Matters of Principle: Religious Truth Claims and Their Logic*. Trinity University Monograph Series in Religion; vol. 6. San Antonio: Trinity University Press.

Whittaker argues that religious truth claims are akin to principles. They are "indemonstrable assertions that sustain and regulate further judgment." As such, their truth depends upon whether they enable the believer to understand new things or to include a greater number of known facts in an overall explanation. The are thus primarily judged by their heuristic value.

Wiebe, Donald. 1981. *Religion and Truth: Towards an Alternative Paradigm for the Study of Religion*. Religion and Reason; 23. The Hague: Mouton.

Wiebe argues that one cannot neglect propositional truth while investigating personal truth. Against phenomenology that would bracket the question of truth in religion, Wiebe maintains that reason demands an explanation for all phenomenon, including religious phenomenon. This work is not so much an exposition of what that truth might be, but rather an argument that the question of truth cannot be left aside. Tillich, Durkheim, Smart, Cantwell Smith, F. Ferré, Hick, and Rahner are all discussed and criticized as the argument proceeds.

Annotated Bibliography: Judaism

Reference Works

Bibliographies

Frank, Ruth S. and William Wollheim (eds.). 1986. *The Book of Jewish Books: A Reader's Guide to Judaism.* San Francisco: Harper & Row.

Holtz, Barry W. (ed.). 1992. *The Schocken Guide to Jewish Books: Where to Start Reading about Jewish History, Literature, Culture, and Religion.* New York: Schocken Books.

Kaplan, Jonathan. 1983. *2000 Books and More: An Annotated and Selected Bibliography of Jewish History and Thought.* Jerusalem: The Magnes Press, The Hebrew University.

Kaplan, Jonathan, ed. 1984. *International Bibliography of Jewish History and Thought.* Kaplan. Munchen; New York: Saur; Jerusalem: Magnes Press, Hebrew University.

Dictionaries and Encyclopedias

Cohn-Sherbok, Dan. 1992. *The Blackwell Dictionary of Judaica.* Oxford [England]: Blackwell Reference.

A concise volume intended as a source for initial entry into the study of Judaica. As such, references sacrifice depth (the average entry length is a mere seventy words) for breadth (over 7,000 entries) of coverage. Although comprehensive, the limited information provided and the lack of bibliographies recommends usage of this volume primarily as quick reference for beginning students.

Encyclopaedia Judaica. 1971. Jerusalem: Keter Publishing House.

An indispensable reference comprehensively covering all aspects of Jewish religion, history, and culture. The sixteen volumes include approximately 20,000 subjects, and are illustrated throughout. Special emphasis is given to developments in Judaism in the twentieth century (most notably the Holocaust, the foundation of the State of Israel, and the establishment of the United States as a primary center of the Jewish tradition), thus setting this new encyclopedia apart from the twelve volume work published in 1906. This reference includes an extensive index (vol. 1) and yearly update volumes since its publication in 1972, and is now also available in a CD-ROM version.

Werblowsky, R. J. Zwi, and Geoffrey Wigoder. 1997. *The Oxford Dictionary of the Jewish Religion*. New York: Oxford University Press.

An accessible single volume reference on specifically religious aspects of Jewish tradition. Extensive cross-referencing and comprehensive bibliographies add to its value for beginning students of Judaism.

Primary Sources

Blumenthal, David R. 1978 and 1982. *Understanding Jewish Mysticism: A Source Reader.* 2 vols. (The Library of Judaic Learning). New York: Ktav Publishing House.

Blumenthal introduces readers to texts from throughout the history of Jewish mystical traditions. Volume one excerpts writings on the secrets of creation and the visionary ascent to God, including the *Sefer Yetsira* and *Pirkei Heikhalot*, as well as the *Zohar* and Lurianic prayerbook. Volume two includes sections of Maimonides' *Guide of the Perplexed,* al-Botini's *Sullam ha-'Aliyah*, and a variety of Hasidic texts. The author's annotations address issues of authorship, chronology, and symbolism, and assist in clarifying central issues in the texts, as well as the meta-issues in the study of Jewish mysticism.

Bokser, Ben Zion, and Baruch M. Bokser (eds.). 1989. *The Talmud: Selected Writings*. Trans. Ben Zion Bokser, introduced by Ben Zion Bokser and Baruch M. Bokser, preface by Robert Goldberg (The Classics of Western Spirituality). New York: Paulist Press.

These selections provide readers with an introductory distillation of the spirituality embodied in the text of the Talmud. It presents the consistent vision of the early rabbis as to the form, content, and goal of Jewish life, with some reflection of the unique role of the rabbi within the religious community. Fifteen Talmudic tractates are briefly excerpted and introduced with necessary background material.

Dan, Joseph, and Ronald C. Kiener. 1986. *The Early Kabbalah*. Edited and introduced by Joseph Dan, texts translated by Ronald C. Kiener, preface by Moshe Idel. (The Classics of Western Spirituality). New York: Paulist Press.

Dan and Kiener acquaint readers with representative and historically significant texts of thirteenth-century Jewish mysticism, some of which are presented here for the first time either in print or translation. These works reflect the creative diversity of Kabbalistic thought prior to the writing of the *Sefer ha-Zohar*. Included are texts from the 'Iyyun Circle, the *Sefer ha-Bahir* (*Book of Brilliance*), the school of Rabbi Isaac the Blind, the Gerona circle, and the Kohen brothers of Castille.

Danby, Herbert, trans. 1933. *The Mishnah.* translated from the Hebrew with introduction and brief explanatory notes. London: Oxford University Press.

Danby proffers a straightforward and highly accessible translation of the Mishnah text in its entirety. Notations are of an explanatory, rather than commentarial, nature, and the glossary, appendices, and lengthy index are designed to assist in making the text available to a broad audience.

Epstein, I. (ed.). 1984. *Hebrew-English Edition of the Babylonian Talmud.* Translated into English with notes, glossary, and indices by Maurice Simon. London: The Soncino Press.

A readable and reliable multi-volume rendition of the entire Babylonian Talmud, based on the Vilna Talmud with corrections from and references to other extant manuscripts. Copious notes, glossaries, and introductions assist the reader in tackling the enormity of the text.

Matt, Daniel C. (ed.). 1994. T*he Essential Kabbalah: The Heart of Jewish Mysticism.* Compiled and translated with note by Daniel C. Matt. San Francisco: HarperSanFrancisco.

Matt offers translations of what he terms the essential teachings of the Jewish mystical tradition. Arranged topically, the translations are designed to be readable and to capture the poetic style of the Hebrew and Aramaic texts. Copious notes clarify more obscure passages and situate the texts and their concepts within the broader tradition.

Matt, Daniel Chanan. 1983. *Zohar: The Book of Enlightenment.* Translation and introduction by Daniel Chanan Matt, preface by Arthur Green. (Classics of Western Spirituality) New York: Paulist Press.

Matt endeavors to capture the lyricism and poetry of the original Aramaic text of the *Sefer ha-Zohar* (*Book of Splendor*), the thirteenth-century classic of Jewish mysticism. Explanatory notes and commentary are placed at the end of the work so as not to impede the reader's course through the primary text. It should be noted that Matt's translation excerpts only a small fraction of the original work.

Montefiore, C. G., and H. Loewe (eds.). 1938. *A Rabbinic Anthology.* Selected and arranged with comments and introductions by C. G. Montefiore and H. Loewe.

Montefiore and Loewe excerpt and translate early Rabbinic texts and arrange them topically. They focus almost exclusively on haggadah rather than halakhah. Chapters treat a variety of subjects ranging from the divine nature and characteristics, to ethics and communal and family order. Supplementary materials and charts trace the intellectual "geneology" of Tanaitic and early Rabbinic thinkers, provide chronologies of the included extracts, and cross-reference biblical, Rabbinic, Greek, and Latin passages.

Neusner, Jacob. 1996. *The Talmud of Babylonia: An Academic Commentary* (University of South Florida Academic Commentary Series). Atlanta: Scholars Press.

This multi-volume work presents the text of the Bavli as a cogent system with organizing principles and a coherent structure, rather than a rather diverse collection of facts and authoritative opinion. Visual clues, such as different typeface and varied indentation, illustrate for the English reading audience the linguistic components (Hebrew and Aramaic) and the structural elements that comprise the Talmudic text.

Neusner, Jacob. 1988. *The Mishnah: A New Translation.* New Haven; London: Yale University Press.

Neusner offers a more literal translation of the Hebrew text into American English than the earlier work of Danby. The intent is to demonstrate, as best one can in translation, the formal and syntactic means by which early/proto-Rabbinic ideas are expressed in the Mishnah. The text in translation is arranged for easy reference and to disclose structural patterns in the prose and poetry.

Secondary Sources

Belkin, Samuel. 1960. *In His Image: The Jewish Philosophy of Man as Expressed in Rabbinic Literature.* London; New York: Abelard-Schuman.

An accessible examination of some of the most fundamental concepts that mold the Jewish definition of man and society, as revealed through the talmudic literature. The basic Rabbinic laws governing various human activities are explored as a means to demonstrating the underlying moral and religious principles that shape Jewish tradition and define humanity. Specific talmudic, mishnaic, and halakhic passages are extensively referred to and discussed throughout.

Berkovits, Eliezer. 1974. *Major Themes in Modern Philosophies of Judaism.* New York: Ktav Publishing House.

A critical analysis of several primary themes of contemporary Jewish philosophy, underwritten by the author's contention that a single unifying theology/philosophy of Judaism is lacking that effectively addresses Judaism as expressed though primary sources and can be reconciled with modern philosophical notions. Berkovitz addresses the arguments of the prominent Jewish philosophers Hermann Cohen, Franz Rosenzweig, Martin Buber, and A. J. Heschel, and also comments on the thought of reconstructionist theologians.

Blau, J. L. (ed.). 1973. *Reform Judaism: A Historical Perspective.* New York. Ktav Publishing House.

A collection of essays culled from the yearbook of the Central Conference of American Rabbis addressing attempts to synthesize past Jewish tradition with contemporary aspects of the American Jewish experience. Diverse means of seeking reform are addressed, including (but not limited to) the re-definition of Judaism through consideration of continuing revelation, practical reconstruction of Judaism aimed at allowing more complete identification of modern Jews with their tradition, and reinterpretation of the tradition though various contemporary philosophical forms. Discussions are largely tailored for the general audience.

Bleich, J. David. 1977. *Contemporary Halakhic Problems.* The Library of Jewish Law and Ethics; v. 4, 10, 16, 20. New York: Ktav Publishing House.

A comprehensive four volume exploration of halakhic responses to various contemporary issues. Emphasis is placed on the ongoing enterprise of halakhah, and the diversity of opinion of modern halakhic thinkers from whose work the bulk of the present volumes are drawn. The vast array of problems addressed here (ranging from issues of general interest such as abortion and criteria of death to the minutiae of specifically Jewish ritual) is intended to convey the seriousness with which contemporary Jews take Halakhah.

Bloch, A. P. 1978. *The Biblical and Historical Background of Jewish Customs and Ceremonies.* New York: Ktav Publishing House.

Bloch, A. P. 1980. *The Biblical and Historical Background of Jewish Holy Days.* New York: Ktav Publishing House.

Two volumes dedicated to detailing various ritual aspects of Jewish life and the biblical and rabbinic literature revealing their historical background and original meaning. A broad survey of ritual is provided, with more in depth treatments of the historical aspects of major Jewish holidays and their associated ritual.

Blumenthal, David R. 1978. *Understanding Jewish Mysticism: A Source Reader.* New York: Ktav Publishing House.

A two-volume textbook designed as an introduction to the field of Jewish mysticism. Translations of primary texts are provided in the context of extensive notes and introductory material to make these texts accessible to the non-specialist. The work is divided equally into four sections, focusing on Merkabah, Zoharic, Philosophic-Mystical, and Hasidic traditions, respectively.

Bokser, Ben Zion. 1993. *The Jewish Mystical Tradition.* Northvale, N.J.: J. Aronson.

A collection of readings from Jewish mystical literature, arranged with extensive commentary aimed at providing basic terms, philosophical concepts, and perspective on the role of mysticism in the larger Jewish tradition. This work is intended as an introductory textbook for the study of Jewish mysticism, and as such provides a varied and accessible sampling of primary sources from that tradition.

Borowitz, Eugene B. 1991. *Renewing the Covenant: A Theology for the Postmodern Jew.* Philadelphia: Jewish Publication Society.

An examination of theological possibilities for the contemporary non-Orthodox Jew in response to the failure of modernity to deliver on the promise of "secular enlightenment" as a means to the betterment of humanity. A postmodern covenant based on God, Israel, and Torah is proffered, with emphasis on Jewish responses to Western (i.e., American) culture, dialogue with orthodox tradition, and practical aspects of theological ideas in contemporary Jewish life. Some familiarity with modern Jewish thought is assumed.

Braiterman, Zachary. 1998. *(God) after Auschwitz: Tradition and Change in Post-Holocaust Jewish Thought.* Princeton, N.J.: Princeton University Press.

An examination of the role of catastrophic suffering (with particular emphasis on the Holocaust) in the development of Jewish views of God, covenant, and tradition. The text focuses primarily on a critical interpretation of the writings of three post-Holocaust Jewish thinkers: Richard Rubenstein, Eliezer Berkovits, and Emil Fackenheim. Their contribution to the theological debate on the Problem of Evil is explored in the wider context of theodic and antitheodic thought throughout Jewish history, beginning with motifs in classical Jewish texts. Special focus is given to the uniqueness of the Holocaust in Jewish history, and its role in fostering antitheodic discourse in specifically religious circles within the tradition.

Cohn-Sherbok, Dan. 1993. *The Jewish Faith.* Valley Forge, Pa.: Trinity Press International.

A concise and accessible introductory overview of Judaism intended to provide general audiences with a guide to Jewish faith and the way of life in the modern Jewish community. The discussion is divided into one section on belief and one on practice, each section exploring biblical foundations, traditional rabbinic interpretations as detailed in the Mishnah and Talmud, and contemporary attitudes of various Jewish traditions. A succinct historical outline of Judaism is also provided.

Cohn-Sherbok, Dan and Lavinia. 1994. *The American Jew: Voices from an American Jewish Community.* London: Fount.

A unique introduction to modern Jewish life in America, offered in the form of a "snapshot" of an anonymous contemporary Jewish community; the story is constructed from over 100 interviews with residents of a "typical Midwestern city," home to over 40,000 Jews. The authors provide a broad spectrum of modern Jewish life and attitudes by selecting voices from varied Jewish backgrounds, ranging through Orthodox Rabbis, pediatricians, high school students, funeral directors, strippers, and even local Gentiles.

Corre, Alan D. (ed.). 1975. *Understanding the Talmud.* New York: Ktav Publishing House.

Corre has assembled essays from leading scholars of the past century that examine the text of the Talmud itself as well as the literature and culture it has inspired. Scholars treat the component elements of the Babylonian Talmud and Midrash, the historical, political, and economic background of the Talmudic period, Sadducee, Pharisee, and Essene movements, *Halakha* and Rabbinic interpretation, and the ethico-religious ideas embodied in the Talmud. Authors include Solomon Schechter, Israel Abrahams, H. L. Ginsberg, and Louis Finkelstein.

Davidman, Lynn, and Shelly Tenenbaum. 1994. *Feminist Perspectives on Jewish Studies.* New Haven: Yale University Press.

A collection of essays from feminist scholars of various aspects of Jewish tradition, from rabbinic study to American cinema. Although wide ranging and disparate in the foci of individual articles, the anthology intends to collectively examine the influence that feminist scholarship has had on mainstream Jewish thought and how gender-based research can effect reinterpretations of Jewish tradition and society. A cross-disciplinary approach to Jewish gender study is argued through demonstrations of the shortcomings of accepted disciplinary boundaries in fostering understanding of Jewish women.

de Lange, Nicholas. 1987. *Judaism.* Oxford: Oxford University Press.

An introductory text aimed at explaining the foundations of Judaism and the development of the tradition, with particular emphasis on Judaism in the twentieth century. The text addresses the concept of covenant, rabbinic tradition, Jewish law and ethics, ritual practice, biblical sources, and Jewish thought as it relates to mysticism, theology, and eschatology. Some familiarity with the general study of religion is recommended.

Eilberg-Schwartz, Howard. 1992. *People of the Body: Jews and Judaism from an Embodied Perspective.* SUNY series, The Body in Culture, History, and Religion. Albany: State University of New York Press.

A volume of fourteen essays exploring a variety of rituals and myths associated with aspects of the Jewish body. Sources range from classical textual passages to contemporary popular culture and folk tradition. The text aims to provide bodily images of Jews as a foil to the traditional image of the "People of the Book," with the ultimate goal of refocusing thought on the Jewish body as a vehicle of Jewish identity and spirituality.

Englander, David (ed.). 1992. *The Jewish Enigma: An Enduring People.* New York: G. Braziller.

A collection of articles aimed at addressing the "enigma" of the intact survival of a tradition and a people physically dispersed throughout the lands of others. The text emphasizes the continuous interaction between Jews and the "host" nations as the primary means by which survival of the Jewish tradition was ensured. Chapter topics include post-biblical history; Jewish peoples in Europe, America, and Islamic nations; religious and secular anti-Semitism; and Zionism and the issue of Palestine.

Fackenheim, Emil L. 1982. *To Mend the World: Foundations of Future Jewish Thought.* New York: Schocken Books.

An in-depth philosophical treatise building on the author's noted "614th commandment" addressing the possibility of "mending" Jewish faith in a post-Holocaust world. Fackenheim contends that not simply Jewish thought, but thought itself must be healed in a world that has witnessed a suffering as unique and unprecedented as the Holocaust. The role of contemporary Jewish theology must be, in the author's eyes, to reinterpret revelation without the traditional foundation of divine sanction and authority, to renew faith in the wake of catastrophic suffering on the scale of the Holocaust, and to resubstantiate the concept of God in a world dominated by secular rationality.

Frank, Daniel H., and Oliver Leaman (eds.). 1997. *History of Jewish Philosophy.* Routledge History of World Philosophies. London; New York: Routledge.

This outstanding collection of essays by thirty-four prominent scholars surveys the breadth and depth of Jewish intellectual history, while calling into question the very category of "Jewish philosophy" by demonstrating its intimate association with and profound contributions to the broader history of philosophy. Part one sifts through the Biblical, Hellenistic, and Talmudic sources of philosophical reflection; part two examines Medieval Jewish thought, and includes essays on Judah Halevi, Moses Maimonides, Levi ben Gershom, and Jewish philosophy in its Islamic context. Parts three and four deal with the tradition's modern and contemporary articulations, treating figures such as Spinoza, Mendelssohn, Rosenzweig, and Buber, and major movements including neo-Kantianism, Zionism, and Jewish feminism.

Friedländer, M. 1891. *The Jewish Religion.* London: Kegan Paul, Trench, Traubner, and Co.

To assist others in interpreting the scriptural and literary sources of religious knowledge, Friedlander offers a comprehensive and detailed summary of the central beliefs and practices of the Jewish tradition. Part one, "Our Creed," outlines thirteen principles of faith grouped under the headings of the existence of God, revelation, and reward and punishment. Part two, "Our Duties," catalogs and explains a broad array of moral, ritual, and spiritual practices. This is an older but still valuable introduction to Judaism.

Friedman, Richard Elliott. 1987. *Who Wrote the Bible?* New York: Summit Books.

Friedman presents a synthetic synopsis of contemporary scholarship into biblical authorship designed for a broad audience. The work offers a brief history of biblical studies, surveys the cultural and historical background in which scriptural writing and redaction occurred, and provides comparative analysis of J, E, P and Deuteronomistic sources. An appendix charts the authorship of the Pentateuch in an easy to read format.

Gilbert, Martin. 1978. *The Holocaust: A Record of the Destruction of Jewish Life in Europe during the Dark Years of Nazi Rule.* New York: Hill and Wang.

In this atlas of maps and photographs, Gilbert records the tragic fate of European Jews. A powerful visual companion to written accounts of the Holocaust.

Gilbert, Martin. 1985. *The Holocaust: A History of the Jews of Europe during the Second World War.* New York: Holt, Rinehart and Winston.

Gilbert weaves the testimony of witnesses and survivors into his historical narrative to present a moving chronicle of the systematic attempt to destroy European Jews. He traces the Nazi program from prewar polemic, through it devastating implementation, to the liberation of the Jews from the concentration camps, if not from the burden of memory.

Gilman, Neil. 1990. *Sacred Fragments: Recovering Theology for the Modern Jew.* Philadelphia: The Jewish Publication Society.

Born of the author's experience assisting rabbinical students and laypersons in their theological quests, this work acquaints the interested reader with central issues in Jewish theological thought and carefully explains alternative approaches in addressing them. Gilman draws on traditional texts, the work of Jewish theologians, and the insights of the social sciences to offer a vision of Judaism that remains true to the historic tradition but attuned to the challenges of contemporary life. Central to Gilman's reflections is his engaging, at times controversial, discussions of myth as the means by which communities structure experience. Modern thinkers must critically and selectively engage the myths of their traditions to express truth and religious meaning. Throughout, Gilman encourages readers to struggle to articulate their own theological vision.

Ginzberg, Louis. 1977 [1955]. *On Jewish Law and Lore.* New York: Atheneum.

This collection gathers together Ginzberg's insights into the halakhic and haggadic traditions. Essays introduce the Palestinian Talmud, reflects on the significance of halakhah for Jewish history, analyze the codification of Jewish law, and reflect on allegorical scriptural interpretation and the Kabbalah.

Goldscheider, Calvin, and Jacob Neusner. 1990. *Social Foundations of Judaism.* Englewood Cliffs, N.J.: Prentice-Hall.

An anthology of articles exploring the relationship of Judaism to society, and how through various forms of Judaism Jews have been able to interpret and understand the social contexts within which they live. The text is roughly divided between chapters dealing with the formative (500 BCE to 640 CE) and classical (640 CE to 1789 CE) ages of Judaism; those concerned with the diversification of Judaism from the eighteenth century to the present; and those focusing on contemporary Judaism, specifically in America and Israel. The creative responses of Judaism to various social, economic, and political influences are examined, taking into account the pluralism within the tradition.

Gordis, Robert. 1990. *The Dynamics of Judaism: A Study in Jewish Law.* Bloomington and Indianapolis: Indiana University Press.

Gordis offers an analytical and prescriptive work that illuminates the vital dynamism of the halakhic tradition. He focuses upon the vital tension in halakhah between seemingly contradictory, but, in fact, profoundly complimentary emphases upon stability and flexibility, between eternal truths and situational ethics. Part one, "Principles," describes the core motifs of the legal tradition which have guided its development into the present, while part two, "Practices," examines the interplay of conservative and innovative forces within the legal tradition in confronting contemporary religious and ethical issues.

Green, Arthur (ed.). 1987. *Jewish Spirituality.* 2 vols. Vols. 13 and 14 of *World Spirituality: An Encyclopedic History of the Religious Quest.* New York: Crossroad.

Green's compendium of articles by leading scholars examines the varied historical paths taken by the religious to live in the presence of God. Volume one surveys Jewish spiritual theory and practice in the biblical, Rabbinic, and Medieval periods. Essays locate Jewish spirituality in its Near East context, explore the roles of the Second Temple and Psalmody in religious experience, compare the contemplative and ascetic paths, and discuss devotional, pietistic and ecstatic traditions in premodern Judaism. Volume two continues the survey, charting the development of traditions in the post-medieval and modern periods. Topics include *halakhah* and Kabbalah as competing disciplines of study, the figure of the Hasidic Zaddiq, HaBaD, twentieth-century interpretations of ritual, revelation and scripture, and the spiritual and anti-spiritual trends in Zionism.

Guttman, Julius. 1964. *Philosophies of Judaism: the History of Jewish Philosophy from Biblical Times to Franz Rosenzweig.* Trans. David W. Silverman. Introduction by R. J. Zwi Werblowsky. London: Routledge & Kegan Paul.

Organizationally similar to Frank and Leaman, above, this work sketches major figures and movements. Essays treat Judaism and the Kalām, Aristotelianism and its opponents, post-Kantian Jewish Idealism, and the nineteenth-century renewal of religious philosophy in the thought of figures such as Hermann Cohen and Franz Rosenzweig.

Harshav, Benjamin. 1990. *The Meaning of Yiddish.* Berkeley: University of California Press.

Drawing on Max Weinrich's *History of the Yiddish Language* (University of Chicago, 1973), Harshav sympathetically examines a rapidly fading component of broader Jewish culture. The author casts light upon the scholarly and devotional layers and tones of Yiddish and the diverse cultural currents reflected in the grammar and structure of the language.

Harshav is particularly eloquent in his examination of the role of analogy and association in Yiddish discourse.

Helmreich, William B. 1982. *The World of the Yeshiva: An Intimate Portrait of Orthodox Jewry.* New York: The Free Press.

Combining direct observation, personal interviews, statistical analysis, and recent academic studies, Helmreich offers a sympathetic, and at times enlightening, introduction to Jewish academies of higher learning in the United States and the culture that has grown up around them. Beginning students of Judaism will benefit from the author's analysis of sociological, cultural, historical, and intellectual currents that have contributed to the flourishing of these Orthodox institutions since the Second World War, and his insight into the daily lives of their students.

Heschel, Abraham Joshua. 1988 [1951]. *The Sabbath: Its Meaning for Modern Man.* New York: The Noonday Press.

In this compelling and insightful classic, Heschel encourages modern readers to turn away from technical civilization's obsession with understanding and dominating the world of space and toward a life mindful of sacred moments. For Heschel, Judaism's unique contribution to the history of religions is its emphasis on the holiness of events and history rather than places and things. Its rituals symbolize an overarching holy temporal architecture, and its goal is the sanctification of time. Through reflecting on and attending to the Sabbath, one becomes more aware of God's presence in this world, not in space, but in time. The Sabbath serves as a token of eternity, meaningful to both God and humanity. Whereas the other six days of the week mark our pilgrimage through the spatial world, the seventh signifies its goal: dwelling in the eternal presence of God.

Heschel, Abraham Joshua. 1959. *Between God and Man, From the Writings of Abraham J. Heschel.* Selected, edited, and introduced by Fritz A. Rothschild. New York: Harper and Brothers.

Rothschild has selected and arranged writings which exhibit the central ideas in Heschel's philosophy of religion and religious philosophy. Entries treat the various means of experiencing and relating the divine presence, the God of the Hebrew prophets, the needs of humanity, reflections on the import of religious observance, and the meaning of history in light of the divine-human relationship. Throughout, the theme of God's quest for humanity is revisited. While hardly exhaustive, this collection is a valuable introduction to the work of a leading twentieth-century Jewish thinker and an invitation to further study.

Jacobs, Louis. 1995. *The Jewish Religion: A Companion.* London; New York: Oxford University Press.

This work offers basic definitions and discussions of key terms, concepts, and figures which students may encounter in introductory studies of the Jewish religion. The dictionary format of the text makes for easy reference, and entries are designed for intelligibility and accessibility.

The Jewish People in America. 1992. 4 vol. Baltimore: Johns Hopkins University Press.

A comprehensive history of American Jews, divided in four volumes covering the years 1654–1820 (the First Migration), 1820–1880 (the Second Migration), 1880–1920 (the Third Migration), 1920–1945 (Entering the Mainstream), and 1945–present (American Jewry since World War II). Five different authors present in-depth historical accounts, exploring common issues such as the varied backgrounds of Jewish immigrant communities, the new social context of America, Jewish political involvement, the evolution of the tradition, and the tension between assimilation and group survival.

Kaplan, Mordecai Manahem. 1994. *The Meaning of God in Modern Jewish Religion.* Detroit: Wayne State University Press.

An examination of how the Jewish conception of God shapes Jewish religious tradition. Underlying Kaplan's exploration of God's meaning is the theme of reinterpretation of Jewish ideas of God in light of maintaining the continuity of Jewish tradition in a rapidly changing modern world. The author seeks to reestablish the relevance of God in modern Jewish life and emphasize the institutions through which God is revealed, through consideration of various categories of religious experience. The attempt is made to suggest the means to this-worldly salvation in the context of a modern scientific rather than a traditional authoritative worldview.

Katz, Steven T. 1992. *Historicism, the Holocaust, and Zionism: Critical Studies in Modern Jewish Thought and History.* New York; London: New York University Press.

With intellectual subtlety and sensitivity, Katz addresses seminal issues confronting contemporary Jewish religious and philosophical thought. The central theme of these essays is an examination of the ramifications of the Holocaust for historiography, philosophy, political theory, and theology. Katz tackles difficult questions concerning the uniqueness of the Holocaust, the problem of relativism in modern European historicism, the possibility of faith after the Shoah, and the criteria for contemporary Zionist ideology.

Katz, Stephen (ed.). 1975. *Jewish Philosophers.* New York: Bloch Publishing Co.

Katz offers a valuable compendium of articles covering major and minor figures in the Jewish philosophical tradition from the ancient, medieval, modern, and contemporary periods. Figures discussed include Philo, Maimonides, Spinoza, and Moses Mendelssohn. A helpful bibliography offers additional readings in the selected topics.

Kepnes, Steven (ed.). 1996. *Interpreting Judaism in a Postmodern Age.* New York; London: New York University Press.

The authors of these essays employ a variety of postmodern hermeneutical methodologies to tackle major issues in contemporary Jewish studies. Often provocative, these essays treat a panoply of subjects, including postcritical scriptural interpretation, narrativity in Kabbalistic hermeneutics, questions of canon, Zionism, and the role of feminist theory in rethinking Jewish women's identity.

Kohler, Kaufman. 1918. *Jewish Theology: Systematically and Historically Considered.* New York: Macmillan.

This classic synopsis of Jewish faith, composed by a leading figure of the Reform movement and former president of Hebrew Union College, emphasizes the ethical and humanitarian character of the tradition. Kohler discusses God, as known in revelation and as conceived in Judaism, human nature and responsibility, the kingdom of God, and the mission and election of the community of Israel. At times ranging from apologetic to polemical in tone, and tinged with optimistic progressivism, this work is nevertheless an illuminating introductory text and a significant historical document of Reform Judaism.

Mendes-Flohr, Paul, and Jehuda Reinharz (eds.). 1980. *The Jew in the Modern World: A Documentary History.* London; New York: Oxford University Press.

This impressive and comprehensive collection of primary materials, many translated here for the first time, surveys Jewish social, cultural and intellectual history from the seventeenth century through the foundation of the modern state of Israel. Throughout, the editors have selected texts representing moments of tension and transformation within the tradition that arise from external pressures and internal dynamics. Excerpts represent a number genres and are translated from several languages. Of particular interest are entries on the Reform movement, Zionism, and traditional Judaism's reaction to modernizing agendas. Introductory materials and annotations assist in situating the texts in their proper sociohistorical milieu.

Neusner, Jacob (ed.). 1973. *Understanding Jewish Theology: Classical Issues and Modern Perspectives.* New York: Ktav Publishing House.

Neusner collects essays by leading scholars and intellectuals, including A. J. Heschel, Emil Fackenheim, and M. M. Kaplan, that bring enduring issues in Jewish theological reflection into clear focus and explore emergent transformations of the tradition. Part one deals with the "fundamentals" of Jewish theology: God, Torah, and Israel; part two examines halakhah and Torah; and part three examines continuities and changes in thought regarding the three fundamentals. The book concludes with reflections on the nature and place of Judaism in a secular age. Neusner introduces each selection, highlighting key issues and raising significant questions for further consideration.

Neusner, Jacob. 1987. *Self-fulfilling Prophecy: Exile and Return in the History of Judaism.* Boston: Beacon Press.

Neusner offers a social history of Jewish traditions wherein the worldview of one particular Judaism has dominated. Arguing that religions shape the world, and therefore that Judaisms create worlds for Jews, the author argues that the central myth of exile and return articulated during the Babylonian exile (597/586–450 BCE) has shaped the development of all subsequent Judaisms. Neusner charts the courses of these various Judaisms through four periods—the age of diversity (586–450 BCE), the formative age (70–600), the classical age (late antiquity through the nineteenth century), and the modern age—and explores the many interpretations of what it means to be an Israel, that is, to be the social embodiment of a given Judaism.

Neusner, Jacob. 1995. *Rabbinic Judaism: Structure and System.* With a contribution from William Scott Green. Minneapolis: Fortress Press.

Neusner presents an analytical and interpretive examination of the categorical structures of normative Judaism, as set forth by the rabbis of the first six centuries CE and embodied in the Babylonian Talmud. After a brief introduction examining alternate approaches to describing Rabbinic Judaism, the author outlines the structure of Judaism according to the tripartite scheme of ethos/Torah, ethics/God, and ethnos/Israel. Part two the surveys the function of this system historically, analyzing the relation of ethos to accounts of social order, ethics to prevailing social attitudes and emotions, and ethnos to issues of teleology and eschatology. While throughout this work attention is paid to external influences upon the tradition, the book concludes with a treatment of Rabbinic Judaism within the Western context.

Novak, David. 1992. *Jewish Social Ethics.* London; New York: Oxford University Press.

Steeped in scriptural interpretation and writing from within the halakhic tradition, Novak offers a coherent and comprehensive statement of his own theological ethics. The goal of these essays is not to discover specific rules for action, but rather to articulate underlying principles within Judaism that may prove invaluable not only for Jews but for the whole of humanity in confronting the problems of contemporary life. Essays discuss the natural law tradition in Judaism, crosscultural ethics, issues of human embodiment raised by current discussions of sexuality and AIDS, environmental concerns, human rights, and the possibility of being a faithful Jew in modern American society.

Peskowitz, Miriam, and Laura Levitt (eds.). 1997. *Judaism since Gender.* New York; London: Routledge.

The twenty-five authors gathered here represent the leading lights in current cultural and gender studies of Judaism. The essays—brief, insightful, and often highly provocative—reflect the authors' deep commitments to both feminist scholarship and the Jewish tradition and manifest a desire to integrate both in transformative practice. Issues addressed include engendering Jewish religious history, the experience of teaching and working in Jewish studies, gender and colonialism, the eroticization of Holocaust survivors' narratives, and constructions of the feminine in Rabbinic Judaism.

Plaskow, Judith. 1990. *Standing again at Sinai: Judaism from a Feminist Perspective.* San Francisco: HarperSanFrancisco.

Seeking to transform the tradition and repair the world, Plaskow offers a compelling new vision of Jewish theology which incorporates traditional sources of theological reflection with a heart-felt and lived commitment to feminist convictions. Applying hermeneutics of suspicion and remembrance, the author scrutinizes the Torah, pointing out its patriarchal biases and recovering women's histories, and articulates a feminist interpretation of halakhah. Through an exploration of the relations among Torah, community, and personhood, she exposes and attacks dualistic hierarchies which have oppressed women and proposes a conception of Israel rooted in the category of distinctiveness rather than chosenness. Chapters also deal with androcentric terms in God-talk and new ways of envisioning the divine, the theology of sexuality, and the relationship of feminist theology and spirituality to social/political action.

Rose, Gillian. 1993. *Judaism and Modernity: Philosophical Essays.* Oxford; Cambridge: Blackwell.

In these essays, Rose examines the intermingling of Jewish and general philosophical thought and the common problems these linked traditions face in confronting modernity. She argues that in both Jewish and Western thought, there has occurred a disruption between ethics and law and revelation and reason. Rather than addressing themselves to this "broken middle, " intellectuals have chosen to gloss over the issue or fly to one extreme or the other. Figures surveyed include Walter Benjamin, Levinas, Rosenzweig, Derrida, and Adorno.

Rubenstein, Richard. 1996. *After Auschwitz: History, Theology, and Contemporary Judaism.* Second edition. Baltimore; London: The Johns Hopkins University Press. [First edition subtitled *Radical Theology and Contemporary Judaism.* Bobbs-Merrill. 1966.]

In this updated and revised edition of his seminal Jewish "death of God" theology, Rubenstein revisits and reinterprets the theological, social, and political significance of two inextricably linked events: the Holocaust and the foundation of the modern state of Israel. He examines the encounter of Christian and Jew, the meaning of the Holocaust, theology, contemporary Judaism, and the problematic of religious faith, relating them to recent events such as the Intifada and the Auschwitz convent controversy.

Rudavsky, David. 1967. *Modern Jewish Religious Movements: A History of Emancipation and Adjustment.* New York: Behrman House.

Emphasizing unity in diversity, Rudavsky sketches the emergence of religious alignments, their intellectual and spiritual influences, and their historical contexts, introducing reader to the ongoing dialogue within Judaism begun two centuries ago. Part one, "Backgrounds," surveys the position of Jews in medieval Europe, the formation of the ghetto, Judaism during the Enlightenment, and the Emancipation and its aftermath. Part two charts the development of traditional, Hasidic, Reform and Neo-Orthodox Judaism in Europe, while part three continues this outline with an examination of Jewish communities in America.

Sacks, Jonathan. 1993. *One People? Tradition, Modernity, and Jewish Unity.*

Writing from a modern Orthodox perspective, Sacks offers a non-polemical account of Jewish disunity and suggestions for overcoming the intellectual and cultural barriers dividing contemporary Judaism. Rejecting both exclusivistic and pluralistic understandings of Jewish religious diversity, he offers a program of halakhic inclusivism that is true to the Orthodox tradition while enabling a great deal of freedom in non-halakhic matters.

Schechter, Solomon. 1910. *Some Aspects of Rabbinic Theology.* New York: Macmillan.

Drawing upon the literature of the Talmud and the "Great Midrashim," Schechter presents historically mainstream Rabbinic opinions on eighteen significant theological issues. This work serves as a useful introduction to a range of topics, including God and the world, the joy of the Law, the source of evil and rebellion, and forgiveness and reconciliation. Throughout, the emphasis is upon the transhistorical consensus of opinion, rather than historical analysis of the development of religious ideas.

Schneider, Susan Weidman. 1984. *Jewish and Female: Choices and Changes in our Lives Today.* New York: Simon and Schuster.

This straightforward and highly accessible work charts the variety of options and challenges that women confront in seeking to integrate their identities *as* Jews and *as* women. Part one examines the relationship of women to religious Judaism and notes movements beyond patriarchal norms. Topics addressed include women's participation in religious services and education, the cycle of festivals, and issues surrounding body image and sexuality. Part two explores women's attempts to redefine their identities and relationships within the contexts of marriage and family. Part three looks at shifting roles and attitudes in the Jewish community and working world. The author has included a "networking directory" and select bibliographic guide to assist readers in discovering resources for education and activism.

Schochet, Jacob Immanuel. 1990. *The Mystical Dimension.* 3 vols. Brooklyn, N.Y.: Kehot Publication Society.

Schochet introduces readers with both mystical aspects of Judaism in general and the specific concepts and practices of Hasidic mysticism. Volume one, "The Mystical Tradition," surveys the general characteristics of Jewish mysticism, locating it within the broader tradition and in relation to non-Jewish mysticism. Volumes two examines the dynamics of *tefilah* (prayer) and *teshuva* (repentance) in Hasidic thought and practice, and volume three explores Hasidic interpretations of *Ahavat Yisrael* (love of a fellow-Jew), the figure of the *rebbe-tzadik*, serving God with joy, religious duty and experience, and the philosophy of Lubavitch activism.

Scholem, Gershom G. 1941. *Major Trends in Jewish Mysticism.* Based on the Hilda Strook Lectures delivered at the Jewish Institute of Religion, New York. New York: Schocken Books.

Scholem offers a superb introduction to historically significant schools of the Jewish mystical tradition, presenting insightful studies of core figures, texts, and concepts. Lectures treat the general characteristics of Jewish mysticism, Merkabah and Gnostic traditions, Hasidism in Medieval Germany, Abraham Abulafia, the *Zohar*, Isaac Luria and his followers, Sabbatianism and its relation to mysticism and heresy, and the modern phase of Hasidism.

Scholem, Gershom. 1974. *Kabballah*. The New York Times Library of Jewish Knowledge. New York: The New York Times Book Company.

Scholem presents a masterful overview of the history, concepts, and key figures of Jewish mysticism and esoteric movements. Part one surveys the historic development of Kabbalah to the twentieth century, charting its spread from the Near East, through Northern Africa, to the establishment of major centers in Spain and Europe. The author introduces basic ideas in the early tradition, including the *Sefirot* and emanation theories, the relation of God to creation, the question of theodicy, and the nature of the human soul, and he examines the influence of Kabbalistic thought on the broader Jewish and Christian traditions. Part two consists of entries on specific topics, most notably the *Zohar*, the *Magen David* (Star of David), the figure of Lilith, and divine providence. The work concludes with discussions of significant personalities in the history of Kabbalah, such as Azriel of Gerona, Moses Cordovero, Isaac Luria, and Moses ben Shem Tov de Leon.

Scholem, Gershom. 1991. *On the Mystical Shape of the Godhead: Basic Concepts in the Kabbalah*. Trans. from the German by Joachim Neugroschel, edited and revised, according to the 1976 Hebrew edition, with the author's emendations, by Jonathan Chipman. New York: Schocken Books. [Originally published in German under the title *Von der mystischen Gestalt der Gottheit: Studien zu Grundbegriffen d. Kabbala* by Rhein-Verlag AG, Zurich, 1962]. This collection of essays drawn from Scholem's lectures to the Eranos Society in Switzerland (1952–61) illuminate central themes in Kabbalistic thought. In each essay, the author traces the historical significance and development of Kabbalistic symbols from ancient texts and medieval treatments to their interpretation in thirteenth- century Spain and in Lurianic and Hasidic schools of thought. Concepts examined include the mystical shape of the Godhead (*Shi'ur Komanh*), good and evil (*sitra ahra*), the righteous one (*tsaddik*), the feminine aspect of divinity (*shekhinah*), the transmigration of souls (*gilgul*), and the astral body (*tselem*).

Schweid, Eliezer. 1992. *Jewish Thought in the 20th Century: An Introduction*. Trans. Amnon Hadary. South Florida Studies in the History of Judaism. Atlanta: Scholars Press.

Schweid argues that the twentieth century, characterized by an increasing acceleration of change and forever marked by the conjoined events of the Holocaust and foundation of Israel, deserves independent treatment in the study of Jewish thought. Initially tracing the connections between and difference in nineteenth-and twentieth-century thought, the author examines emerging orientations in Jewish philosophy. Drawing on the work of well- and lesser-known intellectuals, Schweid addresses subjects including the affirmation of exile and the negation of exile, definitions of Jews and Judaism, the renewal of Jewish society and culture and their transmission, issues of faith and heresy, and theological approaches to repentance, return, and covenant renewal.

Seeskin, Kenneth. 1990. *Jewish Philosophy in a Secular Age*. Albany: State University of New York Press.

An exploration of a number of philosophical problems as they are treated by various thinkers who do or do not conduct "philosophy in a Jewish way." Seeskin emphasizes the primacy of both practical reason (a philosophy of conduct) and transcendence of the rational (the conviction that the ideal transcends the material world) in defining philosophy that is characteristically Jewish. A number of classical and contemporary philosophers are surveyed in this context as they respond to such issues as negative theology and the nature of God, miracle and creation, revelation, ethics, and the Problem of Evil.

Seltzer, Robert M. 1980. *Jewish People, Jewish Thought: The Jewish Experience in History.* New York: Macmillan.

A standard work on the history of Judaism. Intended as a textbook, this volume provides a comprehensive and in-depth survey of the historical development of Judaism, with special attention paid to the scholarly literature on the subject produced in the nineteenth and twentieth centuries. An emphasis on the interrelatedness of Judaism as a religion and Jews as a people is maintained throughout the text. The density of material in this work will likely make it daunting for general readers outside the context of courses on Judaism.

Sherwin, Byron L. 1990. *In Partnership with God : Contemporary Jewish Law and Ethics*. Syracuse, N.Y.: Syracuse University Press.

By applying traditional Jewish learning to contemporary Jewish conceptual and practical problems, Sherwin attempts to foster the ongoing discussion of spiritual, intellectual, and moral issues central to Judaism. The text examines in depth a small number of such problems (ranging from general ethics to specific issues relating to recent biomedical advances), using each to emphasize his methodology (drawing on past Jewish textual scholarship to formulate novel approaches to modern problems) and his advocacy of the continuing extension of Jewish scholarship as opposed to (what he considers) a "voyeuristic" historical approach.

Sklare, Marshall. 1985. *Conservative Judaism: An American Religious Movement.* Lanham, Md.: University Press of America.

A sociological examination of the development and definition of Conservative Judaism in America. The text explores changes in Judaism as they relate to changes in the lives of Jews, thus forcing a consideration of the larger American societal context. Sklare investigated this context as it influenced transitions within Jewish Orthodoxy and the emergence of a Conservative Synagogue, and considers various aspects of Conservative Judaism, including religious and social practice, the institution of the Rabbi, and ideology.

Solomon, Norman. 1996. *Judaism: A Very Short Introduction.* Oxford; New York: Oxford University Press.

A concise introduction to Judaism intended to provide non-Jews with a particularly Jewish perspective regarding the tradition. As such the text often focuses on common misconceptions and attempts to synthesize the images of Jews as a people and Judaism as a religion through discussions of the development of the tradition (considering specifically relationships between God, Israel, and the surrounding world) and central themes of Jewish spiritual and social life, including consideration of contemporary ethical debates.

Trepp, Leo. 1980. *The Complete Book of Jewish Observance.* New York: Behrman House, Inc./Summit Books.

Designed "to help Jews become celebrants of Judaism," this book systematically introduces, describes, and explains Jewish ceremonies, rituals, and their significance. Part one examines conceptions of covenant, the synagogue, and home as focal points of life and worship, prayer, *kashrut*, and *shabbat*, while detailing major festivals and Holy Days of the Jewish calendar. Part two, "The Celebration of Life," discusses rites of passage, including circumcision, bar and bat mitzvah, conversion, and funerals, with reflections upon the role of family in Jewish life and the status of women in the religious community. Trepp offers a solid introduction to both the "hows" and "whys" of public and private religious observance in Judaism.

Unterman, Alan (trans). 1976. *The Wisdom of the Jewish Mystics.* New York: New Directions Books.

This brief book gathers one hundred and twenty-eight sayings and stories from the Jewish mystical tradition. Unterman offers a brief historical and theoretical introduction to Jewish mysticism in general and Hasidism in particular. The sayings themselves hint at the discursive richness of the esoteric branch of Judaism.

Unterman, Alan. 1981. *Jews, Their Religious Beliefs and Practices.* Boston: Routledge & Kegan Paul.

A comprehensive survey of central beliefs and practices which define Judaism, with special emphasis on those areas of the tradition which are uniquely Jewish. Intended as an introductory textbook, this work provides historical and sociological context as well as extensive discussion of contemporary Jewish belief and practice in an attempt to initiate an "acquaintance" with the living faith of Judaism.

Wolfson. 1947. *Philo: Foundations of Religious Philosophy in Judaism, Christianity, and Islam.* Cambridge: Harvard University Press.

A two-volume work representing the second installment in a series of books on the development of philosophy from Plato to Spinoza. The text attempts to systematize the thought of Philo and explore the historical and intellectual context of the growth of that thought, with the goal of elucidating the central themes which would dominate religious philosophic systems until the secular philosophy of Spinoza in the seventeenth century. Wolfson considers the scriptural foundations of Philo's treatment of such issues as the nature of God, creation, nature, and miracle, the soul, free will, and ethics. The depth and scope of this work recommend it either to readers seeking a more advanced survey of religious philosophy, or to those with particular interest in the thought of Philo.

Annotated Bibliography: Christianity

Reference Works and Overviews

Barrett, David (ed.). 1982. *World Christian Encyclopedia: A Comparative Study of Churches and Religions in the Modern World,* A.D. *1900–2000.* Oxford: Oxford University Press.

This work aims to reflect accurately the global character of Christianity in the twentieth century. More than an encyclopedia, it is a multifaceted compendium of reference materials, including a chronology of evangelization from 27 to 1983, a survey dictionary of world Christianity, an atlas of Christian evangelization, and a survey of Christianity and other religions in 233 countries.

Cross, F. L. (ed.). 1997. *The Oxford Dictionary of the Christian Church.* Third edition edited by E. A. Livingstone. Oxford: Oxford University Press.

This dictionary is more like an single-volume encyclopedia, presenting brief articles on each topic.

Ford, David F. (ed.). 1997. *The Modern Theologians: An Introduction to Christian Theology in the Twentieth Century.* Second ed. Cambridge: Blackwell.

This collection of thirty-five specialist articles covers the main theologians of the century, offering sharp portraits rather than bland descriptions. Edited by the Regius Professor of Divinity at Cambridge University, the book devotes slightly more space to British theology than it does to Latin American, African, and Asian theologies combined.

Lippy, Charles A., and Peter W. Williams (eds.). 1988. *Encyclopedia of the American Religious Experience.* 3 vols. New York: Scribner's.

This encyclopedia contains 105 scholarly essays grouped into nine topical and thematic parts, addressing the religious traditions and movements as well as their interaction in North America. The intended audience is broad, including students, clergy, experts, and general readers. The cross-references and the detailed index are of special help to those who want to examine the full scope of the subject.

McGrath, Alister F. 1997. *An Introduction to Christianity.* Malden, Mass: Blackwell.

This textbook aims to introduce Christianity as a set of beliefs, a set of values and a way of life, in an accurate and objective manner, though McGrath's evangelical orientation is inevitably evident. The text is complemented by numerous tables, maps and figures, and each section ends with a set of study questions.

Secondary Sources

Historical Studies

Ahlstrom, Sydney E. 1972. *A Religious History of the American People.* New Haven: Yale University Press.

This is a large and authoritative Eurocentric history that begins with the Spanish missions, devotes considerable attention to the religious development of New England, slavery in the South, and ends with the post-puritanism of the 1960s. Native Americans are mentioned in a footnote on page 1052 in the context of a discussion of the use of LSD by Timothy Leary.

Bays, Daniel H. (ed.). 1996. *Christianity in China: From the Eighteenth Century to the Present.* Stanford, Calif.: Stanford University Press.

This collection of twenty essays is a product of the History of Christianity in China Project funded by the Henry Luce Foundation. Rather than focusing exclusively on foreign missions and missionaries in China, it deals with the topic of Chinese Christianity and accords a high priority to the use of Chinese materials. The articles are grouped into four parts: "Christianity and the Dynamics of Qing Society," "Christianity and Ethnicity," "Christianity and Chinese Women," and "The Rise of an Indigenous Chinese Christianity."

Brown, Peter. 1990. *The Body and Society. Men, Women, and Sexual Renunciation in Early Christianity.* New York: Columbia University Press.

This book grew out of a series of lectures given by Brown in 1982–83 and studies the practice of permanent sexual renunciation that developed in early Christianity up to the time of Augustine. His major concern is the clarification of the notions of the human person and society implied in such acts of renunciation.

Cameron, Euan. 1991. *The European Reformation.* Oxford; New York: Oxford University Press.

This is a comprehensive and synthetic history of the European Reformation. It therefore aims to present a general survey that focuses on the histories of the movements rather than the biographies of individual reformers and to summarize the findings of contemporary scholarship for the reader rather than to present the particular results of the author's own research.

Chadwick, Owen (ed.). The Pelican History of the Church. Harmondsworth: Penguin Books Ltd.

The five books of this series are valuable, though sometimes outdated, introductions to European church history for the generally educated reader. Books in the series include:

- Chadwick, Henry. 1967. *The Early Christian Church.*
- Chadwick, Owen. 1964. *The Reformation.*
- Cragg, Gerald R. 1960. *The Church and the Age of Reason, 1648–1789.*
- Neill, Stephen. 1964. *A History of Christian Missions.* Second edition 1987.
- Southern, Richard. 1970. *Western Society and the Church in the Middle Ages.*
- Vidler, Alec R. 1962. *The Church and the Age of Revolution.* Revised edition 1987.

Cragg, Kenneth. 1991. *The Arab Christian: A History in the Middle East.* Louisville, Ky.: Westminster/John Knox Press.

This history of the intermingling of two strands of identity, "Arab" and "Christian," also documents the continuous interaction of Islam and

Christianity in the Middle East. The author provides a historical survey and then treats Egypt, Lebanon, and Israel in separate chapters.

Crossan, John Dominic. 1991. *The Historical Jesus: The Life of a Mediterranean Peasant.* San Francisco: HarperSanFrancisco.

This book reports on Crossan's attempt not only to rethink the historical Jesus but to rethink the methodological presuppositions of research into the historical Jesus. His strategy is to combine anthropological, historical, and literary research into an effective synthesis. The result is Jesus as a peasant Jewish Cynic.

Dussel, Enrique (ed.). 1992. *The Church in Latin America, 1492–1992.* Maryknoll, N.Y.: Orbis Books.

The contributors of this book are members of the Commission for the Study of Church History in Latin America, whose *General History of the Church in Latin America* (eleven volumes) is being published in Spanish. Written for audiences with little or no knowledge of the church history in Latin America, this book attempts to recapture the history of native peoples since Columbus's arrival. Of the three parts of the book, the first two are chronological and regional surveys, with the last one dealing with more specific subjects. A comprehensive bibliography for further study is provided at the end of the volume.

Finke, Roger, and Rodney Stark. 1992. *The Churching of America 1776–1990: Winners and Losers in Our Religious Economy.* New Brunswick, N.J.: Rutgers University Press.

The thesis proposed by Finke and Stark, two sociologists, is that the history of religion in America is that of the rapid transformation of a largely unchurched population to one that demonstrates remarkable levels of participation and commitment to organized religion. This has been accomplished by aggressive churches committed to "vivid otherworldliness."

Fox, Robin Lane. 1987. *Pagans and Christians.* New York: Knopf.

This erudite and elegant history of the religions of Roman late antiquity ends with the conversion of Constantine. Its achievement is to place the development of Christianity in the existing milieu of Roman paganism. In so doing, the religious continuities and contrasts are sharply and accurately illumined.

Fredriksen, Paula. 1988. *From Jesus to Christ: The Origins of the New Testament Images of Jesus.* New Haven: Yale University Press.

In Part 1 of this innovative introduction to Christian origins, Fredriksen works in reverse chronological order from the Gospel of John, the synoptic gospels, to Paul's letters. In doing so, she aims to avoid the false impression of a teleological development and to end in the Hellenistic milieu of the first Christian churches. Part 2 focuses on the Judaic context. Part 3 aims to reconstruct Christian "prehistory" between the death of Jesus and the beginnings of the documentary traditions so as to account for the diversity of early images of Jesus.

Frend, W. H. C. 1984. *The Rise of Christianity.* Philadelphia: Fortress.
This comprehensive history covers the first six hundred years of Christianity in roughly chronological order. Frend begins his story firmly in its Jewish roots, with extensive treatment of the Jewish background, before moving to concentrate on Latin and Greek Christianity.

Hastings, Adrian (ed.). 1999. *A World History of Christianity.* London: Cassell.
This book is an attempt to correct the Eurocentric bias of other historical surveys. It contains thirteen specialist chapters, beginning with the emergence of Christianity and ending with a history of Christianity in Australasia and the Pacific.

Hussey, J. M. 1986. *The Orthodox Church in the Byzantine Empire.* Oxford: Clarendon Press.
This book is written for the non-specialist reader and aims to introduce the history of the Byzantine church from the seventh century to the downfall of Byzantium in the fifteenth. Part 1 provides a historical survey of the chief challenges in East-West Christian relations, including Christology, iconoclasm, and the crusades. Part 2 documents the organization and life of the Orthodox church in Byzantium.

Isichei, Elizabeth. 1995. *A History of Christianity in Africa: From Antiquity to the Present.* Grand Rapids, Mich.: William B. Eerdmans.
The study of Christianity in Africa has been a central concern for Elizabeth Isichei, who lived there for 16 years. Focusing on what she takes to be the central elements of religion, beliefs, rituals, and community, Isichei delineates the development of Christianity in Africa from antiquity to the present. The book ends with a chapter on Independent Black Africa since 1960.

Jedin, Herbert, Konrad Repgen, and John Dolan (eds.). 1981. *History of the Church.* 10 vols. New York: Crossroad.
This massive history of the Catholic Church from ancient times to the contemporary world is a translation of the German *Handbuch der Kirchengeschichte* completed in 1979.

Kee, Howard C. et al. 1998. *Christianity: A Social and Cultural History.* Second ed. Upper Saddle River, N.J.: Prentice-Hall.

This comprehensive, chronological survey of the history of Christianity focuses on the theme of mutual relationship between Christianity and its social and cultural context. Written by experts in related fields of study, this book retells the story of how Christianity first emerged from the Jewish community and then grew into a worldwide phenomenon.

Latourette, K. S. 1971. *A History of the Expansion of Christianity*. 7 vols. Exeter: Paternoster Press.

This enormous survey of Christian history from antiquity to 1945 was prompted by Latourette's desire to understand why Christianity has spread and by what processes it has been enabled to do so. In the final volume he compares Christianity's expansion with other religions, eventually concluding that it was the value placed upon human beings that was largely accountable for its increasing success.

Lindberg, Carter. 1996. *The European Reformations*. Oxford: Blackwell.

This textbook aims to incorporate modern research in social history into a historical-theological study of the era that came to define the modern West. Beginning with the late medieval period, Lindberg covers the multiple reformations that gave birth to Protestant Christianity, through to the Catholic renewal movement and the Council of Trent.

McManners, John (ed.). 1992. *The Oxford Illustrated History of Christianity*. Oxford: Oxford University Press.

This comprehensive single-volume reference work contains illustrated essays by specialists covering the history of the church to 1800 and then the expansion of Christianity throughout the world. A third section deviates from historical format, considering such topics as "What Christians believe" and "The future of Christianity."

Meier, John P. 1994. *A Marginal Jew: Rethinking the Historical Jesus*. 2 vols. Anchor Bible Reference Library. New York: Doubleday.

Meier, a Catholic scholar, aims to write a balanced, detailed book for advanced students that accurately describes the limits and the possibilities of historical criticism. He claims that his description of a strange, eschatological prophet and miracle worker best fits the historical Jesus retrievable by modern historical methods applied soberly to the data.

Moffett, Samuel Hugh. 1992. *A History of Christianity in Asia. Vol. 1, Beginnings to 1500.*

This volume offers a vast survey of Asian Christianity to around the year 1500. "Asian Christianity" is used in a more cultural than geographic sense, referring to the churches that grew and spread outside the Roman Empire in the ancient kingdoms east of the Euphrates, overland along the Silk Road or by sea along the trading routes from the Red Sea to India. His work sheds much needed light on the neglected story of Asia in the study of Christian history.

Ozment, Steven. 1980. *The Age of Reform, 1250–1550*. New Haven: Yale University Press.

Ozment believes that the Reformation was both a culmination of and a transcendence of medieval intellectual history. He therefore devotes considerable attention to understanding the Reformation from a medieval perspective.

Pelikan, Jaroslav. 1971–1989. *The Christian Tradition: A History of the Development of Doctrine*. 5 vols. Chicago: University of Chicago Press.

This magisterial intellectual history covers twenty centuries of Christian thought. Volume two surveys Eastern Christianity from 600–1700, the remaining volumes focusing mostly on the development of the European tradition.

Robert, Dana L. 1996. *American Women in Mission: A Social History of Their Thought and Practice*. Macon, Ga.: Mercer University Press.

This social history is a contextualized series of case studies of women in mission presented in chronological order beginning in 1812. The books dispels the stereotype of the woman missionary as the long-suffering adjunct of her husband. The work covers both Protestant and Catholic missionaries.

Sanders, E. P. 1991. *Paul*. Oxford: Oxford University Press.

This brief introduction in Oxford's Past Masters series is a swiftly sketched portrait of the founder of the Christian church. Sanders states that Paul's theology was bound up with his understanding of his role as a "minister of Christ Jesus to the gentiles." This leads to the interweaving of a study of Paul's fundamental convictions and his actions to establish gentile Christianity.

Ware, Timothy. 1973. *The Orthodox Church*. London: Penguin.

Timothy Ware describes the history, faith, and worship of the Orthodox Church. It is his belief that the Orthodox Church, because of its different background from other Christian traditions in the West, can open up new ways of thinking and suggest long-forgotten solutions to old questions, and thereby make a positive ecumenical contribution.

Christian Life and Thought

Brown, Peter. 1967. *Augustine of Hippo: A Biography*. Berkeley: University of California Press.

Brown's biography of this seminal Christian thinker turns to the social and cultural context to illuminate Augustine's life and thought. In so doing Brown presents a cultural biography that is a stunning view of Roman late antiquity through the eyes of one of its greatest intellectuals, as much as the other way around.

Byrne, Peter, and Leslie Houlden. 1995. *Companion Encyclopedia of Theology.* New York: Routledge.

This encyclopedic collection of mostly British essays aims to survey the whole of the present situation of academic Christian theology in the West. The five main sections cover the Bible, the tradition, philosophy, spirituality, and practical theology. The sixth section is a collection of essays devoted to the possibility of the future of Christian theology.

Gunton, Colin E. (ed.). 1997. *The Cambridge Companion to Christian Doctrine.* Cambridge; New York: Cambridge University Press.

This British-American joint venture is a handbook of contemporary constructive theology arranged thematically. In Part 1 the authors treat the historical and intellectual contexts for contemporary theology, including hermeneutics, authority, culture, history, and the arts. Part 2 covers the contents of Christian doctrine. In part, the authors seek to summarize the recent developments in theology that have been made possible by contemporary critiques of modernity.

Jones, Cheslyn et al. (eds.). 1986. *The Study of Spirituality.* New York: Oxford University Press.

Containing contributions from over sixty writers, this work covers the theology of spirituality, the history of spirituality and pastoral spirituality. Extensive bibliographies are provided at the beginning of each article to direct interested readers to resources for further study.

Musser, Donald W., and Joseph L. Price. 1996. *A New Handbook of Christian Theologians.* Nashville, Tenn.: Abingdon Press.

This new handbook differs from the old one (*A Handbook of Christian Theologians* edited by Martin Marty and Dean Peerman) in offering extensive coverage on "the shapers of Christian theology at the turn of the millennium," taking special notice of such recent movements as black theology, liberation theology, feminist theology, and womanist theology. One helpful feature is that the editors identify various routes for reading, so that the reader can look for the essays according to the geographical background of the theologian, ecclesial tradition, or theological affiliation.

Oberman, Heiko. 1989. *Luther: Man between God and the Devil.* New Haven: Yale University Press.

In this biography of the "head and heart" of the great reformer, Oberman argues that to understand Luther completely, we must learn to inhabit his late medieval world in which the Devil was as real as God. Then, to understand the relevance of Luther, we must not submit him to the tests of modernity, but rather allow his ideas to challenge "our condescending sense of having outgrown the dark myths of the past."

O'Meara, Thomas F., O. P. 1997. *Thomas Aquinas Theologian.* Notre Dame, Ind.: University of Notre Dame Press.

This accessible, general introduction to Aquinas contains a useful annotated bibliography. Having introduced his life and career, O'Meara devotes most of the book to examining Aquinas's theology both as he conceived it and as it came to influence the development of Catholic theology through to the present day.

Quasten, J. 1953–1986. *Patrology.* 4 vols. Vols. 1 and 2, Westminster, Md.: The Newman Press; Vol. 3, Utrecht/Antwerp: Spectrum Publishers; Vol. 4, Westminster, Md.: Christian Classics, Inc.

These four volumes form an invaluable reference work of the documents of early Christianity. Each text is introduced, summarized, and a small section translated. Bibliographical notes of translations and studies of each text are also provided.

Vatican Council. 1966. *The Documents of Vatican II: All Sixteen Official Texts Promulgated by the Ecumenical Council 1963–1965.* Translated from the Latin. Introductions and commentaries by Catholic bishops and experts, responses by Protestant and Orthodox scholars. Walter M. Abbott, S. J., General Editor. Very Rev. Msgr. Joseph Gallagher, Translation Editor. New York: America Press.

The most important documents of the Catholic Church in this century are collected in this volume. Of particular note are *Gaudium et Spes* on the Church in the modern world, *Nostra Aetate* on the relationship of the church to non-Christian religions, and *Lumen Gentium*, the Catholic church's statement to itself of its own identity.

Welch, Claude. 1985. *Protestant Thought in the Nineteenth Century.* Two volumes. New Haven: Yale University Press.

In these two volumes, Welch offers swift but complex characterizations of the major thinkers and themes that shaped nineteenth century Protestant thought. In so doing, he roams beyond the close confines of theology to illustrate the effect on it of major philosophers and intellectual currents.

White, James F. 1993. *A Brief History of Christian Worship*. Nashville: Abingdon.

White presents a comprehensive chronological survey of the history of Christian worship, but from a contemporary North American perspective. One of his chief concerns, therefore, is to "recognize the cultural diversity inherent in Christian worship as in all human activities." White concludes with a discussion on worship in churches of the future.

Contemporary Christianity

Carr, Anne E. 1988. *Transforming Grace: Christian Tradition and Women's Experience*. San Francisco: Harper and Row.

Writing from a Catholic perspective, Carr argues that feminism and Christianity are integrally connected in the Christian vision. The book therefore combines theoretical arguments with a theological exposition of Christian life, focusing on ordination and feminist spirituality.

Guttiérez, Gustavo. 1988. *A Theology of Liberation: History, Politics and Salvation*. Revised Edition with a New Introduction. Maryknoll, N.Y.: Orbis Books.

This seminal text of liberation theology is Gutiérrez's reflection upon the gospel and the experiences of oppressed Latin American people. Gutiérrez makes it clear that to ponder the significance of liberation is nothing less than "to examine the meaning of Christianity itself and the mission of the Church in the world."

Hill, Brennan. 1998. *Christian Faith and the Environment: Making Vital Connections*. Maryknoll, N.Y.: Orbis Books.

This is a broad introduction to the topic of ecology and Christian theology from a Catholic perspective. Brennan covers not only theology (dealing with Rahner, Tillich, and Lonergan) but also sacramental, spiritual, and ecclesiological aspects of the nexus of problems unearthed by this topic.

Kaufmann, Gordon D. 1996. *God, Mystery, Diversity: Christian Theology in a Pluralistic World*. Minneapolis: Fortress Press.

Kaufmann believes that theology has always been an activity of imaginative construction. Developing the arguments of his earlier book, *In Face of Mystery*, Kaufmann argues that Christian theology must now be radically reconstructed in the light of a historical consciousness and Christianity's encounter with other religions.

Lee, Jung Young. 1996. *The Trinity in Asian Perspective*. Nashville: Abingdon Press.

Jung Young Lee, a leading Korean-American theologian and scholar of Daoism, attempts to reinterpret the Christian notion of the Trinity using the yin-yang symbol as a hermeneutical tool. His argument is that the problem of the Trinity lies not in the concept of the Trinity itself but in the Western, dualistic appropriation of it. Writing mainly for a Western audience, he hopes that his alternative, Asian perspective can help illuminate this ancient Christian symbol.

Mullan, David George. 1998. *Religious Pluralism in the West: An Anthology.* Malden, Mass.: Blackwell.

Although titled religious pluralism, this book is more accurately an anthology of Western texts related to the theme of religious liberty and toleration arranged in chronological order from antiquity to the present. Included are selections from the Bible, Tertullian's *Apology*, Luther on temporal authority, Locke on toleration, and Rawls on liberty, among many others. Each selection is headed by a brief introduction, together with details of the source used and suggestions for further reading.

Tracy, David. 1981. *The Analogical Imagination: Christian Theology and the Culture of Pluralism.* New York: Crossroad.

In this work, Tracy addresses the question of religious truth in the context of ecumenicity and pluralism. He argues for and employs his proposed method, "analogical, theological imagination." Religious truth, Tracy contends, is analogous to the truth of literary classics that articulate universal meanings as interpreted in the particular forms of a culture. The event of Jesus Christ defined as the present liberation of the believer mediated through the theological meanings of the tradition's memory is the Christian classic. Tracy argues that fruitful interfaith dialogue could take place if believers from each tradition could analogically and imaginatively step into and experience the classics of other religions while carefully attending to the similarities and the differences within their own tradition.

Annotated Bibliography Islam

Reference Works

Bibliographies

Ede, David, et al. 1983. *Guide to Islam.* Boston: G. K. Hall.
Geddes, C. L. 1985. *Guide to Reference Books for Islamic Studies.* Denver, Colo.: American Institute of Islamic Studies.
Sarwar, Ghulam. 1983. *Books on Islam in English.* London: Muslim Educational Trust.

Dictionaries and Encyclopedias

Esposito, John L. 1995. *The Oxford Encyclopedia of the Modern Islamic World.* New York: Oxford University Press, 4 volumes, sparsely illustrated.

A general reference accessible to readers unfamiliar with the tradition. Entries are accompanied by convenient bibliographies for further reading. Includes many entries under broad topics (e.g. "economic development," "Islam: an overview," "Sufism") that provide introductions for readers with little or no knowledge of Islam.

Gibb, H. A. R. 1960. *The Encyclopaedia of Islam.* Leiden: Brill New ed. 10 volumes (the tenth volume of the new edition is as yet unfinished), over 10,000 pages, sparsely illustrated.

A basic, comprehensive reference, ostensibly covering all aspects of Islamic religion, history, arts, and culture. Directed primarily at specialists in Islamic studies; knowledge of Arabic greatly facilitates usage, as entries are given according to vernacular terms (searching for terms in English translation will often result in reference to vernacular entries). Includes three extensive indices: proper names, subjects, and technical terms (including glossary).

Glasse, Cyril. 1989. *The Concise Encyclopedia of Islam.* San Francisco: Harper & Row.

A convenient one-volume encyclopedia assuming no experience in Islamic studies. Maps and attractive color plates add to the accessibility of this text as an introductory reference.

Primary Sources

Ali, Muhammad. 1951. *A Manual of Hadith.* 2nd ed. Lahore: Ahmadiyya Anjuman Ishaat Islam.

A collection of Ḥadith relating to practical Muslim life. English translations are given alongside Arabic text with extensive commentary. Hadith are arranged according to major categories of belief and practice, each section being headed by pertinent Qur'ānic verses and the author's summary on the teachings of both Qur'ān and Ḥadith on the subject.

Arberry, Arthur J. 1955. *The Koran Interpreted.* 2 vol. New York: Macmillan; London: George Allen & Unwin.

Pickthall, Marmaduke. 1976. *The Glorious Koran.* Albany: State University of New York Press.

Two widely adopted translations of the Qur'ān. Arberry's translation is indebted to both the Western tradition of critical textual scholarship and a detailed study of the literary and poetic qualities of the original Arabic verse, resulting in an English text which reflects more than most other Western translations the powerful rhythm and literary force of the original. Pickhall, an English convert to Islam, has prepared his translation in concordance with the views of a number of preeminent Muslim scholars and under the auspices of His Exalted Highness the Nizam of Hyderabad and Berar. The result is a translation closely reflecting the standard Sunni interpretations of the Qur'ān. Pickhall's text also provides a side-by-side comparison of the Arabic text and English translation.

Peters, F. E. 1994. *A Reader on Classical Islam.* Princeton, N.J.: Princeton University Press.

A sourcebook of translated texts collected from the Islamic literature of the "classical" period, from Muḥammad to approximately 1400 CE Sources include the Qur'ān, Ḥadith, and writings of various classical Islamic thinkers, broadly addressing all aspects of Muslim religious life and its foundations. Commentary is provided throughout in an attempt to lend historical and ideological context to the selections, and to demonstrate the meaning of particular passages for contemporary Muslims.

Secondary Sources

Abu-Rabi, Ibrahim M. 1996. *Intellectual Origins of Islamic Resurgence in the Modern Arab World.* Foreword by Mahmoud Ayoub. Albany: State University of New York Press.

Abu-Rabi proffers an insightful intellectual history of modern Arab Islamic movements which, while attending to the relation of religion and politics, focuses upon their epistemological, philosophical, and theoretical foundations. Particular attention is paid to the life and work of Sayyid Qutb, a leading theoretician of Islamic resurgence, the changing status of the 'ulama', and the emergence of alternative centers and figures of authority and interpretation of religious and political truth.

Afkhami, Mahnaz. 1995. *Faith and Freedom: Women's Human Rights in the Muslim World.* Gender, culture, and politics in the Middle East. 1st ed. Syracuse, N.Y.: Syracuse University Press.

A collection of essays stemming from the 1994 Washington Dialogue on Religion, Culture, and Women's Rights in the Muslim World. Entries are divided into two categories. The first focuses on the importance of Islam to Muslim women and the need to reinterpret Islamic text and tradition from feminine perspectives while seeking Islamic justifications for female empowerment in the secular realm. The second outlines selected cases of politically motivated violence against women as a means of emphasizing the gravity of contemporary problems.

Ahmed, Leila. 1992. *Women and Gender in Islam: Historical Roots of a Modern Debate.* New Haven: Yale University Press.

A comprehensive study of historical roots of gender discourse in modern Islam, specifically in Muslim Arab societies. The author examines the role of women in the pre-Islamic Middle East and the influence of non-Islamic cultures on the institution of Islamic patriarchy. The book points to the denial of women's rights guaranteed in the Qur'ān, thus challenging stereotypical views of that text's role in removing women from public life. Ahmad proposes a Muslim feminism based on fresh interpretations of the Qur'ān and Islamic tradition and thus independent of Western feminism.

Al-Azmeh, Aziz. 1993. *Islams and Modernities.* Second edition. Phronesis series. London; New York: Verso.

Subverting notions of Islamic cultural and religious homogeneity, Al-Azmeh explores the diversity of cultures, polities, and ideologies subsumed under the banner "Islam." The author critiques modern and postmodern constructions/representations of Islam created by both Muslim and Western intellectuals, activists, and polemicists, and examines the interplay of context and content in articulation of political, philosophical, and religious thought. Essays treat a variety of subjects, including Islamist revivalism and its relation to Western ideology, the concept of utopia in Islamic political thought, and Wahabite polity.

Ali, Muhammad. 1950. *The Religion of Islam: Comprehensive Discussion of the Sources, Principles, and Practices of Islam.* Lahore: Ahmadiyya Anjuman Ishaat Islam.

A general overview of Islam written by a Muslim scholar and aimed specifically at non-Muslim Western audiences. The text covers in three major divisions the classical sources of Islamic teaching, the central doctrines of the religion, and the laws and injunctions governing domestic, social, and international Islamic relations. Although dated, this volume presents a valuable introductory survey of fundamental Islamic thought and practice from a Muslim perspective.

Arkoun, Mohammed. 1994. *Rethinking Islam: Common Questions, Uncommon Answers.* Translated and edited by Robert D. Lee. Boulder, Colo.: Westview Press.

This book makes available in English the insights of this leading Algerian-born liberal Muslim intellectual. Arkoun's brief and often provocative essays offer postmodern criticism of both the mythologized and ideological visions of Islam presented by Muslim militants and apologists and the often static and distorted representations put forth by Western intellectuals.

Ask, Karin, and Marit Tjomsland. 1998. *Women and Islamization: Contemporary Dimensions of Discourse on Gender Relations*. Oxford: Berg.

A reinterpretation of Islamic women for Western readers, aimed at conveying the evolving nature of Islam and overturning the traditional Western view of Muslim women as victims of a fundamentalist and sexist ideology. The included essays by various authors collectively attempt to illustrate means by which Muslim women actively participate in developing a feminine voice in the contemporary resurgence of Islam.

Ayubi, Nazih N. M. 1991. *Political Islam: Religion and Politics in the Arab World*. London; New York: Routledge.

A discussion of the extent to which an Islamic theory of politics and concept of state derives from Islamic religious tradition. Ayubi contends that Islam is not so much a "political" religion as a "social" one and draws distinctions between the collective and communal dimensions of Islam and the development of political theory. The author draws upon a number of contemporary Arab theorists, focusing on responses to fundamentalist and neo-fundamentalist political thought. Case studies of specific Islamic movements are also discussed.

Bakhtiar, Laleh, Abd al-Ra hm an Jaziri, and Muhammad Jaw ad Maghniyah. 1996. *Encyclopedia of Islamic law: A Compendium of the Views of the Major Schools*. [S.l.] Chicago: ABC International Group; distributed by Kazi Publications.

A broad overview of the five major schools of Islamic law: Hanafi, Hanbali, Shafi, Maliki (Sunni), and Jafari (Shi'a). Suitable for readers with little to no familiarity with the field.

Baldick, Julian. 1989. *Mystical Islam: An Introduction to Sufism*. New York University studies in Near Eastern civilization; no. 13. New York: New York University Press.

The text explores historical foundations of Sufism, a broad survey of Sufi writers and thinkers, and the development of Sufism into the modern Islamic world. The author's controversial depiction of the tradition as an amalgam of influences from Christianity, Judaism, Gnosticism, and other traditions is central to the book's argument.

Bogle, Emory C. 1998. *Islam: Origin and Belief*. Austin: University of Texas Press.

This general introduction to the development of Islam in the Middle East closely examines the significant role played by familial politics and early conflicts in shaping the historical and religious course of the tradition. Bogle's overview is distinguished by its emphasis upon the Shi'ite tradition's history and belief structure. Readers will find his chronology, glossary, maps, and charts of use in approaching the study of Islam.

Choueiri, Youssef M. 1997. *Islamic Fundamentalism. Themes in Right-wing Ideology and Politics Series.* Rev. ed. London; Washington, D.C.: Pinter.

An introduction to fundamentalism (defined here as the derivation of sociopolitical principles from what is viewed as an eternal and immutable divine text) in various movements from the eighteenth century to the present. Three separate Islamic fundamentalist movements are examined: revivalist (a reactionary development to European colonialism), reformist (a reinterpretation of Islam in response to Western cultural and political influences), and radical (a reaction to the conception of Western "anti-Islam" movements).

Cohn-Sherbok, Dan. 1991. *Islam in a World of Diverse Faiths.* New York: St. Martin's.

A selection of thirteen papers presented in two conferences on Islam and Christian/Muslim Relations. Essays are grouped according to five focal issues: claims of absolute truth (with emphasis on liberal readings of Christian doctrines); revelation in Judaism, Christianity, and Islam; concepts of apostleship; non-Islamic perceptions of Muḥammad; and the relation of Islam to society. Contributors include adherents of all three Abrahamic traditions.

Denny, Frederick Mathewson. 1994. *An Introduction to Islam.* Second ed. New York: Macmillan.

An introductory text directed at those desiring a very broad overview of Islam and assuming no familiarity with the tradition. Outlines of Islamic historical foundations, religious thought, and mystical tradition are accompanied by an extensive account of pre-Islamic influences, a depiction of Islamic personal and communal life, and a brief discussion of such contemporary issues as nationalism, fundamentalism, and feminism. Includes a brief glossary and suggestions for further reading.

Esposito, John L. 1982. *Women in Muslim Family Law.* Syracuse, N.Y.: Syracuse University Press.

Esposito argues that family law, as that element of the sharia least transformed under the weight of Western influences, serves as both an index of social change within Islamic societies and as an indicator of truly Islamic reforms. He traces the sources of Islamic jurisprudence in its classical articulation and provides a catalogue of significant pronouncements concerning women and families and illumines the impact of social mores upon religious legal development. The author also puts forth a methodology for legal reform drawn from the historic tradition with which to confront the dramatic social changes of the twentieth century.

Esposito, John L. 1987 [1984]. *Islam and Politics*. Revised Second Ed. Syracuse, N.Y.: Syracuse University Press.

Esposito surveys the history of the relationship of Islam to politics in the Middle East, emphasizing the variety of (sectarian) influences, which underlie Islamic and Islamist political resurgence. A review and analysis of the associations of politics and faith in early Islamic history through the modern revival and reform movements reveal wellsprings of both conservative ideology and reformist activism from which contemporary movements draw. Issues addressed include the role of Islam in anti-colonial movements, the rise of nationalism, and the building of modern states, and illustrations are drawn from Mid-East nations as well as organizations such as the Muslim Brotherhood and the Jamaati-Islam movement

Esposito, John L. (ed.). 1987. *Islam in Asia: Religion, Politics and Society.* New York: Oxford University Press.

Designed as an educational text for a broad American audience, this work provides both a historical overview of the diverse roles played by Islam in post-independence societies across Asia as well as studies of specific countries, including Iran, Afghanistan, the Central Asian Republics, and Indonesia. Topics addressed include the influence of Islam upon the construction of minority and national identities, multi-ethnic politics, cultural pluralism and domestic and international relations.

Esposito, John L. 1998 [1991]. *Islam: The Straight Path.* Third ed. New York: Oxford University Press.

Esposito outlines the central beliefs and practices of the faith as well as the history of Islam from its Arabian roots through its growth internationally as a significant religious and cultural force. The author highlights major modern and contemporary religious and political movements within the tradition and draws attention to the challenges confronting the faith in the present and future.

Fakhry, Majid. 1983. *A History of Islamic Philosophy.* Second ed. New York: Columbia University Press; London: Longman.

A standard work in the field of Islamic philosophy. The author presents a comprehensive survey of historical roots, from non-Islamic Middle Eastern influences through to modernity. The text focuses on individual contributions to the development of Islamic thinking and touches on the effects that doctrinal and mystical religious thought have had on that development.

Fakhry, Majid. 1991. *Ethical Theories in Islam.* Leiden: E. J. Brill.

A survey of the development of ethical theory in Islam from its origins into the sixteenth century. Part one examines scriptural morality, highlighting key terms and principles found in the Qur'ān and hadith; part two describes the theological ethics of the Mutazilite and Asharite schools. The bulk of the text is given over to part three, a treatment of philosophical ethics that touches on the incorporation of Hellenistic Greek thought in Islamic ethical theory and the connections among ethics, political philosophy, and psychology. Part four addresses the religious ethics of ascetics, mystics, and theologians as well as the synthetic approach of the al-Ghazālī.

Goldziher, Ignac. 1981 [orig. German ed. 1916]. *Introduction to Islamic Theology and Law.* Trans. Andras and Ruth Hamori, with introduction and additional notes by Bernard Lewis. Princeton, N.J.: Princeton University Press.

The English translation of Goldziher's seminal *Vorlesungen über den Islam* serves as an excellent introduction to the history of Islam, its legal and intellectual schools, and its mystical and sectarian traditions. Sections cover Muḥammad and internal and external influences upon the early evolution of the tradition, the invention of the science of hadith criticism, dogmatic theology and its relation to power politics, asceticism and Sufism, Shi'ism and other sectarian interpretations of the tradition, and more recent historical developments. Lewis's notation and bibliography update the main text in light of later scholarship.

Haddad, Yvonne Yazbeck, and John L. Esposito (eds.). 1998. *Islam, Gender and Social Change.* New York: Oxford University Press.

This collection of essays, principally by women authors, provides insight into the changing status of women and shifting conceptions of gender in a variety of Middle Eastern and Asian societies and the impact of cultural and religious influences upon the daily lives of women. Essays explore women's suffrage, civil rights, access to education, economic empowerment, as well as the history of gender issues in Qur'ānic interpretation and the redefinition of women's religious identity in the midst of political activism. While often critical, the text also illumines the flourishing of women's cultural and intellectual production in Islamic societies.

Haddad, Yvonne Yazbeck, and Jane Idelman Smith (eds.). 1994. *Muslim Communities in North America.* SUNY Series in Middle Eastern Studies. Albany: State University of New York Press.

Challenging monolithic conceptions of Islam, this work surveys the variety of indigenous and immigrant Muslim groups in the United States and Canada. Essays depict the diverse geographic, socioeconomic, cultural, and theological manifestations of contemporary Islam and explore linkages among religion, race, ethnicity, and identity. Groups discussed include the Nation of Islam, Five Percenters, the Bawa Muhaiyaddeen Fellowship, and the Dar al-Islam movement.

Hodgson, Marshall G. S. 1974. *The Venture of Islam: Conscience and History in World Civilization.* 3 vols. Chicago: University of Chicago Press.

Hodgson offers a massive synthetic vision of the history of Islamic civilization, the geographical, historical, and intellectual breadth of which is matched by its depth of detail and balanced presentation. Volume one covers the prehistory of Islam through it development into the tenth century; volume two surveys the mid-tenth through the fifteenth century; and volume three charts the course of civilization into modern times. An extensive introduction provides readers with practical information regarding topics such as transliteration and dating systems as well as insight into and reflection on the challenges of historiography and the dilemma of scholarly bias.

Inayat, Ham id. 1982. *Modern Islamic Political Thought.* Austin: University of Texas Press.

A specialized discussion of Islamic political theory and practice. Both Sunni and Shi'i trends are explored. Special focus is given to the relationship of Islam to the modern political ideologies of nationalism, democracy, and socialism. Also includes a concise historical survey of Islamic political institutions.

Islamic Surveys. 1962–1998. 25 vol. Edinburgh: University Press.

A series of twenty-five texts on various topics ranging from broad overviews (e.g., Shi'ism) to specialized studies (e.g., Muslim neo-platonists). Topics covered include history, philosophy, theology, law, politics, sectarian traditions, medicine, literature, and the development of Islam in specific geographic regions. Likely of greatest interest to readers seeking introductory materials are Islamic philosophy and theology (vol. 1), Shi'ism (vol. 18), History of Islamic law (vol. 2), Introduction to the Ḥadith (vol. 24), Islamic political thought (vol. 6), and Bell's introduction to the Qur'ān (vol. 8).

Kurzman, Charles (ed.). 1998. *Liberal Islam: A Sourcebook.* New York: Oxford University Press.

Kurzman gathers works by significant Islamic thinkers of the past century representing the geographical and intellectual diversity of the tradition. The selected texts are grouped topically and address issues of theocracy, democracy, the rights of women and non-Muslims, freedom of thought, and progress. His introductory essay charts the historical development and interplay of three branches of Islamic thought (the customary, revivalist, and liberal camps) and notes the contributions of liberal Muslims to modern sociopolitical and intellectual movements.

Lapidus, Ira. 1988. *A History of Islamic Societies.* Cambridge: Cambridge University Press.

Lapidus offers a comprehensive developmental and comparative overview of Islamic history focused on the emergence and interaction of political, religious and familial institutions and organizations. Part one surveys developments from the Qur'ānic revelation into the thirteenth century in Arabia and posits the emergence of an Islamic version of Middle Eastern society. Part two charts the global diffusion of this social model in the tenth through nineteenth century and remarks upon its interactions with preexistent sociocultural patterns. Part three concerns the collapse of Islamic empires, the impact of Western imperialism, and the rise and evolution of modern states.

Levy, Reuben. 1962 [1957]. *The Social Structure of Islam.* Cambridge: Cambridge University Press.

Though somewhat outdated, this work serves as a useful introduction to the sociological study of Islam. Levy examines the influence of Islamic belief and ritual upon daily life and social organization in a number of societies.

Lewis, Bernard. 1993. *Islam and the West.* New York; London: Oxford University Press.

Lewis takes critical aim at the postmodern condemnation of Western Near East studies set forth in Edward Said's *Orientalism* (1979) and argues for a more balanced account of the history of European and Islamic perceptions of and prejudices toward the other. This collection of eleven essays, under the headings Encounters, Studies and Perceptions, and Islamic Response and Reaction, probe the mottled history of European-Islamic relations, as well as more recent struggles within the academy to describe and interpret said history.

Martin, Richard C. 1996. *Islamic studies: A History of Religions Approach.* Second ed. Upper Saddle River, N.J.: Prentice-Hall.

An overview of Islamic religion and culture directed at those seeking an introduction to Islamic studies. Emphasis is given throughout to general concepts in the study of religion as they pertain to Western understanding of Islam. Primary focus is given to conveying central themes in contemporary Muslim life, as evidenced by the extensive section on communal life and ritual. A broad survey of historical foundations is also given.

Minai, Naila. 1981. *Women in Islam: Tradition and Transition in the Middle East.* New York: Seaview Books.

This personal account offers insight into the experience of a Muslim woman in a number of cultural and social contexts. Minai provides some historical background, with portraits of historically significant Muslim women, and depicts the present options, opportunities, and challenges facing her peers.

Murata, Sachiko, and William C. Chittick. 1994. *The Vision of Islam.* New York: Paragon House.

This introductory text offers a cohesive Islamic worldview as derived from the classical tradition and the thought of leading historic Muslim intellectuals and Qur'ānic interpreters rather than from the "alien perspective" of Western academics. Using the "Ḥadith of Gabriel" as its organizing principle, the text addresses the topics of islam/submission, iman/faith, including reflections on the divine, its attributes and its relation to the chain of being, ihsan/the beautiful, and the interrelation of history and eschatology.

Nasr, Seyyed Hossein. 1994. *Ideals and Realities of Islam.* Aquarian ed., revised and updated. London; San Francisco: Aquarian.

Nasr provides non-Muslim readers with a illuminating survey of the core tenets of traditional Islam, including the role of the Prophet and the Qur'ān in belief, the foundations of the faith including the Five Pillars, and describes the esoteric and exoteric traditions and the major sectarian branches within the broader community.

Nasr, Seyyed Hossein. 1987. *Islamic Spirituality: Foundations.* World Spirituality Series, vol. 19. New York: Crossroads.

Nasr, Seyyed Hossein. 1991. *Islamic Spirituality: Manifestations.* World Spirituality Series, vol. 20. New York: Crossroads.

Together, these volumes survey the broad historical, geographic, and intellectual scope of Islamic spirituality with a heavy emphasis upon Sufi esoteric traditions. *Foundations* investigates the roots of spirituality in the Qur'ān, the Prophet's life, and in ritual, explores both Sunni and Shi'i traditions, sketches the history of Sufism, and elaborates the Islamic view of the connection between knowledge and reality. *Manifestations* is a work in three parts chronicling the emergence of a number of Sufi orders and heir contributions to Islamic societies, inquiring into the relationship between Islamic literature and spirituality, and examining the connections between spirituality and theology, philosophy, the occult sciences, and the arts.

Nasr, Seyyed Hossein. 1981. *Islamic Life and Thought.* Albany: State University of New York Press.

This collection of essays treats a variety of topics under the headings of Law and Society, Cultural and Intellectual Life, The Sciences, Philosophy, and Sufism. Nasr offers both general surveys of Islamic thought, history and culture, and in-depth, sometimes technical treatments of comparative cosmologies, esoteric traditions, and the works of the Persian philosopher Mulla Sadrâ . A number of essays deal with the complexity of interpreting Islam under the impact of modern Western culture.

Rahman, Fazlur. 1982. *Islam and Modernity: Transformation of an Intellectual Tradition.* Chicago; London: University of Chicago Press.

Responding to the growing intellectual crisis in Islam arising from its confrontation with Western modernisms, Rahman examines the history of Islamic education and Qur'ānic interpretation to reveal the roots of the dilemma as well as possible solutions. He argues for a return to and rereading of classical texts using modern critical techniques to liberate these works from static interpretations and to uncover underlying principles that may guide modern Islamic life.

Rahman, Fazlur. 1980. *Major Themes of the Qur'ān.* Minneapolis: Bibliotheca Islamica.

In this thematically arranged introduction to the core text of the Islamic tradition, Rahman offers a synthetic interpretation of the Qur'ānic vision of life and the world. Topics studied include God, humanity in its individual and social existences, nature, revelation, and eschatology. At times controversial in his pronouncements, Rahman attempts to synthesize the best of traditional Islamic and Western academic approaches to the sacred text.

Rahman, Fazlur. 1979. *Islam.* Chicago: University of Chicago Press.

A general descriptive introduction to the history of Islam covering major events and movements within the tradition. Sections treat the origin and development of scriptural and legal traditions, the birth and growth of theological and philosophical schools, Islamic education, sectarianism, Sufism, and pre-modern and modern reform movements.

Renard, John. 1996. *Seven Doors to Islam: Spirituality and the Religious Life of Muslims.* Berkeley: University of California Press.

Through seven symbolic doors, Renard leads readers on a tour of the more experiential aspects of classical and medieval Islamic spirituality. Along the way, one is acquainted with Islamic traditions of ritual, prayer, literary and visual arts, architecture, and hagiography. Valuable guides to and summaries of significant texts assist the reader's progress and open avenues for further independent exploration.

Richard, Yann. 1995. *Shi'ite Islam: Polity, Ideology, and Creed. Studies in Social Discontinuity.* Oxford, U.K.; Cambridge, Mass.: Blackwell.

A broad overview of the historical development and general ideological foundations of Shi'ism. The author focuses on Iranian Shi'ism and its contributions to Islamic politics and culture, with special emphasis on the intellectual history of modern Iran and the more radical, revolutionary aspects of Shi'a thought. A brief section on Shi'ism outside of Iran is also provided.

Rippin, Andrew. 1990–91. *Muslims: Their Religious Beliefs and Practices.* 2 vols. London; New York: Routledge.

In the first volume, the Formative Period, Rippin explores the emergence, interpretation, and transmission of Islamic identity from its prehistoric and Qur'ānic roots through the period of legal, theological, and ritual development and into the articulation of alternate visions of said identity as embodied in Sufism and Shi'ism. Volume two, the Contemporary Period, resumes the descriptive and analytic task in the late eighteenth century, giving special attention to issues concerning modern interpretations of the life of the Prophet and the authority of the Qur'ān that fuel both a renewed sense of Islamic identity in and conflict with the contemporary world. Rippin draws heavily on recent scholarship and uses literary analysis, source-criticism techniques and structuralist methods in casting his argument.

Robinson, Francis (ed.). 1996. *The Cambridge Illustrated History of the Islamic World.* New York: Cambridge University Press.

A well-appointed historical overview with additional material covering economics, social ordering, education, the transmission of knowledge, and artistic expression in Islamic societies. Introductory readers will find the bibliography a useful guide to resources on a variety of subjects.

Savory, R. M. (ed.). 1976. *Introduction to Islamic Civilization.* London; New York: Cambridge University Press.

This survey of civilization in the Middle East highlights the production of high culture and Islamic contributions to science, medicine, literature, and the visual arts. Essays review the historical and cultural background of Islam in the Middle East; central religious, philosophical, and legal concepts; and explore the impact of Western modernisms upon Islamic societies in general and on Turkey, Iran, and Iraq in particular.

Schacht, Joseph. 1982. *An Introduction to Islamic Law.* Oxford; New York: Clarendon Press.

Islamic law (specifically that expressed in the Sunni tradition) is discussed primarily through consideration of its historical development. The author also provides a comprehensive survey of the system of Islamic law, including sections on legal procedure and penal codes. The practice of law in contemporary Islamic states is not addressed.

Schacht, Joseph, Clifford Edmund Bosworth, and Thomas Walker Arnold. 1974. *The Legacy of Islam.* Second ed. Oxford: Clarendon Press.

A collection of writings from various authors on the impact of Islam (specifically Sunni Islam) on the modern world. The text explores both direct influences on Western nations (including a section on Western images and studies of Islam) and Islamic contributions to "the achievements of mankind in all their aspects" (including sections on economics, architecture, law, political thought, literature, art, music, philosophy, and science). The modes of transmission of these Muslim influences are discussed throughout.

Schimmel, Annemarie. 1974. *Mystical Dimensions of Islam.* Chapel Hill: University of North Carolina Press.

An accessible and comprehensive survey of Sufism. A general overview of the definitions of Sufism and its historical development is followed by an extensive depiction of the mystic path, including detailed accounts of its stages and stations. Other topics covered include Sufi communal life and the formation of the first orders; mysticism in Persia, Turkey, and the Indian subcontinent; and an appendix on feminine influences.

Schimmel, Annemarie. 1994. *Deciphering the Signs of God: A Phenomenological Approach to Islam.* Albany: State University of New York Press.

The author adopts a subjective and phenomenological methodology toward the understanding of Islam, often relying on mystical and poetic aspects of the tradition. A depiction of Islamic religious feeling is developed through the exploration of responses to the numinous aspects of five phenomenological categories: nature and culture, space and time, action, word and script, and individual and society. A special focus is given to the role of language in understanding Islamic religious experience.

Smith, Wilfred Cantwell. 1981. *On Understanding Islam: Selected Studies. Religion and Reason.* The Hague; New York: Mouton.

A collection of 16 papers on various topics, perhaps most valuable for the insight the author brings to studies of Muslim-Hindu and Muslim-Christian theological debates.

Waines, David. 1995. *An Introduction to Islam.* Cambridge; New York: Cambridge University Press.

A broad introductory text covering scriptural and historical foundations of Islam, development of Islamic law and theology, Sufi and Shi'a sectarian traditions, and the role of Islam in the modern world. Includes a brief glossary and annotated suggestions for further reading.

Watt, W. Montgomery. 1988. *Islamic Fundamentalism and Modernity.* London; New York: Routledge.

A discussion of the Islamic "Self Image" and its relationship to contemporary issues facing Islam. Watt portrays fundamentalism as the acceptance of a traditional Islamic world view (one focusing on the ideal, unchanging nature of the tradition), and suggests that as a dominant mode of Islamic belief this conception has hindered the entrance of Islam into modernity). Watt proposes the inclusion of Western methodologies (e.g., scientific and critical historical methods) into Islamic thought as a means of more effectively addressing such modern issues as religious pluralism, international politics, and social problems.

Williams, John Alden. 1982. *Themes of Islamic Civilization.* Berkeley: University of California Press.

A collection of over 180 translated Islamic religious texts selected to convey "the attitudes or the conventions that lay behind [Islamic] institutions." Texts are arranged according to six categories: the community, the perfect ruler, the will of God, the expected deliverer, struggle: jihad, and friends of God. Explanatory text and notations are minimal.

Williams, John Alden. 1994. *The Word of Islam.* Austin: University of Texas Press.

A collection of translated Islamic texts with explanatory notes supplied by the author. Sources include the Qur'ān, Ḥadith, Sharīʿa and Fiqh, Kalām, and writings from Sufi and Shi'a traditions. The accessibility of the explanatory notes makes this work a valuable introduction to a variety of primary Islamic texts.

Wolfson, Harry Austryn. 1976. *The Philosophy of the Kalām.* Cambridge, Mass.: Harvard University Press.

A discussion of Islamic orthodox scholastic theology. Wolfson provides a general overview of the Kalām and traces its historical roots and its influence on Jewish and Christian philosophers. The treatments of seven specific theological problems (attributes of God, the Qur'ān, creation, atomism, causality, predestination, and free will) are examined in detail.

Annotated Bibliography: Classical Religious Categories

Alston, William P. 1991. *Perceiving God: the Epistemology of Religious Experience.* Ithaca, N.Y.: Cornell University Press.

An epistemological account of religious perceptual beliefs. Concerned with accounting for the epistemic value and justification of the perception of God as testified to by the major Western religious traditions, this work focuses on understanding and defending mystical perception and experience, as well as distinguishing various experiential religious perspectives.

Altizer, Thomas J. J., and William Hamilton. 1966. *Radical Theology and the Death of God.* Indianapolis: Bobbs-Merrill.

A collection of expositive essays charting the field of 'radical theology' and its role in contemporary society. Setting forth key concepts such as 'kenotic negation' in arguments developed to oppose classical and modern theism, this collection of works draws from a wide range of cultural resources and is accompanied by a fine selected bibliography covering the various dimensions of radical theology.

Aristotle. 1947. *Basic Works of Aristotle.* Richard McKeon (ed.). New York: Random House.

The contribution of Aristotle's philosophy in demonstrating the interrelations among the sciences, in the development of logical theory and method, and in the general conception and principled understanding of existential reality as a whole is widespread and well known. Clearly influencing major religious worldviews either directly or indirectly in one form or another throughout the course of history, the thought expressed in Aristotle's major treatises (including specifically treatises on logic, physics, psychology, metaphysics, ethics, politics, and poetics) concerned the nature of the soul, epistemology, cosmology, cosmogony, social institutions, and rhetoric generally presents numerous Western categorical distinctions organized within rigorous methodological schematizations. Such Aristotelian notions as the eternal 'unmoved' mover, intellectual virtue, and the relation of essential and accidental attributes continue to influence contemporary religious understanding.

Augustine, Saint. 1958. *City of God.* Vernon J. Bourke (ed.). New York: Doubleday Image.

The quintessential classical account of the notion of a universal religious society, that, for Saint Augustine, was to be brought about through Christian virtue and order. A critical account of pagan society, Christian history, and religious meaning emerges as the dialectical motif of the dual relation between the 'cities' of earth and heaven is made explicit.

Ayer, Alfred J. 1956. *The Problem of Knowledge.* Baltimore: Penguin Books.

An exposition of key philosophical categories including scepticism and certainty, perception, and the relation of self and other in methodological accordance with the theories of logical positivism. Outlined in this work are epistemological concerns relevant to both philosophical and religious problems.

Bell, Catherine. 1997. *Ritual: Perspectives and Dimensions.* New York: Oxford University Press.

This recent work initially develops an account of the contemporary cross-discipline methodological approaches to the study of religious ritual, and then proceeds to outline conceptually the general spectrum of ritual activities for the purpose of examining further the significance and transformative nature of ritual in religious and cultural worldviews. An excellent source identifying the major conceptual frameworks employed by outstanding thinkers for the study of ritual and religious expression, and, additionally, a work that originally systematizes the central issues, debates, and areas of inquiry surrounding the modern study of ritual.

Bergson, Henri. 1935. *The Two Sources of Morality and Religion.* R. Ashley Audra, Cloudesley Shovell, Henry Brereton, and William Horsfall Carter (eds.). London: Macmillan.

As the title of this work indicates, Bergson looks to identify fundamental sources for social morality and religion. Focusing primarily on moral obligation stemming from both the norms and ideals of social conscience and from dynamic models of exemplified morality achieved by individuals existentially appropriating forms of religious knowledge and understanding, an analysis of the categorical constructs associated with static religion and dynamic religion figures centrally into this study of the nature and value of moral obligation as it is related to religion.

Blanshard, Brand. 1975. *Reason and Belief.* New Haven: Yale University Press.

An in-depth presentation of a rationalist-religious alternative to traditional supernaturalism. Claiming reason to be the architect of religion, this work outlines from a Western orientation the relation of reason with the concept of revelation, faith, myth, and belief in view of distinct Christian perspectives. Analysis of the thought of major Western theologians such as Kierkegaard, Barth, E. Brunner and others precedes a constructive cosmology developing thematic critical accounts of an array of religious and philosophical categories including the absolute, goodness, religious sentiment, morality, and more.

Brightman, Edgar Sheffield. 1970. *Religious Values.* New York: The Abingdon Press.

The aim of this work is to identify and interpret central values in religious experience and to reconsider the meaning and value of religion as an actual human experience. Founding this study on the thesis that specific religious values not only presuppose rational belief but entail moral obligation, an account of the nature and validity of religious values is developed to further investigate the experience of worship and its creativity fostered by forms of contemplation, revelation, communion, and fruition.

Buber, Martin. 1958. *I and Thou.* Second ed., New York: Charles Scribner's Sons.

A landmark twentieth-century text examining the dialogical relation between man and God. Developing categorical understanding of the religious and social dimensions of the human personality, this work specifically endeavors to delineate the twofold attitude of man determined by the "I-Thou" (self/transcendent) and "I-It" (subject/object) relation that is construed by Buber to characterize human existential nature generally.

Cusa, Nicholas. 1954. *Of Learned Ignorance.* New Haven: Yale University Press.

Organized into three books or divisions, this work examines epistemological problems associated with knowing the divine, the dilemma of how the divine can be construed as distinct from the world, and, finally, how a limited being maintaining its relative finitude with the created world can be conceived of as being in simultaneous union with God or the *maximum absolutum.* While only explicitly addressing concerns related to Western thought and the Christian tradition, the importance of this work for religious understanding is evident in the novel categorical constructs it employs to further elaborate the Neoplatonic conceptual framework out of which it generally operates. Concepts such as the 'maximum' and 'minimum', contraction, the reconciliation of contraries (*coincidentia oppositorum*), and other traditional religious categories figure centrally in Cusa's philosophical theology.

Davis, Stephen T. 1983. *Logic and the Nature of God.* Grand Rapids, Mich.: William B. Eerdmans.

Endeavoring to critically examine through rigorous philosophical analysis the notion of God—an analysis of the properties and attributes of God from a Christian perspective—this work looks to defend the main aspects of religious understanding maintained by the Christian tradition concerning the nature of God. The logic underpinning the traditional Western categories employed to discuss the nature of God, including time, omniscience, immutability, foreknowledge, omnipotence, and benevolence, is reckoned with in detail.

Dewey, John. 1934. *A Common Faith.* New Haven: Yale University Press.

Making distinctions between organized forms of religion and religious experience, this work discusses the possibility of human experience attaining a religious quality while being emancipated from elements of organized religion which limit the credibility and influence of religion. This position is defended by identifying common denominator values shared by those holding a belief in a supernatural Being and those acting according to the tendencies of natural agencies.

Douglas, Mary. 1970. *Natural Symbols: Explorations in Cosmology.* New York: Pantheon Books.

Developing the thesis that symbols based on the human body are used to express different social experiences, this work looks to examine how the symbolism of the body, empowered by social life, governs fundamental attitudes concerning matter and spirit. The primary approach of this study involves the examination of symbolic concordances of religious expression and their influence in social organizational structures. The role of ritual and religious authority as considered in accordance to Douglas's 'group/ grid' formula of classification figures centrally in this analysis.

Durkheim, Emile. 1965. *The Elementary Forms of the Religious Life: A Study in Religious Sociology.* New York: The Free Press.

This analysis of primitive religion develops standard conceptions for the current sociological study of religion and defends the notion that religious knowledge and understanding is consequently social. Examining the fundamental beliefs of elementary religion, the social character of such belief systems and their origin is made evident through the further analysis of religious ideologies and the principal ritual attitudes of organized forms of religion. Among the many diverse topics explored in this study, attention is specifically focused on the nature of totemic beliefs, primitive conceptions of soul, and religious rites.

Eliade, Mircea. 1961. *The Sacred and the Profane: The Nature of Religion.* New York: Harper Torchbook.

A categorical delineation of specific dimensions of cross-cultural religious experience, focusing on elements of time, space, and religious symbolism. This work argues for the existence of homogeneous cosmic order centered around ritual, theophany, and religious values evolving from primitive forms of religion.

Farrer, Austin. 1959. *Finite and Infinite: A Philosophical Essay.* Second ed., Westminster: Dacre Press.

Concerned with the traditional Western arguments for the existence of God and the examination of rational theology, as well as the general topics of metaphysics developed to support such arguments and defense, this complex work looks to reconstruct the doctrine of finite substance to explore further the dialectic of rational theology and plausible usiological arguments for the existence of God. For his central examination of finite substance, Farrer focuses on the substance of the human will and develops significant categories of understanding concerning the metaphysical nature of the finite self and its relation to the infinite.

Fiorenza, Francis Schussler. 1985. *In Memory of Her: A Feminist Theological Reconstruction of Christian Origins.* New York: Crossroad.

This work seeks to secure the memory of woman discipleship as it is depicted in the Christian gospel. This task, for Fiorenza, is considered to involve the reconstruction of early Christian history as women's history and the further exploration of this Christian history as belonging to both men and women. A feminist critique is developed highlighting categories of the marginalized in early Christian beginnings, outlining the androcentric nature of biblical language, and identifying both historical patriarchal structures and the character of the discipleship of women.

Frazer, James George. 1959. *The New Golden Bough.* Theodore H. Gaster (ed.). New York: Criterion Books.

Frazer's original twelve volume work, *The Golden Bough,* recognized as a pioneer study in magic and religion, is here re-edited and abridged into a single volume highlighting Frazer's most important scholarship. Linking primitive concepts and modes of religious thought to underlying social institutions and folk customs, this work systematically investigates an array of topics including religious authority, death and immortality, the role of ancient myth in religion, religious ritual, evil, taboo, and more.

Goodenough, Erwin Ramsdell. 1986 [1965]. *The Psychology of Religious Experiences.* Reprint. Lanham, Md.: University Press of America.

Concentrating primarily on the experiential phenomena of Western religions, Goodenough develops a general contemporary account of the academic study of the psychology of religion, which, for Goodenough, is portrayed as fundamentally dominated by Freudian models. Goodenough furthermore goes further to describe and consider from a psychological perspective particular typologies of religious experience, including religious legalism, orthodoxy, aestheticism, sacramentalism, and mysticism.

Gutting, Gary. 1982. *Religious Belief and Religious Skepticism.* Notre Dame, Ind.: Notre Dame Press.

Arguing for the validity of religious belief, as it is justified by religious experience, this work critically examines problematic issues associated with various forms of religious belief by means of a methodological skepticism.

Hart, Ray L. 1968. *Unfinished Man and the Imagination: Toward an Ontology and a Rhetoric of Revelation.* New York: Herder and Herder.

This important work looks to develop a 'fundamental theology' as a *via media* between neo-orthodoxy and liberalism, as well as between dogmatic and natural theology. Identifying revelation *qua* fundament as exceeding the founded, this work focuses attention on the cognitive and ontic power of the imagination in its active and passive participation within various existential domains of being. Ontological rhetoric of revelation is developed in notions such as the 'hermeneutic spiral', the 'historio-personal existential', and the 'imaginative existential'. Art and theological symbolics emerge as central to theological 'after-thought' that Hart considers necessarily correlated with the mental faculty of imagination.

Hartshorne, Charles. 1948. *The Divine Relativity.* New Haven: Yale University Press.

Developing a logical analysis of the religious idea of God, this work looks to defend a panentheistic or 'surrelative' account of the nature of God. More specifically, this work argues that divine attributes are abstract types of social relationship, of which divine acts are concrete instances or relations. Accordingly, Hartshorne's text considers the Absolute as definable in positive relational terms.

Hegel, Georg W. F. 1988. *Lectures on the Philosophy of Religion.* Peter C. Hodgson (ed.). Berkeley: University of California Press.

An abridged, single-volume edition of Hegel's four 1827 lectures on the philosophy of religion delivered at the University of Berlin. These lectures present Hegel's understanding and refined interpretation of the concept of religion, as well as Hegel's classification of concrete forms of religion in relation to his broader philosophical vision of the consummation of absolute Spirit in history.

Hick, John. 1989. *An Interpretation of Religion; Human Responses to the Transcendent.* New Haven: Yale University Press.

A phenomenological study of religion developed from an inherently religious perspective, which endeavors to make clear that the viability of religious belief and experience leads to problems of religious pluralism. However, Hick's work furthermore argues that the major religious traditions, supported by specific philosophical distinctions, provide functional resources for resolving such problems. Included in the development of such arguments are discussions of the universality of religion, religious expression of human transformation, the rationality of religious belief, and the future of religious traditions.

James, William. 1902. *The Varieties of Religious Experience: A Study in Human Nature.* New York: Longmans, Green.

The categorical distinctions developed in this psychological study of religious experience have become standard in the study of religion. James's considerations of the sick soul and divided self, conversion, and saintliness among other topics related to the phenomenon of religion lead to scientific and philosophical conclusions respecting and affirming the value of religious experience. Of particular importance in this study, moreover, are the qualitative categories of ineffability, noetic feeling, transiency, and passivity used to discuss forms of mystical experience.

Kalupahana, David J. 1992. *A History of Buddhist Philosophy.* Honolulu: University of Hawaii Press.

This work represents a consolidation of Kalupahana's extensive research and scholarship on early Buddhism and offers an indepth account of the problems and categories of Buddhist thought by utilizing intellectual themes of Western philosophy and religion for their explication. While furthermore developing an understanding of classical Buddhist categories such as the four noble truths, dependent origination, nirvana, and others according to their own distinct meaning within the Buddhist tradition, this historical account of the outstanding philosophical trends and figures of Buddhism is particularly interesting with regard to the categorical analysis developed to give further consideration to the non-substantialist position as it stands related to the general tendency of absolutism held predominantly by non-Buddhist traditions.

Kant, Immanuel. 1956. *Critique of Pure Reason.* London: Macmillan.

A scientific inquiry concerned with the principles of sensibility a priori and the principles of pure thought as developed through the construction of a transcendental aesthetic and a transcendental logic. Specific attention is paid to the deduction, schematization, and experiential potential of pure concepts or categories of reason and the antinomies of pure reason that ultimately involve ontological considerations concerned with the nature of God and human existence.

Kant, Immanuel. 1960. *Religion within the Limits of Reason Alone*. Theodore M. Greene and Hoyt H. Hudson (eds.). New York: Harper Torchbooks.

Kant's last major work explaining his conception of the essence and implications of true and false religion, and further developing his own treatment of rationalistic proofs of God's existence along with his own moral arguments concerning God, freedom, and immortality. Specifically presenting a pietist version of Christianity, the categories and concepts concerning religion dealt with in this work refer far beyond the scope eighteenth-century German Pietism, especially with regard to its treatment of the problem of evil, its approach to the predispositions of human nature, and its theoretical understanding of religious ethics as related to the notion of unconditioned duty and moral dictates of the conscience oriented by the goals of holiness, mercy, and justice. Religion is moreover defended by the author to be a means of furthering the virtuous disposition of the individual by delineating and preserving a course of proper moral action that carries with it rational categorical obligations for both the individual and society.

Kaufman, Gordon D. 1993. *In Face of Mystery: A Constructive Theology*. Cambridge: Harvard University Press.

This work develops a full-scale reconception of Christian theology, revering ultimate mystery in life and articulating the manner by which such mystery is generally treated through expressive forms of Christianity. Outlining the thesis that there exists a kind of conceptual path on which an assent in religious faith can take place in accordance to particular free decisions rationally made and held by individuals, Kaufman also delineates further the categorical nature of monotheistic religion and human agency, while also constructing a theology embracing the notion of serendipitous creativity.

Loy, David. 1988. *Nonduality: A Study in Comparative Philosophy*. New Haven: Yale University Press.

Concerned with the claims of subject-object nonduality proposed by certain Western philosophical traditions, as well as generally similar claims by Eastern religious traditions, this work looks to create a 'core doctrine' of nonduality based on a preliminary comparative study of certain types of 'seer-seen' nonduality articulated by Buddhism, Vedānta, and Taoism. Then, arguing initially that Eastern religious traditions creatively construct metaphysical positions from the perspective of non-duality, rather than from a diametrically opposed worldview that pragmatically assumes a fundamental subject-object duality (i.e., a position dominantly maintained in Western thought), this analysis begins to employ its specific theoretical considerations of non-duality to expose further similarities and differences existing particularly between Mahāyāna Buddhism and Advaita Vedānta. One central outcome of this study involves demonstrating that beneath the surface conflict of concepts and categories given expression by such religious perspectives resides fundamental agreements regarding the phenomenology of the non-dual experience.

MacQuarrie, John. 1981. *Twentieth Century Religious Thought: The Frontiers of Philosophy, 1900–1980.* New York: Charles Scribner's Sons.

A comprehensive survey of the major Western philosophical and theological trends of the twentieth century, including synoptic analyses of the work of their most outstanding proponents. This valuable study outlines the development and evolution of philosophical and religious thought over the past century and introduces the fundamental positions and categorical strategies of a number of Western intellectuals. MacQuarrie's particular classification of the major patterns of philosophical and religious thought also emerges as distinct in terms of the kind of categorical understanding it imparts to expose the general contours of Western philosophy and religion.

Malefijt, Annemarie De Waal. 1968. *Religion and Culture: An Introduction to the Anthropology of Religion.* New York: Macmillan.

This work offers an excellent overview of the anthropological study of religion, its objectives and categorical conceptions, and a full catalogue of the major twentieth-century theoretical perspectives on the nature of religion. Also, taxonomies are developed to discuss religious belief, religious communication, and the functions of religion.

McFague, Sallie. 1982. *Metaphorical Theology: Models of God in Religious Language.* Philadelphia: Fortress Press.

A sequel work to an earlier book, *Speaking in Parables: A Study in Metaphor and Theology* (1975), this text looks to develop theoretical models to speak about and express religious realities from a metaphorical perspective. Initially focusing attention on different typologies of religious language and their potential for generating systematic and relatively permanent theological paradigms, the larger scope of a metaphorical theology is constructed through the consideration of conceptual relationships evident in metaphors and religious language that serve as appropriate theological models indicating ways that religious traditions are to be interpreted as expressing intelligible patterns of life.

Nasr, Seyyed Hossein. 1981. *Knowledge and the Sacred.* New York: Crossroad.

This work endeavors to resuscitate the sacred quality of knowledge for the revival of the intellectual tradition of the West. Nasr looks to the aid of the living traditions of the Orient for this project, claiming that knowledge, for such traditions, has never been divorced from the sacred. Specifically, an examination of the desacralization of knowledge and the nature of tradition precedes a categorical analysis of the sacred, covering such topics as cosmic theophany, eternity and the temporal order, the multiplicity of sacred forms, and sacred knowledge as deliverance.

Needleman, Jacob, A. K. Bierman, and James A. Gould. 1973. *Religion for a New Generation.* New York: Macmillan.

This work contains a wide spectrum of religious writings from numerous important authors illuminating the major directions of the modern religious mind. Included are critical essays on the spiritual revolution of the new generation, religion and social crisis, religious discipline and enlightenment, religious or sacred language, and religious understanding related to the struggle with death.

Nishitani, Keiji. 1982. *Religion and Nothingness.* Berkeley: University of California Press.

This poignant work delves into the ground of human existence through its inquiries into the nature and purpose of religion, its development of categorical assertions regarding personal and impersonal forms of religion, and finally its constructive exegesis of Buddhist concepts and understanding. The general trajectory of Nishitani's work and his individual discussions concerning the nature of emptiness *(śūnyatā)* as related to both history and the noumenal categories of space and time are considered clear and concise by Western and Eastern scholars alike. Also included is a thorough glossary of terms indicating the cross-cultural nature of this work, as well as important categorical terminology developed in Nishitani's positions concerning the dimensions of emptiness and their potentiality.

Otto, Rudolph. 1969. *The Idea of the Holy.* New York: Oxford University Press.

This work ventures to discuss the concept of the 'non-rational' or 'supra-rational', looking specifically at the *feeling* associated with this phenomenon over against its place in and for conceptual thought. For Otto, such an account is construed to involve the analyses of the numinous, the 'mysterium tremendum', the holy as an a priori category, and spiritual experience. Additionally, notions such as these are discussed with regard to their particular schematizations and categorical expression (primarily expressed, for Otto, in Western modes), as they are given further consideration according to their concrete manifestations in history.

Plotinus. 1967. *The Enneads.* Cambridge: Harvard University Press.

This work contemplates and speculates on a wide array of fundamental philosophical concepts and categories related to monotheistic understanding and the existential nature of human being. This particular six-volume text has Plotinus exegetically considering an extensive range of rudimentary human beliefs and ideals, and in the process demarcating the conceptual horizons of classical Western philosophical thought.

Proudfoot, Wayne. 1985. *Religious Experience.* Berkeley: University of California Press.

An examination of important theories of religious experience, offering both an elucidation of the ideas or concept of religious experience as it is presupposed by discussions of such topics as mysticism and reductionism in the study of religion and a consideration of the implications of these theories and this idea for contemporary issues in the philosophy of religion. This work specifically develops a categorical account of conditions and behavior characteristic of the way people understand and interpret religious experience analytically, descriptively, and evocatively. Issues explored include religious expression, interpretation, emotion, mysticism, and explanation.

Rahner, Karl. 1978. *Foundations of Christian Faith: An Introduction to the Idea of Christianity.* New York: Crossroad.

Primarily an exploration of the foundations of Christian faith, as well as a justification of Christian belief, this work more generally focuses attention on the concept of transcendental experience and argues that present in such experience is an unthematic and anonymous knowledge of God. Accordingly, the theological examination of fundamental Christian concepts developed within this "first-level reflection" of the Christian faith proceeds in relation to broader categorical constructs such as the "supernatural existential" (denoting the self-communication of God), transcendental revelation, and communal and individual eschatology.

Ricoeur, Paul. 1969. *The Symbolism of Evil.* Boston: Beacon Paperback.

This work sets forth a theoretical understanding of myth as possessing a symbolic function for human understanding and reality that operates as a means of reminiscence and expectation and as a demarcation of the sacred for mankind. In view of this understanding, Ricoeur proceeds to analyze myths that speak of the beginning and end of evil. Categories of defilement, sin, and guilt are employed to discuss dimensions of evil, and this project is followed by a critical analysis of the symbolic function of myths dealing with the drama of creation and eschatological visions.

Saler, Benson. 1993. *Conceptualizing Religion: Immanent Anthropologists, Transcendent Natives, and Unbounded Categories.* H. G. Kippenberg and E. T. Lawson (eds.). Studies in the History of Religions, vol. 56. Leiden: E. J. Brill.

Preliminarily reviewing different strategies proposed by anthropologists and others for conceptualizing religion, and reflecting on various definitions of religion (i.e., essentialist, monotheistic, substantive) based on particular forms of categorical understanding, this work sets forth a defense of conceptualizing religion according to multifactorial approaches. This standpoint is facilitated, for Saler, by the use of 'unbounded categories'.

Schleiermacher, Friedrich. 1958. *On Religion: Speeches to Its Cultured Despisers.* New York: Harper Torchbooks.

Schleiermacher's five speeches develop a defense for religion as a facet of human experience and establish several categorical distinctions for both the study of religion and for religious human experience. Central to this work is the notion of 'inner' and 'outer' perspectives on religious dimensions and the 'feeling of absolute dependence' characterizing the human creature's relation to the Infinite.

Sharpe, Eric J. 1983. *Understanding Religion.* New York: St. Martin's Press.

This work sets out to explore certain implications of the study of religion, while also developing an account of 'religious studies' that 'excludes nothing identifiable as belonging within the category of religion'. Included in this exploration is an analysis of functional modes of religion, as well as the development of a general definition of religion, considerations concerned with religious or sacred context, and a discussion distinguishing between the supernatural and the transcendent.

Smart, Ninian. 1996. *Dimensions of the Sacred: An Anatomy of the World's Beliefs.* Berkeley: University of California Press.

An analysis of religion as conceived in accordance to its various dimensions. Introduced by an extensive glossary of terms, this work ranges widely over religions and ideologies of the world and looks to identify common patterns in the ways religion manifests itself by classifying elements of religious belief and practice given expression in the world-views of distinct cultures. Specific attention is given to the ritual dimension of religion, as well as religion's experiential, ethical, legal, and social dimensions.

Smith, Huston. 1976. *The Forgotten Truth: The Primordial Tradition.* New York: Harper & Row.

This works endeavors to outline primordial patterns of experience and collective outlooks of the world's religions, focusing particularly on the common values, purposes, and meaning conveyed by religious traditions. A discussion of symbolic space designating levels of reality and selfhood develops categories such as the infinite, the soul, and spirit in accordance to cross-cultural understanding while further examining the relation of religion and science and the quality of religious experience.

Smith, John E. 1995. *Experience and God.* Re-issue. New York: Fordham University Press.

This work first looks to recover the notion of religious experience from various distortions to which it has fallen prey in the modern world and then delineates the religious dimension or mode of experience through which the problem of God first emerges. It understands this particular problem as possessing a dual character, whereas God in one perspective is construed as 'a religious solution to a philosophical problem' and, in another, 'a philosophical solution to a religious problem'. From this position, an endeavor is made to better understand the idea of God in human experience in terms of both historical occasions evoking special insight and apprehensions concerning the divine and the uniting force such conceptions have had in establishing positive religious traditions. Specifically examined is the relation of doubt and reason, ontological and cosmological arguments about God, and the nature of communal religious belief.

Streng, F. J. 1967. *Emptiness: A Study in Religious Meaning.* Nashville: Abingdon Press.

Turning primarily to the religious teaching of the second-century Buddhist, Nāgārjuna, this work endeavors to understand the notion of 'emptiness' and emphasize the central importance of this categorical construct for Indian religious thought. Moreover, Streng looks to relate the concept of emptiness to other expressions of Indian religion, thus developing a wide-ranging account of Indian/Buddhist categories, including nirvana, dharmas, duhkha (suffering), etc.

Swinburne, Richard. 1979. *The Existence of God.* Oxford: Clarendon Press.

The sequel to Swinburne's *The Coherence of Theism*, this work is concerned primarily with the truth claims of arguments for the existence of God and looks to access the weight of such arguments. Concluding that the testimony of religious experience provides the best evidence of proof for the existence of God, an array of other traditional arguments (i.e., induction, explanation, teleological, cosmological, etc.) are also examined for their logical coherence and probability.

Tracy, David. 1975. *Blessed Rage for Order: The New Pluralism in Theology.* New York: Seabury/ Crossroad.

Working initially from a rich understanding concerning the pluralist context of contemporary theology, this text looks to offer a revisionist model for contemporary theology that considers the task of theology to lie in the investigation of its two primary sources—religious (Christian) text and common human experience and language—and the critical correlation of the results of such investigations. The ensuing discussion of traditional religious categories, as construed from the perspective of theological revision, gives general consideration to the religious dimension of human language and its meaning.

Van Der Leeuw, Gerardus. 1938. *Religion in Essence and Manifestation; A Study in Phenomenology.* London: George Allen & Unwin Ltd.

This phenomenological analysis of the objective and subjective manifestations of religion and their reciprocal operation clearly emerges as a standard in its field according to the manner in which it has shaped the phenomenological study of religion generally. Specifically endeavoring to systematically identify and categorize forms of religious expression as such concretely appear in various modalities of experience, this work introduces numerous categorical distinctions concerned with the nature and expression of religion and, more broadly, seeks to identify and make explicit theoretical forms of religion through critical typological analysis.

Wainwright, William. 1981. *Mysticism: A Study of Its Nature, Cognitive Value, and Moral Implications.* Madison: University of Wisconsin Press.

Drawing predominately and broadly from Western sources, this work endeavors to investigate the cognitive pretensions of mystical experience. Developing a conceptual account of the 'noetic character' of mystical experience, this work argues that there are conclusive reasons for believing that some mystical experiences are veridical, and that the truth claims that are built-in to such experience are true as well. Specific issues such as the cognitive status of mystical experience, the forms of mystical expression, and the compatibility of mysticism and morality are explored in detail.

Weber, Max. 1956. *The Sociology of Religion.* Boston: Beacon Press.

A systematic summary of the sociology of religion punctuated by the identification of typological patterns of religious association. Guided by his understanding of religion as a force for dynamic social change and such analytic categories as charisma, prophecy, and taboo, Weber's work looks to uncover the influence of religion on the social dimensions of humanity (i.e., politics, economics, sex, and art). Specifically examined are the origins of religions, the development and expression of religious authority, the idea of divinity in religion, types of theodicy and religious teleology, and the nature and role of religious ethics.

Yandell, Keith E. 1993. *The Epistemology of Religious Experience.* Cambridge: Cambridge University Press.

This work offers a contemporary analysis of the epistemic dimensions of religious belief. Developing phenomenal descriptions and modest typologies of religious experience generally held by the social sciences and subjects of religious experience, issues of self-authentication and verification are examined along with principles of evidence concerning the validity of religious experience. Numerous arguments defending the value of religious experience from a cross-cultural array of philosophical and religious proponents are reviewed as this study investigates how best to formulate a defensible principle of experiential evidence for religious propositions.

Annotated Bibliography
General Resources for the Study of Religion

Bibliographies and Research Guides

Adams, Charles J., ed. 1977. *A Reader's Guide to the Great Religions.* New York: Free Press.

Berkowitz, Morris L., and J. Edmund Johnson. 1967. *Social Scientific Studies of Religion: A Bibliography.* Pittsburgh: University of Pittsburgh Press.

Diehl, Katharine Smith. 1962. *Religions, Mythologies, Folklores: An Annotated Bibliography.* New York: Scarecrow Press.

Holm, Jean. 1992. *Keyguide to Information Sources on World Religions.* Boston: G. K. Hall.

International Bibliography of the History of Religions. 1964–Present. Leiden: E. J. Brill.

Karpinski, Leszek M. 1978. *The Religious Life of Man: Guide to Basic Literature.* Metuchen, N.J.: Scarecrow Press.

Johnston, William M. 1996. *Recent Reference Books in Religion: A Guide for Students, Scholars, Researchers, Buyers & Readers*. Downers Grove, Ill.: InterVarsity Press.

Melton, J. Gordon. 1992. *Religious Information Sources: A Worldwide Guide*. New York: Garland.

Mitros, Joseph F. 1973. *Religions: A Select, Classified Bibliography*. Louvain: Editions Nauwelaerts; New York: Learned Publications.

Walsh, Michael J. 1981. *Religious Bibliographies in Serial Literature: A Guide*. Westport, Conn.: Greenwood Press.

Wilson, John Frederick. 1982. *Research Guide to Religious Studies*. Chicago: American Library Association.

Encyclopedias and Dictionaries

Bowker, John, ed. *The Oxford Dictionary of World Religions*. Oxford; New York: Oxford Univeristy Press.

An accessible reference designed to acquaint beginning students and general readers alike with the fundamental terms, concepts, texts, practices, histories, and personages of all significant world religions. As such, the text devotes its energies to those entries likely to be of most interest to the beginning student of religion, with correspondingly less attention paid to more esoteric aspects of specific traditions. Includes a topical index and extensive cross-referencing.

Brandon, S. G. F. (ed.). 1970. *Dictionary of Comparative Religion*. New York: Scribner's.

A manageable single-volume reference covering aspects of all significant world religions, including prehistoric and ancient traditions, with an emphasis on a comparative approach to their study. Specific topics are introduced generally and subsequently examined regarding their interpretation by and importance to the various major religious traditions. General and synoptic indices, cross-referencing, and individual bibliographies are also provided.

Cooper, J. C. 1978. *An Illustrated Encyclopedia of Traditional Symbols*. London: Thames & Hudson.

Crim, Keith, ed. 1981. *Abingdon Dictionary of Living Religions*. Nashville: Abingdon.

A collection in one volume of a number of smaller dictionaries, each covering one of the major religions being practiced in the modern world. Each section is foreworded by a general introduction providing a description of historical origins, development, and fundamental doctrines and practices. Cross-referencing of terms relevant to more than one of the world's religions extend valuable insight for the student of comparative religion.

Edwards, Paul (ed.). 1967. *The Encyclopedia of Philosophy*. 6 vols. New York: Macmillan.

Eliade, Mircea (editor-in-chief). 1987. *The Encyclopedia of Religion*. New York: Macmillan.

A standard reference for any student of religion. Over 2,500 subject entries in sixteen volumes (including one index volume) ostensibly cover all significant aspects of world religions and their study. The broad conceptual scheme of the encyclopedia, conveniently outlined in the index, covers four general areas: the narrative history and central doctrines of specific religious communities; the comparative investigation of religious phenomena and experience; the conceptual tools essential to the study of religion; and the influence of religion on culture and society. Entries are designed to be generally accessible, and the comprehensive index and cross-referencing, along with extensive bibliographies, make this an invaluable reference for beginning students as well as advanced scholars.

Ferm, Vergilius Ture Anselm (ed.). 1945. *An Encyclopedia of Religion*. New York: The Philosophical Library.

Hastings, James. 1908–1926. *Encyclopedia of Religion and Ethics*. Edinburgh: T. & T. Clark; New York: C. Scribner's Sons.

Hinnells, John R. (ed.). 1984. *The Facts on File Dictionary of Religions*. New York: Facts on File.

MacGregor, Geddes. 1989. *Dictionary of Religion and Philosophy*. New York: Paragon House.

A compact volume broadly covering the philosophical implications of religious belief and practice, focusing almost exclusively on the Christian tradition and related Western philosophical thought. The dictionary is intended as a convenient handbook for quick reference, given the limits that its size places on depth of coverage.

Pike, Edgar Royston. 1951. *Encyclopedia of Religion and Religions*. London: Allen and Unwin.

Smith, Jonathan Z. (ed.). 1995. *Harper Collins Dictionary of Religion*. San Francisco: HarperSanFrancisco.

A single volume reference addressing issues essential to the understanding of the major religious traditions throughout the world's history, as well as issues important to the understanding of scholarly and public discourse on religion in general. Eleven major articles are included which provide overviews of the largest contemporary world religions as well as religions of antiquity and religions of traditional peoples; another offers a survey of the study of religion, including examination of the roles of anthropology, sociology, psychology, and other disciplines.

Swatos, William H., Jr. (ed.). 1998. *Encyclopedia of Religion and Society*. Walnut Creek, Calif.: AltaMira Press.

A survey of contemporary insights of the social sciences of religion, specifically anthropology, psychology, and sociology. This volume does not so much address religion in itself (i.e., fundamental doctrines, historical founders, modern theological thought, etc.), but rather addresses the intersection of religion and society, with emphasis on theoretical concepts, professional societies, and modern thinkers engaged in the sociological study of religion.

General Introductions to the Study of Religion

Capps, Walter H. 1971/1972. *Ways of Understanding Religion*. New York, Macmillan.

———. 1995. *Religious Studies: The Making of a Discipline*. Minneapolis: Fortress Press.

Hall, T. William (general ed.). 1978. *Introduction to the Study of Religion*. New York: Harper & Row.

King, Winston Lee. 1968. *Introduction to Religion: A Phenomenological Approach*. New York: Harper & Row.

Eliade, Mircea, and Joseph M. Kitagawa (eds.). 1959. *The History of Religions: Essays in Methodology*. Chicago: University of Chicago Press.

Kitagawa, Joseph M., and Gergory P. Alles. 1988. *Introduction to the History of Religions*. New York: Macmillan.

Pals, Daniel L. 1995. *Seven Theories of Religion*. Oxford; New York: Oxford University Press.

Sharpe, Eric J. 1983. *Understanding Religion*. New York: St. Martin's Press.

Tremmel, William Calloley. 1984. *Religion: What Is It?* New York: Holt, Rinehart & Winston.

Whaling, F. (ed.). 1983. *Contemporary Approaches to the Study of Religion: The Humanities.* New York: Mouton Publishers.

——— (ed.). 1985. *Contemporary Approaches to the Study of Religion: The Social Sciences.* New York: Mouton Publishers.

General Introductions to Religious Traditions

Cole, W. Owen (ed.). 1996. *Six World Faiths.* London; New York: Cassell.

Earhart, H. Byron (ed.). 1993. *Religious Traditions of the World: A Journey Through Africa, Meso-America, North America, Judaism, Christianity, Islam, Hinduism, Buddhism, China, and Japan.* San Francisco: HarperSanFrancisco.

Fellows, Ward J. 1979. *Religions East and West.* New York: Holt, Rinehart, and Winston.

Hardon, John A. 1963. *Religions of the World.* Westminster, Md.: Newman Press.

Hinnells, John R. 1996. *A New Handbook of Living Religions.* Oxford: Blackwell.

Kitagawa, Joseph M. 1987. *The History of Religions: Understanding Human Experience.* Atlanta, Ga.: Scholars Press.

——— (ed.). 1989. *The Religious Traditions of Asia.* New York: Macmillan; London: Collier Macmillan.

Ling, Trevor Oswald. 1968. *A History of Religion—East and West: An Introduction and Interpretation.* London; Melbourne: Macmillan; New York: St. Martin's Press.

Parrinder, Edward Geoffrey (gen. ed.). 1971. *Religions of the World: From Primitive Beliefs to Modern Faiths.* New York: Madison Square Press.

Sharma, Arvind (ed.). 1993. *Our Religions.* San Francisco: HarperSanFrancisco.

——— (ed.). 1994. *Religion and Women.* Albany: State University of New York Press.

Smart, Ninian. 1977. *The Long Search.* Boston: Little, Brown.

———. 1998. *The World's Religions.* Cambridge; New York: Cambridge University Press.

Smith, Huston. 1991. *The World's Religions: Our Great Wisdom Traditions*. San Francisco: HarperSanFrancisco. Previously published as *The Religions of Man*, 1958, New York: Harper.

Book Series

Boston University Studies in Philosophy and Religion. 1980–1999. Alan Olson and Leroy Rouner (eds.). Notre Dame, Ind.: Notre Dame University Press.

McGill Studies in Religion. 1987–1998 Atlanta: Scholars Press.

Religions of the World Series. Ninian Smart, Series editor. Books in the Series:

- *Buddhism.* Bradley K. Hawkins.
- *Christianity.* Brian Wilson.
- *Hinduism.* Cybelle Shattuck.
- *Islam.* Jamal J. Elias.
- *Judaism.* Dan Cohn-Sherbok.
- *Religion in the Twenty-first Century.* Mary Pat Fisher.

These books provide succinct guides to the major world faiths (except the last volume, which discusses the changing religious scene entering the new millenium). Each book gives a basic introduction to the faith—its history, practices, and beliefs—and emphasizes contemporary developments and the impact of the religion today. They also include brief discussions of the following dimensions: teachings, narratives, organizations, ritual, and experience.

Religious Life of Man Series. 1977–1987. Belmont, Cal.: Wadsworth.

Religious Traditions of the World. 1984–1987. San Francisco: Harper and Row.

Studies in Religion and Society. 1968–1984. Chicago: Center for the Scientific Study of Religion.

Studies in Religion and Society. 1981–1999. Lewiston, N.Y.: E. Mellen Press.

Studies in the History of Religion. 1967–1998. Boston; Leiden; New York: E. J. Brill.

Themes in Religious Studies. London; New York: Pinter Publishers.

Toronto Studies in Religion. 1985–1997. Centre for Religious Studies at the University of Toronto. New York: Peter Long.

The World's Religions. 1988–1991. London: Routledge.

Annotated Bibliography
Theories of Comparison of Religious Ideas

Asad, Talal. 1993. *Genealogies of Religion: Discipline and Reasons of Power in Christianity and Islam*. Baltimore: Johns Hopkins Press.

Berger, Peter L. 1981. *The Other Side of God: A Polarity in World Religions*. Garden City, N.Y.: Anchor Books.

Bleeker, C. J. 1963. *The Sacred Bridge: Researches into the Nature and Structure of Religion*. Leiden.

Brandon, A. W. (ed.). 1970. *A Dictionary of Comparative Religion*. London.

Bouquet, Alan Coates. 1973. *Comparative Religion: A Short Outline*. (9th ed.) Baltimore: Penguin Books.

Charing, Douglas. 1982. *Comparative Religions: A Modern Textbook*. Poole [Eng.]: Blandford Press; New York: Distributed by Sterling Pub.

Clack, Brian. R. 1999. *Wittgenstein, Frazer, and Religion*. New York: St. Martin's Press.

Clooney, Francis Xavier. 1993. *Theology after Vedānta: An Experiment in Comparative Theology*. Albany: State University of New York Press.

Clouser, Roy A. 1991. *The Myth of Religious Neutrality: An Essay on the Hidden Role of Religious Belief in Theories*. Notre Dame, Ind.: University of Notre Dame Press.

Dilworth, David. 1989. *Philosophy in World Perspective: A Comparative Hermeneutic of the Major Theories*. New Haven: Yale University Press.

Eckel, Malcolm David. 1992. *To See the Buddha: A Philosopher's Quest for the Meaning of Emptiness*. Princeton: Princeton University Press.

Edwards, Rem Blanchard. 1972. *Reason and Religion*. New York: Harcourt, Brace, Jovanavitch.
Edwards attempts to apply Wittgenstein's notion of family resemblance to the classification of religions. J. Z. Smith calls this primitive and "al-

most embarrassing," though he applauds Edward's conclusion that there are sufficient but no necessary conditions for calling something a religion.

Eliade, Mircea. 1958. *Patterns in Comparative Religion*, Trans. Rosemary Sheed. New York: Sheed and Ward.

Geertz, Clifford. 1973. *The Interpretation of Cultures*. New York: Basic Books.

Griffin, David Ray, and Huston Smith. 1989. *Primordial Truth and Postmodern Theology*. Albany: State University of New York Press.

Hall, David L., and Roger T. Ames. 1995. *Anticipating China: Thinking Through the Narratives of Chinese and Western Culture*. Albany: State University of New York Press.

James, Edwin Oliver. 1954. "The History, Science, and Comparative Study of Religion," *Numen* I: 91ff.

———. 1962. *Comparative Religion: An Introductory and Historical Study*. London: Methuen; New York: Barnes & Noble.

Lakoff, George, and Mark Johnson. 1980. *Metaphors We Live By*. Chicago: University of Chicago Press.

Larson, Gerald J., and Eliot Deutsch (eds.). 1988. *Interpreting Across Boundaries: New Essays in Comparative Philosophy*. Princeton: Princeton University Press.

Lindbeck, George A. 1984. *The Nature of Doctrine: Religion and Theology in a Postliberal Age*. Philadelphia: Westminster Press.

Mol, Hans. 1976. *Identity and the Sacred: A Sketch for a New Social-Scientific Theory of Religion*. Oxford: Blackwell.

Müller, Friedrich Max. 1873. *Introduction to the Science of Religion*.
This book essentially marks the beginning of comparative religious study, summed up in Müller's statement: "He who knows one, knows none."

Neville, Robert. 1991. *Behind the Masks of God: An Essay Toward Comparative Theology*. Albany: State University of New York Press.

———. 1995. *Normative Cultures*. Albany: State University of New York Press.

Paden, William E. 1994. *Religious Worlds: The Comparative Study of Religion*. Boston: Beacon Press.

Panikkar, Raimundo. 1993. *The Cosmotheandric Experience: Emerging Religious Consciousness*. Maryknoll, N.Y.: Orbis Books.

Parrinder, Edward Geoffrey. 1962/1975. *Comparative Religion*. Westport, Conn.: Greenwood Press.

Platvoet, J. G. 1981. *Comparing Religions: A Limitative Approach*. The Hague.

——— and R. C. Morgon (eds.). 1973. *The Cardinal Meaning: Essays in Comparative Hermeneutics*. The Hague.

Sethi, Amarjit Singh, and Reinhard Pummer. 1979. *Comparative Religion*. New Delhi: Vikas.

Sharpe, Eric J. 1975/86. *Comparative Religion: A History*. LaSalle, Ill.: Open Court.

Smith, Huston, and David Ray Griffin. 1989. *Primordial Truth and Postmodern Theology*. Albany: State University of New York Press.

Smith, Jonathan Z. 1982. *Imagining Religion: From Babylon to Jonestown*. Chicago: University of Chicago Press.

Smith, Wilfred Cantwell. 1963. *The Meaning and End of Religion*. New York.

———. 1981. *Towards a World Theology: Faith and the Comparative Study of Religion*. Philadelphia: Westminster Press.

Swidler, Leonard. 1990. *After the Absolute: The Dialogical Future of Religious Reflection*. Minneapolis: Fortress Press.

Tracy, David. 1981. *The Analogical Imagination: Christian Theology and the Culture of Pluralism*. New York: Crossroad.

———. 1990. *Dialogue with the Other: The Inter-religious Dialogue*. Louvain: Peeters Press; Grand Rapids, Mich.: Wm. B. Eerdmans.

———Tracy, David, and Frank E. Reynolds (eds.). 1994. *Religion and Practical Reason: New Essays in the Comparative Philosophy of Religions*. Albany: State University of New York Press.

Waardenburg, J. J. 1973. *Classical Approaches to the Study of Religion I*. The Hague.

Watson, Walter. 1993. *The Architectonics of Meaning: Foundations for the New Pluralism*. Chicago: University of Chicago Press.

Contributors

FRANCIS X. CLOONEY, S. J., Professor of Comparative Theology at Boston College, is past president of the the Society for Hindu-Christian Studies. He specializes in certain Sanskrit and Tamil traditions of Hindu thought and their implications for Christian theology.

MALCOLM DAVID ECKEL is Professor of the History of Religion at Boston University and does research and teaching in Buddhism.

PAULA FREDRIKSEN is the William Goodwin Aurelio Professor of the Appreciation of Scripture and Professor of New Testament and Early Christianity at Boston University. She has a particular research interest in Augustine of Hippo, and has also published in the areas of Hellenistic Judaism, Christian origins, and Pauline studies.

S. NOMANUL HAQ is currently on the faculty of Rutgers University and a visiting scholar at the University of Pennsylvania. He has published extensively in the general area of Islamic intellectual history, including theology, philosophy, and science.

LIVIA KOHN is Professor of Religion and East-Asian Studies at Boston University. She is a specialist of medieval Daoism.

JAMES MILLER, a graduate of Durham University and Cambridge University, is currently a Ph.D. candidate at Boston University, and an adjunct lecturer in the Department of Theology at Boston College. He is coeditor, with Norman Girardot and Liu Xiaogan, of *Daoism and Ecology*, a volume in the series on world religions and ecology published by Harvard University's Center for the Study of World Religions.

ROBERT CUMMINGS NEVILLE is Professor of Philosophy, Religion, and Theology, and Dean of the School of Theology at Boston University. Neville is the past president of the American Academy of Religion, The International Society for Chinese Philosophy, and The Metaphysical Society of America.

HUGH NICHOLSON is a Ph.D. candidate in the Theology Department at Boston College and is currently writing his dissertation relating Indian philosophical thought to theological and philosophical questions and concerns of the Christian West.

ANTHONY J. SALDARINI has taught early Judaism and Christianity in the Department of Theology at Boston College for over twenty years and publishes in the area of early Jewish-Christian relations.

JONATHAN Z. SMITH is the Robert O. Anderson Distinguished Service Professor of the Humanities at the University of Chicago.

JOHN J. THATAMANIL is a member of the religious studies faculty at Millsaps College, and recently completed his dissertation comparing the thought of Paul Tillich and Śaṇkara.

WESLEY J. WILDMAN is Associate Professor of Theology and Ethics at Boston University. He teaches and does research in the areas of contemporary Christian theology, philosophy of religion, and religion and science.

Index of Names

Plato, 95, 183–84, 200
Plotinus, 114
Popper, Karl R., 142
Porphyry, 114

Saadia ben Joseph, 94–97
Saadia Gaon, 85, 102
Saldarini, Anthony J., xiv–xv, 151–52, 157, 191
Śāliknātha, 51
Śaṅkara, 29, 155, 157, 195
Schleiermacher, Friedrich, 172
Searle, John, 172, n198
Shammai, 93
Sharma, Arvind, xiii
Shepardson, Tina, xv
Sickmann, Laurence, 28
Śaiva, 50, 54
Sivi, 68
Smith, Jonathan Z., xiii, xxiii
Smith, Wilfred Cantwell, 66–67, 69, 79, 129–31, 134, 136, n143
Solomon, King, 88
Sorkin, David, 106
Spinoza, Baruch, 183
Śrīvāsadāsa, 54
Stackhouse, Max, xiii, xvi, 234
Sullivan, Celeste, xv

Tarski, Alfred, 130, 142
Thatamanil, John, xv
Theodosius II, 122
Tillich, Paul, 5
Tsoṅ-kha-pa, 78

Udayana, 49

Vedānta Deśika, 43, 54

Weiming, Tu, xiii, xvi
Wheelwright Bian, 12
White, E. B., 74
Whitehead, Alfred North, 184
Wildman, Wesley J., xv, xvii, xxi, 2, 3, n6, 222–24
Wittgenstein, Ludwig, 153, 172, 183, n200

Xuanzong, Emperor, 35

Yang Xi, 27
Yearley, Lee, xiii

Zhang Daoling, 27
Zhongshu, Dong, 8
Zhuangzi, 38, 151

Index of Subjects

Reality, as a criterion for belief, 96; in Christianity, 109
Reason, 157; in Viśiṣṭādvaita Vedānta, 53–54; in Buddhism, 74–75, 78; in Judaism, 86, 95, 98, 101; in Christianity, 116, 123
Reference, 149–50, 153, 167, 176, 178–80, 182–87, 191, 196; extensional versus intentional, 185–87; iconicity of, 150, 155, 182–84; indexicality of, 150, 155, 182, 184–85; conventionality, 150–51, 155, 177, 182, 184–86, n200
Reform Judaism, 99, 102–3
Relativity of truth, in Buddhism, 72
Religion, complexity of, 204–7, 212; nature of, 204–17; givenness of, 209–11, 215
Religious truth, in China, the dynamic nature of, 8
Republic, The, n200
Revelation, 166; in Judaism, 98, 100–1, 105; in Christianity, 110, 118, 121–22; in Islam, 138, 40
Ritual, 154, 156, 181, 193–94; in Chinese religion, 17; in Judaism, 101
Romans, St. Paul's letter to the, 87–88, n126

Ṣadaqa, 66
Ṣidq, 66, 128–36, n42–43; as faithfulness, 132, 134; as intention or volition, 133; as means to an end, 132–33, as total sincerity, 133, 142
Śaiva Siddhānta, 50
Śiva, 50, 54
Sāṃkhya, n80
Sadducees, 89, 100
Sage, in Chinese religion, 25, 32
Saints, in Christianity, 119
Saṃgha, xviii
Saṃvṛti ("concealment"), 70
Samatā ("equanimity"), 68
Sanhuang texts, 27
Sanskrit, 224–25
Satan, 19, 189
Satyagraha, 69
Satya-kriyā ("act of truth"), 67–69
Schematism, 189, n201
Scholasticism, Medieval Christian, 100, 152–53
Science, 98, 100
Scriptural truth, 154–59; in Chinese religion, 17, 25–28, 35; in Mīmāṃsa, 51, 53; in Viśiṣṭādvaita Vedānta, 54–55; in Advaita Vedānta, 55–57; in Buddhism, 76–78; in Christianity, 110–12, 118, 120–22
Scripture, in Chinese religion, 17, 25–28, 35; in Buddhism, 76–78; in Christianity, 110–12, 118, 120–22, authority of, 120–21, 155–56, 161, 165; in Judaism, 83–5, 92, 98, 101; authority of, 84, 97; exegesis of, 93–4, 102, n106; levels of meaning, 94
Self, in Chinese religion, 32–33, compared to Buddhism, Christianity, Hinduism, and Islam, 33
Self-awareness, in Buddhism, 71–72
Septuagint, 86–87, 121, 155
Shangqing Revelations, 17, 27
Sharīʿa, 109, 138–39
Sheng, 25
Shujing (Book of History), 22
Siddhas (Buddhist saints), 68
Sin, 163, in Christianity, 117–18, 120, 123–24
Sincerity, in Chinese religion, 33
Sites of phenomenological importance, 206–7
Skepticism, 111, 114; in Buddhism and Jainism, 45; about comparison, 227, 231
Society, in Judaism, 90; as embodying or locating truth, in Chinese religion, 33–37
Solipsism, 210
Soul, in Nyāya Hinduism, 49
Specialists, 222